# CRAZY LOCO
# LOVE

# CRAZY LOCO LOVE

# Victor Villaseñor

Arte Público Press
Houston, Texas

*Crazy Loco Love* is made possible through grants from the City of Houston through the Houston Arts Alliance and the Exemplar Program, a program of Americans for the Arts in collaboration with the LarsonAllen Public Services Group, funded by the Ford Foundation.

*Recovering the past, creating the future*

Arte Público Press
University of Houston
452 Cullen Performance Hall
Houston, Texas 77204-2004

Cover design by Pilar Espino
Cover photo by Chuy Benitez, 2008
Author photos courtesy of Victor Villaseñor

Villaseñor, Victor
    Crazy *Loco* Love / by Victor Villaseñor.
        p.   cm.
    ISBN 978-1-55885-315-7 (alk. paper)
    1. Villaseñor, Victor. 2. Authors, American—20th century—Biography. 3. Mexican Americans—California—Biography. 4. Mexican American authors—Biography. 5. California, Southern—Biography. I. Title. II. Title: Crazy Loco Love.
    PS3572.I384Z465 2008
    813'.54—dc22
    [B]
                                                                2008015945
                                                                CIP

♾ The paper used in this publication meets the requirements of the American National Standard for Information Sciences—Permanence of Paper for Printed Library Materials, ANSI Z39.48-1984.

8 9 0 1 2 3 4 5 6 7          10 9 8 7 6 5 4 3 2 1

# DEDICATION

*This book is dedicated to all fathers and sons and to all mothers and daughters.*

*There is no deep, dark, mysterious gulf between fathers and sons and mothers and daughters. There is just a different heartbeat for each generation.*

*Whatever you can do or dream you can do, begin it. Boldness has genius, power and magic.*
Johann Wolfgang von Goethe

*Thousands of geniuses live and die undiscovered— either by themselves or by others.*　　Mark Twain

*It took me a long time not to judge myself through someone else's eyes.*　　Sally Field

*A successful person is one who can lay a firm foundation with the bricks that others throw at him or her.*
David Brinkley

*It's not who you are that holds you back, it's who you think you're not.*　　Author Unknown

*Our deepest fear is not that we are inadequate. Our deepest fear is that we are powerful beyond measure. It is our light, not our darkness, that most frightens us. We ask ourselves, who am I to be brilliant, gorgeous, talented, fabulous? Actually, who are you not to be? You are a child of God. Your playing small does not serve the world. There is nothing enlightened about shrinking so that other people won't feel insecure around you. We are all meant to shine, as children do. We were born to make manifest the glory of God that is within us. It is not just in some of us; it is in every-*

*one. And as we let our own light shine, we unconsciously give other people permission to do the same. As we are liberated from our own fear, our presence automatically liberates others.*

Marianne Williamson, *A Return to Love: Reflections on the Principles of "A Course in Miracles,"* 1992 (commonly misattributed to Nelson Mandela, 1994 inauguration speech)

*We,* los Indios, los mescalados, *the mixed bloods, are like the weeds. The roses you need to water them and give them fertilizer or they die. The weeds you give them* nada-*nothing and they live. You poison them and they come back the following year. You pour cement over them and they will break that concrete, reaching for the sunlight of God. This was my mother's power. She didn't believe in God. She lived with the Almighty, and miracles were her* maíz de la vida.

Juan Salvador Villaseñor

# INTRODUCTION

**M**y mother was so upset she was ready to scream. Once more my dad had made a fool of himself and embarrassed her in public. She wanted me to talk to him and get him to understand that he couldn't go on behaving like this, or it was the end for them. I could see my mother's frustration, but I hadn't seen what happened at the charity function the night before, so I didn't want to get involved. But my mother kept insisting, saying I was twenty years old, an adult, and so I had to help her. Finally I agreed to talk to my father.

The bathroom door was open. My dad was tying his tie and whistling as he looked at himself in the mirror. I don't know why, but my father always put on his pants last when he dressed. First he'd put on his red silk boxer underwear—always red silk—then he put on long black socks with those strap things around his calves that held up the socks and then slipped on his dress shoes. After that, he'd fix himself a drink *para el estribo*, for the stirrup. I guess so he could mount up. Now he went back to the bathroom, sipping his drink, to put on his shirt and tie.

"*Papá*," I said, "*mamá* is mad. She says that you made a fool of yourself last night, and she can't see how you're going to go to face all those people today after having done such an embarrassing thing last night."

He didn't say a word. He just kept right on whistling and working on his tie. It also angered my mother that she could be ready to go in twenty minutes and it took my dad a full hour.

"*Papá*," I said, "please stop whistling and listen to me. *Mamá* is really mad. She says you got so drunk last night that you stepped on the mayor's wife's long dress when you were dancing with her and almost ripped her dress off. Then you told her she looked like she was in pretty good shape and told the mayor he was a lucky man. After that you got mad at the bartender for telling you that you'd had enough to drink, and you threatened to go home and get your horse and rope him by the neck and drag him through town. *Mamá* says that people kept telling her not to worry, that everything was okay, but she could see in their eyes that they felt sorry for her because she had such a drunken fool for a husband. She can't figure out how you're going to face all these people today, and she wants you never to behave like this again, or . . ."

I stopped speaking. My dad was done with his tie. He sipped his drink again and began slipping on his pants, tucking in his shirt, zipping up, and buckling his silver and gold Mexican belt buckle. He still didn't say a word. He just kept right on whistling, happy as a bird in a tree.

"*Papá*," I said, getting a little louder, "I wasn't there last night. I don't know what happened. But if half of what *mamá* says is true, then you . . ."

"It's probably all true," he said.

"Well, then, *papá*," I said, slightly surprised by his open honesty, "*mamá* is right, and you've got to stop this kind of behavior, or else . . ."

"Or else what?" he said, putting on his suit jacket.

"Or else she says it's the end for you two," I said. "*Mamá* is really upset. She can't see how you're going to face these people today."

"Do you want to just keep on talking," he said, "or do you really want to know how I'll face all these people after what I did last night?"

I took a deep breath. He was fully dressed now, and looked very handsome with his lion-mane of white hair, dark maroon suit, and diagonally striped silver and maroon tie.

"No, *papá*," I said, "I don't want to just go on talking. I really want to know how you'll face these people today after what happened last night."

"Easy," he said, "I've done worse."

"You've done worse?" I said, completely surprised by his answer.

"Sure," he said, "I've done a lot worse."

And saying this he turned and left the bathroom and went down the hallway whistling a happy tune. An hour later I saw him take the microphone at the event he and my mother were hosting, and he said, "Good afternoon. I hope you're all feeling okay today. Myself, I understand I got to feeling a little too good last night, and I did a few wild things. I apologize and I want to fix the things I did." He shrugged his shoulders. "But also I want you all to know that I've done worse, and I'll probably screw things up again now and then."

I was shocked. People started applauding. They loved it. And the mayor's wife—of all people—was the first one to come rushing forward to hug my dad, telling him not to worry about anything, that it had given her the chance to get her husband to buy her a new dress. Then a lot of other people came up, including a former Miss Southern California who just couldn't keep her hands off my dad. Hell, she was close to my age, but she paid no attention to me, even though I was all dressed up, too. I guess a lot of people had also done "worse" in their lives and felt glad that someone could admit it openly and not feel bad or guilty or think that it was the end of the world. Even my mother, seeing the people's reaction, calmed down and accepted dad's hand when he asked her for the first dance.

I was flabbergasted and still am today as I write this story forty-some years later. You see, in one great big stroke my dad taught me and everyone else, including my mother, that forgiveness doesn't start with forgiving others their trespasses. It starts within each of us. We all need not to be so hard on ourselves and know how to forgive ourselves before we can begin forgiving other people.

And my mother, she really didn't learn this until just a few days before she passed over to the spirit world. She was eighty-nine years old, and for months she had not been very happy with herself or others. But one morning she was by the birdcage whistling to her canaries with such *gusto*.

"What is it, *mamá?*" I said. "You look so happy today."

"I am," she said. "I'm very happy today."

"What happened?" I said. "Only yesterday you looked pretty upset."

"I've always been a very practical businesswoman," she said, "and last night, while saying my rosary, I decided to forgive everyone everything, even your own father."

"That's fantastic," I said. "Congratulations, *mamá*, but tell me what caused you to do this?"

"*Mijito,* my time is close. I can feel it, and it dawned on me last night that if I want God to forgive me for all the wrongs I've done, then I better hurry up and start forgiving everyone else. I don't want to go to hell because I'm stubborn. I want to go to heaven, and I can hardly wait to get there so I can tell your father how much I loved him all those years. He was a good man, but he made me so mad at times that I'd forget the good things."

Smiling a big smile, she once more began whistling and talking to her canaries in the large outdoor cage. She was glowing with happiness. She'd found peace.

And so there you have it. All of my other books, except for *Macho!*, are about strong women. The heroes of those stories are my grandmothers and my aunts and my mother. The men take a back seat to the powerful women in those books. But in this book—as in *Macho!*—the heroes of the story are the men. In fact, in this book the women are deliberately only developed a little bit. This is a book about fathers and sons and how a boy of sixteen is told that he isn't a boy anymore, but on the verge of becoming *un hombre,* and to be a man one must go out into the world and live and learn and not be afraid of screwing up.

Enjoy! Thank you, *gracias,* from my *familia* to your *familia,*

God bless us all,

Victor E. Villaseñor

# ~ BOOK ONE ~

# CHAPTER ONE

I was just turning sixteen years old when my dad told me that he needed to talk to me. We walked across the grass and past the barn and corrals to the big old pepper tree. This tree was so huge that many of its limbs were as big around as the trunk of some fully grown trees. I'd been playing underneath this tree since I was a child, and I'd helped slaughter and hang and butcher hundreds of steers in its limbs.

"Son," my dad said to me, "in a few days you will have your own driver's license and be driving your own car."

"Truck, *papá*. Pickup truck," I said.

I was all excited about the truck I was getting. It was a 1956 Chevy my dad let me pick out at Weseloh's Chevrolet in downtown Oceanside. It cost a fortune—$1,300.

"Okay, *mijo*, a pickup truck," said my dad to me, "but the point I want to make is this, you are no longer a boy. You are a man now, and to be *un hombre*, a man must not only know right from wrong, he must also know who he is and who he isn't. Because if a man doesn't know who he is and who he isn't, then no matter how much he knows about right and wrong, he will always be like a fish out of water.

"But, on the other hand, if a man knows who he is and who he isn't, then he will have the strength and confidence to do whatever it takes to keep his head above water and create a good life for himself and his loved ones. Do you understand? Am I making sense?"

Suddenly, my gift, the new Chevy pickup—a beaming turquoise— didn't quite seem as important or as exciting to me. What my dad was telling me was kind of scary.

"No, *papá*," I finally said. We were speaking mostly in Spanish. "I don't understand, because, well, to learn what is right and what is wrong, you have the priest and nuns and everybody else telling you which is which. But to learn who you are and who you aren't, I don't see how anyone can teach you that. So, then, how does a man learn this? I don't get it," I added.

My dad smiled a great big beautiful smile. "Exactly," he said, "this is the million dollar question that nobody can teach you and you need to learn for yourself. My mother, a woman, told me this, and I'll tell you, *mijo,* that you will learn who you are and who you aren't in the next four or five years, because not to learn who you are and who you aren't in the next few years, my mother said, is to be missing the most important part of your whole life.

"Myself, I had to learn who I was and who I wasn't at a very early age. Our father had abandoned us and died. The Mexican Revolution was going on all around us, and my old mother and my two sisters were starving. I was ten years old, and all the games I'd played as a child suddenly became the tools for our survival. I knew how to catch rabbits, trap quail, and which wild roots to dig up so we could eat. I knew how to lie and trick the soldiers so that they wouldn't find my sisters and abuse them. All the playful games of my childhood suddenly took on new meaning, and I learned to see and think, here in my *cabeza*-head, not as a child, but as the man responsible for the survival and welfare of his *familia.*"

"I know, *papá,* you've told me this a hundred times," I said.

"Only a hundred? Well, then listen good, because now the time has come for you, too, to put away your thinking as a child and to start looking at life as a man, a person responsible for the survival and welfare of his loved ones. Your brother *José* is dead. He died at sixteen, just as he was coming into his own manhood. You didn't get to see how he was going to make it here in the United States. And how I came into my own manhood in *México* during the Revolution and then here in this country in prison and at different work camps— all that isn't going to be much of a guide for you, either. So, *mijo,* you are going to have to keep your eyes open and learn as you go. You're pretty much on your own now, but you are not all alone, because you have *familia.* Do you understand?"

I didn't know what to say. My mouth was dry. I was scared. My dad must've sensed my fear, because he reached out and put his thick workman's hand on my shoulder and patted me gently.

"A little fear is good," he said. "Nothing wrong for *un hombre* to be afraid. It helps keep the eyes and ears alert like a rabbit in the bush."

Tears came to my eyes.

"Good, go ahead and cry, *mijo,*" he said. "Good men aren't afraid to cry. You are going to do very well. You are already very much *un hombre.* I've seen you handle a horse. I've seen you be kind and patient when we bring the steers from the corrals to this tree to slaughter them.

"I've also seen you work in the hot sun in the fields, as good and strong as any boy from *México.* You aren't afraid of work or sweat or shooting a steer right between the eyes so he never knows what hit him. It is the cowards in life who are afraid of taking on the full responsibility of death who make the cattle suffer, then make their own *familias* suffer, too. You are going to do good, *mijito.*"

The tears now ran down my face. I took a big breath and blew out. My Chevy truck didn't seem very important to me anymore. I could see that my vehicle and driver's license were coming to me at a much higher price tag than I'd ever imagined.

"Also," he said, "remember it is only in making mistakes, and big ones, that you learn to be a man. A man doesn't learn who he is and who he isn't by sitting around and talking. A man learns who he is and isn't by watching, thinking, then stepping into the bullring of life, and taking *la vida* by the horns!

"And a wise man," he added, "learns a lot about life's twists and turns from other people's mistakes. No man has the time in one lifetime to make all the mistakes he needs to make in order to find out who he is and who he isn't. So, *mijito,* you keep your eyes peeled like the newly hatched chick and learn a lot through the experiences of your friends and relatives, and especially from your enemies. In fact, when it's all said and done, my mother always said that a wise man looks back on his life and sees that it was from his enemies that he learned the most.

"Now do you understand? Now are you beginning to see that this is every person's calling, not just for men, but women, too? And people who don't know who they are and who they aren't will leave a string of mistakes behind them like a cat in heat. It takes real guts and responsibility to go through these years that you're about to go through. The body and mind yearn for life. The confusion of love and mating is going on inside of you like at no other time. These are your crazy*loco* years, so you've got to be strong, *mijito,* and keep both eyes open, especially if you're a man. Because, as my mother always said, it is not the men who carry the child in their bodies for those nine months. It is the women. So men have no idea or understanding of what life is really all about. My mother always said if men were the ones who carried the child, our whole world would be different. Oh, she'd go on and on, asking me to just imagine how different the Church would be if the Pope was a woman." He stopped and took a deep breath. *"Mijito,"* he said, "your brother is gone. You are our only male child left, so I say to you, step forth, *mijo,* and become *un hombre de los buenos.* A man who knows how to respect all life and protect his mother and sisters. Do you understand?"

I glanced up into the huge old pepper tree. The sunlight was filtering down between the limbs and leaves. A breeze picked up. I could smell the ocean in the distance. And I'd just thought that my dad had asked me to walk across the grass with him so he could talk to me about transmissions and oil changes and stuff like that. I took another huge breath. This was really tough.

"Do you have any questions?" my dad asked.

I almost felt like laughing or just telling him to keep the truck. But I didn't. I really loved the truck I was getting. I'd picked out the turquoise color myself. It reminded me of all the stars I'd drawn as a little kid. Turquoise was still my favorite color.

"No," I said to my dad, "I really don't have any questions, except maybe one. How does a person know when . . . when they've made a mistake? I mean, sometimes I've been so, well, dumb in the past that I didn't even know that what I'd done was a mistake until a long time later."

He smiled another great big smile. *"Mijo,"* he said, "you've just hit the nail right on the head. This is a question that few people ever ask. And the people who don't ask this question are the fools who never learn from their mistakes or from the mistakes of others. Always go to your heart, here inside, *mijo,*" he said, patting me on my chest with his huge thick hand, "and you will have a much better chance of instantly seeing your mistakes, and then also finding a way of learning from them, too.

"It is the people who don't listen to their hearts and are always listening to other people's opinions that end up with the most *problemas* in life. You listen to your heart, here inside, and trust yourself, and believe me, you will come up with things that at times seem like miracles. This is our power as human beings. This was the strength of *mi mamá* during the Revolution with all that starvation and bloodshed. And this has been my strength, too. If I'd listened to people, I would've never purchased this ranch on which we live. It took guts for your mother and me to step forward and buy this big *rancho.*

"Pearl Harbor had just happened. All of California was trying to get away from the coast, because they thought that any day the Japanese were going to come and attack California, too. But your mother and I didn't run. No, like I've always told you, where there's fear, there's money to be made, especially when the other guy has got the fear and you don't. So we stepped in, took the bull by the horns, and your mother and I bought this ranch for $20,000, with cattle and horses and barns and tractors and new orchards of lemons and oranges and avocados. One year later your mother and I sold one hundred feet by one hundred feet down by the ocean on the 101 highway for $20,000, and the ranch was free and clear. I could never have done all that . . . if I'd listened to people. *Capiche?*"

"Well, then, *papá,*" I said, "are you telling me it wasn't just you who stepped forward to buy this ranch. It was you and *mamá?*"

"Exactly. I value your mother's opinion very much."

"Well, then, are you telling me that in the next few years I not only need to learn who I am and who I'm not, but I also need to learn how to choose the right woman for my wife like you did with *mamá?*"

He smiled the biggest smile I'd ever seen him smile and took me into his arms, hugging me in a big *abrazo.* "You got it! To know how to *escoger,* how to choose the right woman for your wife is the most important thing any man can do in all of his life." He took a huge breath and blew out. "The right woman can help make a man. The wrong woman can destroy a man. But—and this is a big but—before a man can choose the right woman for himself, he must first know who he is and who he isn't. It is the people who don't know who they are and who they aren't that never, never find the right mate. Marriage, understand, isn't for weaklings or . . . built to make you happy. Being happy is a person's own responsibility. Marriage is for building a home. So, *mijo,* you are a boy no more. You are *un hombre* and getting ready to build your own *casa.*"

I felt like saying, "Yeah, dad, this all sounds good. But what if I fail? What if I don't learn who I am and who I'm not in the next few years? Then what am I?" But I didn't say any of this and just kept still.

Seeing my silence, my dad laughed. "Don't worry," he said as if reading my mind, "believe me, if you don't learn who you are and who you aren't in the next few years, then life, *la vida,* will just keep bringing it up into your face until you learn!"

He continued laughing with *carcajadas,* great big belly laughs. But I didn't think this was funny in the least. My God, this was tough! And it wasn't like I could just do more push-ups and get stronger and in better shape to be a man. No, this I had to do from here, inside of my heart-*corazón.*

I took another big breath, blew out, and looked up at the sunlight filtering down through the branches and leaves of the huge tree. The sunlight looked so soft and beautiful. Many a lazy afternoon had I spent alone under this old pepper tree when I was growing up, looking up into its twisted branches. It was easy to see that this tree had seen many storms and droughts in its life, and it also looked like much of its new luscious growth had sprouted up out of these broken, twisted places.

Maybe this was the answer. Maybe it was really okay for me to go out and make mistakes, and even big ones, like my dad had said, and get broken and twisted. The breeze picked up, and the tree's branches began to dance. It felt like the pepper tree was talking to me, singing to me. I smiled and began to breathe more easily.

# CHAPTER TWO

**B**en Weseloh called to say my truck had arrived. My dad said he'd drive me into town to pick it up. Pulling into the dealership, I instantly spotted my truck. It was the only solid turquoise pickup on the whole lot. I rushed up and leaped into the bed of the truck. I couldn't believe it! It was even more gorgeous than I'd ever imagined. I jumped out, got into the driver's seat, and started up the engine, a big V-8. I was careful not to gun it. The salesman, whom we'd known for years, had explained to me that there was a break-in period of five hundred miles before I could really goose it.

My dad paid for the truck in cash and went home. I headed for the beach. I met Dennis Tico by the Oceanside pier. I'd known him since grammar school when we'd both gone to Saint Mary's Star of the Sea Catholic School. Tico was really built and good-looking. He'd been voted the best-looking guy by the girls at Saint Mary's. I showed him my new truck, and he really liked it, but I wasn't able to find Nick Rorick or Little Richard or John Folting or any of my other friends. Little Richard and John Folting went to a private school, the Army Navy Academy in Carlsbad, with me. Dennis and Nick and all of my other friends went to Oceanside High School, where I wish I'd been able to go. But my brother Joseph had gone to the military school and liked it, so my dad and mom decided that I, too, should attend.

I cruised the strand along the beach about half a dozen times, waving at the guys and girls I knew, then headed over to Herb's drive-in across the 101 highway from the old cemetery to get a cherry Coke. I ordered a small one, because I was on the wrestling team at the Academy and had to keep my weight down. Our coach told us to chew ice if we got thirsty or hungry. At Herb's I met a lot of people I knew, and some really liked my new truck, but others, I couldn't believe it, made fun of its turquoise color.

I was just getting ready to leave the drive-in when Little Richard drove up in his cherry-red model-T roadster. Richard was about the coolest guy I knew. He had curly blonde hair and was small and wiry and very strong and athletic. A beautiful girl was sitting right next to him. People said that he looked a lot like Tab Hunter, except better looking. Little Richard and big Ted Bourland, who towered over everyone, were the only non-Mexicans I knew who were tough enough to work with me and the Mexican workers on the ranch. No one, but no one, knew how much guts and strength it took to work in the hot sun out in the fields, until they'd actually done it.

"Is that your new truck?" asked Little Richard.

"Yeah, this is it," I said, proudly. For two years I'd been working and saving my money to buy a pickup. I'd wanted to buy my own vehicle, as my friends had done. But, then, a few months ago my dad had taken me down to Weseloh's and told me that he and my mother had talked it over and they wanted to buy me a new car, the way they'd done with my older sister Tencha. Seeing the turquoise-colored pickup in the brochure, my heart had leaped with excitement, and I'd said yes to my parents' offer.

Little Richard started laughing. He, like my other friends, had worked for years to buy his vehicle. "But why didn't you get it in a real color, like black, or forest green, or cherry red? Nobody drives around in a turquoise-colored truck!" he added, still laughing.

The girl next to him started laughing, too. Several people came around. Most of the local guys who went to the Academy were ostracized by the town kids, but Little Richard was real popular all over town, even though he went there.

"How long have you had it?" asked Little Richard.

"Not long. Maybe an hour," I said.

"Well, then, maybe you can still take it back and get yourself a real truck."

Little Richard was a good friend of mine, so I didn't know what to think or say. Everyone was now grinning and laughing at me. My mouth was as dry as cotton balls. I felt like I was going to cry, but I didn't want to in front of everyone.

"Bye," I said. "Good to see you, Richard, but I've got to get back to the ranch. It's just about feeding time."

"Sorry if I hurt your feelings," he said as I was leaving. "But really, you can't go around in a turquoise truck without expecting people to laugh at you."

"Yeah, I guess you're right," I said.

"See you around."

"Yeah, see you around," I said, and I drove off.

By the time I passed through the front gates of our ranch, I felt so crushed that tears were running down my face. And there were my parents up ahead of me on their horses taking an afternoon ride alongside our lemon orchard. They looked so happy to see me driving in through our big white gates in my brand-new turquoise Chevy. I didn't want to spoil their day, so I quickly wiped the tears from my face and tried my best to give them a great big smile.

Two days later I took my truck down to L.C. Settle's body shop, and I asked L.C. to paint it black for me.

"But why?" said L.C. "This is a factory paint job, and it's brand new and in good shape. I can't do a paint job as hot as the factory does, because when the factory does it, it's just the body. No motor or tires or windows to worry about."

I nodded. I understood what he was saying, but still I said, "Please, paint it. I need it black."

"Why black?"

"Well, not necessarily black," I said. "Just any color different than this . . . this turquoise." I had to fight back my tears.

"How about white," he said. "Black is hard to keep clean and it gets real hot in the summer when you're working on the ranch."

"Okay, white then," I said.

"Does your dad know you're doing this?" he asked.

I started to lie and nod my head, but couldn't. I shook my head. "No, he doesn't," I said.

"Maybe you should talk to him first," said L.C.

I took a big breath. I'd known L.C. all of my life. He was a local cop who ran a body shop on the side.

"Sir," I said, "I really need to do this on . . . on . . . my own. I'm sixteen, you see, and I need to start doing things without going to my dad all the time."

I took another deep breath. I'd already decided what to do if L.C. wouldn't paint it without my dad's permission. I'd simply drive over to Carlsbad or even as far away as Vista and have it done somewhere else.

"Well, all right," said L.C., "putting it that way, I'll do it. But if your dad says anything, you tell him that I warned you. I hate to paint a vehicle that already has a good paint job on it. But you're a good kid, and you must have your reasons. It'll cost you $29. I'm not cheap. I do the best paint job in town. You can get a $19 job done just down the street if that's what you want."

"I know you're good. That's why I came to you first, sir."

"And I appreciate that."

The next day I picked up my all-white truck, and feeling really good, I drove into our local drive-in. Little Richard was there with a different girl at his side. The moment he saw me, he started laughing again.

"What in the hell did you do?" he yelled, walking up to me and my truck. "Trade in your new pickup for a milk wagon?"

"No, I had it painted."

"You had it painted!" he shouted loud enough for everyone to hear. "What's the matter with you? Don't you know factory paint jobs are baked to the metal? You've ruined your truck. Now you can never trade it back in as a new truck."

I didn't even wait for the cherry Coke I'd ordered. I gunned my big V-8, peeling rubber, and drove home as fast as I could. At the gates I took the fork in the road that went up to the barn and I parked my Chevy with all the tractor equipment. I never wanted to see that truck again. Little Richard was right. It did look like a milk wagon. I'd ruined my beautiful turquoise Chevy truck. I'd been the biggest damn fool I knew to have listened to what people thought. I should have just listened to myself, down deep inside, just as my dad had told me to do. I began to cry. I'd failed. I'd really failed!

The following day I called a body shop in Carlsbad—too embarrassed to call L.C.—and asked them if a new paint job could be removed with paint remover. They asked what was under the paint job.

"A brand-new factory paint job," I said.

"Is it a Chevy pickup?"

The question startled me. "Yes," I said.

"Are you the Villaseñor kid?"

"What?"

"Aren't you the one who had L.C. paint your truck over a brand-new paint job?" he asked, laughing. "I'm Ray Chavez. I knew your brother José before he went to that military school. He was a good guy. No, not too much can be done about removal. What you'll probably have to do is paint over it again. What color is it you'd like today?"

I felt devastated. Everyone knew about my stupid *pendejada*. "No, thanks," I said. "I was just wondering."

"Tell your dad and mom hello for me," he said.

"Okay," I said, "I'll tell them," and I hung up the phone.

My hands were trembling. What a stupid damn fool I was. I'd done exactly what my dad had told me not to. I'd listened to other people's opinions instead of listening to what I'd felt inside. I'd loved my turquoise Chevy and I'd ruined it. My dad and mother would never have purchased the ranch we lived on if they'd listened to what other people thought. Here I was only a couple of weeks into my sixteenth year and I was already the most confused, stupid person I knew on the face of the whole earth!

# CHAPTER THREE

Then to make matters worse, that same week we were told at the Academy that we had to take a girl to the next school dance. I'd never taken a girl to a school function in all my life. I was terror-stricken. I didn't know the first thing about how to do this. As long as I could remember, every time I even got near girls, crazy*loco* things happened. Take, for instance, just three years back when I was in the seventh grade and a girl asked me if I'd like to go to the movies with her on a Saturday afternoon. I knew her. Her name was Mary. She'd come over to ride horses at our ranch with her parents a few times, so I said yes, but that I'd have to ask my mom first.

I did. My mom said okay. So that Saturday I biked over to Mary's house, which wasn't too far from the Catholic school of Saint Mary's on Wisconsin Street, where she and I had gone to school the year before. Mary got her bike, and we rode together to downtown Oceanside. It was a wonderful bike ride, but then getting to the ticket window of the movie house, I didn't know if I was supposed to pay or if Mary was supposed to pay since she'd invited me. But then, when she just looked at me and didn't reach in her purse to get her money, I figured that I was supposed to pay for both of us since I was the boy. The tickets cost a fortune, twenty-five cents each, and if I paid for them both, then I'd only have ten cents left and I wouldn't be able to buy us each a Coke and popcorn. This was when Mary finally reached into her purse and said that she'd buy her own Coke and we could split the cost of one bag of popcorn. I thought this was really great, that she'd figured out what to do so I wouldn't keep looking like a fool, trying to count my pennies and nickels.

But then in the darkness of the theater, we just couldn't seem to coordinate our timing and we'd bump our hands together trying to get into the bag of popcorn at the same time. We ended up half ripping the bag and spilling the popcorn all over ourselves. We began to eat the popcorn off our laps. I finished mine first, and she said I could have some of hers. I thought nothing of it, eating the spilled popcorn off her lap. But then she took hold of my hand when I reached for more popcorn and held my hand fast to her lap, right in between her legs.

I got so scared and nervous that my hand began to sweat, but still I had to admit that it felt pretty good to have my hand against her warm legs. We got so hot holding our hands together on her lap that I finally had to get my handkerchief out of my pocket so I could wipe the sweat off of our two palms. I didn't know what was happening. She was having trouble breathing, and she kept pushing my hand in further between her legs. Her hand began sweating even more than mine. She began making tight little sounds and I began to smell something I'd never smelled before. It was a strong smell, too, a little bit like a saddle that has just been taken off a sweaty horse.

I closed my eyes. My heart was pounding so fast that I was getting dizzy. After that, I don't remember anything about the movie. All I remember was that when we came out of the theater, it was still daylight, and the sunlight was so bright that it blinded us. My God, it felt to me like we'd been in that theater for a couple of days.

We had trouble getting on our bikes to pedal to her house. We were both dizzy and disoriented. Something crazy*loco* had happened to us inside the darkness of that movie house. I was feeling so weak and uncoordinated that I had a hard time getting my legs to work right. And she was having trouble pedaling, too.

At her house, she parked her bike next to the garage. We hadn't said a word all the way back to her house. I walked her up to her front door. She started to go in, but then—I'll never forget—she turned, closed her eyes, and puckered her lips toward me. I couldn't figure out what was going on. Did she have something in her eye? Then it dawned on me that she wanted me to kiss her. But I'd never kissed a girl who wasn't my sister or a cousin, and especially not on the lips.

I drew my face close to hers. I could see that her lips weren't all sweaty like her hand had been, so it wasn't disgusting. I closed my eyes and puckered my lips, too, but then when I tried to kiss her, our noses bumped and we hit our foreheads together real hard when we tried to get around our noses so we could get our lips together. The door behind her suddenly opened, and she fell over backwards into her house with me on top of her, and there was her dad with his open newspaper in hand. I was terror-stricken, to say the least, and all the way home I couldn't stop cussing myself out. My God, things just seemed to get crazy*loco* every time I was around girls. And why had our hands gotten so sweaty, and why did she have trouble breathing? Had she gotten sick? And why had I felt so dizzy and had a hard time getting my legs to work so I could pedal my bike?

But then about two months later, I got a lot of these questions answered. It happened at Jimmy Wucker's house, up California Street from our ranch, past the famous rock house, and then around the bend to the left at the top of the hill. Jimmy Wucker's mother took Jimmy and me and his sister Karen into the study and brought out two charts of the human body. Jimmy was two years older than me, and I was two years older than Karen. I'd never seen the human body naked before.

"How old are you?" Mrs. Wucker asked me.

"I'm fourteen," I said.

"No, you're not," said Jimmy. "You won't be fourteen until next year."

"Well, yeah, but that's not too far off," I said.

"All right, you're almost fourteen," said Mrs. Wucker, who was one of the youngest mothers I knew. She was very blonde, just like Jimmy and Karen. Her husband, on the other hand, was a big dark hairy guy who hardly ever talked or smiled. He was a doctor who fitted glasses in downtown Oceanside, and he and Mrs. Wucker had met in college.

"You see," continued Mrs. Wucker, "the human body is very beautiful, and love-making is one of the most wonderful experiences of life. Children should be taught about their sexuality just like they are taught how to ride a bike or drive a car. A lot of things can go wrong if we don't know what we're doing. For instance, just the simple act of kissing has to be done properly or there can be a lot of confusion. Take the nose, you can't kiss if you don't turn your heads sideways or your . . . "

I suddenly realized what had happened when I'd closed my eyes and puckered my lips to kiss Mary. Her eyes had also been closed so this was why we'd bumped our noses, then banged our heads together, hitting the door behind her. And her dad, thinking that someone had knocked on the front door, had gotten out of his chair with his newspaper in hand, opened the door, and that's when we'd fallen through the doorway with me on top of Mary. I should have kept my eyes open, so I could've seen that our noses were a problem and turned my face to one side. Then everything would have maybe been okay.

"This is the male sexual organ," said Mrs. Wucker, pointing to one of the charts. "And this is the female sexual organ," she added, pointing to the other chart. "As you can see, men and women are built alike in most respects and yet quite differently when it comes to their sexual parts."

I glanced at Jimmy and Karen. They didn't seem the least bit embarrassed by what their mother was telling us. Myself, I could hardly look at the pictures, because I couldn't help it, but . . . but now I was beginning to imagine Jimmy's mother naked as she stood alongside the charts, pointing to them. I mean, the way she filled out her blouse and slacks, she looked every bit as beautiful as the nude woman on the chart.

Mrs. Wucker was now telling us about hygiene and washing ourselves properly before we put our private parts together so we wouldn't develop rashes and strong odors, and especially for girls with their something cycle every month. My eyes opened wide. Boy, this was probably why a girl had given me toilet water on Valentine's Day in the third grade so I could wash my private parts. I turned all red.

Now Mrs. Wucker told us that normally it was best if the man was a couple of years older than the girl he married and had some experience because men developed more slowly than women. But it was also okay if it went the other way and the woman was older and had some experience.

"Like you're two years older than Karen," said Mrs. Wucker to me, "so this would be a good relationship, once you two grow up and finish high school and go to college. In fact, one of the main reasons people go to college is to find a mate."

Karen and I glanced at each other, but quickly turned away, we were so embarrassed. I guess that Mrs. Wucker was saying that Karen and I could get married when we got older. But I wasn't really thinking about Karen. No, I was thinking about Mrs. Wucker and wondering if her private parts were blonde and if she had plans to teach me so I'd have experience before I married.

Then, I couldn't believe it, Mrs. Wucker now began to tell us about the different positions that people most commonly used while making love. My eyes got wide once again. I'd never realized that people could do it face to face! How embarrassing! I'd always thought that people did it from behind, like horses and cows.

Suddenly I understood where Mary had been putting my hand when we were at the movies and why it had gotten so warm and all sweaty. We'd been doing it, and I hadn't even known it. That's why she'd kept pushing herself back and forth into my hand and started having trouble with her breathing.

I leaped up and ran out of the study, across the kitchen, down the hallway, and out the front door. I ran across the field to the Wucker's barn and got my horse and took off for home as fast as I could ride. I'd sinned! I'd really, really sinned, and I hadn't even realized it! I had to go to confession as fast as I could! I didn't want to go to hell, in case I died. I'd done it! I really had, and I wasn't even married!

Jimmy Wucker caught up with me when I was getting to our own stables. He'd come chasing after me on his horse. He wanted to know what was going on. I told him that I had to go to confession as soon as possible. He asked why. I didn't want to tell him, but I finally did, and he started laughing and telling me that I hadn't really done it yet.

"You two were just petting," he said. "You petted hers, but she didn't even pet yours."

I nodded. This made a lot of sense. "Then petting isn't doing it?" I asked.

"No," he said.

"Oh, then does this mean that Mary is still a good girl?"

"Is that her name?"

I turned a dozen different shades of red. I should never have said her name. "Yes," I said. "But you've got to promise to never tell anyone."

"Okay," he said. "And yes, she's still a good girl. You see, everyone pets," he added. "It's just natural. People can even pet themselves."

"No."

"Yes."

"Not in my family!" I yelled.

"What do you think, that your parents are virgins? Your father and mother petted themselves growing up, then once they got married, they did it all the way or you kids wouldn't even be here."

"Well, yeah, maybe so, but my parents have only done it five times, so they could have us five kids. My older brother Joseph who died, my older sister Tencha, and me and my two little sisters Linda and Teresita."

Jimmy laughed all the more. "Married couples do it more than just to have kids," he said, "especially if they're happy and love each other."

"You mean like once a year?" I said.

"No, more like several times a week, my mom told me."

I closed my eyes. I'd never be able to look at Jimmy's mom in the face again. Now I'd always see her doing it in all those positions she'd shown us. Oh, I couldn't stand it! I was now sure to go to hell—my mind was so full of all these sinful, awful thoughts. But what could I do?

"Well, maybe so," I said, "but that's because your parents are Protestants. Catholics, I'm sure, don't do it that much."

"You've brought up a very interesting point," said Jimmy, "because I've been reading in *National Geographic* about some very different sexual practices in accordance with different religious beliefs. But I'd venture to say that Catholics, because of their larger families, probably do it even more often than Protestants."

I stopped listening. Suddenly I was flashing on all those pictures of large-breasted naked native women in Africa and South America that Jimmy had shown me in one of his *National Geographic* magazines with the bright yellow border on the cover. Then once more I flashed on his mother standing alongside the two charts of nude people, and she was completely naked as she pointed to the charts, and yes, she had blonde hair on her private parts. I guess that was when I began to fall head over heels in love with Jimmy's mother. I mean, after that, I'd get so embarrassed every time I'd see her that I didn't know what to do. She knew so much and was so beautiful. I began to dream of Mrs. Wucker and her charts, and . . . and of her teaching me all that she knew.

# CHAPTER FOUR

The school dance at the Academy was only two weeks away and I didn't know what to do. Should I invite Karen, Jimmy's sister, or should I invite Clare, my friend Nick's sister, whom I'd gone to St. Mary's with in Oceanside? Or . . . or should I tell Mrs. Wucker that I loved her and that every night I dreamed of her and invite her to the school dance? Oh, it was so confusing. I was a virgin, and yet my head was so jam-packed full of wonderful, awful, sinful thoughts that I couldn't invite any girl to the school dance. I mean, we were going to have to wear our white dress pants to the event and I just knew that if I danced with my date and our private parts brushed against each other, my thing was going to leap out so big that everyone would see my pants sticking out.

My only salvation was to talk to Mrs. Wucker and ask her to please teach me what to do. But what if she said yes, that she'd teach me, then what would I do? Because the priests told us that sex outside of marriage was a mortal sin, and we'd burn in hell for all eternity! Oh, my dear lord God, I didn't want any more catastrophes happening to me like what had happened with Mary at the movies. And I couldn't not invite anyone and just go to the dance alone, because I'd been going to the Academy for three years—since the seventh grade—and I'd never brought a date to any of our dances. I was told that this was it, that I had to bring a girl to the next school dance like everyone else. Otherwise my class would get demerits because I wasn't participating in extracurricular activities. I felt trapped. But what could I do?

Finally, I decided to invite my friend Becky, who also lived up the hill from us past the rock house on California Street. Becky and I were pretty good friends, after all, and her dad knew my dad and so probably, just maybe, I wouldn't get turned down. Plus she was beautiful and had her own horse, so this probably meant that she'd seen her horse do it, so maybe I'd be safe with her because she also didn't know that people could do it face to face.

I asked her, she accepted, and on the night of the dance my parents and I picked her up in our car—we cadets weren't allowed to take our own vehicles to school—and she came out of her house in the most beautiful-looking dress I'd ever seen. She looked spectacular! And her eyes were dancing all over the place.

On the way to the Academy we sat in the back seat together, and my parents sat up front. I didn't know if Becky and I were supposed to sit close together and hold hands or sit far across the seat from each other. I mean, I'd never held hands with a girl since I went to the movies with Mary. But then driving across the lagoon that separated Oceanside from Carlsbad, Becky moved over closer to me and took my hand, which felt really good, but I made sure she didn't put my hand in her lap. After all, I wasn't innocent anymore.

Getting to the Academy, my parents pulled up in front of the main guardhouse and told Becky and me that they'd come back for us at midnight. I got out, walked around the car, and opened the car door. I took Becky's hand to help her out of the car as we'd been instructed to do at school. We said our goodbyes to my parents and went up the walkway along with all the other cadets who'd come down to receive their dates at the curb.

I'd been taking dancing lessons for a month now, so I wasn't feeling too terrified as we went up the stairs and into the gym, which had been decorated to look like a ballroom. The dance floor was set up in the middle of the room, and there were tables with chairs along the sides. Punch and soft drinks had been set up on a table by the entrance. Becky wore a pretty little jacket and gloves. We crossed the dance floor to leave her things on a table. As we walked, I noticed that a lot of cadets were looking at my date once she'd removed her jacket. And I could see why. I'd never seen Becky all dressed up before. I'd always known her in Levis, boots, and long-sleeved Western shirts. But a few months back, I'd come to see Becky in a whole different light.

We'd been riding our horses along the railroad tracks down by Crouch Street when her mare started acting up. Up on a little hill in front of us, a stallion belonging to our friends the Nelsons could smell that her mare was in heat. He was calling to her in wild, screeching horse calls. Becky's mare heard him and started going crazy *loca*, too. This was when her mare suddenly reared up and accidentally hit her in the chest with her neck and head. Becky was almost knocked unconscious. It took all I knew about horses to get that mare to calm down enough so I could get Becky safely out of her saddle and on the ground.

That was when I saw that Becky's blouse had come open and one of her breasts had popped out. I couldn't help myself, I kept staring. I'd never seen a girl's naked breast before, and especially not one this large and up close to my face. Instantly, I swear, without me meaning to, my thing got so big in my Levis that I got dizzy and had trouble breathing. But Becky was oblivious to this. Her hands covered her face as she was crying in pain. I reached out to steady her and helped her sit upright on the ground. Then her other breast popped out of her shirt. I lost my breath at the sight of her two great big juicy breasts and got so dizzy that I had to sit down, too. Her breasts weren't just huge, but mammoth, and I'd never realized that girls' breasts had such big, thick nipples with a little pinhole in the middle. I guessed that the pinhole was for babies to nurse on and get milk just like a calf with a cow. I could never look at Becky the same way after that. Just as I used to undress Mrs. Wucker with my eyes every time I saw her, I now started undressing Becky, whom I was sure had to have the biggest, prettiest breasts on any girl or even a grown woman.

Now at the dance and after putting her stuff down, I walked with Becky back across the dance floor to the punch bowl and soft drink area. The place was really crowded, and I was only a sophomore and had no rank, so Becky and I kept getting pushed back in the crowd of cadets and their dates.

"Wait here," I finally said to her. "I'll just cut in real fast from the side, get us some punch, and be right back."

I did just that. And I was gone no more than a minute, but when I came back, Becky was in tears.

"What happened?" I asked.

"Those two guys over there," she said, pointing to two older cadets, "they spilled their punch on me."

"What? Was it an accident?"

"No," she said, shaking her head, "it was no accident. They deliberately poured their punch on the front of my dress."

My heart exploded. I could now see that the low-cut part of her gown that held her breasts was soaked pink with punch. "But why would they do that?" I asked, still not understanding.

"Guys are always making fun of my . . . my large chest," she said, crying. "Look, they're laughing now and telling those other guys what they did to me."

I turned and saw that the two older cadets were now, indeed, pointing toward my date, and they were laughing. They must have told the other two cadets what they'd done. She was right. This had been no accident. They'd done it on purpose.

My heart began going crazy*loco,* beat, beat, BEATING! My mouth was suddenly dry, and I was in a rage. I knew these guys. They were seniors and one was a sergeant, but I didn't give a rat's ass.

"Come on," I said to Becky, "I'll walk you back to our table and take care of this. This will never happen to you again while you're with me."

I sat her down with both of our glasses of punch, then walked back across the crowded room. I was so angry I was trembling. There were two of them, and they were both way bigger than me, but working all these years on the ranch baling hay and moving horses and pigs and cattle had made me into a pretty strong, capable guy. I'd joined the wrestling team my freshman year, and I'd beaten a lot of guys who were juniors and seniors. I marched right up to the four older cadets.

"You two," I said to the guys who poured their punch on Becky. "We've got business outside!"

All four looked at me, and a couple of them started laughing.

"What are you gonna do, spill punch on us?" said one. "Look, it was an accident. Don't be ridiculous. You don't want to step outside with us."

My mouth felt like it was full of cotton balls. I had to keep licking my lips. "I don't think it was an accident," I said. "I think you two are such chicken-shit cowards that you only pick on girls," I added, kind of liking how I'd said this. I almost sounded like one of those good guys you saw in the movies defending the heroine's honor.

"We aren't chicken-shits," said the other one, laughing. "We just think that you and your cheap date look ridiculous. How'd you ever end up with Big Boobs anyway?"

"Yeah, why don't you turn Big Boobs over to us older guys who know how to handle a girl like that," said the first one.

I was going to kill these two guys right on the spot. This was just the kind of talk my dad had told me that son-of-a-bitch soldiers had used when they'd beaten and abused his sisters in the Revolution.

"LISTEN!" I yelled. "Are you two chicken-shits afraid of stepping out with me or what?"

This was good. My dad would be proud of me. Also, I'd seen this done in many movies when the good guy had had enough. But on the other hand, what the hell was I supposed to do if they really did come outside with me? Maybe I should've yelled a lot louder so somebody on the faculty could hear our ruckus and come over and break us up, because I'd never have a chance against these two big guys at the same time. I should never have brought a date. I should have come alone and let my class get demerits.

"All right, let's go outside," said the biggest one.

Oh, shit, I'd really done it! But what the hell, who was I to complain? My dad had had to step up to the plate of manhood when he'd only been ten years old and I was sixteen. We walked across the room with me leading the way. The whole place was so noisy that no one noticed our argument. My heart was going a million miles an hour. I'd been a fool! What was I, stupid? Going out the side door of the gymnasium, the sea breeze hit me like a cold wall. I was terrified. There were some concrete steps in front of me. As soon as the door closed behind us, I stepped up on the first step so I'd be taller than them and whirled about screaming at the top of my lungs, taking them both by surprise.

"YOU BASTARDS! I'VE KNOWN THAT GIRL SINCE WE WERE LITTLE KIDS! How would you like to have someone do that to your sister? You ever come near her again and I'll cripple the two of you for life! AND DON'T THINK I CAN'T! I was raised on a ranch! I've got guns and knives and axes and know how to use them, and I'll bring them with me to school and butcher you two assholes!"

"She's your sister?" said one, looking slightly concerned.

"No," said I.

"We're not afraid of you!" said the other one, not looking concerned in the least. "There are two of us, and we're both bigger than you!"

"SO IS A THOUSAND POUND STEER bigger than me!" I bellowed, leaping off the step into the face of the one who'd spoken last. "AND I SLAUGHTER THEM!"

Reflexively, he leaped back away from me, and in that instant when they were both stunned, I turned, opened the door, and quickly walked back into the ballroom. I'd done it and it had worked and I'd saved my date's honor and, also, my father's words to me had come true. He'd always told me that if you're scared or outnumbered, just take your enemy by surprise with a scream or a gunshot over his head, because a coward would always back down for a split-second no matter how big and brave he pretended to be. It took a very brave, confident *hombre* to hold steady during a surprise attack.

So this, then, proved that they were, indeed, chicken-shit cowards, which I'd assumed because only sick cowards would pour drinks on a girl's breasts. But my dad had also explained to me that a bluff could only work once, and that was why I'd turned quickly and gone back inside. My dad had told me that he'd seen many a brave man done in by cowards because he hadn't known when to fold his cards and walk away.

Back inside, I had to take several deep breaths to calm down. Then I quickly walked back across the crowded room. The two cowards had also come back inside. I'd have to keep away from them for the rest of the evening, but give them a hard, strong-looking face every time our eyes met, acting like I'd never been afraid of them in the least.

But when I got to our table, Becky wasn't there. I looked all around for her. I guessed she'd gone to the restroom to dry herself off. Or, maybe, she'd gotten so upset that she'd called her father and gone home. And who could blame her.

Then I saw Becky on the dance floor with my friend Nick McLean who was on the wrestling team with me but two weights above me. Nick was one of our best wrestlers, and I could now see that he was also an excellent dancer as he spun around and around with Becky, my date, in his arms. They looked so happy together. This was crazy*loco*! I mean, I'd just risked limb and life for her and she hadn't waited two minutes for me. No, she'd gone off with Nick, my friend, a good guy, and now her eyes were dancing for him with such love as they whirled around and around.

When the dance was over, Becky spotted me and walked toward me with Nick at her side.

"Nick tells me you two are best friends," she said, holding his hand in her hand close to her private place.

"Well, I don't know about best friends," I said. "But we're on the wrestling team together, and we are good friends."

"I didn't know where you went," she continued, "and Nick was kind enough to ask me to dance."

"But, Becky, you knew that I went outside to straighten out that mess about your . . . "

"Let's not talk about that right now," she said, cutting me off. "Everything is okay. Do you mind if Nick and I dance together one more time?"

What could I say? "Sure, of course, go ahead," I said. One more dance became another, and another, and now I could see that the two guys, whom I'd taken outside to defend her honor, were laughing at me and really enjoying themselves watching Nick, a very popular cadet, dance with my date, dance after dance. Finally, I went outside and looked up at the stars so I wouldn't feel like such a stupid damn fool.

At midnight when my father and mother came to pick us up, Becky wanted to know what had happened to me, saying that I'd disappeared so she'd ended up dancing with Nick all night and two of my other best friends. I didn't know what to say. I'd never realized that I had so many best friends, so I said nothing. I was feeling so confused inside that I didn't want her to even touch my hand as we rode in the back seat of my parents' car back to Oceanside.

I didn't know how to explain it, but Becky just wasn't very beautiful to me anymore. Something crazy*loco* had happened to me deep inside when I saw that she hadn't even appreciated what I'd tried to do to protect her honor. I felt so terrible I wanted to cry. When we got to her house, I got out and opened the car door for her, but I made sure not to take her hand or let her touch me as I walked her to her door.

After that, on the way home, I was so quiet that my parents wanted to know if everything was okay. I said yeah, sure, and as soon as we got home, I went to my room and lay down. This wasn't how it went in the movies. The good guy always won, and I'd been the good guy—or so I'd thought. Now these two big seniors were going to be waiting for me at school Monday morning to beat the living crap out of me. And what for?

Tears came to my eyes as I looked out my bedroom window. I could see stars in the night sky and I could also see that my dad had been right once again. Even before I'd started kindergarten my dad had explained to me that most men didn't know beans about choosing the right woman. Yet knowing how to choose the right woman for a wife was the most important thing that a man needed to know.

"Most men are fools," he'd always tell me, "thinking that a pretty face or a great figure is the answer, but these are small potatoes compared to what is needed to make a home. To make a home, a woman must be smart, strong, cunning, and, above all else, have a good heart. Because without a good *corazón*, you can't have trust, and without trust no love can last for long."

My dad was right. I'd lost all trust for Becky before we'd even kissed. Hadn't she realized that I'd been her hero tonight, that I'd stood up for her, and that Nick had lied when he'd told her that he and I were best friends? Good friends, yes. But not best. And those other guys who'd danced with her, saying they were my best friends, too, hadn't she been able to see through all those lies and figure out that they were lying and they'd just wanted to rub up against her big boobs like Nick had done all evening long? Yes, I could now see very clearly that a woman had to be smart and strong to make, not just a home, but even a date.

"Always watch how a woman treats other women," my dad had also told me, "especially when they're working in the kitchen. Is she happy? Does she work with ease? Then watch how she handles her *tortilla* when she eats her *frijoles* and *guizado*. Does she chew her food real good? Because if she doesn't, she'll have an angry stomach, and a woman with an angry stomach will always find every fault she can in her husband. Then, most important, notice how a woman behaves when a man walks into the kitchen. Does she change her ways, or does she continue behaving as she'd been behaving before the man walked in? Strong, confident women don't change their ways. Only weak confused women get all cute and flirtatious and their eyes begin to dance. This is also why you must learn to study a woman's eyes and see for whom they dance, because dancing eyes are always a good indication of *amor*."

I guess that I'd been a fool. I hadn't been paying attention to see for whom Becky's eyes danced when a guy came near her. And why hadn't I been paying attention? I guess because I'd been hypnotized by her gorgeous eyes and big beautiful breasts. Now I was going to pay the price for my stupidity and get my ass killed on Monday.

When was I ever going to learn that I couldn't be around girls without everything going crazy*loco*? Only with Mrs. Wucker did I seem to be able not to screw things up. With her, whatever I said or did just seemed to come out perfect. That night I once more dreamed of Jimmy Wucker's beautiful blonde mother with the greatest smile in all the world. She was so smart and levelheaded and . . . and she knew a dozen different positions.

# CHAPTER FIVE

I was terrified. It was Monday morning, and I knew the moment I got to school those two seniors would be waiting for me to beat me up. But when I got off the bus, I glanced all around and I didn't see them. I quickly made my way across campus to my assigned cottage. We, the day students, were assigned to a room with a couple of boarders and were expected to help our fellow cadets get their rooms ready for our first morning inspection.

I was in a cottage with eight other students, and in my room one cadet was from Mexico and the other from France. The other students in our cottage were from places like Los Angeles, La Jolla, Pasadena, and Hollywood. They were all talking about the things that had happened after the dance on Saturday night. I couldn't believe what I heard. They said a lot of dates had sneaked back on campus after the dance. Then I heard that Nick's date had come back to see him on Sunday, and they'd had a wild time behind the stage in the main building. I couldn't believe it. Did this mean that Nick had a date of his own and that she'd come back to see him the day after the dance, or did it mean that Becky, my date, had come to see Nick the following day? I wondered if anyone even knew that she'd originally been my date.

These thoughts were racing through my mind as I made my way to my last class of the morning. Then suddenly coming around a building, there were those two big seniors. They were grinning and there was nothing I could do. I hadn't been paying attention. They'd caught me flat-footed. And this time I was the one who quickly turned into a coward and got my ass kicked.

In fact, if a cadet officer hadn't stopped them, they probably would've killed me. They were kicking me once they got me down on the ground and telling me that I'd been a stupid fool, that Nick had ended up getting it on with my date just as they'd known was going to happen. The cadet officer, who stopped them from injuring me was named O'Brien. He was a captain and one of the toughest, strongest, and also nicest guys in the school. He was from La Jolla, and at the dance on Saturday he'd brought his sister, aunt, mother, and a beautiful date as well. He'd danced the Charleston with his aunt, who was absolutely drop-dead gorgeous and maybe only ten years older than him. He'd seemed so comfortable with himself, dancing with his aunt and date and sister and mother. I bet that he really knew who he was and who he wasn't, and he didn't keep undressing his date or his aunt in his mind's eye all the time.

"Do you want to report this?" O'Brien asked me, after breaking up the fight.

I wanted to report it. I really did, but I knew that I'd get it worse later on if I did. Also, if I reported it, then the whole business of my defending Becky's honor would come out, then everyone and his uncle would know I was the biggest damn fool in school.

"No," I said, shaking my head, "I don't want to report it."

"Okay, but let me tell you two something," he said, turning back to his fellow seniors. "If you ever harass any lower class cadet again, you'll deal with me!"

They quickly cowed down to him. After all, O'Brien already shaved and looked like a fully grown man. I went back to my cottage to wash my face and straighten up my uniform. My roommate Juan Limberopulos, who was from Guadalajara, Mexico, wanted to know what had happened to me. I told him the truth, that I was the one who'd brought the girl with the large breasts to school. The same girl who ended up with Nick.

"And for that these two guys beat you up?" he asked.

"No," I said. "They beat me up because . . . because," I could hardly say it, "I called them outside to defend her honor. They'd deliberately spilled punch on her breasts."

He started laughing. "And while you were outside defending her honor, Nick picked her up, eh?"

I nodded.

"What honor, you fool!" he said. "Don't you know that girls with big breasts have got to have it and have no honor, because they have extra hormones?"

"You mean only girls with small breasts have honor?"

"Of course. Everyone knows that, you fool! That's why if you're smart, you get all the girls you can with big breasts like Nick is doing, but only marry girls with small breasts."

"That's bullshit," said Lamont, the cadet from France who had come into the room. "Women with large breasts have just as much honor as small-breasted women. I know, I've had both, and believe me, they were all very honorable!" he added, laughing.

"But doesn't honor mean that you don't do it until you're married?" I asked.

"For girls, yes," said Juan, "but for us guys, no. We're obligated to go out and get experience so we'll know what to do on our wedding night."

I nodded, trying to figure out how this new bit of information fit into everything else I'd learned so far about men and women. But it was very difficult for me to make sense of this new stuff. Girls and sex and love just didn't seem to fit together and make sense like things did in chess or math or wrestling. Girls and sex seemed as confusing to me as reading and writing, where the exact same word could be pronounced a whole different way and have a different meaning depending on how it was used in a sentence. I didn't know what to think. It just seemed to me like the whole world was thinking about nothing else but sex, sex, SEX!!

"But, then, what happens to all of those girls who we guys get experience with," I asked my roommates. "Do they find guys to marry, too?"

"Some do, but mostly they don't," said Juan, "because they've been soiled."

"Bullshit," said Lamont, "doing it before marriage or not doing it before marriage has very little to do with getting married or not. It depends how well the girl dresses and how well she can do it. Some women marry rich wonderful men after doing it all over the place."

"You mean it's not just about doing it, but how well we can do it?" I asked. This was astonishing! I'd never heard of this.

"Aren't you a much better wrestler now that you've had two full seasons behind you?" asked Juan.

He was also on the wrestling team with me, two weights below me. Juan was very muscular and well defined, with a six-pack etched on his stomach. I, on the other hand, wasn't that muscular-looking but I was much stronger than Juan and had a very good sense of balance, which our coach, a Marine, told us was the most important thing in wrestling or in hand-to-hand combat.

"Well, yes, of course," I said. "I'm a lot better at wrestling now that I've had two full seasons under my belt, but does this mean that we guys are supposed to practice and work out at f . . . f . . . you know, doing it?"

I wasn't able to say the word. They burst out laughing so much that I turned all red and walked off, feeling even more like a fool than before. All that week the talk was that Becky was coming to school every afternoon to see Nick and that they were actually, really doing more than just petting each other's private parts. They were doing it. They were practicing. And people said that Nick told them that Becky was really experienced and very good at knowing how to do it just right.

I felt crushed.

I felt betrayed.

I felt like such a damn fool! Didn't anyone know that it was wrong to do it before you got married? I just didn't know what was going on. I'd always thought that doing it was a great sin and that you'd go straight to hell if you did it before marriage. I'd thought only "bad" girls did it. And yet, I knew Becky wasn't, well, really a bad girl. I'd known her since we were kids, but maybe Juan was right and big-breasted girls just had too many hormones and couldn't help themselves.

My dad was right once again. For as long as I could remember, my father told me that the relationship between a man and a woman was the greatest of life's mysteries. That he'd seen many a big tough man become nothing but a little weakling when it came to women and that he'd also seen many a levelheaded woman go crazy*loca* over a man. And I knew that what my dad had told me was true, because just last year a friend of my dad's, a big strong-looking man, had killed himself because he hadn't known how to handle his new wife.

He'd been a very successful real estate broker. His first wife had died, and he'd remarried a younger woman with two kids from a previous marriage. I'd met her. She was a dyed blonde with great big boobs. She wanted him to sign over his beach house and other real estate holdings to her. He'd said no, he had three children from his first marriage and they were going to inherit the wealth that he and his wife had accumulated while they'd been married. His new wife had threatened to leave him, and that was when he came over to see my dad. They'd taken a walk together out to the corrals and were gone for about two hours. When my dad came back home, he was fit to be tied he was so angry.

"Lupe, he's a grown man!" my dad had said to my mother as he fixed himself a drink. "A smart man, a tough man, and yet he asked me, 'What should I do, Salvador?' Like he had no brains of his own. 'I'd kick her out immediately!'" my dad said that he'd told him. "Because no man or woman should live under the same roof with someone who threatened them."

"But I love her," my dad said, mimicking the real estate man.

"Bullshit!" my dad said that he'd told him. "Love isn't based on threats or blackmail! You offer her a deal if you want to keep her. Tell her you'll leave her the beach house when you die, but not a penny more, and if she doesn't like that, then tell her to hit the road!"

"But what if she leaves me?" my dad said his friend asked.

"She won't! You yourself said that she didn't have a pot to piss in when you married her. And she's not that young anymore or that valuable at the marketplace of marriage. Hell, you got a better chance than her to find another woman. You're smart, you're good-hearted, and you're clean and dress well. Shit, you don't even smoke, so you don't stink, either."

"You're right, Sal," his friend had said to him. "I'll offer her that deal and if she doesn't like it, she can kiss my ass goodbye."

"Now you're talking," my dad told his friend. "Good for you! Now you're making sense like the good businessman that you are. Not a dumb kid thinking he's in love. Women, I swear, are smarter at separating love from sex and being practical in matters like this. It will work. Just keep your cards close to your chest and hold tight. Because what you're doing is honest and fair. And if a man or woman doesn't keep love based on honesty and being fair, then you just got lust and doubt telling you what to do. And it will be better for her, too. No woman likes to be with a man that she can just push around. Be strong! Get her to respect you! That's *el amor!*"

But, then, two days later our local newspaper reported that a local real estate broker, who had his offices on Hill Street just south of Cassidy Street, had shot himself to death, and he'd left everything to his kids, except for his beach house, which he'd left to his current wife. My dad got so mad he refused to go to the funeral.

"THAT DAMN FOOL!" he roared. "He wasn't in love! To be in love at any age isn't a little kid's game! It's a serious matter! The most serious business any man or woman will ever get into in their lives! The whole heart is open. You feel things you feel at no other time. That damn coward! He knew better here in his heart, but his head had him trapped! He couldn't admit to himself that what he really had going with this woman was a business arrangement. It never had anything to do with love. But here in his head he was still a baby, hoping for love, and not knowing that real love between a man and woman has to have the basis to weather the storms of hate and greed and doubt and passion. A man needs to know how to put his foot down and say, cross this line, *y te chingas!*"

"And a woman?" asked my mother quietly.

"A woman, too! They need to know how to say cross this line and that's it! Men and women both need to know where to draw the line, but this they can't know how to do until they first know who they are and who they aren't. This is exactly what *Benito Juárez*, the Abraham Lincoln of *México*, was talking about when he said, '*El respeto al derecho ajeno es la paz.*' The respect of others' rights is peace. This man was a damn fool! Marriage isn't for chicken-shit cowards! Marriage is for the brave and levelheaded!"

"Salvador," said my mother, "it's not right for you to be talking badly of the dead."

"Bullshit!" said my dad. "We need to talk about everyone, dead or living, so we can learn. In love people need to grab hold of their *tanates* and live. You don't die when love gives you a twist. You dig in deeper, and you know this, Lupe, or you and I wouldn't have lasted all these years."

"Yes, but that man's wife died and he came to you for advice, Salvador. So be kind."

"Kind, hell! We're talking about *amor*! And with love you got to have guts and understanding, not be kind! All these damn fool movies about soft, nice love are bullshit! And our kids need to know the truth about love, if they are to have a chance. Marriage isn't a *matrimonio*. It's *matar los demonios*! But you kill those demons with love like we always do, *mi amor*," he now said softly to my mother as he came close to her and stroked her back gently with his huge thick fingers. My mother smiled.

And my dad was right again. I, too, had needed to hear this, because about a week after the dance Becky came by our house looking so beautiful and she asked me if I'd like to go to the movies with her. I lied, saying that I had work to do. I knew what had happened. She and Nick had become boyfriend and girlfriend, but then the gossip at school had it that he'd dumped her when his girl from Hollywood, a well-known teen model, had come down to see him. I had to be strong. I wasn't going to let myself be taken in this time by Becky's smiles and good looks and especially not by her big boobs.

But, on the other hand, I didn't even really need to be that strong, because the truth was that I didn't see Becky in the same way anymore. And I certainly didn't undress her in my mind anymore, either. She was gone from my heart. I didn't trust her, and I could now clearly see that without trust, love really doesn't last for long. My dad was right. That real estate man had been a fool. With love a person had to be strong and have the guts to keep it based on honesty and fairness in order to survive.

Becky now became my sister Linda's friend, and I'd see her around the house a lot. She'd try to be friendly and nice to me, but how could I ever explain to her that she'd looked so beautiful, so stunning the night my parents and I had picked her up in our car that I'd been ready to fight for her, to protect her, to hug her, to kiss her, to ask her if I could put my hand on her—you know what—but after I'd seen her eyes dancing for my friend, I drew my line and that was that.

I didn't want any more catastrophes happening to me like I'd had happen to me with Mary at the movies, then with me having my beautiful turquoise truck painted white. It was really true. Life, *la vida,* had many dangerous twists and turns, and crazy*loco* things did happen if a man or woman weren't alert. And why was this? I had no idea, except maybe men and women were so . . . so different they just had no way of knowing how to behave around each other.

I was beginning to see that Mrs. Wucker was very wise to be giving her kids advice about love and sex and marriage. Once more I began to have dreams of Mrs. Wucker. Maybe this was the answer. For me to find an older woman like Mrs. Wucker or O'Brien's aunt to teach me about life. I could still see O'Brien's aunt dancing the Charleston with him at our school dance. Brunette, big happy smile, and such wonderful movement to her feet and her fine-looking butt.

# CHAPTER SIX

Then just when I thought I was finally maybe beginning to get the hang of what to do and not do around girls, something happened that was so devastating that it sent me into a wild crazy*loco* spin. It was a few weeks before the end of school, and I was out driving around in my Chevy white milk truck down by the beach in Oceanside.

It was Saturday night, but I was alone. Most of my friends were out on dates or they'd gone to the drive-in movies on Mission Street to hang out and drink beer. I didn't drink beer. In fact, I'd never even tasted one, because, like I said, I was a wrestler, and so I had to keep my weight down and stay in shape year round if I really wanted to be good at the sport.

No one was by the pier, so I drove north on the strand. I could see that there were a couple of cars parked on the beach with headlights on. The moon was full, and the whole shoreline was lit up almost as bright as day. I could see the white of the waves as they came in toward the shore. I parked and got out of my truck. I couldn't figure out what was going on. Normally guys only had beer parties on the beach after the football games, and this wasn't football season. I started across the sand to find out what was going on when two guys I knew came running by me.

"Hurry up!" yelled one with a big grin. "And you can get some, too!"

"Some what?" I said, not understanding what was going on, but I could now see that there was a crowd of people beyond the cars' headlights down by the water.

I walked past the vehicles and saw that the crowd was made up of mostly guys and only a couple of girls. They were standing close together and watching something, just like people gathered together to see a cockfight. This was when my eyes saw something that I couldn't believe was happening. There were two girls on a blanket on the dry sand just where the sea came in with the waves. The girls were naked, and they were having sex with a guy on top of them. Both girls had their knees bent, feet up in the air, going up and down really fast, yelling to the high heavens. I didn't get it. I couldn't understand what was going on, but then to my absolute horror, I suddenly realized that I knew these two girls. They were Mary's cousins. They'd also gone to school with her and me at Saint Mary's Star of the Sea when we were kids. One of the girls was Mary's age and the other was two years younger. They lived in South Oceanside. I knew their parents well. They were devout Catholics, played tennis after church every Sunday, and their father was a big, handsome ex-Marine major.

Now I realized what was going on. The two girls were drunk. Bottles of beer and wine were all over the sand, and a bunch of guys were taking off their clothes and lining up to get their turn at having sex with the two girls. And the guys who'd already done it with the two sisters were down by the shallow surf butt-naked and drinking beer as they watched. This was disgusting! This was awful! These were good girls! I'd known them for years.

"STOP IT!" I screamed. "THEY'RE DRUNK! They don't know what they're doing! I'm taking them home, you BASTARDS!"

I was strong and in excellent shape. I could do sets of forty push-ups with either arm. I quickly knocked two guys out of the way who were stripping, grabbed the guy on top of the younger girl, threw him off her, then went to grab the guy who was humping the other sister to throw him off, too. This was when the older sister saw me and screamed something that I'll never forget for the rest of my life.

"Get the hell away from here!" she shouted at me, her face filled with rage. "Who the hell do you think you are? Mexicans are only good for fucking! And you're a worthless fuckless Mexican!"

I froze.

I didn't know what to do.

The moonlight was coming down all about us, glistening off the older sister's face and neck and breasts and her smooth muscular thighs. People started laughing at me. The guy I'd pulled off the younger sister scrambled back past me, and she quickly spread her legs again, straight up into the air, taking him in again. And she was so beautiful, a very good athlete and an excellent tennis player, just like her mom and dad.

Other guys now pushed me out of the way and got back in line to have a turn. I started back to my truck. I was trembling so much when I got behind the wheel that I couldn't get my key into the ignition. I'd never be able to get that picture out of my brain, especially of the younger sister—fifteen years old—spreading her beautiful well-developed thighs and throwing her feet to the heavens, inviting that guy back. Her whole body looked so muscular and smooth and absolutely gorgeous, with her love-bush glistening wet in the moonlight.

I drove home and went to bed, but I couldn't sleep—I was so upset. If the truth be known, I'd wanted to jump on those two sisters, too. Oh, I hated what I was feeling. I finally got up, got dressed in my sweats, and took off running out of our gates and up California Street. I ran and ran and ran as fast as I could, up past Fire Mountain, and ended up by the cemetery out by El Camino. I jumped the fence and ran over to my brother Joseph's grave. He had always been so smart and brave. The full moon was bright and huge, and I was pouring with sweat. The big white cross with Jesus was only a little ways away.

"JOSEPH!" I yelled. "I SHOULD'VE DIED! Not you! You always knew what to do, just like O'Brien and Hawkins and Porter and some of the smarter, nicer guys at school. I'M STUPID! You hear me! I should've been the one to die! I don't know what to do here on earth! I'm lost, Joseph! Do you hear me? I'm crazy*loco* lost! AND I'M NO GOOD! Because, I, too, wanted to do it with those girls! I can't lie! I did! I really did!"

Crying, I lay down on his gravesite, trying to crawl in to be with my brother in his grave. I didn't want to be having all these awful sinful thoughts going on inside of my head. I cried and cried, and I must've passed out because the next thing I knew, I awoke freezing cold, and the moonlight was all around me and as bright as daylight. This was when I saw that there was a doe and her fawn just a little ways away from me, by the cross with Jesus and His sacred mother

Mary praying at His feet. The doe and her fawn were quietly eating flowers off the gravesites, looking so beautiful that my whole heart suddenly filled up with joy.

"Hi," I said to the two of them, and I swear the little fawn tossed her head and gave me a greeting, too.

I lay there and watched the doe and her fawn for a long while and began to feel a whole lot better. I got up and started for home. I could still see those two sisters on that blanket at the beach so clearly in my head. But also, I could now see that a large part of me really hadn't wanted to do it with those two sisters. Not on the beach with everyone else watching. No, when my time came to do it, I wanted to do it in privacy with kissing and stroking and whispering soft tender words of endearment, the way I saw my parents kiss and whisper to each other. That was what I really wanted.

When I got home, I went straight to bed. For the first time in my life, I petted myself. And oh, my Lord God, an explosion of juices came shooting out of my penis, feeling so painful and good, and it shot halfway to the ceiling. And now I knew what all that glistening wetness had been on that younger sister's love-bush. It had been the semen of all those guys' penises.

I must've played with myself ten times that night, feeling so good and painful each time. Then in the morning, I went to church with my parents. I'd sinned. I'd played with myself so I had to go to confession. And who did I see at church, Mary's two cousins, and the girls were with their parents and their younger brother. And they looked so proper, dressed in long dresses that covered them all the way up to their necks.

Then when it came time to do Holy Communion, I didn't go up because of all the sinful thoughts and petting that I'd done. But to my utter shock, Mary's two cousins got out of their pews and got in line with their father and mother to go up to the front of the church with everyone else to receive the Holy Sacrament of the Sacred Blood and Flesh of Jesus Christ.

I didn't know what to think. Had these two sisters gone to confession earlier this morning? Or had they been so drunk that they couldn't remember what it was that they'd done the night before? I was so upset and confused that I just knew I couldn't go on anymore with all this turmoil that was going on inside me. No wonder that big, strong-looking real estate broker had killed himself in his office down by Cassidy Street. No wonder Mary had put my hand in her lap and pushed her hips back and forth into my hand until she'd gasped and had trouble breathing.

Myself, I'd wanted to SCREAM it had hurt so good when I'd played with myself last night. Sex and love were driving the whole world and me crazy*loco*! I just couldn't stand it anymore! I was going to have to kill myself. But suicide was a mortal sin and I'd go to hell, so I couldn't do that. Then it hit me like a lightning bolt. What I'd do was castrate myself, like we did to the livestock on the ranch, and then this way I wouldn't end up wanting to do something like those guys had done on the beach last night.

I smiled. Sure, this was the answer. After all, my dad always said that the only reason we had any peace on the ranch was because 90 percent of all the males were castrated. And I knew how to do it. I'd helped castrate hundreds of goats and pigs and calves. The young horses, we had the vet do, but I'd watched him do this, too. This was it. This was the only way I could stop all these crazy*loco* thoughts and feelings that were happening inside me. I'd castrate myself. Yes, that was what I'd do. I'd get my dad's castrating knife as soon as we got home and I'd go up to the stables and get that purple medicine we used on the livestock and I'd do myself and then I'd have peace and not have to worry about wanting to do what those guys had been doing on the beach. Because if I didn't, then I'd never be able to get that picture out of my head of those two beautiful sisters doing it on the beach in the bright headlights of those parked cars, screaming with *gusto* to the high heavens!

Yes, this was it! I'd castrate myself, and then I'd be free!

# CHAPTER SEVEN

**B**ut that afternoon I didn't castrate myself, because, well, it was Sunday, so I figured that God wouldn't like me to do it on His Holy Day. I decided to castrate myself on Monday after school. And I'd do it quickly, because I knew if I didn't do it quickly, I'd probably chicken out. My God, just to think about castrating myself was so painful and scary that I got all dizzy and my stomach tightened, pulling my testicles up into my body.

The next day after my last class, I was deep in thought as I walked by the main administration building, going down to the front guardhouse to catch the bus that took us day students home. I could now see that this was probably the biggest decision of my whole life, because after this, I'd never be able to have kids, but, well, maybe this was good, too. After all, I was Mexican, and Mexicans were no good and stupid and only good for the "f" word, so it was best— probably even God's plan—for me to castrate myself. That way, I wouldn't bring anymore no-good stupid Mexican kids into the world.

I was thinking these thoughts and trying to be brave and not chicken out when, out of the blue, Major Terry, an upper-division math teacher, came out of his classroom and called my name.

"Villaseñor!" he shouted.

"Yes, sir!" I said.

"Come in here!" he ordered.

I was still a sophomore. Only juniors and seniors took classes with him. And also I knew that, being one of the slowest in my class, I was never going to be assigned to take trig or calculus with him. I'd probably be told to take algebra or a second year of plane geometry because, as it was, I wasn't doing very well in Commander Ash-more's lower math classes.

I came around the green railing of the walkway leading to Major Terry's classroom. I was surprised he even knew my name. He was considered by a lot of students to be the smartest teacher we had on campus. I'd never been in his room before. It was large and well lit with a lot of equations on the board that I couldn't make heads or tails of, but they did look pretty interesting.

"I understand you play chess," he said.

"Yes, sir, I do." I said.

The year before Bill Coe, a fellow cadet, had really surprised me by giving me a chess set. Coe was one of the toughest, nicest guys in the school, and his grandmother lived in South Oceanside so he was allowed to go off campus on weekends to visit her. He and Lit-tle Richard were best friends and two of the coolest guys on or off campus, so it had really surprised me to get a birthday present from him. And I didn't know how to play chess. Hell, I'd never even seen a chess set before. But Bill taught me a few moves, then Nick Ror-ick taught me some more, and soon I was playing a little bit, but I was never any good until one day it dawned on me that the two hors-es changed to a different color square every time you moved them. And that two horses could control the center of the board, if you knew how to use them, because they were the only pieces on the board that could jump over the other chess pieces.

Suddenly, I don't know how to explain it, but the chess pieces seemed to come alive for me. It was like I could now see the chess pieces moving on the board on their own. I started beating every-body. I, the slowest of the slow, had now gone something like a hun-dred games without losing. I could do no wrong. It was magical how the pieces spoke to me, showing me where to move.

"I understand you're quite good," said Major Terry, turning and going to his desk where he had a chess set all set up and ready to go.

"Yes, sir, I am," I said.

"Did you really beat Drosen?"

"Drosen?"

"Yes, the big rugged-looking cadet in my advanced calculus class."

"Oh, him. The tall guy with the big jaw who has to shave every day?"

"Yes, the handsome lad. He's going to my old alma mater."

"Alma-what?"

"To West Point. I graduated from there," he said, smiling.

"Oh," I said. I'd never heard this word "alma-madder."

"Did he give you a good game?" he asked.

"No, not really," I said, wanting to get out of here so I wouldn't miss my bus and have to walk home. I had to get home as soon as I could so I'd have enough daylight to do what I had to do.

"What do you mean 'not really'?" he said, suddenly changing his tone of voice toward me. "He's a very capable player!"

"Okay. I guess he is. Can I go now?"

"Just hold on," he said to me. "I'd like to play a game or two with you."

"Look, sir, I don't have time to beat you," I said. "I've got to catch the bus home."

"You don't have time to beat me!" he barked at me. "What does that mean?"

"Well, uh," I said, trying to look out the window to see if the bus had already left, "I've seen you play, sir, and you're not very good."

"I'm not very good!" he shouted. "I'll have you know I was one of the best of all the chess players at the Point!"

"Point what?"

"West Point!"

"Oh, good for you. I'm glad to hear that. But I really have to go. See you some other time. Goodbye, sir."

And I turned, running out of the classroom. The bus was pulling away from the guardhouse, but I figured that I could still catch it if I ran across the grass and jumped the hedge where the bus made a U-turn to go north and drop off the Oceanside students.

"Wait!" shouted the major. "I'll take you home! I want to see if you're really as good as they say you are!"

I came back into his classroom. I figured if I beat him real fast I could still maybe get a ride with one of the maintenance men who lived in Oceanside, not far from our ranch.

"All right," I said, "but let's make it fast, okay? Then I can still maybe catch a ride home with *Jesús* in maintenance."

"Fast? You can't play chess fast," he said to me. "You need to think out each move."

"Okay, whatever," I said.

I really didn't want to play. I needed to get home, change clothes, go to the stables, get the things I needed out of the first-aid box, and ride out into the hills. I needed plenty of time to castrate myself, then have enough time to scream and breathe and let the pain subside before I headed for home again. I was trying to think it all out ahead of time.

But just wait. After cutting myself, I'd be too weak to lift my leg high enough to remount my horse to ride home. I'd seen how animals couldn't even move after we'd cut them. That was why it was best to castrate livestock right after they were born. To castrate a young horse or bull was a major operation, so for me to castrate myself at sixteen years of age was going to be . . . oh, my God, I'd have to use whiskey, not just to disinfect myself but also maybe even to drink so I could keep my nerve and ease the pain.

"Which do you want, white or black?"

"What?"

"The chess pieces, which do you want, white or black?"

"Uh, well, I really don't care, sir," I said.

"Well, then, I'll take the white," he said.

"Fine," I said.

He sat down. I did, too. He looked over the chess set real carefully before he took his first move. It always puzzled me when people did this. Whites moved first, and this was just the first move of the game, so who gave a crap? What did they think, that the pieces weren't in the exact same place as they'd been for the last few hundred years of chess playing? He finally moved his queen's pawn two spaces forward. Instantly, I did the same. He glanced at me, then turned back to the board, thought a great deal again, then moved his king's pawn out one space. I did the same thing. I didn't care. Whatever he did I would do for the first few moves, then I'd start lashing out at him with my bishops and knights. It worked. He'd set up such a strong defense that when I ran my bishop across the board, letting him take my bishop free of charge with one of his pawns, he couldn't see what was happening. He was trapping himself. I then came at him with both of my knights, gave up one without even an exchange. He was so happy, I couldn't believe it. He was actually grinning and feeling so good with his two major pieces ahead that he was shocked when I said, "Checkmate!"

"What? Impossible!"

He still didn't see it. So I had to literally move my queen across the board so that he could see what I had in mind. There was nothing he could do about it. His own defense had trapped his ass, and my remaining horse and bishop had stolen his only means of escape.

"That was just luck!" he said. "Let's play again."

"I can't, sir. *Jesús* is my best chance to get a ride home."

"You live in South Oceanside, right?"

"Yes, sir."

"I'll drive you home," he said. "Now let's play! I'll keep the whites since the last game didn't count. I wasn't wearing my glasses. That was my problem."

I got up from my chair.

"Now what!" he said.

"I'd rather stand up to play. I don't like to sit to play chess. I like to move around, if that's okay with you."

"Do whatever you like," he said. "But this time I'm really going to concentrate."

And concentrate he did. It took him almost five minutes for every move. As for me, I'd move the instant he took his fingers off his piece, then I'd walk away so I could look out the open door and smell the sea breeze. I loved the smell of the ocean. Ever since I could remember, riding a horse along the seashore and breathing in the sea breeze was like heaven, especially at night with the sky full of stars. I really didn't have time to play this old guy who just kept thinking and thinking. Hell, he was thinking so damn much that he was probably forgetting what he'd first thought of. I didn't think; that was too slow. I just stared real hard at the pieces, and the whole board came alive. I beat him again quickly.

He arched his hairy old eyebrows at me, saying nothing as he studied my face. "One more game," he said, "and this time sit down!"

he yelled. "You distracted me last time, so that game doesn't count, either!"

I sat down and beat him again, even faster than before.

He exploded. "Dammit!" he yelled. "Stop moving your pieces before I take my fingers off mine! Don't you understand that you have to think before you move? You can't just be playing by wild instincts! It doesn't work that way. You need to think and plan out your game. Sit down and keep still, dammit!"

I sat down and tried to keep still and play a whole lot slower. I could see in his eyes he thought he was winning this time for sure, because he was four pawns and both knights ahead, when I suddenly said "Checkmate," once again.

His eyes went wild, and I could see that—unbelievably—he really hadn't seen it coming this time, either. He stared at me, and the veins came up on his forehead. He knocked the chess set off his desk, screaming at me, "You're not a stupid Mexican! You're just lazy! I'm one of the best chess players in all of Carlsbad and you treat me with no respect!"

I was shocked. All my life I'd been called stupid because I was Mexican, not because I was lazy. This was really good.

"Thank you, sir," I said. "That's really good."

"What's good?"

"That you called me lazy, instead of stupid."

He leaped to his feet. "Can't you stop toying with me even for a moment!" he screamed. "Now you belittle my insults! What are you, some perverted genius who likes to stay in remedial classes to ridicule our educational system?"

"Me? A genius?"

"Yes! Nobody has ever beaten me five times in a row like that, even at the Point!"

"Oh, that point west?"

"Not that point west. West Point!"

"Okay, but how can that be? You're really not that good."

Well, he must not have been used to having people being truthful with him, because he not only screamed at me this time, he literally bellowed! "GET THE HELL OUT OF HERE!"

"But my ride home?" I said. "You said you'd drive me home."

"Damn your ride home! Walk! I don't care, just get out of here!"

I picked up my things and left. I really hadn't meant to insult him. I just hadn't realized that he actually thought that he was good at chess. Boy, I'd had much better games with Nick Rorick, Bill Coe, George Hillam, and Wilbur Rochín, even though in the last few months none of these guys had beaten me, either. I mean, I didn't know what it was, but ever since what had happened to me with my turquoise truck and then with Becky, it was like I was a changed person. I didn't care what people thought anymore, and in not caring what people thought, in some strange way I'd become smarter and able to figure things out that I'd never been able to figure out before.

Hell, I didn't even pay any attention to Becky when she came over to swim and wore a bathing suit. It was like I was so free now that I didn't give a rat's ass what people thought, even when I drove my "milk wagon" around town. And being free felt wonderful! Hell, I didn't even care anymore that my Chevy truck was being used for ranch work and getting all dented up. I could now clearly see that it had been the love that I'd had for my truck and the possibility of love for Becky that had kept me all trapped and confused inside. My dad had been right once again. Love wasn't kid stuff. Love was tough!

Walking home along the beach that day, I started throwing stones into the surf, dancing them on top of the flat shallow water. This was really good. I'd now gone from being a stupid Mexican to just being lazy. I loved it. I began to whistle. I wondered if Jesus had been a chess player. If He had, I bet He'd been really fast and good and hadn't gone into all that ridiculous move-by-move slow-thinking stuff, either.

Suddenly it hit me like a thunderbolt! I now knew what had happened to me and why I'd become so good at chess overnight. I'd lost fear. Simple as that. And once a person lost fear, it was easy to see what other people couldn't see. This was what had enabled my parents to buy the huge ranch we lived on right in the middle of town. They'd been fearless. And this was why I saw things so clearly in chess and why I could move quickly. I was fearless. And Major Terry, on the other hand, was so smart and knew so much about the game of chess that he was trapped by the fear of making a mistake.

I began to laugh. This was really good, so my dad had been right again. For a person to find out who they were and who they weren't, they had to be fearless and willing to make mistakes, and big ones!

I suddenly felt so happy! Big happy! This was when I saw the dolphins, and I began to laugh *con carcajadas*. They were surfing in the waves near the shore. I stopped and called out to them, and I swear to God that the three dolphins called back at me, screeching with happiness, too!

The sun was going down and all around the whole world looked so beautiful and full of magic, and I, the slowest of the slow, had been called a genius—not by someone who liked me but by someone who hated me. I guess it was really true what my grandmother had told my dad. We did learn the most from our enemies. Man, then maybe this meant that Mexicans weren't stupid no-good people, and I, in fact, came from a heritage of smart good people. Maybe even from a whole bunch of geniuses.

I began to jump and dance, feeling so grand and wonderful as the dolphins kept surfing in and out of the waves. We were both having fun! Big, big, BIG FUN!

# CHAPTER EIGHT

The next day Major Terry's pet student, Drosen, was waiting for me when I came on campus. I hadn't had enough daylight to castrate myself when I got home, so I wasn't all swollen between the legs like our livestock, and I was still able to move. Drosen was from Pasadena, and he was real big and hairy and strong-looking. He was a football player, a whole head taller than me, and outweighed me by more than sixty pounds. I could tell he was pissed.

"So you told Major Terry that I'm a moron!" he yelled at me.

"I never said that," I said, getting ready to run. "I just said that you didn't give me much of a game."

"Are you calling Major Terry a liar?" he yelled.

"Well, not a liar," I said, "but a pretty poor loser."

"Do you really think you beat him?" he said, laughing at me. "The man is brilliant! He teaches upper-class calculus. He prepares students for MIT, not just for the military academies."

"What's MIT?"

"What's MIT?" he said, mimicking me. "You better watch your back from now on is all I've got to say. You're not so hot. Remember, you're nothing but a damn Mexican!"

I almost thanked him for not calling me stupid, but I figured that he'd go bonkers if I did, so I said nothing. Man, I was really coming up in the world. It felt pretty good. All that day, I was careful as I walked from class to class so I wouldn't be caught alone by Drosen. It was late afternoon when another teacher called me into his room. It was Olbase, the Spanish teacher who was from Spain. I was getting D's and C's in his class, even though I was fluent in Spanish. It always amazed me that some kids who couldn't speak Spanish at all got A's and B's, but the best I could muster was a C.

"Is it true that you beat Major Terry in chess yesterday?"

"Yes sir," I said.

"Five times?"

"Yes."

Olbase got a big smile. "Good going. I'm glad you beat him badly. He's such an arrogant, pompous son-of-a-gun. Would you like to stay after school and play a game?" he asked.

I looked at him. He was short, balding, and had a happy look of mischief in his eyes. "No, I don't think so," I said.

"Why? You don't have time to beat me, either?"

I was shocked. "How'd you know that I said that to him?"

"Everyone's heard," he said full of *gusto*. "You're really good. My hat's off to you. You cut his balls off before you even began to play with him. Good going. I always knew you had brains and were just pretending the fool."

"Really? You've thought that?"

"Sure. Getting a C in Spanish when it's your mother language. You'd have to be a complete idiot not to get A's," he added, laughing.

I didn't know what to say or think as I watched Olbase go to his desk, open a drawer, and bring out a chess set. The man just had no idea how hard I worked to just get that C in Spanish. It was like language made no sense at all to me. Math, yes; chess, yes; wrestling, yes. Only sex and love were even more confusing to me than language. Like the word "the." Where had that ever come from? The words "this" and "that" made sense. They gave location to objects, like when you said "that" tree over there, or "this" tree over here, but where the hell was "the" tree? Sure, you could use "the" to say "the" tree in front of my house, but you could also just say tree in front of my house.

"Here," "there," "my," "yours," "theirs," all these words made sense, but "the" made no sense, unless it was to intimidate people who couldn't read so you could point to "the" word written on a page and say, here is "the" truth, and they couldn't argue with you because they didn't know how to read.

I was beginning to think that maybe language hadn't just been developed for communication between people, but had also been developed so that the educated could control the uneducated, not just physically, but inside their brains, too. Over and over, I'd seen so many of our best and smartest workers come up from Mexico who didn't know how to read in Spanish—much less in English. They were so frightened of the written word that it was totally sad. It truly amazed me that my dad, who could also hardly read, had gotten as far as he had in this country. My mother, on the other hand, could read very well in both Spanish and English. She was the most educated person in her whole *familia,* having gone to school up to the fifth grade.

Also, I was beginning to see that in Spanish I could say things I couldn't say in English. And it was true the other way around. In English I could say certain things I couldn't say in Spanish. So I was beginning to wonder if my having spoken Yaqui and Spanish before I'd started school was what enabled me to see things that people who only spoke English couldn't see.

I'd never seen a chess set like the one Olbase was setting up. The pieces were old, carved out of wood, and had a brass base. He set up each piece with great care.

"This is the most beautiful chess set I've ever seen," I said.

"Thank you," he said. "It's from Spain. It belonged to my father. He taught my brother and me how to play, and because I could always beat my brother, our father gave me the set," he added, laughing.

I helped him set up the pieces, and just when we were getting ready to play, he stopped.

"No," he said. "I'm not going to play you. What could I gain, even if I beat you?" He laughed, truly enjoying himself. "Maybe off campus I'll play you sometime, but not here."

I nodded, said nothing, and left. It was strange, but I'd seen it in his eyes.

Olbase had gotten scared. My God, something really big had happened since I'd beaten Major Terry. People were now looking at me all differently as I walked around the campus. I wasn't just another stupid Mexican in their eyes anymore. I was someone to respect.


It wasn't until the following weekend that I had enough time to get my medical supplies and saddle up my horse to go up into the hills to castrate myself. I rode east, following the railroad tracks, then crossed

Crouch Street and continued on the trail on the south side of the tracks until I got to the cemetery, just this side of El Camino.

I had decided to stop by to see my brother Joseph at the cemetery and explain to him why I needed to castrate myself. I had tears in my eyes by the time I rode up the hill and tied my horse to the fence surrounding the burial ground. I really didn't want to castrate myself, but what else could I do to get rid of all my sinful, bad thoughts? I was now playing with myself every night, and not just once, but six or seven times, thinking of Jimmy Wucker's mother and O'Brien's aunt and my sister's friends, Carmen and Susan and Camille and Jeannie. My hand and arm were getting sore, I was playing with myself so much, and I was in excellent shape, too.

Walking past the tall white cross with Jesus Christ and His Holy Mother Mary kneeling at the bottom of the cross, I looked up at Jesus and saw all the material gathered about his loins. I wondered why they'd used so much material if it wasn't to hide His erection. Having this thought, I got scared. What was wrong with me? Now I was thinking about God's Only Begotten Son's sex life, too. This proved that I was going bonkers. Sex and love had driven me crazy*loco*! There was just no getting around it. I had to castrate myself immediately, or next I'd probably start getting the hots for the Virgin Mary.

"Dear Lord God," I said, kneeling down before the statues of Jesus and Mary, "I guess You know what's going on down here on Earth with me, because remember You know everything, so You must know what it is that I'm planning to do. I just don't see any other way, dear God. You know what I was just thinking. I mean, just to even think of getting the hots for Your mother Mary must be about the worst sin possible. Look, I'm sorry. I'm just no good and I'm horny all the time. I'm not smart like my brother and able to figure out what to do. Like that new song on the radio called 'Honey Cone' is driving me crazy*loco*. 'Get a piece of bone and a hunk of hair, and you got a walking, talking honey cone.' My God, this is so awful. Sex is everywhere! Even on the radio and on TV, too. I need Your help. I don't want to end up like those guys on the beach, so please, dear Lord, help me to be brave enough to do what I need to do, so I won't be sinning anymore."

Then I thanked God and my brother Joseph and went to my horse. I got everything out of my saddlebags, and I laid it all out on the blanket I'd put on the ground. It was a very beautiful serape with a lot of red stripes that would help hide the blood that was sure to flow. I took a deep breath. This was it. I was going to castrate myself right now.

I put my father's castrating knife to my right along with the whetstone to give the knife a few more passes to make sure it was so sharp that I'd be able to cut myself before I even realized it. I opened the bottle of purple medicine that we put on the calves and pigs after we'd cut them. I brought out the bottle of gin I'd taken from my parents' bar. I decided not to use colored liquor like whiskey or brandy, thinking that clear-looking alcohol like vodka or gin was probably better to clean myself with after I'd done the castration.

I unbuttoned my Levis, pulled them down, then pulled my underwear down, too. I was getting so nervous that I had to sit down. I'd also brought a towel to put on the blanket. Now I was beginning to have trouble breathing. I had to take in a couple of great big breaths to get my hands to stop trembling. I pulled my cock and balls over to my right side and opened the big gin bottle to wash them off, so I wouldn't get any infection. The gin smelled like perfume. It was Gordon's. It had the picture of a boar's head with tusks on the label.

I licked my forearm like I'd seen my father do a hundred times before he castrated any livestock so he could test the sharpness of the blade by seeing if it would shave the hair off of his forearm with ease. But I hardly had any hair on my forearms or on my private parts. I still didn't shave and had such a baby face that most people thought I was too young to be driving, even though I'd been driving alone for almost a month now.

The knife shaved off the few tiny thin hairs I had on my left forearm. I was ready now. Everything was set. I'd also brought thread and a needle so I could sew up the little hole I'd make in the act of castration. You see, when we castrated an animal, we didn't just cut off the sack and the whole business. No, we got hold of the pig's or calf's testicle, one at a time, and pulled on it, so the ball inside the sack would get tight up against the end of the sack. Then, all we had to do was cut a little opening at the end of the sack, and the testicle would pop through. Then, once the testicle was outside of the sack, we would push the sack upward as we held onto the ball, and this way we could cut the cords that held the testicle in place. The ball would now come completely off, looking like a very delicate piece of fine meat.

It had always amazed me that little pigs had such big meaty balls, and calves, who had larger sacks, actually had smaller balls. Also, I'd always noticed that it was more difficult to cut the first ball, because by the time you got to the second, the animal had gone into a kind of semi-shock, lay very still, acting almost dead. This was why, after you cut an animal, you had to make sure he got up and moved around, because if he didn't, he could stay in that semi-shocked state and die. This I knew because the first calf I castrated had died because I hadn't forced him to move. I wondered if this would happen to me, too. I'd have to be careful to force myself to move.

Oh, my God, this was going to be tough! After I cut my first ball, I'd have to keep myself conscious enough to be able to cut my second ball. Because if I only cut one ball, I'd still have all my feelings for women and wanting to mount them. And then, after I'd cut my second ball, I'd still have to be strong enough of mind to force myself beyond all pain and get myself to stand up, pack up my things, and walk home holding on to my horse's side, because there was no way on earth I'd be able to raise a leg high enough to remount. By the time I got home, I figured that I'd probably just about suffered about as much as Jesus Christ Himself getting crucified, and never again would I look at girls with this lust and want that was driving me crazy *loco*!

I wanted to be able to be loving and not just be thinking of sex all the time. Sex was what was driving me so insane I couldn't even conceive of holding a girl's hand and kissing her without getting such a huge erection that I was thankful my Levis were so strong they didn't rip open.

Tears were running down my face. I'd never be able to have children after this. I wished that I'd had sex at least once. Now I was never going to know how any of those positions felt that Mrs. Wucker had taught us. I mean, I really wished that I'd made love at least one time in my life.

I washed the knife off with the Gordon's gin, spread my legs as far apart as I could, and took my left testicle in hand first, because it was larger than my right, and I pulled the sack up tight so that the round piece of meat inside pushed up tight against the sack—so tight that the sack became shiny. Now I came down with the knife in my right hand, and I was starting to cut just a shallow little incision about two inches long, so I could push the ball out. But I couldn't do it. I was shaking too much. Then I realized I'd quit breathing—I'd been concentrating so much.

I took a huge breath, then another, blowing out hard each time. Once more I lowered the blade to my left ball. But my hand just didn't want to do it. I put the knife down. I was getting a cramp in my legs. I got up, pulled off my boots and Levis and underwear, and stretched out my legs. This was when I saw there was a log in the brush just a little way beyond the big white cross at the end of the cemetery grass. I got all my things and moved over to the log area. Sure, this would help. I'd sit on the log so that my balls would hang down freely, then I'd be able to castrate myself more easily and not get cramps in my legs. Also, maybe, I should take a shot of gin to calm me down. But no, I could then make a mistake and cut off my penis, and this I surely didn't want to do. Without my balls, I could still live, but without my penis, I wouldn't be able to pee, and I'd die.

I had everything ready once again, the knife, the bottle of purple medicine, the clean towel, the thread and needle, and the gin. I sat my naked ass down on the log, balls and cock hanging loose, took the knife in hand, and looked up to the heavens.

"This is it, *Papito*" I said. "Never again will I be having all these sinful, awful, disgusting thoughts. I'll be pure. I'll be good. I'll be able to love You with all my heart and soul!"

I closed my eyes, took a huge breath, and felt a smooth easiness come over me. I reached down, gripped my left ball again, pulled it up, and was going down with the razor-sharp knife in my right hand with such calmness this time, such focus, such utter clarity of mind, that I never heard the scream of the huge red-tailed hawk until he came sweeping down by me, almost hitting me with his wings.

I jerked, missed my testicle, and cut the inside of my left thigh. BLOOD WAS EVERYWHERE!

The hawk was SCREECHING!

And I was gone! Gone! GONE!

# CHAPTER NINE

I don't really know how I got home, but I immediately went upstairs to the bathroom, locked the door, and washed myself off with lots of soap and water. I'd failed. I hadn't castrated myself, but I had managed to cut the inner part of my left thigh pretty good. After washing the wound, I dried myself, used a bandage to get the flesh and skin to come back together, and went to bed. I was going to be okay. The cut on my thigh wasn't as deep as I'd thought, so I hadn't needed to use the thread and needle to sew myself up.

All that night I dreamed of that huge red-tailed hawk. And I knew that in our local Indian way of thinking, the red-tail wasn't really a hawk at all, but was the Red Eagle. My dad had always told me that grass-eating animals had their eyes to the side of their heads, so that they could look all around themselves to protect themselves, but that meat eaters, on the other hand, had both of their eyes up front, just like humans, so they could focus with complete power on their prey. And just as I'd passed out, I'd seen so clearly that both of the Red Eagle's eyes had been up front and not to the side as they were on chickens and roosters. And those two eyes of the Red Eagle had come sweeping down out of the heavens. They were huge and shiny and full of intent, like he was telling me something. But what he'd been telling me, I didn't know.

I slept that night as I'd never slept before, and in my dreams I could clearly see that all my life I'd been interacting with hawks and eagles. For instance, when I was twelve years old I went with my father to look at a ranch that he might buy across the border by Tecate, east of Tijuana. I'd been going up a streambed on foot under a canopy of treetops, and a huge red-tailed hawk had come flying down with something in his claws, and I'd shot him so easily. Then

I'd realized why. He had no fear of me, and what he'd had in his claws was a great big rattlesnake. This was when my father told me that hawks, like all predators, had both of their eyes up front just like us humans.

"And who knows, *mijito*," he'd said to me, "maybe that hawk was bringing the snake to you as a gift. Don't be so quick to shoot. Besides, we don't kill what we don't eat, and . . . we don't eat hawks."

I never shot another hawk after that. My dad was right, we didn't eat them, and there was no sport in it. Hawks had no fear of us humans. That was why they sat on the poles of the power lines along the highways, motionless, even if you got out of your pickup with a rifle in hand. I still had the red tail and wing feathers of the Red Eagle I'd shot. They hung on the back of my bedroom door. Maybe my dad had really been right and that hawk had been bringing me that big rattlesnake as a gift. He had looked at me with such regal, fearless majesty, sitting on that low limb across the stream when I'd shot him. And here a Red Eagle had come to me once again. He was the reason that I missed my left testicle and cut my thigh. I hadn't chickened out. I'd been completely focused with my two eyes up front like any killer, to do what I'd been committed to do.

My eyes filled with tears. It was almost like God, Himself, had sent my brother Joseph, in the form of a Red Eagle, to stop me from castrating myself. So maybe this meant that God in His infinite wisdom didn't want me to castrate myself. Maybe the Almighty was telling me that I had to learn how to live as a whole man with my balls and sexual feelings and all. Maybe God didn't think that Mexicans were only good for f . . . f . . . fucking, and I'd been sent down here to Earth for some other reason.

My eyes were crying freely now. So, yeah, maybe I wasn't as smart as my big brother Joseph and I kept having bad, sinful thoughts, but maybe, just maybe God still . . . still loved me. Sure, why not? Maybe I was like what's-his-name in the Bible who God stopped from killing his son when he'd been ready to sacrifice him for *Papito Dios.* I took a big deep breath. The tears were streaming down my face. I'd done good. I'd proved my love to *Papito.* I guess that this was why He'd spared me. I just couldn't stop crying.

"Oh, my God," I said, "it feels like years have passed since my dad took me across the grass to talk to me about the truck that I was getting. I mean all the love that I'd had for my Chevy truck now seems so childish and unimportant. It's like I'm now almost happy that Little Richard ruined my love for my truck for me, because I've grown so much since then. Cars, trucks, they all now seem like small potatoes. Do you know what I mean, God? Please talk to me. I love You and I won't let You down. You do know that I didn't look down at the water like Peter did when he was walking hand in hand with your Son Jesus on the sea. No, I stayed focused and went for it with all my heart and soul!"

"Yes, we know," I heard a voice say deep inside of me.

A chill shot up and down my spine. Who was that? That wasn't my voice. Had God Himself really just spoken to me, or was I so crazy*loco* that I was hearing voices?

I must have gone back to sleep, because the next thing I knew I was dreaming that I was walking side by side with my brother Joseph on the calm rolling waters of the ocean just beyond the breakers. Dolphins were surfing in and out of the rolling waters all around us. I laughed. This was so much fun, to be walking with my brother and the dolphins playing in water all about us.

The next day, I could see that the wound on my leg wasn't healing as fast as I'd thought it would, so I pretended to be sick and stayed home for a few days so I could doctor myself like I'd seen my dad do with the livestock. I mean, on a ranch, you couldn't just call the vet every time an animal went down, or you'd go broke. I got to do a whole lot of thinking while I stayed home. I could now clearly see that something very special had happened to me when I'd been completely focused and committed to castrating myself. It was like there'd been no "me" over "there." All of "me" had been totally "here" with "me." And this was when the Red Eagle had come sweeping down, and this was also when I'd heard that strange voice speak to me. Suddenly I knew whose voice that had been. It had been the holy voice of God's Son Jesus Christ.

I quickly made the sign of the cross over myself. "Thank you, Jesus."

On the third day, I went back to school. I was in Commander Ashmore's classroom when he asked if anyone in the class could solve the math problem he'd put on the board. No one raised a hand. I wondered why and took a closer look at the problem. For some strange reason, I, who was normally the slowest cadet in our whole math class, could see the answer to the problem so clearly this morning. I raised my hand.

"Go ahead," said Commander Ashmore.

I got up and went to the board, and Ashmore went to the back of the class and took a seat. But now with everyone looking at me, I didn't quite see the answer anymore. I breathed deeply, not knowing what to do. A few of the cadets began snickering at me. But I didn't panic. No, I held my ground. I wasn't going to make the same stupid mistake that I'd made with my turquoise Chevy and let other people's opinions rattle me.

I closed my eyes, took a couple of quick big breaths, and pulled myself together so no part of me was "over there" somewhere else. Bingo, when I reopened my eyes I instantly knew the answer once again. It was like all the numbers on the board had come alive for me just like the chess pieces did when I played chess.

I picked up a piece of chalk and went right to work. Now I was seeing the whole thing clearly. This was exactly why I liked to play chess as fast as I could, because when I got to this place "here" inside of me, everything now flashed past my mind's eye like a brightly lit movie in fast-forward, but a zillion times faster. Thinking at this "place" was way too slow. Thinking only worked when you were over "there" lost and not completely "here" within your own self.

I quickly worked the whole right side of the board, and when I was done, all my fellow students started laughing. I felt like yelling the "f" word at them, but I didn't. I put the chalk down and dusted off my hands. I'd done it. I really had, and if they were so smart, why the hell hadn't they raised their hands and come up to the front of the class.

"Quiet down," said Commander Ashmore, getting to his feet. He was a large, tall man, and as he came forward, everyone got quiet. "You're right," he said to the class in a calm tone of voice, "it does look funny how he did it, because he didn't use the tools for solving this problem that I've been showing the rest of you for the last couple of days. But," he added, "he did solve the problem correctly."

Everyone looked totally confused, but then the bell rang, and we all jumped up and started rushing out of the classroom. It was lunchtime, the one period of the day when none of us wanted to be late.

"Villaseñor," Commander Ashmore said as I, too, headed for the door.

"Yes, sir."

"Wait a moment," he said. "I'd like to speak with you."

I was starving, but I liked this man, so I stayed behind. He and a Captain Moffet were my favorite teachers because they never made fun of me, even when they had to flunk me or give me a real bad grade.

"How did you figure out how to do what you did on the board?" he asked.

"I don't know, sir," I said. "It just, well, came to me."

"Just came to you?"

"Yes, sir. I mean, don't ideas just come to us?"

He looked at me a long time, and then said, "No, I don't think so. I believe ideas come to us from the information that we've acquired through study or from experience, not just out of thin air."

"Okay, I can see that. But, sir, is air really thin?"

Hearing this, he raised up his right eyebrow and looked at me for another long time before speaking. "What do you mean by that?" he asked.

"I really don't know," I said. "But could it be that air is really like a sea, a soup full of good healthy, uh, uh, feelings . . . connecting us all together and . . . and the problem is that we humans have become like a dam, you see, holding back all these great feelings that used to just flow freely through all of us when we lived in the . . . the . . . "

Suddenly I remembered my dream. I'd been walking side by side with my brother in the calm rolling waters just beyond the breakers when I'd seen Jesus coming toward us with the biggest smile on His face that I'd ever seen on a human being. Jesus had greeted my brother Joseph like they were old friends, and the dolphins had been all about us, leaping out of the water, screeching with joy.

"We lived in the what?" he asked.

"What?" I said.

"You were talking about air being like a sea, a soup full of feelings, and that we used to live in—are you okay?" he asked.

"Oh, yeah, sure. It's just that, well, it's like a dream, sir. A lost memory I got here within me, and sometimes I get little tiny glimpses of this place."

"What place?"

"That place I sometimes go to that's here within all of us, I guess, but just kind of gets all foggy, especially if we try to think about it. Thinking, I've found out, doesn't really work when I play chess. It's too slow. It's best to trust myself and just go for it real fast, because each move opens up so many other moves that it's impossible to think of all of them. But, if you just trust and let go, then you can fly like an arrow and it's all so, so easy."

"Very interesting," said Commander Ashmore, "a place of memory . . . because what makes how you solved this particular problem so fascinating is that the method you used hasn't been taught for well over a thousand years. Tell me, Villaseñor, do you like math? Have you been reading books on the history of mathematics?"

I started laughing. "No, of course not. I don't read anything, unless I have to," I said. My heart was suddenly pounding with fear. No one at the Academy knew I didn't know how to read. No one knew that I got other cadets to read our assignments to me, pretending that I'd already read them, but hadn't quite understood what I was reading. Also, I paid a couple of cadets fifty cents a day so I could copy their homework.

Commander Ashmore looked at me for a long time once again, then he sat down on the front of his desk and explained to me that the way in which I'd solved this problem was so complicated that most people back then hadn't even been able to comprehend the solution for this type of problem until this great blah-blah mathematician and this other great blah-blah-blah invented these two new easier, simpler solutions. So for me to have been absent on the days that he'd shown the class these simpler ways of doing modern math made it quite astonishing, from his point of view, that I'd been the one to raise my hand and solve the problem.

I asked him to show me these newer tools, and he did, and now I was flying! Oh, my Lord God, I could now see how to solve the same problem I'd just solved, in one, two, three, so easily! Commander Ashmore loved it, and we talked about math as we'd never talked about it before and, little by little, I began to see that math, incredibly, wasn't really about numbers, but was a language just like talking with words. I got so excited that I almost forgot about lunch, and Commander Ashmore ended up telling me that I was now more than ready to go into advanced mathematics with Major Terry next year.

My excitement stopped, and I told him that I didn't want to go near any classroom of Major Terry's. I'll never forget that when he heard this, Commander Ashmore didn't get upset. No, he calmly walked across the classroom, closed the door, locked it, and came back to me.

"Listen," he said to me in a soft, gentle voice, "you have to forgive the man. He's an excellent math teacher, but you see, he always thought that he was going to be a general, and he was never able to get beyond the rank of major. And, for some men, their whole life is the military."

I nodded. I'd never thought of this. Now a whole lot of other things suddenly made sense to me, too. No wonder Major Terry's having gone to West Point was such a big deal for him and also that he'd been one of the best chess players at the Point. I could now see Major Terry in a new light, and I was now able to also see Mary's two cousins in a new light, too. No wonder those two girls had sex with all those guys down on the beach. Those poor girls' father had been in the Marines, and he'd probably only wanted boys and so he'd been putting those two girls down since day one for not being boys. Mary's cousins weren't bad girls. They were just lost girls who'd never once been told about the greatness of women, as I'd been told since I was a child.

I took a great big deep breath. Suddenly I was seeing so many things I'd never been able to see before. Like my dad, who was the nineteenth child born to his mother at the age of fifty, she'd sworn not to make the same mistake with him that she'd made with her other male children and leave his raising to the men. No, she'd sworn to raise my dad in the old Indian way, and in the old Indian way, every male child was raised like a woman for the first seven years of his life, so that, then, he'd know how to see life from his heart like a woman before he learned the ways of men and saw life with his two eyes up front like all the other killers.

I could now see so clearly that this was why my dad respected my mom's opinion so much, and why he knew all the things he knew. His brain didn't just see and think like a male. His brain also knew how to see and think like a female, and . . . and having this ability, my dad had the power of two brains.

All this made so much sense now. Those poor sisters on the beach had been raised with only a male point of view toward life, so this was why they'd behaved like they'd done. Sure, if two brothers could get all the girls of the school to line up to have sex with them, they'd be the most admired two guys in the whole school. This was why Mary's two cousins had spread their legs, taking in guy after guy. They'd done this with a man's point of view toward life, and also, I bet, they'd done it in revenge against their father, because they were girls and he didn't respect women. Sure, of course. This was why the older sister was so mad at me, calling me a worthless, fuck-less Mexican. She really hadn't meant to hurt my feelings. It was just that she'd lost the soft compassionate female part of her brain to the hard no-nonsense male part.

I suddenly got the idea that I'd drive over to see those two girls after school and tell them that they weren't bad girls, that they were good girls, and that there was a reason why they'd done what they'd done. Getting home that afternoon, I got my milk wagon Chevy and drove over to see Mary's two cousins. I had a lot to tell them. I parked in front of their home and walked up the walkway to ring the doorbell. I'd changed out of my Academy uniform and into my street clothes: white T-shirt, Levis, and cowboy boots. No one came to the door, but I thought that I could hear voices inside. I rang the door-bell again. The curtains opened up at the big picture window to my right, and I caught a glimpse of the younger sister's face. She didn't seem very happy to see me, but still she came to the front door and opened it. This was when I heard the scream.

"I said don't open the door!" I heard the older one yell at her sister. "Why the hell is he here! Just to rape us again! Close that door! I don't ever want to see that no-good bastard Mexican near me again!"

The younger sister closed the door in my face. I stood there completely devastated. What was going on? Had they gone crazy or had so many guys been on top of them that they now thought that I'd been one of those guys, too? I was mortified, and turned, going back to my truck. Oh, my dear Lord God, this was awful. And all those guys who'd been in line doing it with them would now never tell the truth and say that I'd been the one who'd tried to stop the whole thing. No, they'd probably love to back up what this older sister was thinking and say, "Yeah, he's the no-good bastard who ruined your daughters."

I got into my truck and took off. What a fool I'd been to have thought I could come over and talk to these two sisters and help right things. Who did I think I was, the Lone Ranger on his white stallion? When was I ever going to get it through my stupid damn head that I was Tonto, the Lone Ranger's sidekick? And *tonto* meant stupid in Spanish. This was who I really was. I wondered if Mary's cousins would now tell their parents, and the cops would come to arrest me. I was suddenly filled with terror. My dear Lord God, I just seemed to be getting into deeper and deeper water everywhere I went.

By the time I got home, I felt so scared and confused that I went upstairs to the bathroom and began to puke. And when my mother heard me and came upstairs to see what was the matter, I lied and just said that I must've eaten something that had made me sick.

"Did you eat at that drive-in?" she asked.

"Yes," I said.

"Was it a hamburger?"

"Yes," I said, lying again.

"We've told you not to eat hamburgers," she said. "You can never tell what kind of old meat they use."

"Okay. Please. Just leave me alone," I said, crying and feeling so terrible, I wanted to die. I'd hit rock bottom. "I'll be okay," I added, but I knew that I was lying and that I'd never really be okay again. This was it. I was destined to be a "fuckless" fuckup all of my life.

# CHAPTER TEN

School ended. It was summer, and I should have been happy, but I wasn't. Now every time the phone rang or I saw a cop car, I wondered if this was the day I was going to be arrested for what had happened to those two sisters on the beach. I could see why that older sister maybe thought I'd been one of those guys who'd had sex with her, because it was my face that she'd seen and yelled at with such hate and conviction.

I prayed for God to help me and not let the cops come to get me, because if they did, I knew that I wasn't going to argue and tell the cops that there had been a whole gang of guys that the girls had sex with and it hadn't been rape at all. No, I would never tell the cops that those two sisters had been spreading their legs on their own and inviting the guys to do it to them.

"Dear God, please help me. I really do want to be a good guy. You know, a hero, and not a worthless fuckless Mexican, so no matter what, I'm not going to cause those girls and their parents any more shame. And also, You, Yourself, know that if truth be known, I wanted to have sex with them, too. So therefore, as we were taught in Catholic school, I'm guilty in thought, God."

I didn't go to the beach all that summer, afraid I'd bump into the two girls and they'd accuse me of having violated them. I began to go to the six-thirty Mass on Sundays so I'd be sure not to let them see me. My God, they might scream at me right there in church that I'd raped them. I stayed on the ranch and worked as hard as I could in the fields so I'd be really strong and able to defend myself in case I went to prison.

I began to live such a terrible secret life that even my friends thought I was getting weird, and they'd ask me if I'd turned queer or what? But then, with the summer half over, something so wonderful happened that my life was changed forever.

I was out bow hunting for rabbits one afternoon after work, in the hills behind our ranch, when I ran into Jeannie Windflow, one of our neighbors. She had been out running down by the railroad tracks. She was fifteen years old, one year younger than me, and blonde and a track star. I guess she was running to keep in shape. She had the strongest, most beautiful, well-defined legs I'd ever seen on a girl. At school, people said she was so fast that her coach had her start running with the boys instead of the girls. And to the boys' embarrassment, she'd wiped them all out, too.

"Come on," she said, "run with me!"

"I'm not as fast as you," I said.

"I'm not running for speed right now, just for endurance. Come on," she said once again, running in place as she spoke to me.

I could see her sincerity. She didn't look like she was trying to get me in trouble. And I really did like to run, so I finally said yes and took off up the railroad tracks with her, carrying my bow and arrows. It was fun. This was really good. I'd never done something just physical like this with a girl before. We were running and dodging in and out of rocks and brush alongside the tracks. I loved it. We weren't having anything to do with sexual feelings or thoughts.

After that, we met and ran together almost every day, and then one afternoon, Jeannie accompanied me while I went rabbit hunting on the golf course across the valley from our ranch. I don't quite know how it started, but near the thirteenth hole we were laughing and having so much fun that we drew close to each other and, just like that, we began to kiss. And Jeannie seemed to know a lot about kissing, even though she was so young, and it was wonderful. Our noses didn't become a problem.

But then, a couple of men in a golfing cart saw us and started yelling at us to get off the grass, that this was a municipal golf course and not a make-out-area. Jeannie and I took off, going down into an *arroyo* for privacy. We were kissing and kissing, and she took my left hand and put it on her chest so I could feel her breasts through her blouse. This felt so good that I used my other hand to massage her you-know-what through her running shorts. And she let me do it.

Oh, it was heaven for me to rub hers and she rubbed mine. Soon every afternoon we'd head for the golf course across the valley, and we'd go down into that *arroyo* for privacy. We were now kissing for hours and learning more and more about how to rub each other's private parts.

I soon forgot all about Mary's two cousins and the cops, and I'd get to feeling so good and wonderful when I was kissing Jeannie that I'd almost pass out. But then, when we stopped, I'd get cramps in my stomach, and my balls would ache so much it would be hard to sleep at night. This was when our neighbor Billy Reddick told me that I was a fool.

"Don't you know," he said, "that you always have to masturbate after you make out with a girl or your balls can get so swollen they'll explode?"

Well, I hadn't known this, but it did make a lot of sense, and so this was the summer that I began to pet myself regularly and not feel bad or guilty about doing it. Soon I found out that petting yourself was an art form, and it worked best with soap and water and both hands at once. One hand on your balls and the other on the gear shift. Then I'll never forget, it was the last part of July and my sister Linda and her girlfriends were having a pool party, I was in the shower by the pool area, petting myself in a frenzy when I found all these little curly hairs on the bar of soap. I stopped and looked at them. They were real black, and I then realized that Camille—who was *una mexicana* and every bit as beautiful as Jeannie—had just showered before going into the pool, so these were probably her black pubic hairs on the bar of soap.

"Did this then mean that she'd been petting herself, too," I said to myself, whacking all the faster, "or had she just washed her private parts real, real, real good?"

Oh, just the thought of Camille doing anything to her beautiful black hairy bush made me dizzy as I kept whacking and looking out the crack of the door at Camille and Jeannie and all of my sister's other girlfriends jumping in and out of the pool.

When I came, I shot so huge that I had to breathe fast to keep from screaming out in pain. I closed my eyes and leaned back on the wall. My knees were weak. I was finished. Then opening my eyes I carefully took each beautiful tiny black curly hair off the bar of soap and went into the house and up to my room. I wanted to keep the hairs, but I couldn't figure out where to put them. Finally I ended up putting them in my Bible for safe keeping, in the section where Moses parted the Red Sea.

I began to pray to God that some day I'd get to do this miracle of miracles and part a girl's pubic hair just like Moses had parted the sea. But I had to be careful because last week, Jeannie and I had been upstairs in the house and we'd gotten so hot and excited that she'd let me actually take her left breast out of her bathing suit top and then told me to lick the nipple. And miracle of miracles, my other hand had gone underneath her bathing suit bottom, and her lovebush was all sticky hot and wet on the inside and we'd been breathing fast and ready to do it when we'd heard someone coming up the stairs. We were just barely able to get apart before my mother came into the room and started smacking us, telling us that she could hear us all the way to the kitchen. And we'd thought that we'd been so quiet. My mother told Jeannie's mother, and it became such a big embarrassing mess that Jeannie and I now were not allowed to see each other alone even for a second. We both knew that our mothers were right, because if we had continued, we were going to end up doing it and getting pregnant.

I now began to collect pubic hair, which I figured was a much safer way to go. I'd look for pubic hair in every bathroom after the girls showered, and in my mind's eyes, I'd try to match up each hair with each girl, all the while imaging her beautiful luscious wet hairy good-feeling bush. I mean, this was the summer that our pool area just seemed to be full of girls all the time. I was quickly becoming a pubic hair expert, even though I was gone from daybreak to late afternoon every day, working out in the fields at our other ranch in the San Luis Rey Valley.

Still, no matter how much I worked in the hot boiling sun, I couldn't stop myself from getting all excited when I'd look at girls, particularly in their bathing suits, where I could make out that little pushed-out-part of their bush. But at least I wasn't going crazy*loco* anymore and thinking that I needed to castrate myself. In fact, I was now beginning to think that maybe there had never been anything wrong with me in the first place, and all this business of sex being bad and sinful had been developed by the Church that was run by men who never married and were afraid of these powerful feelings that we, men, got when we were around women.

After all, my dad had told me that his mother had told him to imagine how different the Church would be if the Pope were a woman. And also when my dad had talked about the real estate man who'd killed himself, he'd said women were more practical at separating sex from love, because of the reality of carrying the baby in their bodies.

"Most men are babies when it comes to understanding love. They think it's all fun and games because they don't know the pains and trouble of carrying the baby. And they don't breast-feed and wake up in the night, no matter how tired, when the child cries. Nature forces women to be a thousand times more practical and levelheaded than men about love and sex and even life itself."

So now, thinking and being practical like a woman, I saw that a guy my age should be feeling all the feelings I was feeling. Hell, if the truth be admitted, these feelings were the feelings every young man and woman my age had been feeling for hundreds of thousands of years. How else would we ever reproduce if we didn't have all these great, wild, crazy*loco* feelings about sex and love?

I began to worship pubic hair, to touch it, to smell it, to lick it. This was when I came to realize that pubic hair wasn't at all like the hair we had on our heads. No, pubic hair was tougher, coarse, and sharp. You could cut your tongue on it if you licked it too hard. The hair on our heads wasn't just finer, but also round, and our pubic hair was thicker and flat, and so this was why it could cut you if you weren't careful.

This was also the summer I once more became good friends with Nick Rorick, whose family owned the local Buick dealership. He and I played a lot of chess. Nick was probably the smartest person I knew. And he'd begun to read books on chess, so he'd beat me now and then with a new strategy he'd learned from the writings of some great master. But after he beat me once or twice, I'd get the hang of it and start wiping him out again, until he'd read about another great new game plan.

This was also the year I began to realize I felt something very strong for Nick's sister Clare. I'd never felt this way about any other girl. I'd first met Clare at Saint Mary's Star of the Sea in grade school when I was eleven and she was nine. Clare and I had the same birthday, May 11th, and we could actually really talk, even when she wore tight tiny shorts and kept stretching her muscular brown legs all over the place.

I was invited to stay for dinner several times with Nick and his family. They used cloth napkins, and Nick would wipe his mouth after almost every bite. Clare would, too. But then she'd deliberately drop her napkin on the floor so she could reach under the table and laugh or pinch her sister Sally when she bent over to retrieve her napkin. She was full of fun and mischief, like her little sister, who I once saw dancing with a broom for a partner. David, the oldest of the four kids, didn't like me and was always correcting my grammar no matter how much I tried to speak in proper English. Clare and Nick and Sally never corrected me.

I was in love! I could feel it in my chest and not between my legs. It was a whole new kind of feeling, one that I'd never felt before. My feeling for Clare was so strong that I stopped masturbating—well, almost—and it turned out to be one of the best summers of my whole life.

# CHAPTER ELEVEN

"**F**ight! Fight! Fight!" cadets were yelling and running to the grassy area behind our cottage.

What happened was that we'd been in line in the hot sun in our itchy woolen uniforms when my roommate Juan Limberopulos, who was now an officer, cut into the front of the line with two of his fellow officers, and a new cadet had spoken up. But instead of admitting his wrongdoing, my friend Juan went berserk, yelling at the new cadet, trying to intimidate him.

"Say what you want," said the new guy, "but because you're an officer, it still doesn't give you the right to cut in line."

"What are you telling me?!" shouted Juan. "Are you telling me I don't have the right to be respected?!"

"This has nothing to do with respect. In fact, if you want respect, you should go to the end of the line like everyone else," said the new student.

"I'm an officer!" bellowed Juan. "You don't tell an officer what to do. Get to attention, private!"

"No," said the new cadet.

"Did you say 'no' to me?"

"Yes, I did."

Juan's eyes went crazy*loco*. "You want to settle this out back?"

"Not really, but if that's what you think is proper, I'll join you," said the new cadet so calmly that Juan should've guessed that this new guy was special. But on the other hand, there were about twenty of us old-timers who'd seen the exchange, so it wouldn't look good for Juan to back down.

"Well, then, come on!" said Juan. He turned on his heels, marching off like a mad bull.

This was when some cadets started yelling, "Fight! Fight!" and most of us left the line and followed Juan and the new cadet to the open grassy area behind one of our cottages. I figured Juan would probably whip this new guy in nothing flat, because he was so mad and pumped up and raging red in the face. But on the other hand, this new guy was so calm and relaxed that maybe the fight would go his way. I felt divided. Juan was my friend, but also I thought that he'd been in the wrong.

Once we were behind the cottages, the two of them stripped to the waist. Juan was really muscular and lightning fast in wrestling, so I thought he'd instantly take this new cadet to the ground and choke-hold him or something like that. But Juan didn't do this. Instead, he stood up tall with his fists cocked up high, and he rushed in on the new cadet, who was slightly bigger than him, but he never threw a punch. The new cadet just backed away, kept his fists down, and hit Juan in the face with a real quick one, two, three combination, then he sidestepped away as Juan barreled past him.

Juan went crazy*loco*. Snorting like a bull, Juan came charging at the new cadet again. But once again he never threw a punch. It was like Juan was so mad that he couldn't remember to punch, much less use his knowledge of wrestling. So I watched as my good friend just kept charging and looking so stiff that he couldn't fight. And this new guy kept hitting him, then bouncing away, keeping relaxed and easy, like he'd been boxing for years and had been in many bouts.

Blood was now coming from Juan's nose and mouth, but he wouldn't quit or change his tactics. He just kept charging like a crazed bull, straight ahead, unflinching, with his nostrils round and huge. And this new cadet just kept punching him in the face until his fists began to hurt and he had to shake out his hands between assaults to keep fighting. A whole crowd of cadets had gathered, and Juan was getting massacred, so I tried to step in to stop the fight. Juan shoved me aside, bellowing like a madman, and charged again, still throwing no punches.

Blood was now all over Juan's chest, and you could see that the new guy just didn't want to hit him anymore. He was backing away, trying to get away from him. But Juan wouldn't let him get away. No, it looked like Juan was in a trance and just kept wanting to fight.

"Stop running!" yelled Juan. "Stand up and fight, you coward!"

"You're crazy!" said the new guy. "Look, I don't want to hit you anymore."

Juan charged again, fists out in front of him, and he knocked the new guy against the back of our cottage. But then, before he could finally start hitting the guy himself, Juan's eyes rolled over backwards, looking all white, and he gasped for air and fell to the ground. Immediately, two other cadets and I jumped forward, got hold of him under his armpits, and lifted him to his feet, slapping him on the back so he wouldn't choke. Then we helped him to his room.

"Tell him that I didn't mean to hurt him," said the new cadet to us. "My God, he's crazy!"

In our room, we lay Juan down on his bed and I got a washcloth, soaked it in cold water, and washed the blood off his face and chest. He'd never lost consciousness. The new guy hadn't been hitting him as hard as he could. He'd been peppering him with real fast jabs and combinations. The others left, and I stayed with my friend.

"Juan," I said after I could see that he was feeling a little better, "why did you do that?"

"What?"

"Get into that fight? That guy was right, you know. In fact, as an officer you're supposed to show an example, not cut into the line, and stop others from cutting in."

"Are you trying to start a fight with me, too!" he yelled.

"What? I'm not trying to start a fight. I'm your friend, Juan. I'm just trying to understand."

"Understand what? That I don't have a right to be respected! He'll never fight me again! Did you see it in his eyes? He got scared. That's why he quit."

"Juan," I said, "he was scared of hurting you."

"¡La tuya!" yelled Juan at me. "He knew I had him, and he wasn't going to have a chance!"

I said nothing more. I could see it in Juan's eyes. He really, really didn't see it. Yes, the guy had gotten scared. That was true, but he'd been afraid he was going to hurt Juan even more than he'd already done.

Then at home that night, I got another big surprise. When I told my father about the fight and how Juan Limberopulos had been massacred because he'd been so mad that he'd been all stiff and unable to move, my dad told me that he admired Juan.

"But what is there to admire?" I asked my father.

"In prison," said my dad, "I saw this guy who wasn't very big or strong, and no fighter at all, just keep coming back and back at this real big, tough guy, who kept beating him to death. But finally the fight was gone from the big, good, capable fighter, and that little man just took the fight from there. He beat that big, tough guy until they had to take him to the hospital, and that tough, big guy was never any good again after that.

"But that little *hombre*, who wasn't very strong or capable, became one of the most respected and feared men in the whole prison, because everybody knew that to go up against him, you better be prepared to kill him. Juan is right, that guy will never fight him again. And the next time that Juan cuts in line, or does anything, that guy and no one else will say a word to Juan. Juan won. He's the winner, and he did it with guts *a lo chingón* and now has respect!"

I nodded. I could see that my dad hadn't understood what it was that I was trying to say. Because I had no respect for Juan. He was my friend and I really liked him, but I had more respect for the new cadet.

"Look, *papá*," I said, trying to explain what I was feeling inside, "I can see what you're saying and how it was good to do it that way in prison, but here at school I don't think that what Juan did is right or to be admired. You see, school is a place for learning, and Juan didn't learn anything, and especially not to be reasonable. There should never have been a fight in the first place, *papá*. As an officer, Juan should be an example of following the rules, not breaking them."

My father laughed at me. "And you think that a prison is less of a place for learning than a school? Prison was college for me!" he yelled. "And I graduated from prison with honors! And no man loses respect for me!"

And my dad went on and on, telling me what he'd told me so many times before. He was tough, and being tough was what had given him the guts to survive the Mexican Revolution and then all the racism and abuses that he'd had to endure in the United States.

I breathed and breathed again wondering if a son could ever really talk with his father. And if he did, could this then hinder the son from growing and learning to see things in his own way and for his own time? This was the real question.

"You just watch and see who goes further in life," concluded my father. "Juan or this other guy who can fight but quit. Because if this other guy had really had guts and was so much a better fighter than Juan, he should've just knocked Juan out and brought the fight to a close. *Mijito,* in life we've got to be tough, and if the other guy is a better fighter than you, then you can never quit. *Capiche?"*

I took a deep breath. This was going to be tough, because I . . . I didn't agree with my dad. And, also, I wasn't going to hold back what I really thought. My heart was beat, beat, beating, going a million miles an hour. "No, *papá,"* I said, contradicting my dad head on for one of the first times in my life, "I don't *capiche.* I don't *capiche* at all," I added with my heart going crazy*loco.* "Because, you see, I still say that this isn't prison. This is a school!"

He looked at me real hard, but he didn't say anything for a very long time. Then he spoke. "Well, I hope you're right for your sake, because my life is basically done, and it is you who now has to know how to be *un hombre* and go out into the world to make his way. So I'll tell you this, don't . . . don't ever underestimate the man who won't quit. Being right or wrong has very little to do with survival in this world. It has much more to do with the type of guts that Juan showed that he has—*TANATES,* AND WELL HUNG ONES!"

I was shocked. Being right or wrong had very little to do with survival? My God, what about Abraham Lincoln? What about Jesus Christ? What about our heroes all through history? My poor dad, he was trying to convince me of a world gone by, just as Major Terry had tried to convince me about needing to think step by step in order to play chess. Thinking move by move was too slow, and fighting just to show your toughness was out of date.

*"Mijo,* understand, you've got to be tough!"

"Okay, *papá,"* I said, heart pounding. "I hear you, I really do, but you yourself have told me that most of the men who are so tough in prison don't become successful like you when they get out. You've told me that most of them learn tools in prison that only work in prison, and that's why they just keep going back to prison. So, *papá,* I don't really think that the things you learned in prison are the things that have helped you do so good out here. I think because you knew how to listen to your mother and you now listen to my mother is what's really helped you become who you are and who you aren't.

"And Juan, with this fight, I think he has shown he's a coward because he didn't have the guts to admit that he was in the wrong. And so he fought for the wrong reasons, got all stiff and couldn't move, because down deep inside he knew that he shouldn't even be in that fight. And *papá,* I'm afraid that he will keep doing this all his life, and he will not do that well in the long run, because he doesn't know how to listen to his heart like you told me that a man must do in order to know who he is and isn't as a complete *hombre.*"

My dad was smiling.

"And that other guy, I bet will go far," I said, "because he'll know how to listen to his heart, not get trapped in his head, and know how to choose his battles. In fact, I think that there is a good chance he'll quit the Academy, because I'm beginning to think that our school isn't really very good at teaching us how to become well-rounded, smart-thinking men."

My father just looked at me and said nothing for a long, long time. Then he spoke. "Let me think on all this," he said. "You've made some very good points. But still I say, I'll bet on Juan."

"How about Abraham Lincoln?" I said. "What about Jesus? He refused to fight and bring the Kingdom of God down and wipe out all those people who were abusing Him."

"Don't bring Jesus Christ into this conversation," said my father.

"Why not?"

"Because, well, then we can't talk about normal, everyday life. And what did it bring Jesus not to fight back? It got Him crucified."

"Yes, but the message that He left with us is . . . "

"Leave Jesus at the church where He hangs on the cross," said my dad, "and listen to me. In the world of men in prison, in business, or in whatever else men do, the going can get tough and so you got to be tough. Jesus wasn't normal. He wasn't married. He didn't have kids. He didn't have monthly bills and a mortgage. His job here on Earth was very different than most men's."

"Then His story isn't important to you?" I asked.

"On Sunday, yes, very important."

"But what about the rest of the week?"

"Not as much as it is on Sundays."

I was shocked. I'd never understood that my dad thought this way. Then he really didn't take all the teachings at the Catholic Church seriously. I nodded. I could now see it so clearly. I was out-to-lunch according to my dad.

The next day back at school, I found out that I was out-to-lunch at the Academy, too. Because when I brought up to Juan what my dad had said, he loved it and started laughing and laughing. He told me my dad was right. He would go far in life and that other guy wouldn't, because the big chickenshit had quit school yesterday after the fight. Then he added that I was dumb and weird, and he wasn't the only one who thought so, that most of the cadets and faculty at the Academy thought so, too.

"Look at you," said Juan, "you bring a girl to school, and she ends up with someone else. You've been here two years longer than me and you still have no rank. And this, my friend, is one of the best private schools in the whole country. Students from here go to all the top universities of the world, and where will you go?"

I nodded. He was right. I probably wouldn't be able to get into any university with my grades. I could see his point, just as I'd seen my father's point the night before. But they couldn't see my point, and I just didn't know how to explain my point, either. Because I could now see that even in prison, it really wasn't best for everyone to be all tough and just out for himself.

I wondered if my dad had forgotten that it was his mother's faith in God that had enabled them to survive as a family in the Mexican Revolution. Yes, my dad had to be tough and cunning and strong in prison and in the Revolution, too, but not abusive. And here at my school, we were in a protected environment, and so, to be as tough as we were being taught to be wasn't a virtue. It could also be just plain stupid. Like one cadet named Wellabussy. He was from La

Jolla, and his family had a feeding pen for cattle in the Imperial Valley east of San Diego County. They were very wealthy, and he liked to tell the story about how he shot illegal Mexicans below their knees with his .22 rifle when they were returning home across the border after they'd worked all day on his dad's ranch.

When he told this story in English class, I was shocked. And after class when I asked him why he would do such a horrible thing, he'd smiled a sick-looking little grin.

"Because it's fun watching them scream," he'd said, "and they're illegal, so they can't do shit about it." He'd laughed, then said to me, "Grow up. We need to be tough and not give an inch or our whole country will go to hell, returning to the Indians who we already whipped."

I'll never forget how he'd grinned at me as he said this, knowing well that I was Mexican and therefore part Indian. There was clearly a spirit of meanness encouraged at our school of "onward Christian soldiers going off to war" that I could see was out-of-date and self-destructive. Oh, how I wished I was as smart as my brother Joseph had been. I had all these feelings deep inside me that I knew were right, but I didn't know how to bring them out and explain them to myself, much less to anyone else.

# CHAPTER TWELVE

'll never forget. It was Wednesday afternoon. The Christmas holidays were upon us, and once more we were required to take a girl to the next dance. But this year I wasn't confused or scared. No, this year I knew exactly who I wanted to invite, and if she said no, that was okay, too. I just wouldn't bring anyone, and they could punish me all they wanted to, but I didn't give a fat rat's ass. Because if she said yes and did go with me to the dance, it would be heaven on earth. I would ask Clare, Nick's sister. She was home for the holidays from her private school up in the Bay area near San Francisco. We were on the beach by the pier just below their two family homes.

"Clare," I said, "there's a dance at the Academy this weekend. Normally I don't go to the school dances, but I was, well, wondering, I guess, really hoping that if I, well, asked you, would you maybe, just maybe . . . "

"Sure. I'd love to go with you," she said, her eyes dancing.

"You would?" I said. "I mean, are you sure?" I was shocked. She was Irish and so beautiful that I'd assumed she'd turn me down.

"Yes. I've never been to a dance at your school, and some of my friends from Bishop's have gone, so I'd like to go, too."

The year before, Clare had gone to Bishop's private school for girls in La Jolla, so she still had a lot of local friends.

"Okay, that's great," I said. "I'm really happy. My parents and I will come by to pick you up about six thirty."

"When? This Saturday?"

"Yes," I said, "this Saturday, but also I want you to know, Clare, I don't have any rank." It was real hard for me to say this. "I've been going to the Academy for over four years, but I'm not a sergeant, or an officer, or anything. So if you decide that you don't want to go with me, that's okay. I'll understand."

She must've seen my worried look, because she now said something that I'll never forget for the rest of my life.

"Can anyone at school ride a horse as well as you?" she said.

"Well, no, I don't think so," I said, slightly surprised.

"You see," she said, "school isn't everything."

This was so beautiful! And her look of concern for my feelings sent me shooting across the heavens! She was right, nobody at school could touch me on horsemanship. I'd taken the California State Championship in the Stock Horse and Western Pleasure classes when I was fourteen years old, competing against boys and girls who were two and three years older than me. There were sixty-five contestants, and it had finally been narrowed down to ten of us. These kids had come in from Pasadena, Rancho Santa Fe, Los Angeles, Santa Barbara, and Sacramento. I'd beaten them all. But then I quit horse show competition when I took up wrestling. I wanted to shout with joy and hold Clare in my arms to thank her for helping me to feel good about myself.

"Okay," I said, "then you'll go to the dance with me?"

"I'd love to," she said, her eyes still dancing. "And you and your parents will pick me up this Saturday night at seven o'clock."

"But it starts at seven," I said, suddenly getting scared, "so I thought we should pick you up at six-thirty."

Her eyes filled with mischief, just like when she'd deliberately dropped her napkin at the dinner table. "Let's be late!" she said, with a delicious tone in her voice.

I'd never thought of that. But it was true. Why did we have to be on time? When you got to a dance on time, it felt kind of stupid anyway for the first hour, until things got going.

"Okay," I said. "That sounds great. We'll be late, then."

"Yes, we'll be late together."

The word "together" sent me flying through the heavens! All week I was so excited I could pop, and on Saturday my parents drove me to pick Clare up at the two large brown houses near the pier in downtown Oceanside. I was in my dress whites. My parents stayed in the car, and I went up to the front door—the door we kids never used. We always went around to the back and came into the house from the garden area. I knocked, and Clare's father came to the door. He cheerfully invited me inside. I had a beautiful orchid corsage that my mother had made from her hot-house garden.

When he saw the flowers, Mr. Rorick called out in a booming voice, "Someone come down and get the corsage for the party girl!"

Clare's aunt came down and took the corsage upstairs. Mr. Rorick kept talking to me, asking me about my parents, but for the life of me, I didn't know what to say. Then I heard Nick say something in the kitchen. I guess that he was going to stay out of sight and not get involved with this situation of me taking his sister to a dance. And who could blame him? I'd be all confused if someone came over to take my little sister Linda to a dance.

Finally, Clare came down the stairs in a long beautiful baby-blue dress with the corsage that I'd brought pinned over her heart. She looked so tall and regal and absolutely beautiful. I'd never seen her all dressed up like this before. She walked down with the dignity of a queen, but then on the last step, she suddenly tripped.

Instantly, I lunged forward to catch her so she wouldn't fall. But I couldn't believe it, as I caught her in my arms she winked at me. I started laughing as we went to the door.

We said our goodbyes and went out. The ocean was just across the street and the sea air hit me like a cold wall. I opened the car door for Clare, helped her into the back seat, then I walked around the car to get in the back with her, too. Looking over, I saw Mr. and Mrs. Rorick standing side by side watching us from the doorway. I'd never seen a more grand-looking older couple. I nodded goodnight to them once again but I was so self-conscious that I yanked the car door too hard and hit my knee, yelping in pain.

As we drove off, heading south toward Carlsbad, Clare moved close to me and rubbed the hurt spot on my leg. "Are you okay?" she asked.

"Yes, I'm fine," I said.

"It really hurts when you smack your shin, doesn't it?"

"Yeah, it really does."

"I hope you'll still be able to dance," she said, taking my hand in hers.

The warmth of her hand felt wonderful, and yet to my surprise, I didn't get that horny and crazy*loco* feeling inside. It actually felt kind of relaxing to hold Clare's hand.

By the time we got to the lagoon between Oceanside and Carlsbad, I felt like I'd never felt before while holding a girl's hand. Our hands were warm, but not all sweaty, and I swear that I could feel my heart beating through our touch. I forgot all about my hurt leg. This was heaven, just holding hands.

Arriving at the guard house at the Academy, we said goodnight to my parents and started up the walkway to the main building. Going inside we could see that we were clearly late. People were already on the dance floor, but I wasn't feeling scared or stupid and clumsy. No, we'd come late on purpose, and together.

I glanced around and found two empty seats for us at a table near the dance floor. This time it was easy for us to get punch when we went to the refreshment table because there wasn't a long line waiting to get a drink. I could see that Clare had been smart to have us come late.

We were sipping punch when Clare spotted a couple of girls she knew from Bishop's, and we went over to greet them. I didn't know any of the girls, but still I thought that everything was going very well until we started to dance. I don't know what happened, but with Clare's body so close to mine, I forgot all of my dancing lessons and kept stepping on her feet. I began to sweat, then to add to my embarrassment, the front of my pants began to jump, and I had to pull my body away from her so she wouldn't feel my erection. I think she did, though, because she glanced down at my pants and gave me a little smile. I could've died. But once more she said something that I'd never forget.

"Don't worry about it," she said to me, taking over the lead in our dancing. "We'll catch on before the evening is over, or if not, then we'll just do better next time."

My eyes opened wide. "Next time?" I said.

"Of course," she said. "You're going to invite me again, aren't you?"

This was music to my ears. She wasn't going to dump me, even when she could see that almost everybody was a better dancer than I was.

"Yes," I said. "I'd very much like to invite you again."

She smiled a beautiful smile, and we began to dance a lot better with her leading. Then, I couldn't believe it, just when I was beginning to think I'd gotten the hang of dancing once again, here came Wellabussy, the guy who'd told the story in English class about shooting Mexicans below the knee with a .22 rifle.

"Hi," he said to Clare, cutting between us and completely ignoring me. "You remember me. We met in La Jolla at the Evans' house," he added, laughing with great charm.

Clare reached out and took my hand. "I know Margaret Evans," she said, "but I don't remember meeting you. Excuse me," she added, "but this is our dance."

She turned and quickly led me back to the dance floor. "I don't like him," she said to me under her breath as we began to dance. "There's just something about him I don't trust."

I loved it! She was really smart. She'd used the word "trust" and hadn't been taken in by a guy just because he was tall and handsome and charming. I was suddenly dancing much better and could lead without stepping on her feet.

After the dance, Clare told me that she was going to the bathroom with a couple of her girlfriends. I watched her cross the room with two girls from Bishop's and I was left alone. But I didn't feel alone. No, strangely enough, I felt like we were still "together."

I glanced around the room and saw that there were quite a few cadets who hadn't brought dates. Then I saw Wellabussy with three other guys. They were talking together, and then they came walking across the room toward me. My stomach tightened. I didn't like the feel of this.

"Is this the guy?" asked one cadet, pointing at me.

"Yeah, he's the one," said Wellabussy. "Last year he brought a local girl with big boobs to a dance so Nick McLean could get it on with her. This year he's brought a local carpenter's dream for us, except none of us want her."

"What's a carpenter's dream?" asked the first cadet.

"A girl that's as flat-chested as a board," said Wellabussy, laughing and never taking his eyes off me.

I almost went for his throat, but I stopped myself. I could see they'd set me up and were ready for me. They'd actually worked out the whole dialogue before they'd come across the room. I took a huge breath and turned and walked away. They started laughing and laughing, but I didn't run off and hide. No, I crossed the room and stayed by the door to the girl's restroom waiting for my date. Why was Wellabussy so mean? Why had those seniors poured punch on Becky's breasts last time? Oh, I just didn't know what to think. Maybe I should just never bring another date to any function at the Academy. I didn't like how girls were treated. If I wanted to see Clare again, I'd invite her to one of our celebrations at the ranch. After all, it was almost that time of year when all of my aunts and girl cousins came to our *casa-grande* to make *tamales* for Christmas.

I laughed and got to feeling better, thinking about my life on our ranch. Making *tamales* for Christmas was part of our yearly celebration of *Las Posadas,* a reenactment of Mary and Joseph looking for shelter. My father and my uncles and cousins and I would kill a pig and prepare the meat, and some of the younger kids in our extended *familia* would dress up like Joseph and Mary and the three wise men. Joseph would lead one of our smallest horses carrying Mary, and the three wise men would follow behind. They'd go from structure to structure on the ranch, looking for an inn to take them in. The rest of us would be waiting with lit candles, singing traditional songs in Spanish. This pageantry of the Christ Child's birth was a Mexican tradition called *Las Posadas* and had become such a huge event at our *rancho* that it was no longer just a family affair with a few friends. Now hundreds of people came to carry candles and sing songs, then eat our homemade *tamales* and drink *margaritas.*

When Clare came back from the bathroom with her girlfriends, she was laughing just like I always saw my mother and aunts laugh together around the kitchen table while they made *tamales.* I could see so clearly that Clare was very much at home with her girlfriends, just like I felt very much at home on our ranch. She was confident and sure of herself and trusted her . . . her feelings. This was why she hadn't become all cute and flirtatious when tall handsome

Wellabussy had come over. I could trust her. She didn't change when a man came up to her being all charming. I felt so happy, I could shout!

Going home that night with Clare in the back seat of my parent's car was one of the happiest nights of my life. When we got home, I went right up to my room and removed all the pubic hair I'd been keeping in my Bible. And it wasn't because I was now going to start looking for Clare's pubic hair, either. It was that . . . well, I wanted to get to know all of Clare, inside and out, and not just her you-know-what.

# CHAPTER THIRTEEN

Every year right after the Christmas holidays, our I.Q. scores were posted on the bulletin board at the Academy. We, the juniors and seniors, had taken our tests several weeks ago, and for the last few days we were all nervous wrecks waiting to see our results. Of course, we were all told that what was really crucial for us to get into the college of our choice was the grade point average of our last two years of high school, plus our S.A.T. scores. But we knew that our I.Q. score could also make a big difference, because our I.Q., we'd been told, was what gave us a true measure of our intelligence. So if we hadn't worked real hard in school or hadn't tested well in our college entrance exams, then our I.Q. could make all the difference.

I quickly ran to the bulletin board with the other cadets to see my test score. This was my only hope of ever getting into—not the college of my choice—but any college. Maybe Olbase was right and I wasn't stupid and it's just that I'd been fooling around all these years. Maybe Major Terry was right, too, and I was a genius who'd been ridiculing our educational system all this time. I hoped so. My grade average was a D+ or C- at best. In fact, if it hadn't been for a couple of mistakes of two teachers giving me B's instead of D's, I wouldn't even have as high a grade average as I did.

There was a shark frenzy of cadets looking at the bulletin board when I got there. The cadet at the top of the sheet was, of course, Nill, and this made a lot of sense because everyone already knew that Nill was going to go to MIT and become a great engineer or scientist. Then the next few guys listed on the board were also very bright and had scored high on their college tests. Then there were two or three guys, whom no one thought were that smart, but they had also scored real high. Thinking about it, this also made sense, because these were the cadets everyone knew could do well in school, if they wanted to.

I didn't push to the front of the line with the other cadets who were all anxious to see their scores. I was hoping I'd maybe, just maybe, scored high enough in the math part of the test so that someone would see my name and read it off. Everyone I knew was going on to college, and so I hoped to God that I could also say that I was going to go to college. I didn't want to be the only one in my whole class who wasn't, but I was getting pretty scared as people kept reading off their scores, then giving each other the high five. Soon there weren't very many of us cadets left who hadn't found their names on the bulletin board. This was when George Hillam found his test score down toward the bottom, and he said that he'd gotten 112. Wilbur Rochín now found his up toward the top and said that his was 124, which meant that he was really smart. Everyone had found their score, but I couldn't find mine.

Then, I'll never forget, I came closer to the board, carefully going down the list. There were sixty-some juniors and seniors in our two classes, and then there I was, the third name from the bottom.

My heart CRASHED! I couldn't breathe! The two guys below me hadn't even bothered to come to look at the bulletin board, because they both were into gambling and smoking and really didn't give a flying shit about school. I mean, everyone knew these two guys were so rich that the need to prove anything to anybody was beneath them.

But I'd tried! I really had. I was SHOCKED!

Tears came to my eyes and I think Rochín and Hillam saw me, but I didn't care. This was it. My life was over. I was done, finished. I had no future.

"Well," I said, taking a deep breath and wiping the tears from my eyes, "I guess that I really am stupid after all, but . . . but . . . at least I'm strong!"

And I turned and ran and went to my room and changed my clothes and went down to the wrestling room. I did my stretches, warmed up, and took off running. I ran and ran, out to the field on our point near the sea. I hit the track and came up on Walrick, our school miler, who was one of our fastest middle-distant runners at the school. To my surprise, I was able to keep pace with him lap after lap, and when he tried to leave me behind on the last lap, I stuck to him like glue. He looked at me and began to panic. He was one of the best milers in all of North County, so he knew he should be able to easily jump out in front of me. But he couldn't pull away. I stayed with him stride for stride to the finish line. He'd tested high on our I.Q. test and was going to get a track scholarship at college, and yet he hadn't been able to beat me, a nobody, a retard who wasn't even a runner. I was a wrestler, and I only ran to get in shape.

He collapsed at the finish line, but I just kept on going. Hell, I wasn't even tired. These two or three miles that we'd run were just a warm-up for me. I ran around the track a few more times, and I saw Walrick, a guy taller and much leaner than me, look at me in disgust and walk off, going back toward school.

I laughed. I was pouring with sweat, but I could go on forever just as *mi papá* had done when he'd run after the train back in *México* without food or water. And he'd been a child of ten.

"The Mexican Revolution had been going on all around us," he'd told me, "but my mother and sisters were on that train so I was never going to give up. I couldn't, because I had fear pushing me and love pulling me, and when a man or woman is sandwiched between fear and love, we humans can do miracles."

I ran off the point, hit the beach, and ran south toward the Carlsbad power plant, never slowing down. I was crying. I was screaming, but I just kept running. My mother's people were Yaquis, some of the greatest runners in the entire world along with the great Tarahumaras from La Barranca del Cobre.

Reaching the power plant, I turned around and came running back up the beach, never slowing down, and hit the bluff at our school campus at a full run. Then I went back to the basement, and in the terrible heat of our enclosed wrestling room, I wrestled my heart out. I took on guys two or three weights below me for a speed workout and guys two and three weights above me for strength, and I beat them all. I was on fire! And that night when I got home, I never told my parents about my test results. Instead, I did over 500 push-ups, 500 sit-ups, and cried and cried in the upstairs shower.

I WAS STUPID!

I WAS A MORON!

And now everyone knew it! Now there was no doubt about it! I'd never be able to get into any college, and suddenly I came to the horrible realization that I'd never be able to see Clare again, either. Because if I did, she or Nick might ask me what college I was going to go to, and I'd have to be truthful and say none. I fell down in the shower, hoping to God that no one could hear me crying, so I wouldn't have to explain to *mi familia* what was going on.

"What college have you decided to go to?" Clare would ask me all innocently, if I ever saw her again.

"I'm not," I'd have to tell her. "Because you see, I'm a moron. Didn't you know? You're smart. You should have figured it out. I'm stupid and I don't know how to read. Hell, Clare, I still can't even make heads or tails of the directions of the manual I was given when I was eight years old and I got an electric train set for Christmas. I'm stupid, Clare! Get it? I'M A STUPID *PENDEJO!* That's why all these years I've just been pretending that I don't like trains when your brother Nick talks to me about his trains. Clare, understand! I STILL CAN'T READ the directions to assemble my train set that's for little kids!"

"Do your parents know that you're a stupid *pendejo?*" she'd most likely ask me.

"No," I'd have to tell her truthfully, because I loved her and in love my dad told me that you always had to be truthful. "I've kept it a secret from them, too. They have no idea that I'm a stupid *pendejo,* and I've never learned to read. You're the only one who knows, Clare," I'd tell her, wanting to die as I spoke these words.

I could never, never, never see Clare again, or Nick, or Sally, and especially not their older brother Dave, who I was sure had figured out how stupid I was because of the way he always kept correcting my grammar.

My I.Q. score was 101, and we'd been told that it took at least 105 or higher to complete high school. The next day at school I gathered up all my strength and did one of the bravest things of my entire life. I got up the nerve to ask if I could take the test again. I was told that normally this wasn't allowed, but because of my low score and seeing how upset I was, they would allow me to do it.

I prayed all that night as I'd never prayed before, asking *Papito Dios* to help me. Then the next morning Captain Moffet, my English teacher, gave me the test. I got such a headache, just trying to think carefully so I wouldn't make any mistakes, that my test score dropped to 96. I couldn't breathe. This meant that I was mentally slow, that I'd been lucky to even get into high school.

My eyes filled with tears. I didn't know what to do. I asked Captain Moffet if my parents needed to know this. I felt so ashamed. I should've been the one to die, not my brother Joseph. He'd been smart, just like my little sister Linda, who at six years old could read better than me.

"Look," said Captain Moffet in a kind tone of voice, "not all people score well on tests." We were alone in his classroom. Why, I don't know, but he'd been the one who'd volunteered to administer my testing. "Some of the people that I've seen score the highest in life, never did well in school. Even one very well-known general who's presently active and we all know."

He put his hand on my shoulder. "I know you're upset and disappointed and it's hard for you to hear what it is that I'm saying, but you're a good, decent, young man," he said. "I've seen the dedication that you've put into your wrestling. I've seen you running out on the point after hours to get in shape. Not many young men have that drive. And you're probably the best chess player we have on campus. Have you beaten Nill yet?" he asked with a big smile.

Nill was the "most likely to succeed" student in the whole school. He liked to play chess, too, but he always refused to play me, saying that he was too busy studying. In the last three months I hadn't lost one single game of chess. It was crazy*loco*, but sometimes I thought that I was so brilliant because I could see what other people couldn't see or understand even after I'd explain it to them. Playing chess wasn't about making single moves. It was about seeing patterns, then backing up inside of your mind and seeing the last five and six moves of your opponent, then flashing forward real fast. And bingo, the whole chessboard became alive in living patterns. My dad told me this was what happened to him when my mother and he went to

Las Vegas and he played dice. The dice table would become alive just like the desert had become alive for his mother when they'd been dying of thirst in the middle of the Mexican Revolution. The clouds had gathered overhead and given them water. The dice would talk to my dad and do as he asked of them. But then I'd lose it, just like Peter when he'd looked down at the water, and the chessboard would go dead on me and I'd now be the stupidest person in all of the world, completely unable to understand or explain all the things that were going on inside of me. I just didn't know what to do. I felt so stupid and crazy*loco* and completely worthless.

I took a big breath. It was really good that Clare was now up at her school in the Bay area again. I didn't ever want her to see me again. I could never invite her anywhere, not even to the *fiestas* at our *rancho*.

I was DONE!

I was FINISHED!

I really, really should've castrated myself that day!

There was no hope of me ever being able to make a living, except maybe by being strong. Being able to dig a ditch. Being able to work in the hot sun and not get sick or pass out.

I thanked Captain Moffet for his kindness and went into the new wrestling season with a vengeance. I won my first two matches in the first round with a power and speed I'd never had before. I'd moved up a weight. I was now at Nick McLean's old weight of 145. He was no longer with us. He'd quit the Academy and was going to school in North Hollywood. The rumors were he was doing great and dating a famous model. Myself, I no longer thought of girls. No girl would ever want to be seen with a moron. Hell, I had nothing to lose, and so I'd just rush into a match with such wild abandon that I'd sometimes beat guys who were way better than me within seconds. But, other times I'd take such risks, and I'd get out-pointed by guys I should've beaten easily.

But I didn't care! I didn't give a shit! I didn't give a flying f—f—f—FUCK! I wasn't going anywhere anyway. I'd be working on my dad's *rancho grande* with the workers from Mexico for the rest of my life. At least these people didn't know I didn't know how to read and was a stupid *pendejo*. In fact, they assumed I could read and did very well at school because I spoke English. I felt like such a liar and a sneaky hypocrite.

Then a cadet named Johnny Cota, who'd been a year above me, got sick and died. He'd been the most muscular, toughest cadet the school ever had. He was a *mexicano* from East L.A., and almost single-handedly he'd turned our losing football team around and made us into a winning team. But, then, after football season, he'd been caught with a six-pack of beer in his room and expelled. He'd loved the Academy. It had broken his heart when he was kicked out. He'd gotten sick and died up in L.A. We had a moment of silence at one of our assemblies to honor Johnny Cota's death.

I wrestled my next two matches in Johnny's honor, and in one match I tied the best wrestler in the county at my weight. We went into overtime. I went out of my head, doing a reverse hold after reverse hold, every time he tried to take me into a pin. I was out of my mind. Then I almost pinned him, this guy who hadn't lost a match in four years of wrestling in high school.

All the other matches stopped. This was going to be the biggest upset of the whole wrestling season. I was wrestling like I never had before. Then it hit me: Johnny Cota was here with me! He, the strongest and most muscular and physically talented cadet ever to have come to the school, was here within me, taking this guy into a pin, helping me wrestle far beyond all of my own natural abilities. I was flying all over the mat with this super athlete. Then it was over, just like that, and the more experienced guy had won on points, even though I thought that I'd pinned his ass three times.

I'd lost! I couldn't believe it!

The referee tried to raise my hand, too, for having wrestled the greatest match he'd ever seen. But I jerked loose, ran to the lockers, and fell down on the floor weeping. I really thought that I'd pinned him and won.

I'd failed once again.

I'd failed for Johnny Cota.

I'd FAILED! FAILED! FAILED!

I was still on the floor crying when our wrestling coach came in to try to comfort me, telling me that next year, my senior year, I'd be sure to go to state. I ignored him and rolled up into a ball. I felt like a little baby who wished he'd never been born.

I never wrestled very well again all that season. My heart was gone. I had no more power inside. And when we wrestled against Oceanside, a Mexican guy from the barrio of Pozole Town, whom I'd known since kindergarten, beat me with such ease that it was totally embarrassing. I was a shell of a human being. My life was over, done, gone!

Then, I don't know how to explain it, when the wrestling season was over, I'd lay in bed, and a dark, deep hole began to come up all around me and I'd begin to tremble uncontrollably. The realization hit me that I, a man, *un hombre* was never, never, never going to be able to make a living and build a home like my dad had said that it was time for me to start doing hit . . . hit . . . hit me. No one paid anyone to play chess or wrestle. I'd been a fool not to castrate myself. If I had, then there would be no way of spreading my seed and bringing more stupid worthless no-good Mexicans like me into the world!

The tears poured down my face, and I just hoped to God that my dad and mom didn't find out. It had been hard enough on them when I'd flunked the third grade two times. They had absolutely no idea I still didn't know how to read. This was the darkest, deepest secret of my entire life. Keeping different girls' pubic hairs in my Bible had been small potatoes compared to this.

I quit playing chess, and at school, I don't know why, but I began to lay down on the ground every chance I got by the two big rubber trees in front of the mess hall. Their roots protruded a foot above the ground and gripped the earth like huge, long, grey-brown octopus legs, getting smaller and smaller as they extended out twelve and fifteen feet away from the tree trunk.

I'd lay down between the protruding roots of the two trees and I'd get to feeling a whole lot better. There were a few other cadets who liked to come and sit in the shade of these two huge trees and relax, too. It was like these two trees could speak to us, sing to us, comfort us like the big pepper tree did for me back home on the *rancho*.

# CHAPTER FOURTEEN

I was sound asleep when the wind and rain came tearing in through my open window. I got out of bed to close the window, but I could barely make it across the room with the wind blowing the rain in through my window with such force. In all of my years of living on our ranch, I'd never seen a spring storm come roaring like this into our beach communities of North County San Diego. The storm lasted for days. Power lines were ripped down, trees were uprooted, streets were flooded, and most of the houses down at the beach had their large picture windows shattered by rock and sand and seawater.

One of our horses got caught in the middle of the flooded waterway below our house, and there was no way to get to the animal with our tractor to pull him out. On the third day, I watched my dad take aim and shoot the gelding through the head with his 30/30 Winchester to stop his thrashing and screeching and suffering. We lost the whole side of one of our barns, and fifty tons of hay were ruined. Then one day the storm suddenly ended. The sun came out so strong and beautiful it almost felt like summertime. That year we recorded more than eighteen inches of rain at our ranch, where we normally only recorded about eight to eleven inches.

I couldn't believe what happened at school. The great big tree that stood so huge and majestic all these years—right next to the mess hall—had been split in half. Its huge beautiful limbs lay jagged and broken on the ground. It looked like a whale that had beached and been gutted.

I was devastated. I loved this big tree. She and I had been best friends ever since I started at the Academy. If it wasn't for this great tree, I could never have survived at school as long as I had. I hugged the huge old tree, telling her that I loved her, and for her not to worry, that she'd been a good tree and had given so much love and comfort to so many of us cadets over the years that her soul was sure to go straight to Heaven.

I immediately felt the great tree respond to me. I could feel her heart beat, beat, beating in the palms of my hands as I hugged her. Tears came to my eyes. This was what I'd felt when I'd held Clare's hand in the back seat of my parents' car, and . . . and I could never see Clare again. I decided to go to the school administration and tell them that we should have a moment of silence for this mighty tree, like we'd had for Johnny Cota. Some cadets came by and saw me hugging the tree. They started laughing and making catcalls at me, but I paid no attention to them. I knew what I was doing. My Yaqui Indian grandmother had taught me how to talk to plants and trees.

Our school maintenance men came up with chain saws and axes to start cutting up the tree so they could dispose of it. My Mexican friend *Jesús* was with them.

"Please don't," I said to the boss of the maintenance crew. "Give me time to get hold of someone at administration, so we can have a ceremony before you start cutting up the tree."

"I wasn't told about any ceremony," said the crew chief, starting up his chain saw.

"HOLD ON!" I yelled above the screaming sound of the saw. "PLEASE! JUST GIVE ME A FEW MINUTES!"

*Jesús* saw my concern, and he walked over to his boss and spoke to him.

"Okay, yeah," said Bill, turning off the chain saw, "we can first work on the drain in the basement of the main building."

"This will give you about an hour," said *Jesús* to me.

"Thanks," I said, and I took off running.

I didn't even bother going to my next class. I ran directly into the two-story administration building and flew up the stairs. I'd never been up here before. I always kept away from all administration people because it seemed as if I was always in enough trouble as it was. I told the woman at the front desk that I needed to talk to the dean. She said that he was out and wouldn't be back until late afternoon. She asked me if I wasn't supposed to be in class. I said yes, but that an emergency had come up.

"At your home?" she asked.

"No, here in school," I said.

"What kind of emergency?" she asked.

I didn't want to tell her, I really didn't, but I went ahead anyway. "You know that huge tree, the biggest one of the two big trees by the mess hall? Well, it got knocked down by the storm."

"We know that," she said. "Maintenance is taking care of it."

"Yes, that's the point," I said, anxiously. "We can't let that happen. We need to first honor that tree."

"Honor a tree?" she said.

"Yes, like on our ranch, we give a ceremony before and after we kill a steer, or clear an area of trees and brush."

"Are you okay?" she asked.

"Am I okay?" I said. "What's that got to do with anything I'm saying? The tree is what I'm talking about. Don't you get it, it's been so beautiful all these years and giving us cadets . . . ."

I could see it in her eyes, she thought I was crazy*loco*. I turned, walked down the hall, then leaped down the long steps in one bound. My heart was POUNDING! Going a ZILLION MILES AN HOUR! I didn't know where to go next, but I had to do something! That tree's whole heart had cried out to me. I decided to go to Commander Ashmore's classroom. Maybe he'd be able to understand what I was trying to say. But when I got there he was teaching. I turned and ran to Captain Moffet's room, but he was also busy teaching. I didn't know what to do. And I had to do something, and real quick!

Running down the sidewalk of the administration building, I noticed that Mr. Olbase didn't have a class in session. I ran into his room, all out of breath.

"Mr. Olbase!" I yelled. "I need your help! Please, it's important!"

"What is it?" he asked, leaving what he was doing at his desk and coming over to me.

"The maintenance men," I said, trying to catch my breath, "they're going to . . . to . . . going to . . . ."

"Slow down," he said. "Just take a big breath and slow down and tell me what's going on. I'll help you. Everything is going to be okay."

I could see the sincerity in his eyes and hear it in the tone of his voice, too. Immediately, I began to feel much better. "That big tree, you know, by the mess hall."

"Yes, I hear you, the big tree by the mess hall."

"There were two of them, you see, and . . . and the biggest one was knocked down by the storm. Actually almost split in half down its main trunk, and . . . and the maintenance men are going to . . . to . . ."

"Yes, the maintenance men are going to do what? Cut it up and dispose of it?" he asked.

"Yes!" I yelled excitedly. "That's it exactly! But you see, sir, we need to have a ceremony for that tree first. We can't let them just cut that tree up in little pieces until we've said goodbye to the spirit of that great tree who's been so good to us and given us shade and good feelings all these years."

He looked at me. Olbase really looked at me, then out of the blue, he started laughing and laughing.

"Oh, you're really good!" he said, laughing all the more. "You're the best! You really had me going for a little bit. I was actually, really listening to you, thinking you had something important to say. You're the best!" he said once again. "You thought you could come in and checkmate me one, two, three like you checkmated Mr. Terry, and then that player that Major Terry brought up from San Diego to beat you."

A few months back Major Terry and his pet student Drosen had brought in a guy from San Diego to play chess with me. I'd had no idea that he was rated and was really good, so I'd beaten his ass real fast. He'd gotten all mad at Major Terry and Drosen for not telling him that I was as good as I was. He'd accused them of setting him up to publicly embarrass him. I'd had no idea what the big fuss was all about. I hadn't even realized that there was such a thing as tournaments and championships for chess just like we had in wrestling.

I'd quit playing chess at school after that incident. Now I only played at home with my dad's older friends, Roberto and Salvador Montoya, who'd both been very good chess players in Mexico City.

I beat Roberto almost all of the time, but his older brother Salvador beat me pretty regularly. And I'd recently been told that Salvador had been so good that he'd once gone to Cuba to play and that he'd come in third among some of the best international players in the world.

Olbase was still laughing. "Ha, I got you, eh? I wasn't a fool and fell for your move of the bishop cutting across the board! You really thought I'd fall for your trap and go up to administration and tell them that we needed a voodoo ceremony for that tree's great spirit, so you could just laugh at me behind my back like you did with Major Terry and his big city chess whiz.

"What's going on? You think I don't know about you getting them to give you a second chance at your I.Q. test, so you could do worse than you did the first time?" he yelled.

His face was suddenly red with anger. "The whole trouble with you is that your father is rich, like so many of these spoiled kids, so it doesn't enter your minds that you guys are going to have to go out into the world and fend for yourselves!

"Checkmate you!" he shouted. "I'm no fool! Now get out of here, and stop wasting my time! All I can say is that you better shape up next year! It's your last chance before you get out into the real world!"

I turned. I was devastated. I'd never expected this. I felt totally helpless. I walked out of his classroom and down the sidewalk along the building. I no longer had the energy or presence of mind to run anymore. I went up to the great fallen tree to tell her that I'd failed her, too, and I began to cry.

It was Captain Moffet who found me.

"What is it?" he said. "I saw you come by my window when I was giving a class."

"I don't know, sir," I said, wiping the tears off of my face. "I guess I'm not just, well, stupid, but I'm crazy, too. Because you see, I love this tree and . . . and my grandmother, she . . . she . . ."

I could hardly talk. My grandmother had been a full-blooded Yaqui, and the Mexican army had massacred her people so they could take their fertile lands. She was the one who'd told me, when I was a child, that every woman needed her own crying tree and that every man needed his own big boulder. That women came from "tree" and men came from "rock," and the Spirit of the Deer, she'd told me, was the Spirit that enabled us human people to go from one world to another, just as the Spirits of the Tree and Rock were the Spirits that kept human people grounded on Mother Earth so they could do their holy work that they'd brought with them from the Stars. "You see, all us human people are walking stars," my grandmother used to tell me. "We all came across the heavens, gathering stardust to plant here on Earth for *Papito Dios.*"

But I didn't know how to explain any of this to Captain Moffet without sounding even more like a crazy*loco* stupid moron.

"Look," I finally said, "I think we should have a ceremony for this tree before we let the maintenance men put their axes and chain saws to it."

Captain Moffet looked perplexed, and he reached out and put his hand on my shoulder. "You're having a rough time of it, aren't you?" he said in a soft, kind voice.

"Yes, sir, I am," I said.

"I don't know why they insist on posting those I.Q. test results. Education doesn't have to be this way," he added. "In the time of the Greeks, students were taught with dialogue, and there wasn't a grading system. It's still done much in this same way in Cambridge and Oxford in England today."

"Dialogue?" I said. I'd never heard this word before.

"Yes, conversation. You see, knowledge was drawn out of the individual. Information wasn't just crammed into the brain."

I had no idea what he was talking about, but I did know that he cared and was being kind to me.

The very next day in Olbase's Spanish class everything was answered for me when Olbase said something under his breath but refused to repeat what he'd said until one of the cadets insisted that he repeat what he'd said.

"Okay, I'll say it again, but in Spanish," he said to us in Spanish, because, I guess, we were in Spanish class, "but many of you aren't going to like it. I said it's a good thing the Spanish and English eradicated most of the natives in the Americas, because wherever there are Indians left, these are the very places where civilization hasn't been able to advance."

Right away, Wellabussy began to whoop it up and stomped his feet with excitement, saying that he'd always known this. And a couple of other cadets agreed with him, too, but most of us were stunned by such open racism.

"You see, I told you many of you weren't going to like what I said," continued Olbase, "but it's true. Whenever I leave the U. S. and travel through Mexico and Central and South America, I can see very clearly that the places with the most European-looking people are the places where civilization has succeeded. The Indians of America had nothing to offer, just like the Blacks of Africa. Neither one of them had a worthwhile civilization.

"The truth is that worldwide, native people are backward and ignorant, and it's the European blood that runs in the veins of the Mexican people and the Blacks in the U. S. that has given these people any intelligence worth speaking about. I know these are tough words, but as the future leaders of our country, you need to hear and understand tough words. As for myself," he added, with a big smile, "I'm proud I'm pure Spanish-European and have absolutely no Indian blood in my veins."

By now more of the students were agreeing with what he'd said and joining Wellabussy and his group of cadets. I couldn't stand it anymore. They knew nothing of what they were talking about. My father's mother, a pure-blooded Indian from Oaxaca, had been a gifted fifteen-year-old when Benito Juárez won Mexico's independence from France. They'd taken her to the Academy of blah-blah-blah in Mexico City, and she'd astonished her European professors by learning French in six weeks. And my dad and my mother were some of the smartest, bravest people I'd ever met, and their mothers had both been full-blooded Indians. Also, year after year I saw that some of our quickest-learning workers on the ranch who came up from Mexico were Indians.

I wiped the tears from my eyes and leaped to my feet!

My heart was beat, beat, BEATING, GOING CRAZY*LOCO*! I was ready to grab Olbase and tear out his jugular! I was ready to take on Wellabussy and all his racist friends at the same time! But NOT IN WRESTLING! With GUNS! With WEAPONS!

I didn't shoot defenseless unarmed people below the knee. I hunted game that was fast of hoof and great of eye and hearing and smell. And I honored what I killed. I loved and respected what I killed. And I brought it home, and we ate of its flesh!

Everyone was looking at me. I stared at Olbase, eye to eye. Now I finally understood what it was that I'd failed to understand all these years, ever since I'd first started going to kindergarten. The entire western movement from Europe across the Americas and the whole globe was a racist, arrogant, self-righteous movement of mean, ugly intent!

For the very first time, I understood what *mi papá* had been telling me all these years about his very own father, the great Don Juan, straight from Spain, and how he'd only liked and loved his blue-eyed children, the ones like himself, and had never even recognized his dark Indian-looking children like my dad.

I SCREAMED!

I BELLOWED TO THE HIGH HEAVENS, scaring the living shit out of everyone else in the classroom, knocked two desks out of my way, and ran at Olbase. He bolted, running behind his desk. I saw fear in his eyes. I loved it, decided not to kill him, and turned, running out of the classroom.

I was finally FREE!

FREE of all ILLUSIONS and PETTY HOPES!

I now understood EVERYTHING IN ONE GREAT FLASH!

I ran to the huge tree that was still being worked on, scooped up a bunch of sawdust from the chainsaw waste, got a handful of leaves, and took off, running toward the sea. Never again would I ever come back to this school, or any other school!

I was finished with my European-based brainwashing!

I was DONE!

I was FINISHED!

*NO MÁS! NO MÁS!*

I could see that I'd never, never really belonged here. Nick McLean had been smart to quit the Academy. Nick Rorick had been absolutely brilliant to have refused to come to the school in the first place. And that cadet, who'd quit after fighting Juan Limberopulos, had been a genius to leave that same day.

Running up the beach toward home, I stopped at the lagoon, ripped off my tie and shirt, and threw them away. Then I took off my shoes and socks and threw them away, too. I was barefoot, and it felt great to feel the sand under my feet.

I kept running, racing, screaming with joy!

Up ahead, I stopped, faced the Mother Sea and said a prayer for the great tree. Then I walked slowly out into the surf, scattering the sawdust and leaves.

"Thank You, *Papito Dios*," I said, "for having bestowed on us so much *amor* through the Spirit of Your Great Tree."

Instantly a humming began behind my left ear, and I was so happy. Big happy! I'd forgotten how good it felt to give thanks to the Almighty.

I watched the sawdust and leaves mingle with the sea as each wave now took the remains of the great old tree further and further out. I made the sign of the cross over myself, blowing a kiss to the disappearing leaves and sawdust. Then, magically, the dolphins suddenly appeared, surfing in the waves. They began calling to me as they'd done the year before. I called back to them, and the humming behind my left ear quickly spread across the back of my head to my right ear, too. *Papito Dios* still loved me and was staying by me.

When I got home, my parents were waiting for me. They already knew everything. The school had called and told them about my crazy behavior.

I didn't deny it. No, I welcomed it. But, then, when my parents told me that I'd have to go back to school, I SCREAMED AT THE TOP OF MY LUNGS!

"BEAT ME! KILL ME! PUT ME IN PRISON FOR THE REST OF MY LIFE!" I bellowed. "But I will never, never, NEVER GO BACK TO SCHOOL, just to be proven that I'm stupider than the year before!"

I felt GREAT!

I was FREE! FREE! FREE!

I could still feel the humming behind my left ear, and in my mind's eye I could see the dolphins surfing in the waves. But, also, I could see that my poor parents had no idea what was going on.

I took a big breath, blowing out hard, and began to weep, because what could I say? Tell my dad and mom that it had begun for me as far back as the first day of school when our kindergarten teacher had yelled at us, "English only," and all the other teachers had looked down their noses at us Mexican kids, telling us that we were inferior, no good, and didn't even belong in this country, much less in school?

I loved my parents, but what could I say without telling them that they, too, were dark, Indian-looking, stupid Mexicans and that, yeah, sure, they'd been very lucky to have gotten rich and have a big house and ranch and a big, long Cadillac, but . . . when push came to shove, they, too, were nothing but stupid, backward *indios sin razón*! That was why the Oceanside Elks Club had never admitted my dad, even though he was one of the biggest movers and shakers in the whole area. And Jack Thill, our insurance agent, had tried to sponsor my dad into the Elks Club again and again.

So what could I tell my parents? That I'd just learned at school that Spain and England should have killed all of their mothers' people off, so that civilization could advance?

I said nothing and cried silently. My poor parents just looked at me. They had no idea what to do. And I didn't either. We were dead ducks, as far as I could see. I continued crying and crying, feeling so bad, especially for my parents who worked so hard and come so far and yet . . . it really meant *nada, nada,* nothing in the end.

# ~ BOOK TWO ~

# CHAPTER FIFTEEN

I awoke. I could hear the surf calling to me. I got up quickly, dressed, and headed for the corrals. I saddled up Dick, one of the fastest and hardest running horses that we had on the ranch, and took off at a run down the canyon to the sea. The sun was just coming up when I barreled past Carlsbad toward Encinitas. Clare had been absolutely right: Get me on a horse and nobody could touch me, no matter how high an I.Q. they had and how well they performed at school. Get me on a horse or working in the hot burning fields and I was more capable than almost anyone I knew.

When I got back home, I decided to go down to Johnson's Sporting Goods store in downtown Oceanside to buy myself a .357 magnum Smith and Wesson. I wasn't going to take it anymore. This was it! THIS WAS WAR! Olbase and those bastards who'd applauded deserved to die. For the next couple of weeks I stayed home and practiced pistol shooting every afternoon after I'd worked all day on our ranch. Our workers didn't know I was stupid, and we'd work side by side sweating and laughing and speaking in Spanish. Then after work, I'd get in my milk wagon Chevy truck and go out to our other ranch by the San Luis Rey airport to practice shooting my .357 magnum.

Ted Bourland, my *amigo,* who lived in the Fire Mountain area just up the hill east of us, would sometimes go with me, and we'd shoot our two .357 magnums until dark. He'd bought his right after I bought mine. He wanted to become a cop, and shooting would be part of his job, so this was why he was willing to put in shooting time. Ted was six-feet-five and had forearms as large around as most people's legs. He told me that when he was a kid, he'd seen a movie with a scene of a cop knocking the hell out of a couple of bullies beating up on a little kid. The movie had touched his heart, especially when the cop spoke gently to the little kid after running off the bad guys.

He asked me what I wanted to be when I finished school. I said that I didn't know and just kept shooting. Ted was one of my few friends from the Oceanside-Carlsbad area who hadn't gone to the Academy. Bill Coe, who'd given me my first chess set, had also quit the Academy, was going to public school, and started shooting with Ted and me. Bill Coe was super lean and muscular and smoked cigarettes. He had an Army Colt .45, and he told Ted and me that he'd decided to join the Marine Corps and become an M.P., then he'd get on the pistol team so he could whip our asses in shooting—which he eventually did.

John Folting, who was still going to the Academy, would sometimes go shooting with Ted and me. He told us that he'd decided to become an airline pilot and travel the world. And Bill Coe's cousin, Eddie O'Neill, who'd never gone to the school, surprised us all by one day taking off and joining the Army. Little Richard, who'd also quit the Academy, took off and joined the Navy.

Everyone I knew was either going to college, joining the military, or knew what they wanted to do with their lives. Terry Watson, another local guy, and I were the only ones who hadn't decided what to do. But Terry did say that for a while his calling was music and having a good time with girls, so as soon as school let out, he was heading up north to San Francisco to hang out at the North Beach coffeehouses and check out the whole beatnik poetry scene.

Myself, I had no idea what I was going to do. I only felt good when I was working on the ranch, where no one knew I was stupid, or shooting and working out. My wrestling weight of 145 was up to 156, and I'd gone from a 180-pound bench press to 220. I was working out with a vengeance. I was preparing myself for war.

Then one afternoon, when I was at the horse corrals by our house—not shooting but practicing throwing my knife—my parents came up and told me that they wanted to talk with me. They'd talked to the dean at school and he'd said that if I went to summer school for six weeks, they could still give me a high school diploma.

"You see, this way you don't have to go to school next year," said my dad, "but you'll still graduate."

I didn't mean to, but I screamed, "NO!" and I kicked at the huge tree on which I'd leaned my targets.

I hadn't meant to, but I'd startled my parents. For the last couple of weeks I could see that my behavior was tearing them apart.

"*Mijito,*" said my mother, "at least please think about it. It was our dream that all of our children finish high school," she added.

I took a deep breath. I could see my mother was really hurting. "Okay, let me think on it, *mamá,*" I said.

They left, and I took my big Bowie knife, concentrated real hard, and threw it with such force I split another one of the 2 x 6s I was using for practice. There was just no talking to me. I was all crazy*loco* inside, ready to explode like a bomb at any moment. But still that night I prayed, asking *Papito Dios* for guidance, and in the morning I awoke remembering that Captain Moffet had said something about education not needing to be as it was, that the Greeks had drawn knowledge out of the individual instead of . . . I didn't quite remember what else he'd said.

I met my parents at breakfast and told them that I'd thought about it and that I would maybe go back to school, but that it depended on what classes they wanted me to take and who would be my teachers, and also that I wouldn't wear any tie or uniform.

My mother didn't like my answer, but my dad took her hand and said they would look into it and see what could be done. They came back that same afternoon and told me I could choose my teachers and that uniforms were not worn at summer school. The classes I'd have to take, my mother told me, were English, chemistry, and biology, so they could still give me a college-acceptable diploma.

I took a big breath, because I knew I'd be sure to flunk these courses. But my parents assured me I wouldn't flunk, that I'd be given extra help and all the tutoring I needed until I passed.

I started laughing. Now I got the real picture. It was going to be the same old thing my parents had done for me with my third grade teacher, but this time it wasn't a case of avocados and an envelope full of money. It was probably a good-sized donation to the Academy. They were going to buy me a high school diploma. But I didn't want this. What were my parents going to do, roll the dice in my favor for the rest of my life? When was I ever going to get to accomplish something on my own?

Suddenly I wondered if they'd set up that event when I'd been fourteen years old and won the California Championship in horsemanship. Then I wondered if they'd set up my wrestling matches and chess games, too. Could it be that Major Terry could really have beaten me the day I'd wiped him out five times in a row? Had my parents paid him off?

I started laughing! Oh, I really was the best, just like Olbase had said. Here I was now making myself crazy*loco* with doubt? There was no way on God's little green apple that Major Terry, who'd graduated from West Point, could have thrown those games. He'd been out to get me with all he had, then he'd brought in that chess whiz from San Diego to beat my ass, because he was so pissed off at me. And I'd beaten them all! So, no, I wasn't crazy*loco*!

Going back to the Academy for my first day of summer school, I couldn't believe what I saw. The smaller tree, the one that hadn't been demolished by the storm, was flourishing, and in such a short time. Soon, I bet, she'd be a giant, too. My heart filled with joy. Life really did go on.

I ran up and hugged the tree, and I just knew I was going to be okay going to summer school at the Army Navy Academy. And it did turn out fine. It was like going to a whole different school. No one wore uniforms, and I was allowed to drive myself to school in my beat-up old-looking milk truck. It was crazy, but I loved my Chevy in a whole new way. I loved that it had gotten dents while working in the fields and corrals and it was strong and dependable. Little Richard's cherry-red roadster now seemed phony to me. I actually thought my Chevy milk wagon looked pretty damn good.

I got Mr. Lawrence, the varsity football coach, for chemistry, old man Jacobsen for biology, and Captain Moffet for English. I didn't recognize Moffet in his street clothes. I was used to seeing him in his army uniform. Each class would be two hours long each day, and at the end of each week, I'd be tested. Each week would be the equivalent to a month of regular schoolwork. It was heaven. I didn't have to march to class, and I could wear my Levis, in which, of course, I felt at home. Best of all, since my classes were one on one, I could ask all the questions I wanted to ask, no matter how stupid they might seem, because my teachers had been hired especially to help me with each subject. Like in biology, which I'd taken before and flunked, I now got to ask—even before we opened the textbook— something that had been really bothering me since day one. That was, what was biology? Old man Jacobsen told me that biology was the science of plants and animals, then he calmly suggested that we look up the word together in the dictionary. I'd never realized the dictionary could be used for this. I'd always thought that a diction- ary was only used to find out how to spell a particular word.

So we looked up "biology," and he read me the dictionary defi- nition. Biology was the science that dealt with the origin, history, and physical characteristics and habits of plants and animals, and it included botany, zoology, and then the subdivisions of these. Sud- denly biology made more sense to me. I'd never realized that it was the study of both plants and animals. I'd always thought that biolo- gy only had to do with animals, so I'd been all mixed up, wondering why we kept jumping all over the place, like mixing up checkers with chess. So now when we opened up our textbook and old man Jacobsen began to read to me, I could understand where we were going and why we were going where we were going. It was beauti- ful. I could relax and begin to learn.

The same thing happened with Mr. Moffet—we weren't sup- posed to call him captain during summer school. I told him I didn't see why we kept dividing up each sentence and putting the subject on one line, the verbs over there on the other line, then the adjectives and adverbs someplace else. And why did some words, like "read," change their pronunciation but not the spelling when the tense changed.

Then I asked him where the word "the" came from. It made no sense to me. "This" tree over here and "that" tree over there made a lot of sense to me, because they gave location to a tree, but "the" tree gave no sense of location, but a sense of importance that hadn't been established, and so it seemed entirely false to me.

He started laughing and said he loved my way of thinking and that he was finally beginning to understand how my mind worked. He explained to me that even as recently as the last century, the rules of the English language hadn't been set in stone, as they now seemed to be. He said that the journals of some of our most world-renowned adventurers and scientists were quite primitive in spelling and English usage. He added that English, as opposed to most Latin-based languages—was pretty screwed up at best. He also didn't know how and when the concept of the word "the" had begun, but he did agree with me that this word gave a sense of unestablished importance, especially when coupled with the word "truth."

Hearing this, my heart soared and I felt a great pressure come off my chest, a weight I'd been feeling ever since my very first day at school. Here was one of the smartest teachers I'd ever met, telling me he didn't know some things and that he agreed with my feelings.

"Then English isn't a better language than Spanish?"

"No, of course not."

"Then why do we get all of our education only through English?"

"For convenience. For laziness. For control. Most European people speak two or three different languages. In China people speak four different dialects."

My mind was reeling. This was all so new to me. I'd thought that English was superior to Spanish and that was why they'd hit us on the head when we were little kids and we were caught speaking Spanish.

"And it's also okay to not know?" I asked.

"Of course. In fact, it is only when people realize how much they don't know that they are capable of taking in new information."

I felt a chill go up and down my spine. This was wonderful! My father's teachings came bursting into my mind. All my life he'd told me that thinking that you knew was the enemy of all learning. That looking was not seeing. Hearing was not listening. And repeating information was not thinking.

"In fact, always remember, *mijito,* that only in not knowing and admitting it, do we have any chance in hell of seeing and learning and finding the wisdom with which to get through the twists and turns of life."

Here at long last I had a teacher who was validating what I'd been taught at home, instead of making the things that I'd been told at home sound inferior and stupid.

I thanked Mr. Moffet from the bottom of my heart. I didn't feel divided deep inside myself anymore. I was able to start listening and learning English for the very first time in my life. Before, I'd never really wanted to learn English. Hell, on our first day of school, we Mexican kids had been slapped and shouted at if we didn't speak "English only." It had felt like the tongue with which my mother had sung me to sleep had been torn out of me, making me feel ashamed even to remember the *amor* that my mother had given me in Spanish.

And so here I was, eighteen years old, and I finally felt safe enough inside myself that I could begin to learn in English. I felt invited, not invaded. I felt trust, not abuse. But then all of this trust and feeling of invitation went flying out the window in chemistry class with Mr. Lawrence, the varsity football coach.

We were in our third session of the first week when I realized that I still couldn't get the swing of things in chemistry.

"Look, sir," I said to the football coach, "I still just don't get it. Maybe we should look up the word 'chemistry' in the dictionary like I did with Mr. Jacobsen for biology, so I can understand where it is that we're going."

"You look it up," he said to me. "I know what chemistry is. I've been teaching the subject for over twenty years!"

I could see he was angry. But I kept calm and tried to explain. "All right, then, since you know, could you tell me why it is that $H_2O$ makes water? I don't see why."

"That's what it does," he said. "You take two parts of hydrogen and one part of oxygen and you get water. That's it."

"Yes, but why? I mean, could it be that there is something else going on between these two elements, like an attraction or—I don't know how to say it—a something else that's maybe even invisible between all elements, and it is this something else that causes the creation of a totally new substance when we combine elements, and so then . . . "

"Look," he said, cutting me off, "you know I'm going to have to pass you at the end of this six-week period one way or another, so can we please stop all this nonsense and get to the point!"

Now he wasn't just angry, but really pissed off. And I knew I should have stopped, but I couldn't. Because I really, really had to get this fact straight in my head or I'd be forever lost in chemistry, not knowing where we were headed.

"I have never really known what the word nonsense means," I said to him. "Because maybe nonsense to one person could be making a lot of sense to another, so what I'm asking is simply this, why do these elements do what they do?"

He SCREAMED!

He BELLOWED!

He JUMPED to his feet behind his desk, and the big cords of his short, thick neck rose up until they looked like they might burst. He threw his big thick chemistry textbook at me from across the room. I ducked, and the book hit the wall behind me with a thunderous bang!

"ASK GOD!" he yelled, his chest heaving and the white of his eyes turning red with rage.

But I wasn't going to take this shit from him. I took a big breath and stood up, too. "YOU'RE FIRED!" I yelled at him.

"I'm what!?! YOU EGOTISTICAL PUNK!"

I looked at him and repeated my words. "YOU'RE FIRED! I want someone else to teach me chemistry!"

He came around his desk like he was out on the football field and he was going to make a rush at me.

I took up my wrestling stance. "I wouldn't, sir," I said, "if I were you." And I almost added, "Because you're old, and fat, and out of shape, and even on your best day, I don't think you would've had a chance against me." But I didn't say any of this. Instead, once I saw him back off, I gathered my things and left his classroom.

I went up to the administration office and said that I didn't want to take chemistry with Mr. Lawrence anymore and that I wished to do it with Mr. Moffet, if I could. They asked if anything had happened between me and the football coach. I lied and said no, because I didn't want to get him in trouble. I shouldn't have pushed him. He was too old and set in his football mentality. He wasn't smooth and easygoing and smart like old man Jacobsen or open-minded like Mr. Moffet.

That same day I took a chemistry class with Mr. Moffet, and when I asked him the very same question I'd asked Mr. Lawrence, he said, "We don't know why $H_2O$ makes water. In fact, we don't really know anything ultimately in science. We just know that if we do this and that, we get these results, and when we observe this long enough, getting the same results each time, we call this scientific proof. But it's not really a proof. Science never gets into the realm of knowing the why or the understanding of anything."

"Then science isn't really about learning and understanding," I said. "Science is really all about memorizing if you do this and that with these and those, then you get this other."

"Exactly."

THE WHOLE WORLD EXPLODED OPEN FOR ME! All these years I'd been expecting to learn, to understand, never just to memorize and then call what I'd memorized knowledge.

I was FLABBERGASTED!

What a fool I'd been!

Now I understood why Mr. Lawrence had gotten so mad at me when I'd asked him "why" in chemistry. He hadn't known the answer. And I could also see why he'd gotten so mad at me years ago when I'd once asked him why we called football football. It wasn't played with the foot, so why didn't we call it throwball or runball? He'd gone crazy with rage.

Now I got it. He'd gotten mad at me both times because he hadn't known the answer. Simple as that. And he'd been terrified to admit that he didn't know, especially after teaching chemistry and coaching football all these years.

I took a big breath. I was now beginning to "see" the whole system of our American education so differently. Why hadn't I just been told all this at the beginning, that I wasn't being expected to learn or understand, that I was really just being asked to memorize. So then our style of education was really all about cramming information into our heads. That was why Nill and some of our other top students referred to their preparation for a test as "cramming," because that was exactly what our educational system wanted and was geared to, simply cramming information into our brains.

No wonder my dad, who'd never had a day of school in all of his life, could "see" things so clearly that educated people couldn't see. He had never been brainwashed into cramming, into filling his mind with so much unnecessary information that he had no room left in his brain to think and be creative.

Suddenly I flashed on the day I'd done that math problem in Commander Ashmore's classroom, and he'd said that people hadn't solved those kinds of problems in the way I'd done for well over a thousand years. He'd asked me where I'd gotten my idea and did I like math and had I been reading books on the history of math. I'd said no. The idea just came to me.

Well, I now wondered where that first guy, the big famous blah-blah-blah mathematician had gotten his ideas. Could it be that I'd been right when I'd suggested to Ashmore that air wasn't really thin and was like a sea, a soup, and it was from this living-sea-soup that we all got our ideas?

Could it be that there was a living glue, a force, a something invisible or maybe even spiritual between all elements that caused them to be attracted to each other, and it was this "living attraction" that caused a totally new substance to come into existence?

I began to tremble. This was so exciting. Then could it possibly be that . . . that there was also something going on between all of us human people that did the same thing, and if we could grasp this "something," we would then suddenly "see" all of life come alive like I did with the chess pieces and my dad did with the dice in Las Vegas?

I held. I breathed. I closed my eyes. "Then could it be," I said aloud to myself, "that when I quit thinking, let go totally, and breathe in deeply with complete trust, I am combining this something within me just like $H_2O$, and this is how I am able to get to that magic place and . . . and be such a good chess player and . . . and last year become such a great wrestler?"

I held, then breathed again and again, and gently, smoothly I came to know that this was it. There really was a living-sea all around us, but we could only "see" this sea when there was no us "over there" and all of us was "here within us," right now, completely connected together forever.

Tears came to my eyes, I was so happy. Then this was the "place" Jesus had come to earth to tell us about when He'd said we all had the Kingdom of God within us.

Oh, I loved Mr. Moffet! He was WONDERFUL! He'd given me hope! I felt fearless once again, and I could clearly see it had always been fear that had kept me dammed up all these years. Fear of sin, fear of hell, fear of what people might think of me, fear of . . . of . . . I didn't quite know how to say or even think all these thoughts I was having, and yet . . . it was like I was now so excited with all these thoughts racing around inside my brain that I was on fire. Maybe I wasn't really stupid after all. Maybe I'd just been misled all these years from the very beginning. OH, A FIRE FOR WANTING TO LEARN ALL I COULD LEARN WAS NOW BURNING INSIDE OF ME!

Quickly, easily, I memorized all of the elements and what they did when they were mixed together, and I got an A in chemistry on my first week's test! I was FLYING! School was EXCITING! I got A's in all of my other classes, too. And it was so easy! Now all of my focus was simply on memorizing and not on trying to learn or understand.

Hell, this was so simple compared to what I'd been trying to do all of these years. I didn't need to know or understand shit to pass a test. In fact, trying to understand actually slowed the mind down and didn't help at test time. Oh, this was so beautiful! I was FREE! FREE! FREE!

And English was not superior and didn't have to make sense, either. All I had to do was memorize the different words, their spelling and their definitions. But this part was really hard for me, because after five minutes of trying to read, I'd get a splitting headache. It was a good thing that Mr. Moffet and Mr. Jacobsen kept reading all my material to me in each class. I wondered if this had also been arranged by my parents, but I didn't want to ask.

# CHAPTER SIXTEEN

**S**ummer school was almost over when my cousin Victor Astorga came to visit us. He was a year younger than my older sister Tencha, which made him nine years older than me. He'd been in the Army, then he'd gone to college up in the Bay area of San Francisco with his G.I. Bill money.

My parents told Victor—we'd both been named after our mother's father, *Don* Victor—about my situation, saying they'd barely been able to get me to finish high school. They now wanted me to go to college to study business, they told him, but didn't know how to even approach the subject with me. Victor told my parents he was on his way to San Diego to register at the new Catholic university that was just opening up above Mission Bay. He suggested that they talk to me about going down to San Diego with him.

That night my parents told me what my cousin had suggested. I said no, absolutely not! I turned and walked away as fast as I could. My parents really had no idea how much it had hurt me all these years to go to school. I was done with all book learning. I'd worked so hard during summer school that I had nothing but splitting headaches for the past two weeks. But the matter didn't stop there. My cousin Victor spent the next few days talking to me every afternoon, trying to convince me that he was sure I should go to college.

"The school is new, so they need students," he said, "and you can go down with me. I can help you fill out the forms and see you through the procedure. Look," he added, "I'm family. I know what you're going through. I, too, never thought I could go to college. How could I? No one ever has in all of our family. But the Army opened up my eyes, and I've completed two years of college with the

Jesuits up in San Francisco, so I know what I'm talking about. You can do this, and your parents are willing to back you financially."

I took a big breath and almost leveled with him about the fact that I didn't know how to read. But there was just something about my cousin I didn't quite trust. And besides, now that I'd finished high school, all I wanted to do was to stay on the ranch and work with our workers from Mexico. These were my people. This was where I belonged and felt at home.

"What are you going to do," said my cousin, as if reading my mind, "stay on the ranch for the rest of your life? It's a big world. You need to get out. You're not a child anymore."

I took a great big deep breath and blew out. We were under the huge pepper tree where my dad had spoken to me just before I'd turned sixteen. I was eighteen now and part of me knew he was right and I couldn't just stay on the ranch for the rest of my life, especially if I wanted to build my own home. But I also knew that—oh, I just didn't know how to explain it—school wasn't teaching me anything. It was destroying me!

"Look," he said, "at least go down to San Diego with me and look around. Okay?"

I kicked the dirt, pushed back my western hat, glanced up and saw all the broken, twisted branches of this huge old tree and how new growth had started at the broken, twisted places. I took another deep breath. "Okay," I said, "I'll go with you, but I'm not promising anything."

The following day Victor picked me up in a little baby blue convertible, and we drove down to San Diego together. I'd never been in a convertible before. It was fun driving down the coast with the top down.

The Catholic university was on a hill across from the Presidio and Old Town. All the buildings were still under construction, but I could already see that this was really going to be an incredible place once it was completed. The chapel was way bigger than our church in Oceanside and was still under construction, too. The ground lay bare around the buildings where I assumed gorgeous gardens would one day be installed.

I'd followed my cousin into the administration building. I couldn't make head or tail of the form they gave me to fill out. I didn't know what the words "marital status" meant. I thought maybe these words had something to do with martial arts. I asked my cousin what these two words on the form meant.

Victor laughed and said that it "pertained" to marriage. I told him I didn't know what the word "pertained" meant, either. He laughed again and called me a simple pumpkin from the country, and when he went to rough up my hair in a friendly happy way, I grabbed his hand, spun him about, and yanked him into a wrestling hold.

I didn't give a shit that he was older and stronger and had been in the Army. I jerked him in tight and had him in complete control. But then I saw that people were watching, so I let him go. I turned and walked out of the building. Once I was outside, I screamed to the high heavens and took off running. He finally caught up with me in his car.

"Where are you going?" he yelled at me.

"Home."

"You plan on running all the way?"

"I'll walk, too."

"It's forty miles."

"So what. I've gone farther when I go hunting out by Palomar Mountain."

"Look, I didn't mean to embarrass you," he said. "Get in. I'll drive you home. But please, let's just complete the forms. I found out they're still not officially accredited, so they told me that they can make allowances for you on admissions."

I didn't want to hear any more. What were my parents going to do, buy me a college degree, too? I looked up and saw the series of long ladders resting against the towering tower of the chapel. I had a sudden urge to go inside. But there were signs everywhere saying nobody was allowed to go in, that the place was under construction and dangerous.

I ignored the signs, left Victor waiting in his car, climbed over the mounds of raw dirt surrounding the chapel, and walked inside. There were no doors or windows installed yet, and pigeons fluttered about in the empty space.

Then I saw him.

I saw his huge dark eyes as he sat on the cross alongside Jesus in all of his wide-shouldered regal beauty. The huge red-tailed hawk and I stared at each other eye to eye, and my whole heart filled with so much feeling that I just knew that I belonged in this place.

"Hi," I said to this large-eyed wondrous creature.

And I swear the Red Eagle nodded his head, giving me a sign of welcome. Instantly, I knew that yes, yes, yes, a thousand times yes, I was supposed to be here.

But the office of admissions wouldn't let me in. My cousin told my parents that they'd have to drive down from Oceanside to meet with the people in charge of admissions. My parents drove down in their Cadillac, had a private session with Bishop Buddy himself, and it was agreed that if I took a few classes from their affiliated Catholic high school across town, I could attend the University of San Diego at the same time. I agreed to do it, but I couldn't pass the English entrance exam, so I was put in dumbbell English. I brought my stuff down and got a room in the dormitories on the campus along with a bunch of football players who'd been recruited from across the country. Bishop Buddy clearly wanted to make this new Catholic university the Notre Dame of the West.

I only went once to the Catholic high school across town. They didn't know anything about me taking classes there, so I never went back. Little by little, I came to realize that the whole university was still so new and in such chaos that what was decided on one day was forgotten the next.

I took logic, theology, world history, business, and dumbbell English. I was shocked to learn that in college a student didn't take the same class five days a week. Some classes met twice a week, others met three times a week. Also very differently from high school, we were now encouraged by our professors to study in groups. I soon found out that in every study group there were always one or two guys who liked to play the role of the professor, and this person would read aloud to the rest of us what we were studying. This was great! Fantastic! Wonderful! All I had to do was just open up my book and follow along, pretending that I, too, knew how to read.

In the second week our logic teacher, Dr. Nacozi, said that anyone who needed extra help could stay after class. Two of us stayed after class every day, and we got to ask a lot of questions. I'd already looked up the word logic in my Webster New World Dictionary of the American Language that I'd purchased in downtown San Diego. I found out that the word logic came from *logike* in Greek and that to be logical was an act; it was the science of reasoning and that this science dealt with criteria of valid induction and deductions of thought. It was the system of principles that underlie any act of science, as through the working of cause and effect. I read this definition over and over, but couldn't make head or tail of it. So I asked a student in our logic study group, the one who liked to play the professor, if he could tell me what "criteria of valid induction and deduction of thought" meant. He loved it. His name was Berry. He thought that maybe he wanted to become a priest. He sat up, took on a bishop kind of look, and read the whole thing to me, explaining each word as he went along. He was very good, but I still couldn't quite get a handle on it. Because didn't logic have to start first with listening, then thinking about what you'd heard? Wasn't this why the definition had started out by calling logic an act? But an act of what?

This was also when I began to find out that to look up one word in a dictionary only caused me to have to look up the five or six words that had been used to describe the meaning of the first word. It was endless. It would take me about two hours to just look up one word. And I couldn't very well keep asking different students to read all these different definitions to me, so once more I began to get splitting headaches after fifteen minutes of trying to work with my New World Dictionary—not of English—but of the American Language.

Then one day an explosion took place in theology class. I asked how we knew what Jesus had really said, since He hadn't spoken English, much less American.

"I mean, it's now nearly two thousand years later, so what we really have is more of an opinion—and in English—of what He said and in a very different kind of language."

The big guy sitting in front of me whirled around in his seat and looked at me like he wanted to tear me apart.

"Look," he yelled at me with exasperation, "just be smart and use the tools that we've been taught in our logic class. Jesus was an honest man, right?"

I glanced at our priest. He'd been the one to whom I'd asked my question, but I could see he wasn't going to answer my question. He was enjoying what was happening.

"Yes, of course," I said to my fellow student.

"And honest men don't lie, right? So, then, everything that Jesus said is gospel and the truth, because honest men don't lie, and Jesus, you agreed, was an honest man. Now do you get it?" he said. "You can't be questioning Jesus if you're logical!" he added, then turned back around as if the discussion was over and he'd explained everything to me.

I took a deep breath. I knew this big guy very well. He was one of our blue-chip football players, recruited from the Midwest, and a very handsome well-liked guy. I liked him, too. And I wanted our professor-priest to speak up and tell us what was obviously wrong in the other guy's understanding of logic. But I could see I wasn't going to get any help.

"Well," I said, taking the bull by the horns as Dr. Nacozi always told us in our logic class, "I can see what you're saying, but my question wasn't about honesty and even what Jesus said. I'm saying that Jesus didn't speak English. He spoke Aramaic, we've been told. And I speak English and Spanish, or you could say American and Mexican, and so I know that each language has its own . . ."

"But Jesus is the Son of God and God can do anything," said the big football player, cutting me off. "And no loving father would ever abandon his only begotten son, and God is loving, right? You'd agree with that, wouldn't you? So it's then only logical that God would be sure to inspire each translation of His Son's Holy Words! Do you get it now? Or are you saying that God isn't all-powerful and doesn't love his Son? Which is totally illogical!"

I took another deep breath. My heart was pounding, and everyone in the class was staring at me. I could see that our professor-priest was still not going to step in. I suddenly felt like I was back at the Army Navy Academy, and instead of the football coach throwing his chemistry book at me, this professor-priest was going to let this big powerful student intimidate me. It was a setup.

"Look," I finally said, "I'm Catholic, just like you. I believe in Jesus, too. But . . . but I've also seen honest men make mistakes. So I'm not saying that these translators who translated Jesus' words weren't really trying to be sincere and do their best, but maybe they just couldn't comprehend what it was that they were translating, because . . . "

"Are you saying that Jesus was ignorant?!" he yelled. "Is that what you're really saying?"

He was furious. He hadn't heard a word I'd said, and he was ready to leap out of his seat and come at me. I closed my eyes, heart pounding, and worked hard to stay focused, to go to that calm, magical place within me. I wasn't going to allow this guy to bully me. Sure he was much bigger than me, but I was a wrestler, so I wasn't afraid to defend myself or my position.

"No," said I, opening my eyes, "I'm not saying that at all and you know it. You just like getting mad and keep changing the subject. You haven't really listened to one word I've said. You twist everything I say. You use logic and words to intimidate. Not to think. Not as a way of using induction or deduction, which are the very tools of logic. Because, if you really want to use deductive reasoning, you would have been better off to simply say that faith is beyond reason, and so it is with faith and not reason that we know that Jesus' words are true even today."

"But you don't really believe that either! Do you?! That's why you questioned what Jesus said in the first place!"

I glanced at our professor. I didn't know what to say anymore. I knew this student well. He was normally calm and good-natured.

"Don't you get it?" he now continued in a much softer voice. "Religion isn't something to question. That's wrong."

I looked at him and almost said, "Yeah, but then why doesn't religion just stop at faith, instead of jumping into being all-knowing, and then is willing to start religious wars and slaughter native people all over the world." But I said nothing, because I didn't really have the tools to say all I was feeling inside. My God, this guy—a good guy—was using religion just as Olbase had used racism back at the Academy. This hadn't been Jesus' message. Hope had been His message. Forgiveness had been His foundation. I felt helpless.

"All right, enough. Calm down," our professor-priest finally said, laughing lightheartedly. "I believe we've just witnessed a classic dilemma. One person is using impartial reasoning for proving something that, at its very basis, is really a matter of faith. And faith is a matter beyond all logic. We can't mix water and oil."

"Then if our beliefs can't be talked about or discussed even between fellow Catholics," I said, "why are we even in this theology class in the first place?"

"That's it!" yelled the football player, turning about in his chair to me once again. "Now you got it! We can discuss, see, but we can't question!"

"But my New World Webster Dictionary says that the word discuss means to question, to take apart, to scatter, to consider and argue the pros and cons with varying degrees of . . . ."

The whole class was staring at me. Even our professor. I had no idea what was going on. I knew this definition by memory, because I was so slow that I'd had to read the definition a dozen times, even after I'd asked our study group to look up the word "discuss" in the first place.

"Why are you even at this school?" said another student. "Why didn't you go to Berkeley?" He was angry, too.

I didn't know what this Berkeley was, so I figured he was saying that I was too stupid to be in any university. I said nothing more and our class continued, but people were no longer treating me like they had before. Now they would glance at me every time our professor said anything. But I said nothing more. Then in my next class with Dr. Nacozi, I stayed after class to see him.

To my surprise he immediately asked me what was the matter. I guess I still looked pretty shook up because of what had happened in our theology class. We were alone, so I explained the situation to him. He asked me if I'd like to take a walk with him. I said sure, of course, and we went out of the building and into the rose garden that had just been planted. The place smelled of heaven.

"First of all," said Dr. Nacozi to me, "I want you to know that I realize you have a brilliant mind."

"Me?" I said, feeling shocked.

"Yes, you," he said. "And maybe you haven't done that well in school in the past, but this is all about to change very rapidly for you, because the further you go in university life, the more apt you are to find minds like your own. I never had many friends until I got into graduate school. Before that . . . well, I always felt confused and lost," he said, laughing. "And not very capable with the girls and in my social life, either.

"But since then, I've married a beautiful woman. A queen. And I've come to realize that the mighty oak always takes much longer to grow than the pine, but once the oak has grown, it can weather the worst of storms, because it is so much stronger than the pine. That is why we make our floors of oak, which is a much harder wood than pine, so that our floors can endure the years and years of people walking and jumping on them. And a mind like yours and mine is the type of mind on which society builds its floors. Ideas are the foundation of any society," he added with *gusto* in his heavily accented English. "Ideas that have been put through the fires of discourse and have the strength to endure the tribulations of . . ."

I'd quit listening. He was going way too fast for me. I was still way back at having heard him say that I had a brilliant mind. I mean, I'd never had anything like this told to me in all my life. Then he'd said that he, too, had felt confused and lost and not very capable with the girls or socially. This was WONDERFUL! Then maybe there really was hope for me! I began to listen once again.

"What happened to you and that other young man in your theology class was simply a matter of fear," continued Dr. Nacozi. "Tell me, what is the most frightening and dangerous act any human being can ever do?" he asked as he stopped and bent to smell a beautiful red rose.

"I guess war?" I said.

"No," he said. "if this were true, then we wouldn't have so many wars. Risk of death?" he added. "Could this be the most frightening and dangerous of acts? No, or we wouldn't have so many daredevils with motorcycles. To think," he said with his face full of joy as we continued walking once again. "Thinking is by far the most frightening and dangerous act any human being can perform. People would rather die than be forced to think. A whole nation would rather blow itself to pieces than question its basic values. Whole groups of religious sects all through history have preferred committing mass suicide rather than face the possibility of error or change. And all of these people prided themselves on doing what they did in the name of principle."

It had never entered my mind that it took guts to think. All these years, I'd always thought that I was a weak, lost, stupid coward to have all these questions flying around inside of my head. Well, then, if this was true, maybe I really was brave and smart and maybe even . . . even brilliant.

Dr. Nacozi continued on. "What does the term 'principle' really mean?" he asked. "Is it a natural fundamental truth, a law of nature, a doctrine, a motivating force, a rule of conduct, or is it a belief? And what does it say about the human mind that it is ready to forsake all for such an idea as a principle?

"The human mind, I tell you," he continued with his heavy European accent, "is our greatest unexplained, unexplored territory, far greater than all of outer space. Because once we begin to travel this interior road, then suddenly we come to the realization that inner space is the key—the reflection—with which we process the information we receive of the outer world through our five senses. 'I think, therefore I am,' as the great genius Descartes said so well."

Here he stopped, but I was still sailing, shooting inside my mind like an eagle shooting through the heavens. I was reeling inside my brain. "But do we really have only five senses?" popped out of my mouth.

He stopped and stared at me, then started laughing. He got to laughing so hard that his laughter was contagious and I started laughing, too. "There, you've done it again!" he said. "You've just questioned one of the very pillars on which our entire western—if not the whole world—is based. Now, what caused you to ask this question? Do you think there are, in fact, other senses?"

"Yes," I said. "I'm a wrestler, see, and in wrestling we were always told that . . ."

"So you are a wrestler?" he said, going into a wrestling stance. "So was I, a thousand years ago!"

"Really?"

"Yes, Greco-Roman. Do you know that style?"

"No, I don't," I said. "I only know American."

"Too bad," he said, "but that's all right, too, so go on. You were saying that in wrestling you were always told . . ."

"We were always told that balance comes first. That you find your center, your spot, your stance, like the one you just took up, and that our sense of balance is the key to all wrestling."

"This is true," he said. "Balance is everything in Greco-Roman-style wrestling, too."

"We were told a person can be blind, can be deaf, or even both, but once they touch, their balance is the most important sense of all. So then, why isn't finding our center, our balance, the most important sense we have? Because until we know how to center ourselves . . . understanding that this spot, this place is everything, we can't hold . . . hold . . ."

I suddenly had this very strange feeling as I was speaking that I wasn't completely "here." That there was another part of me that was "over there," and it was this "other me" from where all these great thoughts came.

I smiled. That great genius Descartes had been right, but it wasn't "I think, therefore I am." It was, "I think, therefore we are!" Yes, yes, yes! Because all of us are connected to each other and together we are the power! Oh, I was truly traveling through unexplored dark deep canyons and crevices within my own mind, and as the words continued to come out of my mouth, I could see that my thinking was illuminating my way. "So yes," I was now saying, "balance must be the key to all our other senses, because without it, then . . . well, it's so easy for anyone or anything to knock us off our feet."

He couldn't stop laughing. "Stop! Stop! Slow down! This is what Einstein was talking about when he said that the imagination is the most important asset we humans have!

"Now go on, please, I'm listening. Why isn't balance our most important sense? And why is it that Aristotle, that giant, that genius of geniuses, didn't even name balance as one of our senses? Could it be that . . . that balance is our sixth sense?" he said. "This must be how Galileo felt as he searched the heavens for understanding."

The man was beaming, he was so excited! There was absolutely no fear in him as there had been in the big handsome football player. And so together Dr. Nacozi and I took off on another roller-coaster ride of the mind, and it was wonderful! Maybe this was what it had been like to live in the Garden of Eden. To question, to think hadn't been seen as frightening, but . . . but instead viewed as our ongoing conversation with God Himself.

I took a great big deep breath. Then could it be that this center, this balance within us was the "place" where we found out who we were and who we weren't? And could it be that this "place of balance" could only be reached when . . . when we used both our male and female brain?

SUDDENLY IT HIT ME BETWEEN THE EYES LIKE A THUNDERBOLT! Jesus Christ had been a balanced male and female human being and He hadn't come down to earth to save us from sin! No, He'd come down to teach us how to get into this Kingdom of God that was within each of us. This was why He'd been smiling that great big smile the day I'd seen Him come walking across the rolling waters beyond the breakers to greet my brother like an old friend.

I laughed.

I giggled. This was so much fun and made so much sense and felt so good deep, deep inside of me. Then Jesus Christ had allowed Himself to die a horrible death to show us that even a horrible death was better than living a life full of fear, because it was, indeed, only fear that was holding us human beings back from making this whole planet into a PARADISE ON EARTH!

Oh, His message was beautiful! Fantastic! And totally uplifting!

I smiled. And this was when I, too, was at my best and happiest, when I was fearless. And this was Jesus' power. He'd been fearless. He hadn't died on the cross with a long frightened face. NO! A THOUSAND TIMES NO! He'd died, going to the Father in one glorious great feeling of PURE LOVE! And so it was wrong for us to be sad or feel terrible about His crucifixion. We should be JOYFUL! And willing to live without fear just like Him.

Oh, I felt so happy! BIG, BIG HAPPY! And I could now clearly see that it was balance that was the "key" to getting us humans
into the Kingdom of God that Christ had come down to Earth to tell
us about. And in order to have a balanced brain, we had to be open
to both parts of our brain. This was my dad and mom's power.
They'd both been raised by their mothers, and so they had balanced
male and female brains. Oh, my Lord God, I WAS FLYING!
GOING A ZILLION MILES AN HOUR! I was "here" and "over
there" at the same time and "over there" was my direct connection
to God.

Getting back to our dormitories, I looked up the word genius in
my Webster New World Dictionary and it said guardian spirit or spirit of a person; spirit, natural ability; according to ancient Roman
belief a guardian spirit assigned to a person at birth.

I LEAPED!

I SCREAMED!

I POUNDED my feet on the floor in a frenzy of joy! My grandmama, the Yaqui, had told me that I'd come to Earth with a guardian
angel at my side. And that any time I felt lost or confused, all I had
to do was close my eyes, place both of my hands over my heart, and
my guardian angel would speak to me, showing me my way. Then
this "other me" was my guardian angel. I'd been right when I'd said
that this "other part of me" was directly connected to God.

I laughed. I went out on the terrace of our apartment that over-
looked the beautiful bay of San Diego and took a big deep breath of
the clean, crisp ocean breeze. This was wonderful! Then being a
genius didn't necessarily mean that you were smart. No, being a
genius really meant that you could get quiet enough inside of yourself to listen to the voice of your own guardian angel.

Tears were streaming down my face. It was all right that I had a
low I.Q. It was all right that all these years I'd felt so stupid and lost
and confused. It was all right that I was Mexican and Mexicans
weren't just good for f . . . f . . . fucking. They were good capable
people, too.

I took a big deep breath, held, then blew out real slowly. I placed
both of my hands over my heart and took another big breath.
"Hello," I said to my guardian angel. "Hi, there."

Instantly I felt a warm, smooth, easy feeling come to me, and I could now see that all these years my angel, my genius, had been guiding me, but I'd just never quite seen it before. I breathed in again and again, and the warm, smooth easy feeling expanded all through me. Little by little I began to know to the marrow of my bones that my guardian angel had always been with me. Like when that new cadet at the Academy hadn't wanted to keep hitting and hurting my friend Juan, my angel had been with me and had let me know that the new cadet wasn't being a coward like Juan and my dad had said. No, he simply hadn't wanted to hurt Juan anymore. Why? Because he had a balanced brain. Half male and half female, just like Jesus, and hence he'd been able to listen to his guiding angel spirit. And when we listened to our genius guardian angel, then we automatically didn't want to hurt one another. No, we wished to be kind and gentle and loving.

I could now see my friend Juan so differently, and I could also see Wellabussy and his friends differently, too. They had all been lost and disconnected from their angel, and so they had seen no other way to behave. Because it really did look like a dog-eat-dog world when we weren't angel connected and able to hear the voice of the kingdom within us. My God, what would have happened if Juan had listened to his angel? How would Wellabussy and his friends have behaved if they'd listened to theirs? And how would that blue chip football player have behaved in our theology class if he'd been able to hear his genius? The possibilities were endless! A whole new world! Dr. Nacozi was the best! There really was hope for us to make a paradise on Earth, and it began with thinking fearlessly. With having a balanced brain and then listening to our genius. My dad had said that hearing wasn't listening, and looking wasn't seeing. Oh, *mi papá* was a genius! And he was *un puro mexicano de* Los Altos de Jalisco.

I SHOUTED!

I LAUGHED!

Then I heard a TREMENDOUS SCREECH, and I glanced up and there above me was a huge red-tailed hawk circling in the sky. Instantly I knew who this red eagle was. He was my brother Joseph. And he was the same wide-shoulder hawk I'd seen in the chapel sitting on the cross alongside Jesus the first day I'd come to this university.

The great bird screeched again and again. I'd entered heaven. I really had. And I could now clearly see that heaven was right here. All around us. A reflection of what we perceived of ourselves "here inside" placed "over there" on the outer world as Dr. Nacozi had so well said.

"Thank you," I said to my guardian angel and to my brother Joseph and to my Yaqui grandmama. "Thank you, all of you."

"Thank you," I heard a collective voice say back to me.

The humming began behind my left ear. I was not alone. None of us were. We'd all been sent here to Earth with a whole *familia* of spirits. We'd come as well equipped with knowledge as any frog, duck, or goat. The red eagle continued screeching. I grinned. Sure, of course, mix two parts hydrogen and one part oxygen and you've got water. Mix two parts genius and one part living and you've got the Kingdom of God here within us—a place so beautiful, once we get beyond our fears.

The tears continued running down my face, but I wasn't sad. No, I was happy! Big, BIG HAPPY! Dr. Nacozi had opened up a whole NEW BRAVE WORLD FOR ME!

And the Red Eagle Hawk, my brother, continued SCREECH-ING! I was blessed. And had always been blessed, because this was also the very same magnificent bird who'd come screeching out of the heavens and had stopped me from castrating myself.

"Thank You, *Papito Dios,*" I said, "thank You, thank You, THANK YOU!"

# CHAPTER SEVENTEEN

A whole new life began for me. I was brilliant. I wasn't stupid. I was really okay. I was an oak. Not a pine. And I had a guardian angel and my brother Joseph in the form of a red eagle guiding me. I began getting up every morning before daybreak to go to confession and to Bishop Buddy's private mass, then I had breakfast with the bishop in his private dining room with about five other students. I figured that now that I was brilliant and listening to my angel, my next step was to become a saint. The bishop's private mass and breakfast were open to the whole student body, but it took place so early that hardly anyone ever went. Within a week I began to feel dizzy. I didn't know what was going on with me. After all, I was being almost perfect.

Then late one afternoon I spotted a large stand of trees just across the valley from our campus. I hitched a ride there with a fellow student who was going downtown. The place was called the Presidio. It was much larger than I'd thought, with a big grassy area on a slope. There were families picnicking all over. I took off my shirt and began working out on the grass, trying to get over my dizziness. After I had a good sweat going, I felt like playing, so I began to roll down the hillside on the grass the way I'd done in the hills behind our home when I was a little kid. People looked at me like I was crazy *loco,* but I didn't care. I wasn't feeling dizzy anymore. I was having fun.

An elderly lady with wild red hair came up the slope to me. She'd been down at the bottom of the hill with a younger woman and some kids. She lay down on the grass next to me and started rolling, too. The younger woman with her yelled for her to stop, that she could hurt herself and that she was getting her grandkids all excited.

The old lady just ignored the younger one—her daughter, I guess—and took my hand. She was out of breath and asked me to help her back up the slope so we could roll down again together.

"Mom!" shouted the younger woman. "There could be dog poop! Please, don't do it again!"

"Maybe you better not do it," I suggested.

"You just help me back up the slope," she said, petting my hand. "I'm old enough to figure out what I want to do. Don't pay attention to her."

The old lady and I went back up the hill hand in hand, then lay on the grass, and went rolling back down the slope like two little kids, laughing all the way. Her grandkids wanted to join us, but their mother, an extremely attractive woman in her thirties, kept telling them about dog crap and that maybe they'd get hurt. Then she added that their grandmother was misbehaving and making a fool of herself.

I flashed on the guy in my theology class who had been so upset with me. I could see this younger woman was equally upset with her mother. Obviously, something was bothering her far more than her mother rolling down the grass with me, just like there had been something else bothering that guy in my theology class far more than what I'd said about Jesus.

"Don't mind her," the old lady said to me. "She's married to a big hot-shot judge in town, so she thinks she has to be prim and proper all the time. Myself, I'm a waitress in Phoenix at a truck diner, so I'm free of all that crap!"

Three more times the old lady and I went back up the hill hand in hand and then rolled down the grassy slope, laughing and having a great time. By now her daughter was going crazy.

"We better stop," she said, "or I'll never hear the end of it. Boy, this was fun. Come on over and I'll introduce you to my grandkids. They haven't been totally brainwashed yet."

Her daughter was one of the most beautiful women I'd ever seen, but she was so upset with her mother that it made her look ugly.

"All I can say is, it's a good thing no one we know is here," she said to her mother, completely ignoring me.

"Yes, wouldn't that be terrible, seeing your old mother having fun," she said. Turning to me she said, "Thank you." And she took me in her arms and gave me a great big kiss. "Also, she's never liked it that I love to get my hands on nice strong young men," she whispered in my ear, gripping my ass with her right hand.

That night I didn't dream of being brilliant and almost perfect and wanting to be a saint. I dreamed of that old woman. We were naked and her breasts were as saggy as an old milk cow, and yet her smile was so great and her eyes were so full of fun and mischief that I couldn't keep my hands off her as we went rolling through white clouds up in the heavens and all the while she was kissing me as she gripped my ass, pulling me to herself in a tight embrace, teaching me a dozen different wonderful great feeling positions!

I awoke screaming and found I'd wet my bed. But it wasn't pee. It smelled strange and was all sticky. I leaped out of bed! I'd done it in my sleep! I had to go to confession before God condemned me to hell. No wonder Adam had been so willing to blame Eve for everything! IT WAS WOMEN WHO DROVE US MEN CRAZY*LOCO* INSANE!

When I got to the chapel to do my confession, I found that the doors were still locked, and to my surprise there were three other students waiting to go in, too. One of them was Berry, the guy in our study group who was thinking of becoming a priest and liked to act like a bishop when he spoke. Berry and one guy were giggling and looked all hung over. The third one, whom I didn't know, was trembling and looked terror-stricken.

"Did you just get back from T. J., too?" Berry asked me.

"No," I said.

"So you got some on this side of the border, eh?"

"Well, not really," I said. "It's just that . . ."

"Oh, you were using the old fist, were you? Which one, right or left?" he said, laughing all the more.

We heard footsteps inside the chapel, and the mammoth doors opened. Inside we found that we weren't the first guys to have come for confession. Half a dozen of the seminarians, the guys who were already studying to become priests, were ahead of us.

I followed Berry and the other two guys inside. Immediately the one who looked the worst off rushed to the side altar to light a candle and started praying as fast as he could. I knelt down and began to pray, too, but I couldn't get into it. I mean, I'd never seen so many guys so full of fear. It pissed me off. When the hell were we ever going to get past all this fear crap that we carried around inside us? Were we going to continue to live in Adam's fear forever, blaming women for everything?

*Mi papá* always said the only reason the Jews had lost the Garden of Eden was that they hadn't had any tequila. "Because if Adam had had a couple of good shots of Herradura before God came down and asked him about what he'd done," said my dad, "like any good *mexicano*, he would never have blamed his wife. Hell no, he would have pounded his chest and said, "Yeah, I did it, God, *¿y qué?* And so what?

"Then God would've seen that Adam was a stand-up guy," my dad always added, "and He would've been proud of him and shook hands with him, saying, 'What are you drinking, Adam?' Adam would've said, *'Tequila* from *Los Altos de Jalisco'* and God would've said, 'Hey, I've never had *tequila.* Let me try some.' And so God would have had a couple of good shots with Adam, and we'd all still be in the Garden, laughing and drinking *tequila* with God."

I got up, saw all this fear-based praying around me and went out of the chapel. I wasn't going to confess. Hell, I hadn't done anything wrong. All I'd done was have a great juicy dream of rolling through big fluffy white clouds with an old lady, laughing and having so much fun that my body had automatically, on its own, released itself in my sleep. If God wanted to send me to hell for this, then I welcomed Him to come and do it. I wasn't going to live in fear any longer. I was done with that. There had to be another way. I could feel it deep inside of me. Life had never been meant to be lived with all this fear-based crap. Somewhere, somehow, I just knew there was a way of living where all hearts opened and life flowed easy and full of *amor.*

The birds in the sky flew freely. The deer and the lion each did what they did. So why was it that people just couldn't do what came naturally, too? That old lady and I had just been having so much fun hugging and kissing. And if she liked to grab young strong men by their asses, as she'd said, what was wrong with that? It was her daughter who was so worried and uptight who needed to go to confession. Not me. Not her mother. But that drop-dead gorgeous daughter who was destroying her kids' lives before they even began to live.

I walked out. I didn't go to confession, and then that same afternoon I went back to the park across the valley from our campus. Maybe it was time for me to really let an older woman teach me all those positions that Mrs. Wucker had told Jimmy and Karen and me about. But that happy, sexy old waitress from Phoenix was no where to be found. I began to get dizzy. I had to lay down on the grass. Oh, I had so much stuff dammed up inside of me that I was going crazy*loco*! That night I dreamed of that old woman once again, and this time I deliberately played with myself again and again, shooting great wads of semen.

Now I knew what those poor seminarians were going through. I mean, some of them had looked like pretty big, strong, healthy guys. We were all going crazy*loco* insane! And it was sex, sex, SEX THAT WAS DRIVING US CRAZY*LOCO* INSANE! No wonder Mary had put my hand in between her hot young juicy thighs when we'd gone to the movies in the seventh grade. No wonder those two sisters had taken on all those guys at the beach in high school. Mrs. Wucker was right. We had to get educated about sex just like we did about riding a bike and driving a car. And not by our parents, who'd we'd be all embarrassed to listen to, but by our school, our church, our . . . somebody who was married and happy and knew what the hell—I mean, what the bed—they were talking about. Not by priests who didn't know crap about sex. Not by old nuns who were probably even more frustrated than the priests. But by happy, healthy, married couples with both parts of their brains working!

I could clearly see I didn't want to be a saint and have a perfect life. I wanted to have a real life. A life full of sex and fun and laughter like the old lady and I had when we'd gone rolling down the grassy hillside.

# CHAPTER EIGHTEEN

The next morning I was in my business class when our professor, a very successful local businessman, said, "Reach in your pockets and bring out a one dollar bill. Read what it says on each side."

We followed instructions. On top of one side were the words "Federal Reserve Note." In the center of the other side, over the word "one" it read "In God We Trust."

"Is money, then, a religion?" he asked.

Some of my fellow students laughed, but our professor didn't.

"If money isn't a religion, then why does our dollar bill ask us to have trust in God? Or could it be," continued our professor, "that trust in God is really at the root of every human endeavor? Not just in religion, but in politics and science and business, too."

My mind exploded! This was fantastic! This made perfect sense. Then everything was, indeed, a religion and based on our trust of God. That was why Mr. Lawrence, the football coach at the Academy, had thrown the chemistry book at me and screamed, "Ask God!"

God and trust were everything! We trusted the gas station when we pulled up to the pump and got our gas. We trusted that the water was clean and good when we got a glass of water from the sink. We were surrounded by trust! We couldn't live without trust. And trust in God was our biggest, most conclusive trust of all. This was why that big football player had gotten so mad. He'd thought that my questioning threatened his very foundation of God and trust. He hadn't understood that only in questioning our beliefs can we strengthen our trust. Because we're not stagnant. We're growing, changing, advancing.

Our professor-businessman continued. "Tell me," he said, "what is the Federal Reserve? Is it a reserve of the federal government or . . . could it be something else all together?"

A student raised his hand.

"What has any of this to do with business? I took this course so I could learn how to make money, not how to philosophize about what money is or isn't."

I was shocked that this student wasn't interested in what was being said, but I could also see that quite a few others were agreeing with him. They didn't want to know the "why" or "what." They simply wanted to know the "how." I raised my hand. Our professor called on me.

"Sir," I said, my heart pounding with fear with what I was about to say, but still I had to say it. "Can we really ever know the how, if we don't first examine the 'why' and 'what'?"

He smiled. "Go on."

"My dad," I said, "a very successful businessman, always says that a lot of rich people are really poor." I could hardly speak I was so nervous. I had never said in public what my dad told me in private. "They don't have any money, says my dad. Money has them. So this is why they don't know when to retire. My dad retired at the age of forty. He didn't wait until he was too old to enjoy his money." I took a big breath. "And he always says that any man who thinks that making money in itself is the goal and he thinks that money is what he really wants, then this man is a fool, because money is just paper and nothing else."

I stopped. I could see I'd spoken way too long. Everyone in the classroom was staring at me.

"What does your father do?" asked our professor.

"He owns liquor stores and . . . and ranches."

A couple of students laughed.

"Which is the most lucrative for him?"

"The liquor stores," I said. "He says that a liquor store with a gas station on the corner of a busy boulevard with easy parking and a few groceries and free hot coffee is the future, because he says every day people have less and less time."

Our professor nodded. "I can see his point. This makes sense. Where was your dad educated?"

I froze. I knew I should never have opened my mouth. What could I say, that he'd done his college in prison? I tried to think of something else to say as fast as I could, then it hit me. "He was educated in Arizona," I said, "and then in California."

"Oh, the University of Arizona in Phoenix or U of A in Tucson?"

I shook my head. Tears began to come to my eyes. "No," I said, taking the bull by the horns, as Dr. Nacozi kept teaching us to do, "in Florence, Arizona."

"Florence?"

"Yes, at the Arizona State Penitentiary."

A few students laughed. Instantly the tears stopped and my heart started pounding. I wasn't going to cry or panic or fall apart. I was my father's son, and I was going to hold strong inside myself.

"Then he studied in Tulare, California," I added. "That's where he learned to make first-class whiskey. In jail," I added.

I heard snickers and the word convict, but I didn't turn to see who had said it. After all, this had been all my fault. What had ever gotten into me to talk about my family? Didn't I know my place and my *familia*'s place in American society by now? We were nothing but a bunch of ignorant uneducated Mexicans. What in the world had gotten into me?

"Quiet down," the professor said to the class. "How many of you realize that whole settlements of our original thirteen colonies came from the prison system of England? How many of you know that almost all of Australia was settled by people from the penal system? We have no idea why this young man's father went to prison."

"His . . . his mother and two sisters were starving to death," I said, "and my dad stole six dollars worth of copper ore from Copper Queen Mining Company in Douglas, Arizona, so he could feed them. My dad was thirteen years old, and he was put in the penitentiary," I added, with tears running down my face.

"There, you have it," said our professor. "To judge is to close your mind and to put blinders over your eyes. What else has your father told you about business and money?"

I couldn't speak.

"Please, we're listening. Do go on," said my professor. "Your father sounds brilliant. Free coffee, I love it. And you, young men, if you really want to learn about making money, and not just business theory, then listen carefully. Real-life experiences can be very advantageous. Please, do go on," he said, turning back to me.

I took a big breath. I could hear his sincerity. "Well, my dad says that money is like water," I said, "and when you got no water that's all you can think of, water, water, water. But then you get some water, and other things become more important than water. So money, like water, must be respected, but also it must be understood that it's not salvation, and it's not happiness. Money is just a tool like a hammer or an axe. It's not to be worshipped or loved, or you'll always come up feeling empty.

"And he says that he doesn't care if it's gold or silver or paper money. It's still nothing but a tool that can put you in the driver's seat of your business, but not in the driver's seat of your life. And he says that most people don't get this. They think that once they have lots of money, their problems in life are all going to be over and they are going to be happy. He always says that this is bullshit of the worst kind. Because happiness has very little to do with money.

"In fact, he says money is the start of most people's serious problems. He says if you give money to a fool, that fool will lose it before the first full moon. You give money to a greedy, mean person, and they will spread meanness and greed. He says lack of money is what really helps keep most people alert and honest and respectful. The lion isn't just given the deer on a silver platter, and the deer isn't just given free grass, but with the price tag that she has to keep watch over herself or she will be killed and eaten by the lions. And the lion that gets fat, my dad says, will always starve. So lions must also be alert and attentive and stay 'on the come.' That's a term in dice," I added. "My dad is also a professional gambler, and he wins on an average of five times out of six when he goes to Las Vegas. Many times, I've seen him win $10,000 in a single night."

No one was laughing anymore. In fact, several classmates now wanted to know if my dad was still alive and if they could meet him. Others wanted to know if he was a millionaire. I got real embarrassed, but had to admit that he and my mother were multimillionaires. I suddenly realized that I'd done the right thing. Sure, I'd taken a big chance, but it had worked out good in the end, because I'd . . . I'd stayed centered, focused, in balance, and I hadn't let fear get to me.

Our professor-businessman asked me to stay after class so he could speak to me privately. I hoped to God I wasn't in trouble.

"You're very proud of your dad, aren't you," he said once we were alone.

His question threw me. I hadn't expected this. "Yes, I guess I am," I said.

"Good," he said. "It took a lot of nerve for you to say where your dad acquired his education. I'm sorry I put you on the spot. Please accept my apology. I had no idea where my question would take us."

"Thank you, sir," I said.

My God, it was really coming true, the higher and higher I climbed in education, the more I was finding people I could talk to. I sure was happy I'd gone to summer school at the Academy and that I'd gotten to ask Mr. Moffet all the questions I'd wanted to ask without being laughed at or made to feel stupid. I could now see that feeling free to ask questions was what freed the mind and allowed us to learn the real juicy stuff in life.

That afternoon back at our dormitories I looked up the Federal Reserve System in my Webster New World, but I couldn't understand what I read, so I went down the hall and asked Berry to explain it to me. He said sure and read the definition to me, but I still couldn't get it. Yeah, I understood that the Federal Reserve was a banking system of twelve banks, with each acting as the central bank for its district, and that there were over 10,000 affiliated banks, and that they were the ones who managed our currency, which fluctuated with the demands of business. This part I understood. This part made sense. But . . . who owned these original twelve banks? It didn't say that the federal government owned them. I began to wonder, to suspect that this was a little bit like putting the fox in charge of the hen house. It began to look to me like the deck had been cut in the favor of business in the United States from day one, and it had been cut from the top to the bottom. And it had been done very sneakily, because by naming it "federal," it made it sound like it was part of our government, but it wasn't, so far as I could tell. Then to put "In God We

Trust" on one side of our dollar bill, this was really slick. Money instantly locked in both sides of our mentality, God and country. I smelled a big fat rat.

I guess my dad had been right once again. Every group had their own racket and two sets of rules: one for the public to see and believe and another so that the insiders could do whatever they damn well pleased without the general public knowing anything about it.

Because in my estimation, I could now see it was the Federal Reserve System that was the real power behind our whole government. What a con job. And who had done this? It hit me like a lightning bolt! That big hot-shot judge, the one who'd married that very attractive woman in her thirties who hadn't wanted her mother rolling down that grassy slope with me. It was his type of mentality that had pulled off this kind of con job, and he'd done it without blinking an eye. Why? Because CONTROL WAS EVERYTHING for him! That was why he'd terrorized his wife into becoming such a proper uptight mother that she was willing to destroy her own kid's basic fun.

I remembered how angry Jesus had been with the money lenders at the entrance to the temple. To those He had not said that He forgave them for they didn't know what they did. I took a deep breath and made the sign of the cross over myself. "God help us," I said, and the very next day when our professor-businessman asked us who had looked up the Federal Reserve System, only two of us raised our hands. The other guy was tall, wore glasses, and people said his uncle was the banana king of the U. S., meaning that his uncle was also a multimillionaire. Our professor asked what the two of us thought about what we'd found out. I said that I smelled a big fat rat, that we should change "In God We Trust" to "God Help Us." Only our professor laughed. The banana king's nephew said he didn't agree with me. He thought it was important that the Federal Reserve System was kept above partisanship, so there could be monetary stability even during a change of political parties in government.

"And what do you think of that?" our professor asked me.

I took a deep breath. "I say, yeah, that sounds real good, but still my dad always says, 'Sure, I trust you, just cut the cards,' and here there's no one to cut the cards."

When a couple of the other students wanted to know what we were talking about, our professor-businessman simply said, "Look it up. Have initiative. That's the key to success. In fact, if I were hiring, these two, who showed initiative to look up the Federal Reserve, are the only ones I'd hire out of this whole class."

A huge collective groan came up from the class, but the nephew of the banana king and I felt pretty good. He asked me out for lunch. I said sure. He had a beautiful open-engine hot-rod convertible. But the doors didn't open. We had to jump in. He took off flying, and we went in the back way of a golf course to the clubhouse. I'd never seen so many Cadillacs, Jaguars, Mercedes, and rich-looking people in all my life. I guess you could say that I'd arrived.

# CHAPTER NINETEEN

I was home, and my dad and mom said they wanted to talk with me.

"So we understand you're doing very good at school," he said.

I guess my cousin Victor had talked to my parents.

"Yeah," I said, "I'm doing pretty good."

"So, then, you like going to college?" asked my mother.

"Yeah, I do. I'm really learning a lot," I said.

"Good," said my dad. "Your mother and I are very proud of you and, well, we've been talking and we think it's time for you to get your own car. We can't just keep asking John to drive you back and forth on the weekends."

For months now my friend John Folting had been driving me down to San Diego on Sundays and then picking me up on Fridays to drive me back to the ranch.

But I couldn't hear what my parents were saying to me. Instantly all my old fears about my Chevy truck came crashing up inside me. My mouth went dry. I had to lick my lips several times before I could even speak. "I don't want another truck," I said.

"It doesn't have to be a truck this time," said my dad.

"John told us," said my mother, "that there's a Ford car that you told him you like."

"Yeah, I did," I said to my mother, "but it's so . . . so . . ." I didn't have the words to describe the Thunderbird that John and I had seen going up the hill at Torrey Pines. It had been so beautiful with the sea and hills behind it.

"Let's drive down to Dixon Ford and have a look," said my dad. "We don't have to buy anything if we don't want to. We'll just go look. That's all."

"Okay," I said. "But I don't want a car, *papá*. I can always take the bus. I don't need a car."

"I understand," said my dad. "But let's just go down anyway."

At the Ford agency in downtown Oceanside, two Thunderbirds were in the showroom. One was golden-bronze and the other was turquoise-blue like the one John and I had seen go shooting past us by the sea and up the steep Torrey Pines grade.

"So these are the cars?" asked my dad. I guess he had seen it in my eyes as we walked into the dealership.

I nodded. I couldn't help it. They were so beautiful. And their name alone gave me chills: THUNDERBIRD!

"Which color do you like?" asked my dad.

"Both," I said. I'd never seen this color of gold before. It had a tint of red. And turquoise was still my favorite color. It was a hard call.

"Yeah, they're real beauties," said the salesman, coming up to us. My dad and I were both dressed in Levis and cowboy boots. My dad was wearing his beat-up old ranch hat. "But they are expensive," added the salesman, arching his eyebrows as if telling us that they were out of our price range.

Hearing this, my dad reached in his right front pocket and brought out a roll of money large enough to choke a horse. The salesman's mouth dropped open, salivating like a dog. Quickly he asked us if we'd like to step into his office. We did.

"Okay, what's the best deal you can give my son and me on one of those two cars right now?" said my dad.

The salesman went right to work, and I wanted to stop my dad and not let him buy me another vehicle. But I was helpless. I was in love, just as I'd been in love with my Chevy truck.

"Okay," said my dad, glancing over the figures the salesman had written down. "Then this is the best deal you can give us?"

"Yes," he said.

"Are you sure?" said my dad. "Because now we're going to go down to Encinitas and see the Ford people there, and if they're one hundred or two hundred dollars cheaper, I won't go with them, because I like to do my business in my own hometown. But if they're four or five hundred dollars cheaper, I won't be back."

The salesman didn't look so happy anymore. He tried to explain to my dad about how good their service department was and how they'd take good care of us after the purchase.

"Don't bullshit me!" snapped my dad. "Your service is just another moneymaking racket, and you know it! So don't sell me pie in the sky. Just stick to what we're talking about right here, right now!"

The salesman got nervous and said that he had to talk to his manager. My father winked at me. The salesman came back and said that this was the best deal that they could give. My dad put his roll of money back in the right front pocket of his Levis and we left. And on the way to Encinitas, I told my dad that I really didn't want the car. It was too beautiful.

"I haven't earned it, *papá*, and I'll just be laughed at by everyone for having such a fancy car."

"Is that why you painted your truck white? Because people were laughing at you for having such a nice turquoise-colored truck?"

I froze. I didn't know what to say. We'd never spoken of this before. But finally I nodded. "Yes, *papá*," I said.

"And then after you painted it white, they still laughed, didn't they? So this was why you turned it over to the workers to use on the ranch?"

"Yes," I said once again, tears coming to my eyes.

"And after all that, you still care what people think? Didn't you learn anything from those two experiences? Eh, how many times is it going to have to take, *mijito*?"

I took a big deep breath. I felt like such a fool. *"Papá,"* I said, "but can we ever really get beyond that? Don't we always worry about what people might say or think?"

"To the degree that a man knows who he is and who he isn't, to that degree he doesn't care what people think or say. And also to this same degree you will be respected. No one respects anyone who doesn't know who they are and who they aren't. You like to talk about Jesus. Well, what do you think His power was? He, above all others, knew Who He was and Who He wasn't, and then He had the *tanates* not to care what people thought, even as they crucified Him. That's *un hombre!"* my dad added with power.

"But *papá,* you told me not to bring Jesus into normal conversations, that you only believed in Him on Sundays."

"Is this a normal conversation?" he said. "Or is this a Sunday kind of conversation, where we are wrestling for your very soul?!!"

I was shocked. My dad was never going to fail to astonish me. He'd just twisted everything around that he'd told me last time . . . and brilliantly!

"It took Christ-like guts for your mother and me to build the biggest and most beautiful home in all of Oceanside. She was worried what our friends in the *barrio* would think. Would they think we were just being show-offs, now that we'd come into money? We struggled for months, but finally we did it, and your mother was right, some people now hate us and still talk badly about us; but others respect us and wish us well. Opinions, *mijito,* are like assholes. Everyone has one and they all stink. You are a rich kid, so your job isn't to hide from that. Your job is to figure out what to do with this great opportunity that fate has given you, and go into life with the power and dignity and honor of a great *matador."*

"But, *papá,*" I said, feeling all this fear come screaming up inside of me, "what if I, well, just don't have it in me? What if I don't find out who I am in the next few years? What if I don't . . ."

"If my aunt had balls she'd be my uncle. There are no 'ifs' in life. It is just another one of those words invented to keep us full of doubt and confusion."

"Okay, I can see that, but . . ."

"Don't 'but' me!" he said. "Just know this, do you love this car?" he asked.

"Yes, I do," I said.

"Then go with your love. You hear me? Always go with your love and that's how you will find honor and dignity and who you are. And let me help you today, since I can. Who knows, maybe tomorrow your mother and I will need your help."

"But *papá* . . ."

"*Mijo,* you've got to stop this 'but' business. I've told you a million times, there are no buts, only assholes. If you were the kind of kid who was always wanting me to buy you things, I wouldn't have even brought you down here in the first place. But you don't do that.

You're like your mother. All the money in the world could never spoil your mother, because she lives—not in her head with wanting and wanting—but here in her heart, where all the riches and jewels of the world don't matter. *Capiche?"*

I didn't know what else to say. I knew that he was right about my mother. She loved her *familia.* She loved her flowers. She loved her birds. She loved to hum and sing and whistle and attend to her flowers, birds, and *familia.* So we went to Encinitas, and they were five hundred dollars cheaper than Oceanside. My dad counted out the one hundred dollar bills to the salesman, and I drove home in a brand-new Thunderbird, gold in color. I was still too self-conscious to have bought the turquoise car. Driving back toward Oceanside along the beach, people kept looking at me. I had to stare straight ahead so I wouldn't panic.

I hid the car in our barn and sat in it all afternoon, looking at it, stroking it, trying to get up the nerve to drive it again. The next day the salesman from the Oceanside Ford agency called. He said they could come down six hundred dollars. My dad was furious and told me to bawl the man out. And when I wouldn't, he grabbed the phone from me and gave the man hell.

"You're one day late and a dollar short, and friend, this is a very stupid, dangerous way to handle business! Goodbye!"

On Sunday, John Folting came over, and we decided to cruise the beach in my T-bird before I drove back down to school. We went by Herb's drive-in, but we didn't stop. Most of our high school friends were gone, so John and I didn't know a lot of these kids anymore. We headed for the beach. Down by the pier we ran into a few of our friends. They smiled and waved as we cruised by. I took a great big breath. It had gone a lot easier than I'd expected.

Dropping John off, I headed back to San Diego. I parked my golden bird several blocks from our apartments. I didn't want to draw attention to myself, but it didn't work. My roommates had seen me drive by. They told me I should park my car in front so it wouldn't get stolen. I hadn't thought of that, so I did what they suggested. I quickly came to realize my T-bird was no big deal. There were quite a few other rich kids going to this Catholic university.

# CHAPTER TWENTY

**G**ripping my penis, I leaped out of bed and rushed across the room to the bathroom before I peed all over myself. The first semester was over, and exams were going to start next week. I was so scared I was ready to pee in bed. I was having such terrible nightmares.

"Dear Lord God," I said to myself as I peed in the toilet, "help me. I can't do this alone. I feel like I'm back in the third grade and I'm going to flunk again. I need Your help. Please, dear God, don't abandon me now!"

I didn't know what to do. I didn't want to become a bed wetter all over again, the way I'd been all through grammar school. In those days I'd been so terrified of tests and people finding out I didn't know how to read that I'd been going crazy*loco!*

Then it hit me. I'd hire my cousin Victor to take my tests for me. He was in his third year. He already had two solid years of college testing under his belt, and he liked to brag about how he looked forward to test time. Yeah, sure, I'd hire him to do my exams.

I drove over to visit Victor that very day, at his apartment in Ocean Beach. His two roommates were out for the day. I told him about my plan. He laughed.

"You've got to be kidding," he said. "I can't take your tests for you."

He offered me a glass of wine. I didn't drink, but I accepted the offer.

"Why can't you take your own tests?" he asked.

I looked at him and tears came to my eyes. "I'll tell you," I said, "but you've got to promise never to tell a soul."

"I promise," he said.

"I'm serious," I said. "Do you really, really promise?"

"Yes," he said. "I promise."

"I can't read," I said.

"What do you mean you can't read. I've seen you read before."

"I can read," I said, "but only to a third, or maybe a fourth-grade level. I flunked the third grade twice. I only got into fourth grade because my *papá* and *mamá* put me in San Luis Rey Mission School and made a deal with the nuns and priests."

"So that's why you didn't want to go to college," he said. "And that's why you couldn't fill out the forms for admission."

I nodded.

"You know, my older brother Chemo has trouble reading, and my oldest brother—the one in Mexico—he can't read at all. I wonder if it's genetic?"

He asked me to stay for dinner, and we had several glasses of red wine. I'd never drunk before, and it went right to my head. Then after dinner Victor asked me to show him how I'd grabbed his arm and spun him around that first day in the administration building. I showed him. He became intrigued and asked me to show him some of my other wrestling moves.

"I hear you pinned one of our best football players?" he said, laughing.

"Yeah, I did," I said, and it was true. After the outburst in our theology class, that big football player had tried to manhandle me when we got back to our dormitories. I guess he was still pissed at me for having questioned Jesus' words. It had shocked him when I'd ducked, swept his legs out from under him, and pinned his ass in less than two seconds.

"And he was way bigger than you, right?"

"Yes, but wrestling isn't based on size or strength," I said. "It's based on balance and speed. He actually pinned himself, because he didn't know that I knew anything."

"Show me what you did to that football player, and maybe I'll reconsider helping you with your exams."

"Okay," I said, and I took up my stance.

"But don't hurt me," he said with a giggle, "like you did last time."

I thought his giggle sounded funny, but I ignored it and instantly took him down. Then we pushed back the dinner table and the couch. I now explained to him the way our two Marine Corp wrestling instructors had explained to us at the Army Navy Academy that the basic stance in wrestling gave us a circle within which to work.

"And our stance is our center of balance within that circle," I said, moving left and right, then whirling and sweeping an imaginary opponent's leg. He was impressed.

"I've never seen you move like that," he said. "It almost looks like a dance. Can you wrestle with me? In the Army we'd work out in pairs in hand-to-hand combat practice."

"Sure," I said. "Our Marine instructors told us that it's basically the same in combat training."

Once more I took my stance, and he came at me. Instantly I took him down again. I released him, and he came at me again and again. Each time I took him down and pinned him, but I could see he wasn't really trying to defend himself. I began getting annoyed. He was bigger than me and had been in the Army. He played a lot of tennis, so I knew he was strong and fast, but he just wasn't trying.

Then out of the blue, he hugged me, but it wasn't a wrestling move. It felt all different. My whole world exploded, and I knocked him away from me!

"IT WAS YOU!" I screamed, seeing all these images go flashing past my mind's eye. "IT WAS YOU, wasn't it?!?"

"What are you talking about?" he asked.

"When my brother Joseph was sick and in the hospital, you got in bed with me when I was asleep and you kept trying to touch me!"

"Are you crazy? I don't know what you're talking about!" His eyes started jumping about all over the place.

"BULLSHIT!" I yelled. "YOU TRIED TO MOLEST ME! I remember now! All these years I'd thought that maybe it was all a dream, but it wasn't! You son-of-a-bitch. I was eight years old, crazy with grief for my brother Joseph and you—how could you?!!"

"I was overseas," he said, "in the Army. You have me mixed up with someone else."

"You weren't in the Army yet! Now I remember EVERY-THING! You kept spitting on your dick and trying to push it at me.

I yelled and yelled, and you'd get back into my brother's bed and say, 'Are you okay? Are you having a bad dream?' pretending like it hadn't been you! But it was you, YOU BASTARD! Don't say another word! I'm leaving, and don't you ever come near me again, or I'll break your FUCKING NECK!"

I slammed the door on the way out, got in my Thunderbird, and took off. I began to cry. Over and over, he'd tried to molest me when I was a little kid. He'd done it under the pretense that he'd stay overnight to help take care of me while my parents went down to La Jolla to see my brother Joseph in the hospital.

I drove down to the beach and parked by the bathrooms. I suddenly felt dirty. I opened up the trunk of my T-bird and got the sweats I kept in the back. I stripped down to my shorts, changed my clothes, then went into the men's room and threw the clothes I'd been wearing in the trash. I never wanted to touch those clothes again. I washed my hands again and again. I hated my cousin. How had it ever entered his mind to try to take advantage of a little kid?

I breathed deeply, held my breath, then blew out. I'd completely forgotten all about those memories until he'd touched me in that funny way. I went out of the men's room and walked across the sand to the water's edge. The sun was going down. I took another big deep breath and held it, held it for well over two minutes before I blew it out. What did all this mean? Was my cousin Victor a homo, or was he a child molester? Or was he both? I had no idea.

I took off my shoes, rolled up my sweatpants, and walked out into the shallow water. And why had he come on to me? Did this mean I was a queer, too? Is this why I'd been repulsed seeing all those guys' gangbanging those two sisters on the beach that night? Was I really a homo, too, but I was refusing to admit it, and this was why I was still a virgin and yet almost all of my guy friends had already had several girls or they'd gone down to T.J. to lose their virginity to a prostitute?

Could it be that I was full of shit, thinking that I was so holy and good and trying to understand everything, and the truth was that I'd been hiding from this big truth all these years?

Tears came to my eyes. And why did I cry so easily? My own sister Linda often said I acted more like a girl than she did. What was wrong with me? The other day, some of the guys in my logic study group had said homosexuality was an accepted and common practice in ancient Greece and that even Alexander the Great had been a queer. I was all mixed up. I had no idea what to think.

I walked along the seashore in the shallow water until it was dark. In the darkness, I stripped and went for a swim. The water was freezing, and I was shaking like crazy by the time I got back to my car. It was a good thing I always kept a towel along with my sweats in the trunk.

The next day my cousin came up to me in one of the hallways at school and asked me if I'd called and told my parents.

I looked at him. This hadn't even entered my mind. I felt too ashamed to ever say anything to anyone, and especially not to my parents.

"No, not yet," I said.

I could see he was really scared. Suddenly, I got a flash and remembered back to my old days of blackmailing people when I was in the third grade.

"Look," I said to my cousin, "I won't tell, if you help me with my tests."

"But how can I help you?" he asked.

"I'm not sure," I said. "Maybe you can do something like you did for my registration, like walk me through my textbooks and figure out for me what I'll be tested on."

He agreed, and in the next few days he taught me how to prepare for an exam. I'd never known any of this. Then he managed to get hold of some old tests the school had gotten from Loyola in Los Angeles and Santa Clara in San Jose. He went over these tests with me and made me memorize the spelling of the key words. It was beautiful. He suggested I drop the courses I felt weakest in, like dumbbell English and business, and this way we could concentrate on the courses in which I felt strongest.

He convinced me, so I did what he suggested even though it was too late to get my money back. When exam time came, I felt more prepared than I'd ever felt in all of my life, but still I was so scared I could hardly think straight. I began to sweat. All those memories of my first few years of school were still haunting me like great dark demons.

# CHAPTER TWENTY-ONE

The night before our exams, I was cramming with my study group when Berry, our leader, threw down his books and said we should take a break and go over to "The Food's." This was the nickname Berry had given the women's college on our university campus. Everyone agreed and said okay, they'd go, but I immediately got apprehensive.

What if I was a homo? Or what if I wasn't and the sight of girls got me so excited that all my preparation for my tests would go flying out the window? I'd been avoiding all contact with girls for months and working out two and three times a day so I wouldn't get dizzy. I was up to 160 pounds, and I could now bench-press 265 pounds with ease and standing-press 145 with either arm. I was working out day and night, so I could keep my mind on our tests and not be thinking of being a homo or liking girls.

We all piled into Berry's silver Dodge convertible and went over to the Catholic women's college up the street, around the corner, and down the block. The women's campus had beautiful, well-tended gardens everywhere, and the buildings were much closer to completion than ours. Then I saw the girls, a group of them on the other side of the large indoor courtyard. They were all laughing and looking as happy and beautiful as well-groomed race horses in the main barn.

I froze. My pants were jumping out in front of me. I quickly turned my body away so that nobody could see my erection, then I took off running. I guess I should have brought a sweater or jacket or something that I could keep in front of me to hide my reaction when I came into contact with females. Just the sight of girls was intoxicating! Did this mean I wasn't a homo? Or did girls excite homosexuals, too?

I ran all the way back to my room, got a sweater, and drove back to the girls' campus in my own car. Now I had a sweater to keep in my hands in front of me. After all, I couldn't just avoid girls all of my life. One of the girls looked a lot like Clare. My whole heart filled with joy! Suddenly it dawned on me that I could see Clare over the holidays when she came home from up in the Bay area of San Francisco. I felt so happy, I could SCREAM!

We got our exam results. I had an A, two B's, and a C. I was in ecstasy! I didn't need to hide anymore. At Christmastime I could go over to see Clare and Nick. Driving home that weekend in my golden T-bird, I decided to cruise by the Army Navy Academy. I couldn't believe how little and insignificant the school now looked to me. I thought of stopping to visit Captain Moffet, but decided against it. I still felt a little too uneasy about too many other things that had happened to me there.

At home on the ranch, the first thing I did was jump on a horse bareback and go riding down to the beach. I hadn't been on a horse in months and it felt wonderful! I galloped my horse in the surf from Buccaneer Beach to Carlsbad, then back up to the Oceanside pier. It was heaven to be on a horse once again. From just south of the pier, I looked up at the two two-story houses on the bluff where Clare had been born and raised. I'd never forgotten that when I asked her to the dance at school, she'd gotten a delicious little look in her eyes and she'd said sure, she'd love to go and we could be late "together." Then when I'd stepped on her feet while we were dancing, she'd said not to worry about it, that we'd do better next time. Oh, those words "together" and "better next time" gave me such warmth deep inside of me! She was definitely a girl—no, a woman—a man could marry; she would help him build a home with a strong foundation of trust and love and . . . and tears came to my eyes, but I wasn't sad. No, I was happy! BIG HAPPY! I thought of charging up the bluff on my horse and sweeping Clare off her feet like a knight in shining armor, but . . . but I decided I wasn't ready yet. I kissed my fingertips and threw a kiss to her home, then started for the ranch, racing in the surf.

Then it was time to help make the *tamales* for the holidays. I invited Nick and Clare to come over to help. They did. And their little sister Sally came along. I was a nervous wreck being around Clare and ended up picking a fight with her. She got mad, and I apologized. I just didn't know how to behave around girls.

The next day Nick and I went out shooting at the rifle range in San Luis Rey. We shot all afternoon. That night I went to Clare and Nick's home, and I played chess with Nick all evening. I never won a game. Every time Clare walked through the room, I got so dizzy and light-headed I'd have to grab a pillow to put on my lap to hide my erection.

After church on Christmas Day, my family and I took flowers to my brother Joseph's grave, and our dad and mom told us kids that they'd purchased the two grave sites next to Joseph's grave for themselves. I didn't want to hear this, but my mother went on, saying how she wished to be buried alongside Joseph and our father. I breathed deeply. She'd never made any mention of where my sisters and I would be buried.

This was the first Christmas dinner I was asked to carve the ham and turkey. It was now almost three years since my Uncle Archie's death, and he'd always been the carver. He'd given me his huge butcher knife and cutting board just before he died, telling me that of all of his *familia,* I was the only one who was a hunter, so he was leaving me his shotgun, butcher knife, and cutting board, because he knew that even in bad times, I'd bring home the bacon.

I carefully carved the ham and the turkey with his huge butcher knife, putting the meats on the two different platters just as I'd seen my Uncle Archie do time and again. Archie had been a giant of a man, and he'd always been the best carver of our family, much better than my dad. My dad was best at outdoor cooking in an earthen oven when we did a whole steer, enough to feed over five hundred people. After I'd carved the turkey and ham, I took the two huge platters to the dining room, placing them at the center of the long table. My sister Tencha was married now and had two children. Our family numbered well over twenty-five people.

My cousin Victor showed up just as we were sitting down to eat. Everyone was happy to see him, but it was very difficult for me even to look at him. He immediately started bragging to my parents about how well I was doing at the university and how much he'd helped me. I felt like belting him in the mouth or at least running him through the groin with the big butcher knife I had in my hand. I didn't give him a hug or shake his hand. I pretended I was too busy.

Then as soon as I got back to the university, I drove over to my cousin's place in Ocean Beach and confronted him.

"Look," I said with my heart pounding, "just because I agreed not to tell my parents anything doesn't give you the right to come up to me and act friendly!"

"Well, how am I supposed to act? We're cousins," he said.

"You should've thought of that before you tried molesting me!"

"But I didn't molest you."

"ONLY BECAUSE I SCREAMED, you son-of-a-bitch!"

He grinned. "What's really bothering you? Are you beginning to think that maybe you're also . . ."

"YOU DON'T STOP, do you?!" I screamed.

"Stop what? Are you afraid to think about the possibility that you might also be . . . "

"VICTOR, YOU ASSHOLE!" I screamed. "I'm not afraid of any possibilities in my life! What I am is disgusted with you!"

"Are you sure?"

"DAMN YOU!" I said, shoving him so hard that he went flying on his ass over his coffee table, landing on the floor.

"DON'T GET UP! I warn you! You get to your feet, and I'll beat the living shit out of you!" I was heaving with rage! "You sneaky bastard! I was a little kid, and you were big! How did you ever get into all of this? Honestly! Don't bullshit! Talk! Were you born like this?"

His eyes started jumping all over the place, and he began to sweat. "I don't know," he said, pulling himself up and sitting on the couch. "My mother, she'd go from man to man. I was just a little kid, and we never had any home for long until we got that little ranch over in Vista."

He was talking about my aunt Mary, who had a restaurant on the corner of Vista Way and Hill Street in Oceanside. My dad always said he had nothing but respect for Mary, that she was a hardworking woman and tough as nails. My mother admired her sister, too, even though she also thought she was pretty rough.

"But Victor, your brothers Joe and Andy, they go with women."

"You don't know everything," he said.

"STOP IT, Victor! You don't have to try to turn everyone into a queer to justify yourself! Just stick to you! What happened? I'm trying to understand, so I don't hate your guts!"

"Really, is that what you're trying to do?"

"Yes!"

He sighed. "I don't know," he said. "You tell me, what comes first, the chicken or the egg? All I know was that I saw all these men coming and going. I was little. Then this priest, he became my friend . . . no, I will not talk about it!" A terrible fear came onto his face.

"It was a priest, then, who showed you . . . you . . ."

"Love," he said, tears coming to his eyes.

"What?" I said. "How can you call that love?"

"Easy, because that's what it was."

A million zillion pictures began flashing past my mind's eye. The young priest who'd gotten so mad at me when I was in the fourth grade and proposed marriage to a beautiful young nun. He'd gone crazy*loco* and locked me in a broom closet, calling me evil. The mean old nun who'd gone bonkers when she heard my proposal and knocked me out of my chair and started hitting the little nun who'd been nothing but kind to me as she tried to help me learn how to read. Everyone, everywhere was trying to find love, and love seemed to always lead to sex.

That real estate man who'd shot himself had also been trying to find love with his second wife with the three kids. And so had Becky when she'd dumped me at the dance and she'd gone with Nick McLean. Wherever *amor* went, then sex seemed sure to follow, or if not . . . then there was a huge confusion of body and mind that could drive a person crazy*loco*.

I flashed on all those poor seminarians who'd been lined up before daybreak to go to confession. I flashed on Berry and the two guys waiting outside the chapel. One of the guys with Berry had looked terror-stricken and once inside, he'd rushed to a side altar, lit a candle, and started praying in a frenzy of fear.

"Talk to me," I said to my cousin, "talk, damnit! Talk! I'll listen!"
"Will you?"
"Yes! Just talk! Explain! Give me something so I can understand and not just be hating you," I said.

And so we talked, or precisely, I kept asking him questions, and little by little Victor began to open up. I soon had a picture of a lost little kid who'd been touched by some of the men who'd come to the house with his mother. Then he'd become an altar boy, and the priest had been so kind and thoughtful to him that his whole world had begun to go that way. I suddenly wondered if this was the same priest who had begun to befriend me, but I was so dumb that I hadn't been able to learn my catechism lessons well enough to become an altar boy.

We talked for hours, and little by little I began to see that I wasn't the only one who had a whole secret life. Maybe everyone had a secret life that they hid from the world. That young priest, that old nun, and even Major Terry, who thought he should've been a general.

Everybody and his uncle seemed to be hiding something. I began to hate my cousin less and less, and then, finally, I began to start to forgive him. I could clearly see that this was the greatest message of Jesus, forgiving them for they didn't know. People really didn't know. We all really didn't know.

But still when I was ready to go, I didn't let my cousin touch me, even in a handshake to say our goodbyes. I felt repulsed by him just as I'd felt repulsed by all those guys gangbanging those two sisters on the beach. I remembered Altomar, a big Mexican guy at the Academy, would come into our cottage after lunch, and he'd pick up the picture of my roommate's mother, who was an ex-dancer from Las Vegas. He'd take the picture and rub it into his crotch, moaning the whole while.

My roommate, Lukler, a really good guy from Point Loma, would pretend like it didn't bother him. But, my God, that was his mother! And why had she sent her son a picture of herself in her Las Vegas costume when he was going to an all-boys school? And why did Lukler keep that picture of his mother on his desk for everyone to see? Our whole planet was a big screwed up mess when it came to love and sexuality. And why? Because we didn't talk about it, like Mrs. Wucker had done with her children.

Suddenly I remembered Jeannie Windflow, who'd taught me how to kiss when we were kids. At the age of seventeen, she'd run off with a Mexican guy from Pozole Town who was nineteen years old, had a job, and was one of the handsomest guys I'd ever seen. He was a semiprofessional boxer and real dark. She was a track star, a straight-A student, and real blonde. They were the first people of our age group to move in together, not be married, and be openly having sex for the whole world to see. They'd been watching Elvis Presley on T.V. when her brother and I went over to visit them one day.

It had been crazy*loco.* She was wearing a short little dress and sitting on her boyfriend's lap when we'd come in, and she hadn't gotten off him. No, she'd stayed glued to him like a bear on honey, and Elvis was singing and wiggling on the T.V. screen beside them. She'd told her brother and me that for as long as she could remember, she'd just known that she was going to get herself a Mexican, marry him, have a bunch of kids, and wait for him every day for a nooner.

"What's a nooner?" I had asked.

"A drive-by shooting," she'd said, and they'd all burst out laughing.

But I didn't get it, and so she'd finally explained to me that a nooner was a Mexican-American lunching, and she added that she'd always wanted to be a stay-at-home mom while her man went out into the world and worked his ass off to keep their kitchen full of *frijoles, tortillas,* and *carne asada.* And she'd looked so happy saying all this. Not the least bit confused or scared or ashamed of what people might think. Not even her parents who'd refused to sign the papers so she could marry before she was eighteen, because they wanted her to go to college—being so smart and beautiful—and marry a college graduate.

I could now clearly see that Jeannie, with the strongest, most well-defined legs I'd ever seen, had known who she was and who she wasn't at a very early age. And so she'd been able to take the bull of life by the horns and go for it full bore ahead! Wow, she was GREAT! No confusion there! No hidden secrets! Everything out in the open and full of healthy good love and sex and life just like that grandmother from Phoenix and Mrs. Wucker. THOSE WOMEN WERE MY HEROES!

# CHAPTER TWENTY-TWO

Then it happened. Not exactly as I'd hoped, but it definitely did put me into the middle of the arena of life, *la vida.* For nearly a month I hadn't allowed myself to think of girls or masturbate. All my waking hours were completely dedicated to working out, doing my studies, and the greater glory of God. But still I knew something was amiss deep inside of me, if I would just admit it. I went to confession.

"Bless me, Father, for I have sinned," I said.

"When was your last confession?"

"About three hours ago."

"Three hours ago?"

"Yes."

"And what sins have you committed in the last three hours?"

"One, Father. One terrible sin," I said, feeling my stomach tighten.

"And what is this terrible sin?" he asked.

I could hardly speak, I was so upset. "I haven't really done it yet, Father."

"You haven't done it yet?"

"No, Father, but I'm thinking about it all the time."

"Go on. What are you thinking about all the time?"

"Father. . . I'm . . . I'm thinking about . . . about . . . and I get so excited that I . . . I . . ."

"So go on. What have you been thinking about? Is it girls?"

I almost laughed. I wished it was that simple. "No," I said. "I mean yes, but girls are only a small part of it." I took a big breath. "It's really about . . . about . . ." My heart was pounding, I was so terror-stricken.

"Tell me, what have you done!" said the priest.

"I told you, nothing yet."

"Then is it about boys? Is this what you want to confess about, that you haven't done as of yet? That you want to be with boys?"

"I wish it were," I said. "But no, it's not about boys, either," I added.

"Well, then, if it's not about girls or boys, what is it? You can't just go around confessing and getting absolution to sins you haven't committed."

"Why not?"

"Because, well, the structure of our Catholic belief system would—what is this sin you are about to commit!" he yelled. "Is it murder?"

I could feel that he was getting really scared. But I couldn't stop. This was it. I was taking the bull of life by the horns, and I didn't care if I got gored or killed. I couldn't go on like this anymore. Tears were streaming down my face.

"No," I said. "What I've decided to do is a much larger sin than murder or wanting girls or boys. Because once I voice what it is that I am about to do, Father, there will be no turning back. Ever." I took a large deep breath, held, then blew out fast. "It is the sin of . . . of arrogance, Father," I said.

"Arrogance?"

"Yes, because I've decided that I will not live in fear of God any longer," I said. "Because I believe that it is this fear of God that is holding us humans back all over the earth in everything we do, and . . . and I refuse to live like this any more."

"Do you realize what it is that you've just said?" asked the priest.

"No, not fully," I said, "because I've been living in fear of God for so long that not to live in fear of God would be so new to me, that, well, I don't really know if I do understand what I'm saying. But . . . but I don't really need to know, do I? In fact, all of these years of thinking that I needed to know is what has kept me weak and stopped me from jumping in and just living."

"Are you saying that our belief in God holds us back from living? This is an outrage! Our belief in God is the only thing that helps humanity to continue living through tragedy after tragedy even though we were born in sin."

I laughed. I couldn't believe what he'd just said. "Oh, that's great, Father, just great. Can't you see that this is exactly what I'm talking about? How do you really know if we were born in sin or not? Myself, I've decided that not knowing is wonderful! Do you see what I mean? To not know, and yet still just to jump into life is what sounds really juicy, Father. Eh, am I making sense?"

He didn't answer me and I gripped my forehead and took another great big deep breath. Lately, it seemed like I was getting so many flashes coming into me so fast all at the same time that it was frightening. It was like the dam that had been holding everything back all these years had broken inside of me.

"Father," I continued, "I'm beginning to honestly believe that God is pure love and more female than male, and all this stuff that the church tells us about the wrath of God is a bunch of . . . of, well, not true. In fact, I no longer believe that we're made in God's image. I think that we made up God in our own screwed up human image, and that's why we're all f . . . f . . . confused and lost and full of fear."

"Young man, you can't speak this way!" said the priest.

"Yes, I can. Remember, we got free will, Father. Look, from now on when I say the Act of Contrition, I don't want to say 'For I dread the loss of heaven and fear the pains of hell.' Because, you see, Father, I've decided that I don't dread the loss of heaven and I don't want to be a saint and perfect. I really don't. I want to live and have a real life, and if this means that I'm going to hell when I die, then good. Bring it on, because I also don't fear the pains of hell. In fact, I invite God to come flying down right now and send me to hell this very instant for all eternity if I'm wrong. Because I'd rather go to hell right now," I said, raising my voice, "than keep living IN FEAR OF OUR LORD ALMIGHTY, WHOM I LOVE WITH ALL MY HEART AND SOUL!"

I could hear the priest breathing fast. "THIS IS BLASPHEMY!" he shouted. "Not just a sin of arrogance! Do you realize who last spoke to God like this?"

"Who?"

"LUCIFER!" yelled the old priest.

"But he challenged God," I said. "And I'm not challenging God. I'll say in my Act of Contrition, 'Oh, my God, I am heartily sorry for having offended Thee, Who are all good and deserving of all my love, and I promise that with the help of Thy Grace to confess my sins, do penance, and amend my life,' all this I'll say," I said, "because I do love God with all my heart and soul, but never again will I ever say that I dread the loss of heaven and fear the pains of hell. Because . . . because, Father, I'd rather go to hell right now, than to believe THAT GOD IS FULL OF WRATH AND IS BLACKMAILING US!"

The priest jerked open the little screen between us. He was speechless. He was having trouble catching his breath.

"How old are you?" he said.

"Almost nineteen," I said.

"Young man," he said to me in a voice full of righteousness, "you can't talk like this and remain a Catholic!"

"Oh," I said, "I never thought of that. All right, then," I added, "I'm no longer a Catholic. Thanks. Goodbye."

And I didn't even bother to make the sign of the cross as I pushed away from the little shelf on which I had my hands pressed together in prayer.

"Wait!" he said. "You were baptized and confirmed! You can't just throw your soul into the flames of hell."

"Why not? With all my heart and soul I'd prefer to go to hell right now than live in fear of God." Tears were streaming down my face. "Thank you, Father. Goodbye."

I got up off my knees and stepped out of the confessional. He came out as well.

"But wait," he said again.

"No," I said, "I'm no longer a Catholic, so I don't have to listen to you anymore."

I went out of the huge university chapel. I'd never seen the sunlight so bright and the sky so blue. I was free! TOTALLY FREE AT LAST! I could now love my Lord God without any limits or boundaries! The whole world was finally open to me! Why hadn't I thought of this before? It was fear of God that was the biggest fear we had going on all over the globe. In fact, it was fear of God that drove us into more wars than anything else in all the world! Oh, why hadn't I seen this before. It was so simple. Christians, Muslims, Mormons, all of us could come together with love and peace once we were free of the fear of the Almighty.


How Father William, who'd become a close friend of mine, found out about my confession, I'll never know, but . . . he came over to my dormitory that very afternoon, knocked on my door, and asked if he could speak with me. I said sure, of course. He asked if I'd really used the term "blackmail" in reference to God.

"Yes, I did," I said, "but what I'd really meant to do was to use the term blackmail in reference to how the Church wants us to believe in God."

"Are you suggesting," he said, "that the Holy Roman Catholic Church is misrepresenting God?"

"I hadn't thought of it that way, but yes, I guess I am."

"That's pretty dangerous stuff," he said.

"Why? Because the Pope is infallible and hence everything the Church says is gospel? Well, I don't buy that anymore. I think God is pure love and just as much female as male so She-He can be in balance, and anything else is just a bunch of . . . of . . . well, stuff made up by the Church and men to keep us all full of fear, so that they can control us and get us to do terrible things to each other without any . . . any compassion and balance and . . . and personal responsibility."

I stopped. My heart was going crazy*loco,* and once more I felt like part of me was "here" and yet another part of me was "over there." I took a deep breath, and the humming began behind my left ear. I now knew how I'd solved that math problem in Ashmore's class. Everything, every thought that came to us came from heaven through our guardian angel, our genius, when we were at peace in our hearts and in balance in our brains. So yes, I was barking up the right tree with all these thoughts and words that were coming out of my mouth. And with such ease. No, one million times no, I wasn't going to back off. No, I was going to "trust" this Kingdom of God that was within all of us and go for it full steam ahead!

Also, I could see that Father Williams was looking at me in much the same way that Ashmore had looked at me. He wasn't condemning me. Part of him was, actually, fascinated by everything that was coming out of me, and yet another part of him looked quite cautious. He was hearing his own angel and yet not quite ready to listen to what he heard.

"Do you have any idea," he said, "what would happen if everyone just chose to believe whatever they wanted to believe? There'd be utter chaos."

I took a great big deep breath. No, I wasn't going to be knocked off of my center. "Okay, I can see that maybe you're right," I said. "But, on the other hand, could it be that just like the storms twist and break the limbs of a mighty tree and . . . and that tree bursts forth with new growth at these broken, twisted places, so does the Church—if she really is of God—needs chaos from time to time to grow new growth. Because, Father, we're at the end of our rope.

"I mean, why didn't Adam stand up and defend Eve? Why was he such a wimp? If I was married and living in paradise, you can bet your boots I would've faced up to God and said I did it. Me! Here! Right now! Especially if it had been Eve who'd done it. Because love, true love, makes a man brave and willing to die for his wife and kids, and also I do believe that God," tears came to my eyes, "would be more proud of me to be a stand-up guy, instead of a chicken-little wimp of a human being."

I stopped my words. The tears were streaming down my face. Maybe I was going too far, too fast. But it was like I just couldn't stop myself. The dam inside me had broken wide open and my river waters were running wild and free. I could see that Father Williams was thinking. He'd really heard what I'd said. He wasn't jumping to quick conclusions like the old priest at my confession.

"Tell me," he said, "do you have any comprehension of where all these ideas might take you?"

"No, of course not. But I am beginning finally to understand why my father says his mother didn't believe in God. You see, Father, to believe is weak, but to know is strong, and my dad says this was his mother's power. She was a short, dark, little Indian from Oaxaca, and she didn't just know God. She lived with God, and this was what enabled her never to lose faith or fall apart even in the middle of war and starvation. That's what I want, Father. That's what I need. And I can't get there by thinking that God is full of wrath. Can you see what I'm trying to say? It's out of date for us to fear God. We don't live in the dark ages anymore, and yet, Father, we still treat each other with all this out-of-date hate and revenge and wanting to get even."

"That's the devil's work," he said.

"Really, Father," I said. "Or could it be that we've made up the devil just as we've made up God, and now we're stuck, trapped, imprisoned between these two great forces. Father, let's get real for a moment. From one side of our mouth we say God is a mystery and beyond all reason and understanding, but then from the other side of our mouth we say that we know who God is and isn't so well that we're willing to go to war and slaughter people who have different beliefs than us. We can't keep having it both ways, Father. It's driving us crazy*loco.*" Tears began to flow from my eyes once again. "How can we ever hope to become better people, Father, if the God we worship is . . . is so judgmental and mean and . . . and . . . and. . ."

I took a deep breath. "What we need, Father, is a new improved God so we can get out of the Stone Ages of our male-based thinking brain—that always gets us into war and slaughter. Hell, in history class I learned that during our Crusades, we killed more fellow Christians than Muslims because they looked different than us. We need, Father, to start seeing God, not just as a strong male, but also as a compassionate female with large loving breasts full of rich, juicy, warm milk and all cuddly, big arms and thick thighs."

Father Williams closed his eyes and took a deep breath. "I do believe that you'd better stop," he said, opening his eyes.

"Stop?" I said. "But how can we stop, Father? We've got to go on. Look, only yesterday we thought the world was flat and we were the center of the universe. We've been wrong about so much for so long, so why can't we be wrong about God? Domain over the land and fish and animals, what a self-centered, self-serving, out-of-date righteous bunch of sh . . . sh . . . "

I stopped. I could see that Father Williams was looking at me in a way I'd never seen a priest look at a person before. He was shook up, but still his eyes weren't jumping around like the old priest's.

"I hope you realize that you're not the first to have gone this way," he said, "and you will not be the last. Be careful, Victor. There's a reason for structure and time-proven beliefs. The winds of hell and heaven aren't earthly winds, but torments of heart and soul that can drive even the most brilliant of minds to the brink of insanity."

"Exactly. I agree," I said. "And that's why I refuse to be part of this insanity about the pains of hell and the loss of heaven any longer. I want to go directly to God and not be led by anymore of this male-based fear stuff we got going."

Father Williams took a deep breath, but still his eyes held steady. He wasn't getting angry or leaving me. He was truly a man to respect.

"Have you ever heard of the poet Arthur Rimbaud?" he asked.

"No."

"This is where you seem to be headed. Rimbaud was a brilliant young French poet, and yet his brilliance killed him by the age of thirty-three."

"Same age as Jesus, eh?"

He nodded, brought out his rosary, and asked if he could give me absolution.

"No," I said, "no absolution. I've done nothing wrong. But you can give me your blessing."

He did so and left.

Then my cousin Victor showed up. He was all upset.

"Now what have you done!" he yelled at me.

"Nothing."

"Nothing? You told a priest that God is a blackmailer? I'm calling your parents!"

I started laughing. "Calling my parents? What have they got to do with this?"

"Everything! They paid your tuition! They pay for your room and board. I'm not going to let them down and have them think I had anything to do with this!"

"Look, let me get this straight," I said. "It's okay for you to be a queer and do something that Catholics are told is against the laws of God, but for me to question God and ask the Church to knock off all her crap about threatening us every Sunday with damnation and hell is wrong? Hell, Victor, I'd thought that you, of all people, would be happy I'm questioning the very basis of all this fear crap that's been shoved into our brains ever since we were little kids."

His eyes widened, and he raced across the room, getting as far away from me as he could. "It's him, God! Not me, who's saying all these blasphemies!" He opened the front door.

"What the hell are you doing?"

"I'm keeping away from you in case a bolt of lightning comes down from heaven and zaps you!" He began to giggle that nervous laugh that he'd done in his apartment. "In North Africa, when I was in the Army, I was . . . was assigned to intelligence. We were writing up material for counterintelligence, and . . . and I, too, began to have all these thoughts, not too different from yours, but I learned my lesson!" His eyes were moving about nervously, and he was staying by the open doorway, as if he was ready to run on a second's notice. "They . . . they found me wandering in the desert. I would've died, you hear me, died, if they hadn't found me! You can't, I repeat, you can't go out into these far-out regions of thought without supervision and structure or you'll fry! I know! I'm going to tell Uncle Sal and Aunt Lupe about you!"

I started laughing. "What are we, in kindergarten, and you're going to tell my parents on me? Good. Do it. I'd rather burn in hell once and for all than live in fear of . . . " I started crying again. I couldn't help it. "Don't you get it?" I said. "I LOVE GOD! I LOVE THE ALMIGHTY! And I will not be blackmailed by the fear of hell or anything else!"

"Don't say that! God could be listening!"

"Damnit, I hope He is! Our whole planet is so full of fear that it's driving us crazy*loco* with wars and greed. Can't you see it? It all starts with how we see the Holy Creator. We really, really do need a better God. Hell, half the time I think I'm a better person than this God that has been presented to us."

"Oh, oh, oh, you're going to go to hell!" he yelled, going out the open door. "Who do you think you are?" he added once he was outside. "Jesus Christ?"

"Wouldn't we all be better off if we all started thinking that we were?"

"Oh, you are crazy! You really are!" he said, running.

"Victor, come back here! Think! Who else is there worthwhile to strive to be, if not Jesus?"

He threw up his arms. "I'm out of here! You're insane!"

He ran further.

"Victor," I shouted after him, "we're at a university! We're being asked to think, to figure things out, so what could be more important than to figure out who God is?"

"Stay away from me!" he yelled. He ran to his car, got in, and started the motor.

"Okay, run, but I'm not turning," I yelled after him. "I'm going to keep going and going and going until I find out what it was that Adam and Eve ate from the tree of knowledge, SO I CAN SPIT IT OUT!" I bellowed.

Yelling this, I closed my eyes and part of me wanted to make the sign of the cross over myself and ask God for help, but I didn't know how to do this without sliding back into all the structure of the Church that I'd just left behind.

# CHAPTER TWENTY-THREE

It was almost noon when Father Williams came to see me a few days later. He said he wanted to speak to me privately. I should have realized that my cousin had called my parents and my parents had come to see Father Williams and Father Spain, both of whom lived with us in our all-male student dormitories. I'd become good friends with both of them.

Father Williams and I decided to go out for lunch. We went to the Cotton Patch, a very nice little restaurant down the hill from the university. He ordered a martini. I ordered a glass of orange juice. He told me my parents had come to see him and expressed their concern for me. Then he asked me where I'd gotten all my wild ideas? Had someone at the university been talking to me like this? I laughed. What did he think? That I couldn't think for myself? Or did he also just see a stupid Mexican sitting across the table from him? But I really didn't care if he did or didn't, so I changed the subject.

"Father," I said, "I'd like you to know that the other day I drove out toward Point Loma, and for the first time in my life I went inside a Protestant church. And you know, nothing bad happened to me." I took a deep breath. "I just sat quietly in a pew, and it felt real good. Next, I'd like to go to a Jewish temple, and then maybe even a place of the Buddhists, and a Mormon place, too."

"Is this why you decided to relinquish your Catholic faith?" he asked.

"Partly," I said.

The waitress came with our drinks and was ready to take our order. I told Father Williams to have anything he wished, since my parents had obviously set up this luncheon. He ordered a New York steak. I did the same, and I noticed that our waitress was acting very friendly toward Father Williams, even though he was wearing his collar. But who could blame her. He was in his thirties and was one of the handsomest men I'd ever met.

"You were saying?" said the priest after the waitress had taken our order.

"I was saying that I've been feeling very happy ever since I quit being a Catholic," I said. "I'm not carrying around all that stuff about hell and damnation and God's awful wrath anymore. Father," I added, "I truly enjoyed going into that Protestant church the other day. I could've never done that before. Ever since I can remember, I've been told that it's a great sin, one of the most dangerous kind, to go into a Protestant building and hear their words."

"We could arrange this for you," he said, sipping his martini. "You don't have to renounce Catholicism to be allowed to study other forms of worship."

"I could?"

"Yes, you're going to a university, and at this level, it's quite all right for a student of theology to study different beliefs."

I nodded, but then thinking this over, I said, "No, it wouldn't work."

"Why not?"

"Because I'd still be thinking like a Catholic, passing judgment on every little thing that was said or done. I could never really hear or see anything as new and a real possibility, because of the filter through which I'd be viewing the . . ."

Our waitress came over with another martini and told Father Williams that this one was on the house. He smiled and thanked her. She reached out and touched his shoulder, then left with a very suggestive walk.

"Father," I said, "what do you do about women who come on to you like this?"

He flinched, then he sipped his drink, acting all innocent. "Why are you asking this?" he said.

"Father," I said, "our waitress, she's crazy*loca* over you. Do you go out with women, Father?" I asked.

He looked at me with his large blue eyes. "I do believe, Victor," he said, "that you're stepping over the edge."

"The edge of what?"

"The edge of what is proper and improper."

"And who defines what is proper and not proper? This is exactly why I said it wouldn't work. Because as long as I'm a Catholic, every time I start to ask or even think of the really good, juicy questions, a wall of fear will come up inside me. And I believe that it is this wall of fear that's holding us back."

My heart was beat, beat, beating as I spoke these last words. But I'd made my decision, and so there was no turning back. I was going for it all the way.

"Father," I continued, "our waitress is coming on to you, and you know it. So what are you going to do about it? I saw you glance at her butt when she walked away. She's extremely good-looking. What's going on inside of you? Myself, I'd be going crazy*loco* with feelings if I were you."

"I took the oath of celibacy," he said.

"Yeah, but so what? I'm asking how are you feeling. Not what you are thinking. Sex, Father, is a very large part of us. My God, just the scent of her is . . . is intoxicating!"

And I almost told him about the summer I'd collected pubic hairs and put them in my Bible, but I didn't. I figured that I'd maybe gone too far as it was. For the first time, Father William's eyes began to jump around like my cousin Victor's had done. He didn't answer me. And he was right to not answer me. I had lost my sense of what was proper, and the worst part was that I liked it. It felt pretty darn good deep inside to talk and think freely.

We continued to sit in silence, and the silence got so thick you could cut it with a knife. Then our steaks arrived, and we began to eat, forgetting to say grace.

"Tell me, Father," I said, halfway through our meal, "what do you think about the parting of the Red Sea? Do you think that it really happened?"

"Yes, of course, it's Scripture," he said.

"Yeah, sure, of course, but do you honestly believe it happened and, if you do, then do you believe that other humans can do this, too? Because Moses wasn't the Son of God like Jesus. He was just another human being. So then, it follows that if he could do this, then the rest of us should also be able to do—if not this—then at least something quite similar."

He took a deep breath and signaled for another martini. "Are you now comparing yourself to Moses?" he asked with that well-practiced priestly look.

I took a deep breath. I knew what he was doing. With this question and that look, I was supposed to quit what I was doing. But no, I wouldn't fall for that old trap priests had been using on us kids since day one.

"Absolutely," I said, slipping past his noose. "Why not? Don't you compare yourself to Moses? You're a man of the cloth. You're a sworn-in representative of Jesus Christ, Himself, who was the Son of God, so shouldn't you be at least as full of grace as Moses if you really believe. I mean, why shouldn't you be able to do miracles, too, Father?"

"Because I wasn't chosen," he said.

Immediately, my heart started beating faster. I'd thought of this, too. My chess pieces were all alive! "Or could it be, Father, that it's not about being chosen, but just the opposite. It's for each and every-one of us to step up and choose." Tears came to my eyes. I flashed on the day that I'd tried to castrate myself. I'd truly, really stepped up. "Because, Father, if I understand it correctly, Peter wasn't able to walk on water alongside Jesus because he looked down and lost faith. And Jesus said, 'All this I do, you will do and more.' So what I'm saying is that it's our responsibility, as true believers, not to look down and lose our faith, but instead to step forward and reach up for the heavens with all our Christ-like powers, and do miracles here on earth every day. It's our choice, see? We've got free will. So I choose with all my heart and soul to be like Moses and not be like Peter," I added.

"And part the Red Sea, too?"

"Yes, Father, absolutely!" I said. "Part our Red Sea of all this fear and doubt that's strangling us all over the world! And I'm sure it can be done and that it needs to be done. We can't just sit around anymore and keep calling all these old things of the Old and New Testament metaphors and symbols, because those kinds of words just soften our brain and take us off the hook from taking on the full responsibility for who we really are!"

"And who are we really?" he said, sipping his martini and giving me that well-practiced priestly look once again.

I took a big breath. I could see that he was toying with me once more. He was still well within the comfortable boundaries of his educated Catholic beliefs. I took another deep breath.

"That I don't know yet, Father," I said. "But I will tell you this, we certainly aren't who we've been led to believe we are. We're much better people than that all over the world. And I don't believe that we were born with sin and that we're the only ones who have souls. I was raised on a ranch. I've seen horses who have more soul and honor and dignity than a lot of the people I've met."

"I thought you said that people are much better than we think they are."

I looked across the table. He was playing chess with me. I took hold of my queen. This was it. "They are, once we get rid of all the crap inside our brains that has been crammed into us since day one. Father, I'm not going to have my kids baptized. Original sin is a bunch of . . . of, well, crap. Can't you see that when you look at children? Kids are a blessing! It's all the crap we put into their heads that turn them mean and greedy. Only in an organization where men are separated from women and children can all this misinformation exist."

There, I'd hit his king between the eyes with my queen. Or more precisely in the groin of his king. He wasn't sipping his martini anymore.

"Look, Father, believe me, I'm not out to get the Church or you or anyone. It's just that if for one day, we could all step forth as human beings, as one united people all over the world, made in the image of a pure, loving, newly improved God, balanced in both male and female energies, then all our different religions—and not just Catholic and Protestants and Jews and Muslims, but also our religions of football, chemistry, and love of country and money—would flow into one mighty river of forgiveness and understanding, and collectively we could then part the entire Pacific Ocean!

"Moses, the way I see it, is small potatoes compared to what we can now do with modern communications, and we've got to do it, Father, we really do! We can't just keep passing the buck."

I could see it all so clearly, like when the chess pieces came alive for me on the chessboard.

"It's time, Father," I said, "for you, for me, for all of us to stop thinking we're so smart and have all the answers and open up ourselves to the voice of our genius, of our guardian angel, and see possibilities never imagined before! Look around, Father, see our freeways, see our airports, our T.V.'s, we've come so far so fast that . . . that old scary story of a male-based mean God is COMPLETELY OUT OF DATE!"

I stopped. I was trembling, and the tears were streaming down my face. I'd finally said everything I'd been feeling deep inside me for months.

"Tell me," said Father Williams, "I don't understand how you've come up with all these ideas. I've met your parents. They're not theologians. They're very practical businesspeople. So how is it that all this is so important to you?"

I took a huge breath. This was a good question. "I don't know," I said. "Maybe it's because ever since I started school, I've been an outsider. Or maybe it's because when I was sixteen years old my dad told me that to be a man, it wasn't enough to know right from wrong, that a man also needs to know who he is and who he isn't. Then here at school one day, when I was praying by myself in the chapel, it dawned on me I could never really know who I was and who I wasn't until I first found out who God was and who God wasn't, especially since I've been told since childhood that we were made in His image."

Father Williams nodded. "I'll speak with your parents. Maybe you're not as lost as we've been led to believe. Be careful what you say to your cousin Victor in the future. He feels very responsible for you, and you frighten him."

I almost said, "Good. The bastard is a child molester," but I didn't.

Father Williams was pretty tipsy by the end of our meal. And I saw our waitress almost grab him and give him a kiss. She was so hungry for a good man, and good he was, and yet he wasn't admitting who he was, especially when it came to women. He'd liked her ass. I'd seen it in his eyes.

# CHAPTER TWENTY-FOUR

That weekend when I drove home, my parents and my cousin Victor were waiting for me. My mother was crying.

"Did you really tell the priest that you don't believe in God?" she asked.

"No, I never said that," I said.

"Yes, you did!" shouted my cousin Victor. "You said that God is a blackmailer!"

"Shut your damn mouth!" I yelled at him.

"See! I told you, he gets violent! He's gone crazy!"

"All right, enough," said my dad. "No more! Let Mundo talk for himself." Mundo was the nickname given to me by my family, because my middle name was Edmundo, and also "mundo" in Spanish meant world. "What did you say to the priest?" asked my father.

"I said that I won't live in fear of God anymore, and I won't be blackmailed by the Church, which is always preaching to us about the pains of hell."

"Okay, so then what's the big deal? Sounds pretty good to me," said my dad. "Who doesn't want to stop living all their lives on their knees?"

"But, uncle," said my cousin Victor, "he thinks he's Jesus Christ! You can't say things like that! It's blasphemy!"

"Who says so?"

"The Church."

"The Church says we shouldn't be like Jesus? Then why in the hell is she always telling us so much about Him?"

"Well, yes, but to compare yourself to the Son of God is . . . "

"You know, we've got to be careful about what we believe that this Church tells us," said my dad. "Remember, she's the one who stole all the best lands *de México* for herself and enslaved all the Indians that she didn't kill off. I agree with him. I wish I'd thought of this myself. Why live our whole lives on our knees? It's about time we stand up and want to be the Son of God like Jesus, too. But a practical Jesus and not get our asses crucified. My mother, she would've thought of this," he added with a big smile. "Nothing frightened that little bag of Indian bones!"

"But you don't understand," said my cousin, beginning to sweat. "His soul is in great peril!"

"And so are the souls of all the rest of us, too? So why not call the Church's bluff. After all, didn't that great thinker—what's-his-name—say that *la vida* we don't examine isn't worth a shit?"

"Where'd you hear that?" asked my mother.

"In my college in Arizona," said my dad. "Now, the question that I've got is this, where do you go from here, *mijito?*" he said, turning back to me. "You have opened up a whole can of worms and you're not just going to be able to put them all back in the can again."

"Exactly!" said my cousin. "And I warned him! I warned him!"

I closed my eyes and took a few deep breaths before I spoke. "I don't know, *papá,*" I said. "It's like I'm now in a whole new world, and I don't really know what comes next."

"Did you actually say that you're no longer a Catholic?" asked my mother.

"Yes," I said.

"Oh, my God," said my mother, making the sign of the cross over herself. "How could this have happened? We sent you to a Catholic university. Where did we go wrong?"

"*Mamá,*" I said, my heart aching for her, "this has nothing to do with you. I'm just so sick and tired of all the lies and hypocrisy that I could . . . could . . ." I didn't say the word kill, but it was exactly what I was thinking.

"What lies?" my mother was saying. "Who has been lying to you, *mijito?*"

"Everybody," I said.

"Everybody?" she said.

"Yes," I said. But I didn't know how to explain what I was feeling inside. It had started with my first day of kindergarten. Everything was a manipulation of separation and conquest, just as we'd been taught to do at the Academy. It was part of our basic way of life to put down everyone and everything different from us and ours. It was a planetary sickness, politically, socially, and religiously, for each to think that theirs was the only way. Then it hit me like a lightning bolt. The word "only" was the seed of this entire sickness. Because you added "only" to "the" and now you had solidly cemented separation and imprisoned the mind. I wondered who had invented these two words.

My mother was looking at me with tears streaming down her face. My cousin Victor went to my mother and put his arm around her. I felt like belting him. Why had he even told my parents? He didn't want me to say anything about him being a child molester and yet, he'd told them about my confession.

Suddenly I saw what was really going on. Victor was trying to separate me from my mom and dad. He wished that he was their son. Divide and conquer. This sneaky son-of-a-bitch. I grabbed him by the neck and yanked him away from my mother.

"*Mamá*," I said, with tears streaming down my face, too, "don't worry, everything is going to be okay."

"You're damn right," said my dad, going to the bar. "When he was two years old he pissed on me, and he's still pissing, that's all!"

Saying this, my father brought out a bottle of tequila and served himself a good size shot. "*¡Para el estribo!*" he said, belting down the drink. "Hell of a good life! Hell of a good time! Plenty of room to screw up and down and just keep going and going and laughing the whole way with *carcajadas*! Want a shot, *querida*?" he asked my mother.

"No," she said, shaking her head.

He served himself another and shot this one down, too. "Aaah, damn good!" he said. "You've got to FEEL IT 'til it hurts real good or it ain't living!"

My dad loved using the word "ain't." He said it was the best damn slang word invented by the Americans. He capped the bottle and came across the big high-ceilinged room and took me in his thick strong arms, giving me a big *abrazo*.

"Still pissing, eh, *mijito*?" he said to me.

I smiled. I guess it was true. When I was little my dad had spanked me and I'd thought that was totally unfair, so I'd stalked him, following him around the house and yard all afternoon. Finally he laid down to take a nap in the living room. It was Sunday. We'd gone to church in the morning, and when my dad was asleep, I'd gotten up on the coffee table in front of the couch, pulled down my diapers, and pissed in his big open snoring mouth.

Suddenly, out of the blue, I knew where I'd gotten the nerve to challenge the Catholic Church and everything else that I'd been taught since a child. Hell, when your own dad allowed you to challenge him, while still in diapers, this was power! And I'd been raised like this since day one and so had my dad, because his mother had raised him as a girl for the first seven years of his life. This was the key. People like my cousin Victor, the youngest in his *familia,* who'd never had a father figure growing up as his older brothers and sisters had, was lost here deep inside his heart and soul and afraid to make waves. Yes, I now saw it so clearly. I was still pissing, just as my dad had said. I felt like walking over to the bar and having a shot of tequila with my dad, but no . . . I wasn't quite ready for this, either.

# CHAPTER TWENTY-FIVE

School was out. It was Saturday, and I was driving our *familia*'s big Cadillac. We were on our way to Brawley, east of San Diego, to visit my godparents, Manuelita and Vicente Araiza. Manuelita was best friends with my mother. They'd known each other since they were little kids back in the Rain of Gold canyon in *Chihuahua, México*.

After dinner, my godparents' son Raul asked me if I'd like to go with him and his friends across the border to Mexicali. He was a couple of years younger than me, and he'd just gotten a brand-new Chevy Impala.

"Sure," I said, "but I don't drink liquor, so I don't want to just go bar-hopping like guys from San Diego do when they go to Tijuana."

"I don't drink alcohol, either," he said.

I went with him and his friends, and we walked the streets. It was fun. I'd never been out with the guys like this before. Also, we were all Latinos, and so we were speaking Spanish instead of English, and this felt super good. We went into a nightclub. It was a strip joint. I was nineteen years old, and I'd never been in such a place before.

The manager sat us down by the ramp where the dancers came out of the back. The woman who was already dancing was in her thirties and chubby and really funny, especially when she started to take off her clothes, whirling them and tossing them to us. Once, when one of the guys at our table reached out to grab hold of her, she turned her ass at him and farted. We almost died laughing. I'd never seen a naked woman fart before. And it really smelled, too. Everyone tossed her money. She was the greatest show in town.

Then the second dancer came out. She was so young and beautiful that it was a good thing the place was dark or everyone would've seen the front of my pants start jumping.

Our drinks arrived, but I hadn't ordered one. Our waitress told us it was a three-drink minimum, whether we drank or not. I didn't touch my drink. A group of girls came over and sat down with us and told us we had to buy them drinks, too. I didn't know what to do, but Raul winked at me and ordered more drinks for the girls. Then it happened. I'd never had a girl reach down and grab hold of my private parts before. I almost freaked out. One of the guys got up and went off with the girl who'd sat down on his lap.

"What's going on?" I asked Raul in English, so we couldn't be understood.

The girl, who'd grabbed hold of me, said in perfect English, "Fuckie-fuckie, that's what's going on, *papacito.*"

I got scared, and not because it was a mortal sin to have sex before marriage and I'd go straight to hell, but because I was in love with Clare and I wanted to save myself for her.

"No, not me," I said to her in Spanish, but she'd already put her tongue in my ear and pushed the table away, so she could straddle me face to face. "No," I pleaded. "Please, no," I added weakly.

"What are you, one of those others?" she said, laughing. "I don't think so," she said, stroking my erection.

I began to sweat. My penis had double-crossed me. "But please, you don't understand," I said, whispering. I really wanted to grab her, but I wasn't going to. "I'm . . . I'm . . . you see, saving myself for when I get . . ."

"This one is virgin!" she yelled loud enough for everyone to hear.

"No, I'm not!" I said. I didn't want Raul and his friends to know. After all, I was nearly two years older than all of them. She got off me and left. Raul and his last two friends got up and went off with the girls who'd gotten on their laps. I was now the only person left at our table. I took a deep breath and glanced around. I'd never seen so many women dressed with so little clothing. Some were chubby, some were skinny, some were really young-looking, and some looked older, like maybe in their thirties. But it was hard to tell, with the lights so low.

Then I spotted one, way over by the far corner. She was sitting on a stool at the bar reading a book. She didn't seem to care about doing any business.  Another woman, an older one, must have seen me looking at her, because she yelled "College Girl!" in English to the one who was reading the book and pointed to me.

College Girl stopped her reading and looked at me. She put her book down, got off her stool, and came walking toward me with a slow sensual gait. She never said a word. She just came up to me, put her hands on her lean young hips, and looked at me in the eyes, all the while smiling a quiet little smile. Then, still without saying a word, she reached out to me with her right hand and motioned with her index finger for me to get up and come to her.

I was mesmerized. Before I even realized it, I was on my feet, had taken her hand, and I was following her. Just the scent of her young slender body sent shocks of molten fire shooting all through me. She led me across the large bar and out the back door. The desert air of Mexicali was cold, and the sky was filled with a million stars. Her tall spike-heeled shoes clicked on the cobblestones. It was music to my ears. She led me across the alley to a shabby little motel and took me into a room. On the nightstand were three little candles in front of the statue of the Virgin Mary and a picture of baby Jesus and Joseph. She closed the door behind us. At first I couldn't get my eyes off Jesus and His Mother, but then College Girl began to undress. She was so young and beautiful that by the time she got to her bra and panties, I forgot all about the Virgin Mary and her *familia*.

I mean, I'd never seen a woman take off her undergarments before. It was so fascinating as her hands went behind her back to undo the snap of her bra. Both her shoulders turned downward, and her elbows danced at her sides like the wings of a bird. Smiling, she tossed me her bra, but I didn't try to catch it. Her breasts had leaped out, and I was goggle-eyed seeing these beautiful mounds of human flesh.

Laughing, she reached for her panties, started to take them off, but then stopped. Instead, she slowly, carefully licked her lips, then came to me. She took my hands in hers and placed mine on her underwear. Her legs were long, and I felt the warmth and smooth-ness of her skin as she helped me slip-slide her underwear down her hips and legs. I lost my breath. I'd never seen a naked bush before, and especially not this close to my face. Her bush was beautiful. I wanted to pet it, to part it, to kiss it, but tears came to my eyes. We weren't married, and I'd always wanted to be in love and married when I did this.

"It's okay," she said, unbuckling my belt buckle, then unbuttoning my Levis and pulling them down. "I'll be gentle. How old are you?"

"Nineteen," I said.

"Me, too," she said, pulling off my boots so she could get my Levis off my feet. "Where are you from?"

"San Diego."

"I'm from Guadalajara," she said, putting my boots and pants on the chair by her bed.

It felt so natural and wonderful to be doing all this with a naked woman. I wiped the tears from my eyes with the back of my hand. "My father's people come from that part of Mexico, too," I said. "How long have you been in . . . ah, well, this kind of work?"

"I've been doing this for almost a year," she said, coming back to me and unbuttoning my shirt. "I have a little girl. He never married me like he promised, so I have to support my child and my mother, who takes care of her for me. This is your first time, no?"

"Yes, of course," I said.

"Don't worry," she said. "I'm clean, and I remember my first time, too. I'll be much gentler with you than what was done to me my first time."

"What happened?"

"No more talking," she said, taking off my shirt. "Very nice," she added, gently running her right hand over my muscular torso. She smiled and reached for my underwear and gently, slowly began slipping them down. My penis leaped out. She laughed. *"Papacito,* you've been hiding a very nice present away from the girls."

She took my penis in hand, gave it a little kiss, and finished getting my underwear off of me. She went across the room and put on some music. She started laughing, dancing, and having fun. I couldn't help it. I started laughing, too. Then she came back to me and drew me to herself, and our whole bodies came together, fitting so well that my erection instantly, all by itself, reached for her warm luscious bush.

She began kissing me and whispering to me in Spanish in my ear as she backed up and lay down on her bed, pulling me down on top of her. My cock seemed to have a mind all of its own as it kept searching and feeling. Then the tip of my erection touched something that was all moist and sticky and warm, and BINGO, she pulled me in a little, then a little more, and . . . and suddenly, miracle of miracles, she pulled her legs up and apart, and I slid-slipped in DEEP, and even DEEPER INSIDE HER!

IT WAS HEAVEN!

I ALMOST PASSED OUT, IT FELT SO GOOD AND JUICY-HOT!

It could never get any better than this, but then she got hold of me by my ass, and she began to move under me in a slow, twisting strong, lean body rhythm of movement that I just knew was HOLY! Was SACRED! And men and women had been doing this for hundreds of thousands of years. No, millions and millions of years. It felt so good and totally natural. I couldn't believe that all my life I'd been trained to think this was bad and sinful and that Jesus had never done it.

This was BULLSHIT OF THE WORSE KIND! Jesus Christ had done this too! I just knew it with every fiber of my moving, twisting, FEELING, BEING! This was too good for Jesus not to have done it with Magdalena every chance they got!

This is LIVING!

This was FEELING THE WHOLE DELICIOUS MIRACLE OF LIFE, *LA VIDA* ITSELF!

Then miracle of miracles, she rolled me over on my back and began riding me like a bucking bronco with a ramming, turning, twisting action, faster, faster, and then, oh, my dear Lord God, something BIG WAS HAPPENING!

SOMETHING VERY BIG WAS COMING!

Shooting down my spine and through my whole body!

Coming!

Coming! Coming! COMING!

And now the whole shaft of my thick cock suddenly EXPLODED INTO A ZILLION BILLION GOOD-HURTING PIECES, coming out the tip in awful stinging pain!

Someone was SCREAMING!

But I had no idea who it was until I realized that it was me SCREAMING BLOODY MURDER, because it hurt so, so, SO GOOD!

AND SCREAM I DID! Again and again! I couldn't stop screaming! I could never stop! And so I didn't, and we continued again and again, COMING and COMING and COMING until someone was knocking on our door!

She shouted for them to leave us alone, that it was my first time, and she had to show me the whole *milagro del amor a lo mexicano!* And show me she did, half a dozen more times, and each time I died! I died! And I came to know the miracle of half a dozen different positions.

Adam had never chickened out. No *hombre* could ever chicken out and blame his wife once he'd known the miracle of making love. That was all a bunch of crap made up by mean old dried-up men who'd forgotten the wonders of being with a gorgeous, luscious, juicy, great singing, moving bush!

It was long after midnight when we got dressed. I tried to give her all the money I had, but she said I only owed her ten dollars.

I asked her what her name was.

She looked at me, and said, "You don't really want to know."

"I don't?" I said. "Why not?"

"Because this isn't my life," she said, "so the name that I'll give you has nothing to do with my real name, and you're asking me for my real name, aren't you?"

"Well, yes, I guess I am," I said.

"So no, I will not tell you."

"Okay," I said. "I love your honesty. And here, this isn't for you, it's for your daughter."

I put another forty dollars on her little altar of Jesus, Mary, and Joseph. She began to cry, but silently.

"What is it?" I said. "Did I do something wrong?"

She shook her head. "No, you did something very right, and that's what's so terrible."

"I don't understand."

"Like Jesus showed respect to Magdalena, you have shown me respect, too. My true name is Magdalena Villaseñor," she said.

My knees went weak. I had to sit down. The name Villaseñor was not a common name. In all of my life, I'd never met a Villaseñor who wasn't a relative.

"What is it?" she asked.

"That's my name, too," I said.

"Villaseñor?"

"Yes," I said, gripping my forehead.

Her eyes got large, and she made the sign of the cross over herself. I guess we were both thinking the same thing. We were probably cousins. Sure, why not? From the very beginning we'd felt so comfortable together. I took all the money I had in my pocket and handed it to her. It was about fifty more dollars. My dad always insisted that I carry at least a hundred dollars on me at all times.

"No," she said, "please no more."

She was crying. I was crying.

"Yes, please. And give me your address, and I'll send you money every month. You don't need to keep doing this. You can . . . "

"GET OUT!" she screamed. "Get out!"

With trembling hands, I got dressed and left.

# CHAPTER TWENTY-SIX

**D**riving back across the border, I couldn't understand what Raul and his friends were saying to me. I was gone. I was spent. And the next day driving home, I also couldn't understand what my parents said to me. I was still all gone, spent, confused, and so pissed at God I couldn't hear or comprehend anything that was said to me.

It hadn't been one little bit funny! Of all the prostitutes in the whole world, why had the Almighty set it up that I'd lose my virginity to a person who was a relative? Did God have a sick sense of humor?

The moment we got home, I went upstairs and locked myself in my room. I was completely bananas with rage. What was God trying to tell me? Had I been wrong to leave the structure of the Church? Was I now a lost human being? I spent the next few days going up into the hills on horseback and shooting and shooting, and this was where I finally got my answer.

I was with big Ted Bourland, and we were out at our ranch in the San Luis Rey Valley shooting at some old barrels and washing machines when I suddenly got my answer. It hit me right in the gut with such force that all the wind was knocked out of me, and I thought I was dying.

"Ted," I said in a whisper as I hit the ground, "I've been shot."

Ted thought I was joking and started to laugh, but when he saw me on the ground gripping my stomach in terrible pain, he stopped laughing and his face turned white.

"You're serious?"

I nodded. I couldn't say a word. Everything was going black. Then in the darkness, I felt Ted take my hands away from my gut so he could examine me more closely, and he then said the craziest thing I'd ever heard.

"You've been shot," he said, "but I don't think you're dying. Your belt buckle saved you."

I had no idea what he was talking about, but I was starting to get my breath back and my vision was clearing. I sat up, and . . . and I saw my brother Joseph's big, thick, western belt buckle had taken the hit from the bullet and was all dented in at the center. Instantly, I realized what had happened. One of our bullets must have hit the inside part of an old hand-turned washing machine and ricocheted right back at us. It was a good thing we weren't shooting .357 ammo, and instead .38 special—because it was cheaper and we wanted to save money—or that bullet would have probably penetrated the buckle and killed me.

Ted helped me to my feet and drove me home in my old Chevy, which now had patches of turquoise coming through the white paint because of all the wear and tear it got working on the ranch. I went right to bed when I got home. I couldn't get it out of my mind. If that bullet had come flying back at me just one inch higher, I'd be dead. If it had come back one inch lower, I'd be dead. Two inches to the right or left, and I'd be dead. I began to cry. Maybe this meant God still loved me, and my brother Joseph was still looking out for me.

"Forgive me, God," I said, "for being angry at You. I didn't mean it. I'm just, well, all mixed up. What are You trying to tell me, that sex is bad and I should be dead? Is this why You set it up for me to do it with a relative? Please help me to understand, dear God. I don't know what to think, and I'm lost and I miss You." Then I added, "God, You are my . . . my EVERYTHING!"

I began to tremble like I'd never trembled before in all of my life. My whole body was vibrating in quick little jerks. I remembered what my cousin Victor had said about wandering in the desert and almost dying. I flashed on what Father Williams had said about the place where I was going not having earthly winds, but torments of heart and soul. Had I bitten off too much? Then I remembered what my dad said that his mother had told him when they'd gotten caught in a sandstorm at Ciudad Juárez across the border from El Paso, Texas.

She'd been blinded by the blasting sand. My father was twelve years old and sure they were going to die. But his old mother had gripped him and jerked him close and told him they were not going to die. They were going to live and for him to not give up. That for every broken, lost human being there was in the world, there was another who'd seen worse and had not given up. That people could go on and on no matter what, if they kept their faith in God. And she'd promised my dad they would live, and she, herself would live long enough to see him grow into manhood and marry. And she did it, old and broken she'd lived long enough to complete her word.

"You are not quitting," I heard a voice say deep within me with utter clarity. "We were blind. We were unable to breathe. The sand came through *mi sarape* and tore the skin off our bodies, and yet we never ever lost faith. How could we? A whole army of people are within each of us, helping us, guiding us. You are not alone, *mijito,*" I heard the voice say. "YOU HAVE *FAMILIA!*"

Then I must have gone to sleep, because the next thing I knew I was under the large pepper tree where my dad had spoken to me when I'd turned sixteen years old, and in my dream I saw Magdalena Villaseñor all dressed up and looking so beautiful as she lit the three candles in front of her little altar with the statue of Mary and the picture of Joseph holding the Christ child. The whole room had a golden glow. She knelt down and prayed, then she got up and began packing her belongings.

I smiled. She was quitting her job. She was going home. It had been no mistake for me to leave her all that money. When she was packed, she took the statue and picture off her altar, put them in her luggage, and blew out the three candles. She hurried out the door. It was night, and the stars were out by the millions. Across the alley a cab waited for her. But two men suddenly leaped out of the dark shadows and went to grab her. She didn't panic. She was prepared. She pulled a gun, firing at their feet. They quickly retreated. I started laughing. She truly was a crazy*loca* Villaseñor.

I didn't come out of my room for three days. I kept dreaming. And I once saw Jesus walking across the rolling waters just beyond the breakers with my brother Joseph at his side. Then I saw that Jesus and my brother were in the cab with Magdalena, sitting on each side of her as the cab took flight like a shooting star up into the star-studded heavens. I couldn't stop laughing. I was pregnant with God. I was a cow chewing her cud.

The Love Force of Creation was germinating within me.

Each and every moment was a miracle.

Each and every second was Sacred and Holy.

My parents were knocking on my door, but I wouldn't let anyone in.

Then I finally began to understand what God was telling me. My parents' wealth, no matter how large, was temporary. If fate moved my parents just an inch to the right or left, they, too, could be poor, and my very own sisters could be doing what Magdalena Villaseñor was doing.

We were one family all over the world. That prostitute, that wino, that lost bum on the street, was my very own brother and sister, too. I began to cry. I now understood. I really did. My guardian angel genius was still guiding step by step, illuminating my way.

The knocking continued, and I remembered that Magdalena had explained to me why they called her "College Girl." She had been in medical school in Guadalajara studying to be a nurse when she became pregnant and her father threw her out of the house. He'd never believed her when she'd told him that she'd been raped by a doctor. Her dad knew the man, and the doctor was a very respected and important figure in the state of Jalisco, and so her dad had blamed her just as Adam had blamed Eve.

The knocking continued, and I now knew in no uncertain terms that the time had come for us to throw off the yoke of men blaming women. I saw it so clearly, judgment day was coming, and IT WAS THE DAY WHEN PEOPLE ALL OVER THE EARTH STOPPED PASSING JUDGMENT ON ONE ANOTHER!

The knocking continued. This was what Jesus had come to earth to show us. Even as they'd nailed Him to the cross, He hadn't passed judgment and blamed them. In fact, He'd said to turn the other cheek. Like my dad had said, Jesus was *un hombre* Who truly knew who He was and who He wasn't.

The knocking continued. I got up to answer the door. I was ready to come out of my room. I, too, had wandered in the desert as my cousin Victor had done, but I hadn't stopped when I'd felt myself on the edge of going insane. Hell, no, I was already crazy*loco,* and so I'd just kept going and going as my *mamagrande* had done in the desert and . . . and so had Jesus Christ, my best friend.

"Thank You, God," I said. "Thank You. We're doing okay. We're going to make it. We just got to stick together."

*Casa grande* at rancho, 1947–1977.

Home 1977

My parents Sal and Lupe, 25th Anniversary.

In my Army/Navy Academy uniform, 1957.

My sister Teresita dancing.

My sister Linda with Honest Bee.

Deer hunting with John Folting, 1956.

La Bonita, the baby of Honest Bee.

Me, relative, my parents, and Linda (left to right), Acapulco, Mexico, 1960.

With my sister Linda, 1960.

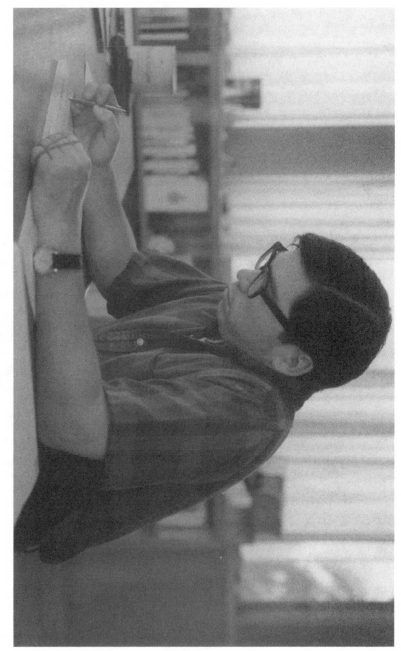

Writing at *rancho,* 1960.

# ~ BOOK THREE ~

# CHAPTER TWENTY-SEVEN

I was running barefoot in the surf on the beach and feeling wonderful! I was no longer the person I'd thought I was. I was a totally different person. I was seeing a whole new world. It was like I'd been wearing blinders all my life. I was finally beginning to glimpse who I really was and who I wasn't. And, simply, I could now see that I was a human being. No more and no less, a human being, and God was the Supreme Being, so when we were together we were Being.

That evening when I got home, I found that Raul's older sister Marina was visiting us from Mexico. I'd always liked her and I guessed my dad and mom had a talk with her, telling her I spent all my time either locked up in my room or out in the hills shooting, and they didn't know what to do with me. Because the moment I came in, Marina asked if we could talk.

"Sure," I said.

"It's cold," she said, shivering. "Could we go to the living room and you build a fire for us? I guess I've become accustomed to the warmer weather in *San Miguel de Allende*," she added the town's name with a Spanish flare of pronunciation that sounded so exotic and romantic.

"Makes sense," I said.

We went to the huge living room, a room we hardly ever used. I built a little fire for us in the fireplace. Long ago I'd learned that a big fire meant white man far back and a little fire meant Indian up close. I liked little fires. You used a lot less wood, and you could get so close to a little fire that the flames became hypnotic. My dad was still in the dining room smoking his big cigar and sipping his cognac. My mother was in the kitchen. I could hear her doing the dishes. She always said that it helped her to relax to do the dishes after dinner, even though she had help to do them for her.

Marina was about eight years older than my sister Tencha, so this made her about eighteen years older than me. She was presently a reporter for the *New York Times*. When she was in high school, she'd won the Underwood Typewriter typing contest, doing well over a hundred words a minute without a single mistake, setting a national record that still holds to this day. She attributed her fast hands to her cotton-picking days as a young girl in Scottsdale, Arizona.

Marina toured the country for Underwood and was given a full scholarship to the University of California at Berkeley—the first *Latina* ever to have such a scholarship, and she'd graduated with honors. For half an hour she told me all about herself and how difficult it had been for her, as a woman and a *mexicana* on top of that, in the United States.

"Living in *México* helps me tremendously," she said. "I couldn't live in New York. I would lose my soul in no time at all. Go to *México*," she said to me, "and find your soul!"

I nodded, not quite knowing what to say. "My parents have talked with you, haven't they?" I finally said.

"Yes, of course. Why shouldn't they? They're very concerned about you. First, you quit high school, and now you don't want to go to college anymore, and you spend all your time in your room or on horseback, riding and shooting. You don't even go out with your friends anymore. This isn't normal. You're a young man. You should be going out with girls and with your friends."

"*Marina*," I said, "I don't know how to explain this, but . . . well, everything I say or do or even think just doesn't seem to work out for me. Except when I'm totally alone." I almost added, "Totally alone with God," but I didn't, because I knew how crazy*loco* this might sound, especially since I wasn't a priest or a monk.

"When did this start happening? I've always seen you as a very capable person with horses and tractors and all those manly things."

"Yes, I do seem to do pretty well on the ranch, but somehow, when I go off the ranch, everything I do just, well, turns to . . . to shit," I said. "Take for instance the Chevy truck my dad got me. I loved it. It was turquoise, my favorite color, but my friends ridiculed it so much, telling me I should have gotten a real color, like black or red or forest green, that . . . "

"Now that's exactly why you need to go to *México!*" she said full of excitement. "Everyone loves turquoise in *México!*"

"What?"

"Of course. Don't you understand that when the Europeans came to the Americas, they came—not just to conquer—but to force their ideas and beliefs on all they came in contact with. This is a German-English-based country, and at one time it looked as if we were going to have German as our national language instead of English."

"Really?"

"Most people would disagree with me, but I can make a good case for what I say. And wherever the English or Germans go, they obliterate the indigenous people. In Latin America, where the Spanish and Portuguese went, *los indios* became part of mainstream society, but, of course, only up to a point. So go to *México, Mundo,*" she said, calling me by my nickname. "Visit the museums, see the art, hear the music, and find people who'd love to have a turquoise truck, too!"

I couldn't stop smiling. Now she was telling me I came from strong stock, that my parents were her greatest heroes, next to her own mother, so I should be able to do something very important with my life, and not just be locking myself in my room and going up into the hills riding and shooting.

I took a big breath and part of me could kind of agree with what she was saying, but I also felt like I should explain to her that I couldn't read. But I didn't. In fact, the closest I came to saying this was when I told her that I was a slow reader.

Still, she insisted I go to Mexico and attend the University of the Americas in Mexico City. It was a private school, and they could give me special help with my reading. Finally, I agreed to give education one more try, but this would definitely be the last time. Every time I got near books, I just seemed to get splitting headaches and feel more confused than I'd felt before.

The night before I left for Mexico City, my dad took me aside.

"*Mijito,*" he said, "I want you to know that México is a very different place than the United States. Things are going to happen to you in *México* that haven't happened to you in the States. And in Mexico City, which is a huge city, you will come across situations you wouldn't come across in the smaller towns of *México* or out in the country. Because in big cities all over the world, it's dog eat cat, and there are a lot of people who will try to take advantage of you. In fact, in Mexico City you will be walking down the street and a man will come up to you acting like he knows you, talking with great charm and a happy smile. He will say he has a deal for you and will open up his coat, which is lined with wristwatches. He will tell you to pick one out, that they are a bargain at two or three dollars.

"And the watches will look good and shiny and new," continued my dad. "But you must keep walking, *mijito,* and not stop even for a second. Because it will be late at night when this happens and there will be no one around. This man with the watches will look small and not too strong or dangerous, but as soon as you take a better look at the watches, another man, bigger and stronger, will come out from behind the shadows and hit you across the head. And the guy with the watches will then take out his knife and they will rob you and maybe even kill you."

"But *papá,*" I said, grinning, "how can you know this?"

"DON'T 'BUT *PAPÁ*' ME and grin!" he roared in a sudden bellowing voice. "I've told you a thousand times, there are no 'buts,' only assholes! So you listen good, because . . . this is going to happen! Do you understand?! It happens everywhere in every big city! Then, also, once you've been there a few weeks and people know you have money, two *americanos* will invite you to a nice little private poker game. Do not go. It is a setup. Even the fight at the end of the night and the chips being knocked all over the place in case you are winning, was all planned out," he added. "And that guy that steals the money and runs off, he's part of it, too. Get it? I know what I'm talking about. Just like you've learned about horses and know how to size up a good horseman just by the way he sits in the saddle, I know the ways of the underworld. *Capiche?*"

Suddenly I remembered . . . why my dad always used this Italian word "capiche" instead of the word "*entiendes*" in Spanish to ask if I understood. My dad knew the underworld. For the Chinese he'd smuggled doctors and teachers, professionals from China, into the United States, people that the American Chinese community was willing to pay top dollar for. And my dad had also done the jobs for the Italians that nobody else was willing to touch or didn't have the connections to get them done. He'd explained to me that he was perfect for these delicate jobs, because being a Mexican, he'd been able to filter into key positions in American life as a gardener, a plumber, a garbage man, and nobody ever noticed him until it was too late and the job was done. Being an underrated nobody was power, he'd told me time and again.

Well, I really didn't *capiche,* but I said nothing and the next day my parents drove me across the border to Tijuana with my two little sisters to put me on a plane. My mother gave me a hand-embroidered handkerchief.

"Always remember, *mijito,* that a gentleman carries a handkerchief and doesn't—"

"And doesn't wipe his nose on his shirtsleeve. *Lo cortés* doesn't take away from bravery and bravery doesn't take away from good manners."

"Exactly."

"And *mijito,*" said my dad, "about that guy with the watches and those two *americanos* with the poker game, it was *mi mamá* who came to me in my sleep and told me to tell you these things. Always trust your heart and listen to your dreams. It is in our sleep that we humans are able to hear from our ancestry on the other side speaking to us," he added.

"Your father is right," said my mother. "Over and over it was my mother's dreams that gave us the faith and wisdom with which to keep going in the face of disaster."

"Okay, okay," I said to my parents, "you've both told this a hundred times."

"Only a hundred," said my dad, laughing. "Well, then, *querida,* we've got about nine hundred more times to tell this son of ours."

"Yeah, that's what I'm afraid of," I said, smiling.

I hugged and kissed my sisters Linda and Teresita, said goodbye, then I turned going through customs. I'd only been in a big plane once before in my life. The takeoff was scary and yet a powerful, wonderful sensation. I truly enjoyed it. Looking out my window, I wondered why the wings of the plane didn't rip off, the pressure was so tremendous.

The stewardess offered us free drinks. I accepted a *margarita*, thinking of my dad's mother, *Doña Margarita*, who'd come to talk to him about me in his dreams. I made a toast to my *mamagrande*. The drink tasted so innocent, and yet my head immediately started to spin; the roar of the plane's engines numbed me to the bone. I had three more *margaritas*, and a nothing-*nada* airplane dinner. I was starving by the time we landed in Mexico City, and I wanted a good dinner of *mole* or *carnitas con nopalitos en salsa colorada*.

I got my luggage and took a taxi from the airport to the hotel on Reforma Boulevard that *Marina* had suggested. The restaurant in the hotel was closed, but I was told there was a good place across the street that stayed open 24 hours a day. I was just crossing the wide boulevard when a man came rushing up to me with a long coat and opened it to show me hundreds of watches.

I almost laughed. This was so weird. And it was late at night, too, and there were no people on the street just as my dad had told me that his mother had told him to tell me.

"Only three dollars for any watch you want," he said to me in a very broken English.

I couldn't believe it, he was also thin and small like my dad had said.

"No, *gracias,*" I said in Spanish.

"Oh," he said, "you speak Spanish, then only two dollars for you, *amigo.* Here, take a good look," he added with a big charming smile.

Suddenly, I remembered my dad's whole message, and my heart started pounding. I could already feel-hear silent footsteps rushing up behind me. I whirled about. And there was that bigger, stronger guy.

"NO, THANKS!" I shouted, but in English this time, and I quickly took off, going through the traffic to Sanborn's, the all-night restaurant where a few people were standing outside. I couldn't believe it. My dad had been absolutely right. But how could he have known all this? Had his mother really come to him in his dreams and told him?

"Yes," said a voice deep inside of me. "And *Marina* was a godsend and *Raul* was a godsend and *Magdalena* was a godsend, too."

"Then everything is a godsend?" I asked.

"Yes, once we open our hearts and see and hear with our souls."

Inside Sanborn's, the talking stopped. The place was big and brightly lit and ultramodern looking. It felt like I'd returned to the United States. I walked past the magazine racks and knickknack glass counters with jewelry and fancy perfume bottles to the restaurant. An extremely beautiful young Mexican woman escorted me to a table and handed me a menu. I was glad to see they had some Mexican food on the menu and it wasn't all just American food. I ordered *tortilla* soup and had a *flan* for dessert. It felt so relaxing to hear everyone speaking Spanish and no one yelling "English only!"

I wondered why the voice inside me had stopped so abruptly when I'd walked into the place. Was it the bright lights that had stopped the voice or . . . or had I just gotten too distracted to hear anymore? A chill snaked up my spine. There was truly a very fine line between being with your angel and . . . and just being crazy*loco.*

I took a big deep breath. The *tortilla* soup arrived and it was delicious. Immediately I began to feel better. Maybe I'd just been hungry. I put my spoon down, didn't make the sign of the cross over myself, put my hands together, and began to pray, giving thanks. Instantly I began to feel a whole lot better. This was good. I'd left the Church, but this didn't mean that I couldn't keep on praying and giving thanks to the Almighty.

# CHAPTER TWENTY-EIGHT

It was expensive, but for the next five days I stayed across the street from Sanborn's in the beautiful rustic old hotel. The manager knew Marina very well and told me how to get around the city by bus. I'd never been on a city bus before. Oceanside was so small that I walked or biked or drove everywhere.

I took the bus out to the University of the Americas to register. It was fun. It was a real adventure getting packed in with so many people. My grades from the University of San Diego looked pretty damn good. When I was on the plane, I'd looked at my transcript, and after my third *margarita*, I'd gotten this wild idea. I decided to doctor my grades a little. My one F became an A, my two D's became B's, and dumbbell English—which I'd taken for two semesters and was never able to pass—I changed from "incomplete" to "complete."

I signed up for only three courses. One in Philosophy of Reason, one in the History of Mexico, and another one called Art Appreciation. I wasn't going to get cocky like I'd been in my second semester at San Diego when I took so many courses that I flunked out.

I walked the streets of Mexico City every afternoon after class, and everywhere I went, people spoke Spanish. It felt so good to hear the language my mother had sung to me when I was a child and she put me to bed. And I saw turquoise everywhere. On the buildings around the windows and doors and in people's clothing, especially the Indians from Oaxaca, where my grandmother Doña Margarita had been born.

Then one day I saw a huge semitruck painted completely turquoise. I yelled at the trucker, pumping my fist for him to blow his horn. He did, and his horn played the tune of *La Cucaracha*. I almost died laughing. Marina had been right. I was finding my soul in *México*, and my soul's color was turquoise, a healing color, as I found out from a street vendor. This was why people wore turquoise jewelry around their necks and wrists and ears, to bring in the healing spirits of the sea and the sky.

Everyone in *México* was an artist, and everything was a piece of art. The way the people laid out their mangoes on a stick in the street was art. The way the Indians from *Oaxaca* laid out their blankets and jewelry on the sidewalk was art. I went to the museums in downtown *Zócalo*. I saw the paintings of *Diego Riviera* and *Orozco* and *Tamayo*. I was stunned. I sat for an hour before the painting of a short little black dog howling to the full moon, done by *Tamayo*.

For the first time in my life, I was able to relax enough to slow down and just sit and drink in all the beauty I saw around me. And in the parks I watched mothers nurse their babies and young couples stroll by together, hand in hand. And no matter how much I walked and searched, I couldn't find any stupid, chile-belly, illegal greaser Mexicans. Everywhere I went, I just saw people. Old people. Young people. Fat people. Skinny people. Poor people. Rich people. Mexicans were just normal everyday human people like everyone else.

Tears came to my eyes. I'd never truly understood how much I'd been brainwashed back home in the United States. I could now see clearly how the structure of a society completely dominated the way we viewed the world. No wonder there were wars. Each nation brainwashed its own: politically, religiously, and socially. Little Richard hadn't really been out to get me when he'd laughed at my turquoise Chevy truck. He'd just been expressing what he'd been raised to think, and he'd thought that turquoise was ridiculous.

On Sunday, I listened to classical music in the park. I'd never realized that classical music could massage the brain and actually dissolve the knots of anger I'd been carrying inside my gut ever since I started school and was humiliated for not speaking English. In fact, I'd never really realized how much my stomach had been hurting all of these years, until now . . . that I was in *México* and the knots started dissolving.

One afternoon, some little kids came up to me and asked me what part of the United States I was from. I was shocked. I asked them in Spanish why they thought I was from the United States. They laughed and said it was because I walked funny and dressed funny and spoke Spanish in a funny way, too. I felt crushed. And here I thought I'd finally found my home, fitting in without being different.

One evening I found a towering glass structure, taller than any building in downtown San Diego. It was beautiful! There was a cocktail lounge on the top floor. From up here I could look out on the whole city. But not all of Mexico City was lit up like San Diego. There were whole sections without electricity. I asked the guy sitting next to me if he knew who'd built the skyscraper. He told me that Mexicans had built it.

"Yes, of course, the workers," I said, "but who were the brains, the architects responsible for the design? Americans, right?"

"No, *un mexicano,*" he said in Spanish. "He's world famous. In fact, he does work in the United States and in Germany."

I couldn't believe what came out of my mouth next. "Really," I said, "a Mexican can do this?"

In that split-second, I suddenly understood how prejudiced and truly brainwashed I was about my own people. No wonder those kids had asked me what part of the United States I came from. They'd seen right through me.

At the university, I was told I could rent a room in a house where two other students were staying with the family of one of our professors, a woman from Spain. I moved in the next day.

It was lust at first sight. The professor's oldest daughter was visiting from Venezuela. She had two children, was in her late twenties, and was drop-dead gorgeous. When we glanced at each other, our eyes would immediately start dancing. But I kept away from her, because I understood she was married, even though her husband had left her.

There was only one bathroom on the side of the house I shared with the two other students. Every afternoon when I got back from school, I'd quickly shower before the others arrived so I could go out to walk the streets. As always, nobody was home this afternoon and the door to the bathroom was partly open, so I walked in to take my shower, and there she was, getting out of the tub.

I froze. She was naked, and her bush was the darkest and fullest I'd ever seen. She covered herself with her towel and walked around me, but she didn't leave the room. She closed the door and locked it. She never said a word and took me in her arms. I'd never smelled a freshly bathed woman. We fell together to the floor, and she was as hungry as a wild mare in heat. We tried to keep quiet and not scream out, in case someone else came home.

After that, we couldn't keep our hands off each other and every time she was as wet and hot and hungry as our first time. I'd never realized women loved sex just as much as men. And her bush was beautiful. I kissed and licked and tasted every hair and . . . and those large full lips of her Red Sea. But then one night her husband from Venezuela showed up. He was really handsome and well-built, and he'd come to take her back home with him.

That night when we, the three students, and the family had our dinner together, he kept looking at me across the table as if he could sense something had happened between his wife and me. He kissed her, acting as if they were newlyweds, then he'd smile at me like letting me know she belonged to him once again. Maybe I had lust for his wife, but it was all over now, because he, the great husband-lover, was back. But she, on the other hand, kept giving me little suggestive glances when he wasn't looking. That night, my roommates and I could hear them going at it, with the headboard of their bed beat, beat, beating against the wall so hard and for so long that we feared the house would cave in. Then I heard her screams, those wonderful screams that we had never allowed ourselves to have when we'd been together.

I had to move. I just couldn't get her out of my mind, and we could never be together again. I found a pair of her panties that I was sure she'd left behind for me in the bathroom. I slept with them every night, smelling of them and dreaming of her. But now she was sleeping with her husband on the other side of the wall.

Two days later I met a big rugged-looking guy named Jack Gulliver at the university. He was from Massachusetts. He told me that he had been going to Princeton, an Ivy League university on the east coast, before coming to Mexico. It turned out he and his two roommates were looking for a fourth guy so they could afford their big

fancy place in the *La Zona Rosa* district. He was in my Art Appreciation class. That same afternoon he drove me over to see their place
in his sleek, black convertible. I told him about my T-bird. He suggested I fly home for the weekend and drive my car down.

"It's only about 2,000 miles," he said, "you can probably do it
over the weekend."

"Over the weekend!" I was surprised. "But I was told," I said to
him, "that you can't drive at night in Mexico because of all the *bu-
rros* and cattle on the roads. So the most a person can hope to drive
is four or five hundred miles in a day."

"Well, you might be right," he said, "but I drove all the way
down from Massachusetts with my mother in three days, and we
drove late into the night each day."

He also told me he'd been a wrestler in high school, and his
younger brother, whom he said looked a lot like me, had been a state
champion. We became fast friends, and everywhere we went people
would stare at Jack because he looked a lot like Clark Gable, except
younger and taller and better-looking despite his thinning black hair,
even though he was only twenty-three years old. One of his roommates was from Canada, the other from Idaho. They told me that
what they all had in common was that they'd decided to get away
from the cold country and do their studying where it was warm all
year around. They all agreed with our history professor that the war-
like Aztecs had been geniuses to fight their way down out of the cold
country of the U. S. and settle in Mexico City, the world's Garden of
Eden, where it only rained for an hour a day in the rainy season and
never got too hot or too cold and had no mosquitoes, like the coast-
lines of Mexico.

Jack and his two roommates liked me, and I liked them, so they
accepted me as a roommate. The guy from Canada said that his dad
was a fight promoter, and so he knew a lot of famous world-class
boxers. The guy from Idaho said his dad was a contractor, and he'd
built Hemingway's house in Ketchum, Idaho. I asked who Hemingway was, and they all laughed and thought I had a great sense of
humor. They started calling me the writer, but I had no idea why.

A couple of days later I was feeling pretty damn good, and I
stepped into the elevator of our apartment building to go up to our

floor when a slender, older woman came rushing around the corner with her arms full of grocery bags.

"Please hold these for me," she said, handing me her two bags. "I still have my basket just around the corner! Don't go! Hold the elevator!"

She was all out of breath when she came running back with a large basket. In Mexico, the markets didn't give out paper bags. Everyone took their own bags and baskets to do their shopping. She was a brunette and very slender and delicate-looking, with large dark eyes. She had an Audrey Hepburn kind of elegance, and yet she also looked like a doe who'd been caught in the middle of the road in the headlights of an oncoming semitruck.

"Thanks," she said with a great big happy smile. "You do speak English, don't you?"

"Yes, I do," I said.

"Oh, good! My Spanish isn't that good yet, but I am working on it. By the year 2000, I should be bilingual, I'm sure."

She laughed uproariously, then pushed the button to the fourth floor. I guess because it was 1960 and the year 2000 was still far off, she thought this was really funny. Or maybe she was just nervous.

"What floor do you live on?" she asked.

"The fifth."

"Oh, that's where they have all those wild parties, isn't it?"

"I don't know. I just moved in."

When we reached the fourth floor, I helped her with her bags of groceries. She carried the basket. Her place was small with lots of plants and books and large colorful pillows on the floor.

"Would you like a cup of tea, neighbor?" she said.

"No, not really, but I would like to look out your window," I answered.

"Sure. That's why I took this place. I fell in love with that view the first day I came here," she said, putting on water for tea. "The fourth floor puts you right at treetop level; and you can enjoy the birds and the occasional flock of afternoon parrots. They're wild here, you know. Coming from La Jolla, I never thought I'd ever find a more beautiful place to live. My kids and I just love it here."

"You mean you're from La Jolla, just north of San Diego?"

"Yes! How'd you know that? Where are you from? I assumed you were from here. You are Mexican, are you not?"

I almost laughed. The Mexicans thought that I was an American and the Americans thought that I was a Mexican. "Both my parents are from Mexico," I said, "but I was born in the U. S. In fact, just north of you in Carlsbad."

"Really?"

"Yes, really."

"Then we're also neighbors back home. Are you sure you don't want some tea?"

"Well, okay," I said, finally coming away from the window. She was in the kitchen, putting things away, and I could see that she was very attractive in a skinny kind of way. "How old are you?" I asked.

"Gulp!" she said, surprised, and yet not really too offended. "Is it my late afternoon wrinkles showing that caused you to ask such a question? Or is it your nature to be this blunt and you really want to know? And if you do, then why?" she said, smiling. "Twenty-nine, I am," she added. "How old are you?"

"I'm nineteen."

"I must look like a very old lady to you," she said, laughing.

There was a knock at the door.

"Would you get that?" she said.

I went to the door and opened it. A little red-haired girl and an even smaller red-haired boy stood there. They both had freckles and big brownish-red eyes. They looked like dolls, they were so cute.

"Who are you?" asked the girl as she entered with a bookbag over her shoulder. She had the same wonderful voice inflection as her mother. "I'm Lauren and this is my brother Peter."

"I'm your neighbor, Victor, from upstairs," I said. "I helped . . . I guess, your mother with her groceries."

"Oh, good! We have food!" said Lauren to her brother.

They both rushed past me to the kitchen. They quickly hugged and kissed their mother, tore off their packs, went to the table, and began to eat.

"Well, I'll be going," I said.

"Oh, let me see you out," said the mother. At the door she added, "My name is Eve."

"Really."

"Yes. And yours is Victor, I heard you tell my children. Well, very glad to meet you, Victor. Do you still live in Carlsbad?"

"No, but almost. Our home is in South Oceanside, just a couple of miles north of where I was born."

"Really, in Oceanside. Near the beach?"

"Yes, I was raised on a ranch by the beach."

"A ranch on the beach? You mean with horses and cattle and all that?"

I nodded. "Yes, and big orchards of lemons, oranges, and avocados."

"Do you hear that, children?"

"Yes," Lauren said. "Do you have goats?" she asked.

"Yes, we do."

"Could we pet them?"

I laughed. "Yes, of course."

"Do you have rabbits?" Peter asked.

"Absolutely," I said.

"I like rabbits," said Peter. "I was once given one for Easter, but it died."

"Ours don't die," I said. "In fact, they have babies. Baby goats and baby rabbits are some of the cutest of all our animals."

Lauren and Peter screeched with joy.

"Well, you've obviously made a big hit with my kids. Tonight, a girlfriend and I are going to hear some music after I put the children to bed. Would you like to join us? It will be about nine."

I didn't really know what to say. Nine was pretty late for me. That meant they probably wouldn't get back until way past midnight. But what the hell, there was something about the tone of Eve's voice and her inflection of each word that was so captivating. And her daughter Lauren had that same beautiful inflection in her voice. It sounded slightly British.

"Did you ever live in England?" I asked.

"Yes, that, and half the rest of the world."

"Why?" I asked. I was curious, since for me, Mexico City was one of the first times I had ever been out of San Diego County.

"My father was in the military attached to Army intelligence, so we traveled the world."

"Oh, was he an officer?"

"He could have been. He was offered that many times. But he preferred to remain an enlisted man so he could be attached to the Chief of Staff, but not put up with all the nuisance of being an officer."

"I don't understand."

"He was the real brains behind what the generals said to the public," she said.

"Oh."

"But all that is in the past. How about now? Would you like to join us?" she asked again. "My friend is younger than me. It really won't be like going out with two old ladies," she added, laughing good-heartedly.

I laughed, too. "But I don't have a car here."

"I don't either," she said, pronouncing the word "either" with a long "i" sound at the beginning. "We'll take a cab. Cabs are so cheap, and they don't get lost. My husband was always getting lost after we crossed the border. But he refused to ask for directions, even though he knows Spanish quite well. Are you afraid of asking for directions?"

"No. Why?"

"Because, my dear, most men are, you know."

"Afraid to ask for directions?"

"Of course. One of the main differences between men and women is that women don't feel it's a threat to their ego to admit they don't know something. So they ask. You didn't know that?"

"No, I guess I didn't."

"Very interesting. You feel comfortable asking a woman past her teens her age, and you don't feel threatened asking directions. Please, do come with us tonight. I think you'll enjoy it."

"Okay," I said. "See you at nine. But one more thing."

"Yes?"

"If your husband came down with you, does this mean that he's still down here and . . . and does this mean that you're still married?"

I was beginning to like her, so I wanted to get this straight from the start. I didn't want to end up with the situation I had with the professor's daughter. She'd told me she loved me the very same afternoon her husband showed up. And I think I had, well, started falling in love with her, too. Sex, I was beginning to understand, was so good, so fantastic, that it changed people.

"Yes, he is still down here, and yes, I am still legally married. But we are separated and completing our divorce."

"I see," I said. "And, also, since he was always getting lost, does this mean that you two came down in a vehicle?"

"Yes, we did."

"How long did it take you to drive down from San Diego?"

"Almost a month."

"A month?"

"Yes, like I said, we kept getting lost, and he refused to ask for directions. Then we camped for a week south of—I think you call it *Mazatlán*. We got sick, but my kids didn't. They loved it and would have loved to stay there on the beach for the rest of their lives. By the time we got here to Mexico City, I didn't want to be with him anymore. He was scared of everyone and everything and just kept calling his dad and mom to send him more money. And they did. It was tragic. We were on our honeymoon. We'd just gotten married. Now he's living with a *torero* and has decided to become a bullfighter. It's the Hemingway thing to do, you know, when you're not sure of your manhood."

"Who is this Hemingway?" I asked. "My roommates also mentioned him."

"You don't know who Hemingway is?" she said, her eyes getting large.

"No, I don't. Is he a local bullfighter?"

"Oh, my, you really do not know. This is wonderful! He is a world famous writer, who a whole generation of want-to-be *macho* men have adopted him as their hero."

"Oh," I said, "I didn't know. See you at nine. Bye now."

"*Vaya con Dios,*" she said in Spanish.

Her pronunciation was terrible, but I appreciated her attempt.

# CHAPTER TWENTY-NINE

I went to the gym with Jack. We worked out, showered, had a bite to eat at the snack bar in the gym, then I left while Jack stayed behind, letting the girls go goggle-eyed over his body and great looks. I went back to our place to get dressed. I was the first guy I knew to wear Levis with a navy-blue blazer. I also wore cowboy boots and a beautiful good-feeling white shirt. Mexico City was at 7,000 feet above sea level, so it got cool enough in the evenings to wear a jacket.

I took the stairs down to the fourth floor and knocked on Eve's door. She answered immediately. She looked stunning. She was no longer a deer out in mid-road, startled by oncoming headlights. She looked relaxed, comfortable, and extremely elegant. She gave a couple of last minute instructions to her babysitter, a young Mexican girl, using the worst and yet most charming Spanish I'd ever heard. Her children seemed to be accustomed to being left alone with a sitter at night. I guessed that they were about eleven and nine, but Lauren seemed much older.

We caught a cab outside on the street and went to her friend's place, a very plush-looking apartment building with a uniformed doorman at the entrance. We buzzed the apartment, and her friend's voice filled the speaker box, telling Eve to come up, that she was almost ready. The elevator was smaller than ours, but much fancier. We got out on the seventh floor and went down a long hallway. The next to last door was partially open.

"Doris?" called Eve.

"Come right in! I left the door open for you!"

We walked in, and there, in mid-room with two glasses of white wine in hand, stood a naked woman. I couldn't take my eyes off her.

Doris was blonde, head and bush, and had the most well-developed shoulders and . . . and calves I'd ever seen on a woman. And her thighs were magnificent, too.

"Oh, you didn't say you had company with you," said Doris, not knowing what to do with her nakedness, but only for a split-second. Then she came right to us and handed us each a glass of golden white wine. "Here," she said, "you two have these while I get some clothes on."

"I'm sorry," said Eve, taking one glass. "I assumed you'd be dressed. I'm really very sorry."

"It's okay," said Doris. "I mean, if your friend isn't too—"

"Victor," I said.

"If you're not offended, Victor."

"Oh, no. Believe me, oh, no." I took a deep breath. "You must be a dancer or an Olympic-class sprinter, to have calves as developed as yours."

"Oh, my, you are special, aren't you? To have noticed that, of all things."

"He is. He doesn't know who Hemingway is," said Eve. "And right off the bat he asked me how old I was, without any malice intended."

"Really?"

"Yes."

Doris took another good look at me. "You do sports yourself, don't you?"

"I'm a wrestler."

"I danced for the New York—but, well, that was a long time ago, and yes, I was also a track star, but never quite at an Olympic level. Well, well," she added, taking a deep breath, "I'll put on some music for you two while I get dressed."

She crossed the large spacious room and bent over to put on a record. I had never in my life seen a bush of golden hair rise up between two long legs surrounded by a heart-shaped butt with a little space between the thighs, then held there, like a human sculpture, as she fiddled with the dials and the record. My heart soared! The absolute beauty of naked women was astonishing!

Doris dressed quickly, and we took another cab to the artsy part of the *Zona Rosa* district, where there were little restaurants and art galleries and a few small crowded nightclubs. But these weren't strip joints. They were classy-looking places.

The lights were low, and we were given a small white linen-covered table not too far from the musicians. There were about thirty of us in the club. Quite a few people seemed to know Doris and Eve. I heard the word jazz used a couple of times, and there were two black guys, one white guy, and a Mexican-looking guy playing. No one sang. They just played instruments. At first I didn't get it, but then I closed my eyes and began to feel the music more than hear it, and it was really wonderful.

We had a round of drinks, and the music seemed to go deeper and deeper into me. The horn began to sound like a lone coyote calling to the full moon. A tickling sensation began to snake down my spine. I'd never experienced anything like this in all of my life. When the break came, I walked up to the two black guys and asked them what part of the United States they were from.

*"No hablamos inglés,"* said one of the black guys. "We don't speak English."

I got confused. "But aren't you two guys black?" I asked.

"No," one answered in Spanish. "I'm *cubano y mi amigo* is from *Panamá.*"

I nodded. My head was swimming with music and alcohol. "Oh, I thought you were black," I heard myself say.

I went over to the blonde guy and asked him in English what part of the United States he was from.

"I don't speak English," he also said in Spanish.

"But aren't you white?" I heard myself say. My whole head was turning and swirling.

"No, I'm Mexican," he said. *"¡puro mexicano!"* he added with real *gusto.*

"Well, then, how in the hell did you get so blonde?" I asked.

"I'm of German ancestry," he said, "but we've been in Mexico for five generations, so I'm *un mexicano a puro dar*! We're all *Latinos* here. *Puros hermanos* jazzing together! What is it with you, eh? You got a problem?!!"

I took a step back. He was right. I did have a problem. I . . . I . . . I was racist. I'd become that which I'd hated all my life. These guys didn't see themselves as Black and White and Brown as I did. They simply saw themselves as Latinos, as *cubanos* and *panameños* and *mexicanos*, and . . . and as brothers.

I gripped my head. My mind was reeling. I decided to go outside to get some fresh air. The air was crisp and clean. I took a big deep breath. Then it hit me like a sledge hammer between the eyes. Then words weren't reality. They were "labels" that were placed on reality.

I began to shiver, this thought WAS SO GREAT! Then words were like maps, and a map could tell us about a state or nation, but a map wasn't that state or nation any more than words were the person or place we were referring to.

I mean, I could get a map that laid out the freeway systems of California, the towns and cities, and I could get another map that laid out the rivers and mountain ranges, the valleys, the different types of vegetation at different elevations, and yet all this information would still never give me the reality of California.

I could get ten different maps of California, brilliant maps, and they still wouldn't be worth beans compared to the actual experience of getting up before dawn and going up a draw on horseback and feeling the delicious air currents as I climbed, smelling the brush and dampness of the coming day, then up ahead hearing a little stud quail calling to his covey as dawn broke all about me.

Words were empty! Empty! EMPTY!

Words were HOLLOW, and yet it was through these hollow labels called words that I viewed the whole world. I called a person Black, and I assumed that . . . that I knew everything about that individual. I call a person a Protestant, a Catholic, a Jew, a Republican, a Democrat, a homosexual, and I immediately assumed that I knew everything about them, too.

I suddenly understood with utter clarity that I saw no one or anything, because all I saw, I saw through a filter of words.

My eyes filled with tears. I was one great big *PENDEJO*! No wonder I'd locked myself in my room after that miracle of the belt buckle. I hadn't wanted to talk to anyone or . . . or to put into words what had happened to me. It was too precious, and to talk about it, to put it into words would have destroyed it.

I could now see that we, humans, destroyed all we touched because we attached words to . . . to everything, even to God.

I held, and my whole body began to tremble.

"Oh, my God," I said aloud, "that's how we destroyed You. We attached a label to You, and then we backed up that label by using words of description to define You, to limit You, to . . . oh, my dear Lord God, forgive me," I said. "Please FORGIVE US ALL! We humans destroyed You, my Lord, by squeezing every ounce of joy and love out of You, and imprisoning ourselves in our heads. This is what words do. They put us in our heads, just as Major Terry was trapped in his brain when he'd played chess. He couldn't see beyond one or two moves."

The tears were streaming down my face. "My dear Lord, never again will I imprison You with words. No wonder my dad always said that his beloved mother so wisely always called You her Everything. Because that's Who You are . . . our EVERYTHING!" I wiped the tears from my eyes with the tips of my fingers. "I can now see that You, God, are more like the Sea. The Oceans of the world. And it's us humans who put the label Pacific on You, Atlantic, Sea of Cortez, Gulf of this and that, then we say that the only way for anyone to know You is through the label we placed on You. We're so smart that we outsmarted ourselves with our invention of words and beliefs and principles. And why? So we'd feel more . . . more comfortable with our own fears and . . . and shortcomings."

Then it hit me like a BOMB! God Almighty had been a genius not to have given me the tools with which to learn to read. Because . . . because it was in the act of putting words into print that we then cemented these word-labels into the deepest crevices of our brain. This was why I could go where my cousin Victor feared to go. He was so well-read that words owned him, and words didn't own me.

I suddenly knew what the Bible was referring to when it said that we'd eaten of the Tree of Knowledge. Language, itself, was that Tree and the written word was the Forbidden Fruit that . . . that we ate and that caused us to lose the Garden. Yes, this was it! I saw it with UTTER CLARITY!

The jazz group had started playing once again, but I stayed outside. So then maybe this meant that prior to language, all people must have seen each other and the whole wide world in an entirely different way. No words or labels existed that entrapped the mind and separated us from . . . from our heart and soul and *Papito*. In fact, *Papito Dios* hadn't been *Papito*. She-He had been beyond all words, all description, all sexuality, all boundaries and man-made limitations. She-He had been the soup, the SEA-SOUP BETWEEN ALL ELEMENTS! God was the Attraction, the Force, the Power, the . . . the . . .

Then I saw it. I mean, I heard it. They were playing jazz together once more. Brothers. *Amigos.* Without boundaries or limitations and I saw-heard it so clearly. The Holy Creator had been jazzing, making music when She-He had Created the Universe.

I don't know when Eve came outside. All I know was that my eyes were pouring like rivers, and yet I wasn't crying. No, I was soup-seaing. I was jazzing with the Holy Creator and Everything was Alive and Holy all around the two of us like when I played chess. It was all those heat waves of our blacktop road of words that had entrapped me in my brain.

Eve was talking to me, but I couldn't hear her.

Eve was saying something, but I didn't understand what she said.

"Are you okay?" I finally heard her say.

I smiled. "I've never felt better in all of my life," I said, with the tears still running down my face.

"Oh, you're crying," she said. "How beautiful! You're not afraid to show emotion."

She took me in her arms and held me close. It felt so good and warm and safe. I dried my eyes and tried to tell her how this jazz music had touched me, especially the horn. Then I explained to her what had happened to me when I'd gone up to the musicians and spoken to them in English, assuming that they were from the States. I told her that for the first time in my life, I could clearly see that I'd become that which I'd hated all my life—racist—and I'd also seen that words weren't reality. Words were labels placed on reality and that they basically worked like a map.

"So now I can see," I said to her, "that in reality I see no one or anything, because I view the whole wide world through such a thick filter of words that . . . that I'm blind."

"It sounds like you had an epiphany," she said.

"I had a what?"

"An epiphany, e-p-i-p-h-a-n-y," she spelled out the word for me with a great big happy smile. "It means an appearance or manifestation of God or other supernatural beings. Historically, in most Christian churches, it was seen as the yearly festival in January, commemorative of the revealing of Jesus as the Christ of Bethlehem to the Gentiles. But now it is mostly seen as the light or . . . or the appearance of God that many saints say they experience."

"Wow, that's quite a word, epitahmee."

"No, epi-fanee," she said without malice or a condescending tone.

"Okay, thank you. I got it. Because that's exactly what happened to me. God appeared to me in a whole new way, beyond all words, which I can now see are just labels, but we take them so seriously that they imprison our minds, and God can best be realized through music, through the . . . the feeling that we get through music." I held, not breathing. "I'd never heard jazz and . . . and those guys opened me up, here in my heart." I began to breathe again.

"Look," I said, taking out the hand-embroidered handkerchief my mother had given me and wiping the tears from my eyes. "I can now see that we never lost the Garden of Eden. It's here all around us. Every child still comes into the Garden at birth, but . . . but then when that child grows up a little and begins to learn language, one day he or she will run up to her mother or father saying, 'Come, look! It's an angel! It's a dancing flower! And it loves me! Hurry, come and look!' And that father or mother, who's tired and feeling half sick doing their taxes, doesn't want to go, but does and sees and says, 'Oh, that's nothing! It's just a butterfly!' then he or she goes back inside to finish their work.

"That child is left all alone outside and feels so crushed inside that after that this child will also say, 'Oh, yeah, nothing. Just a butterfly!' That child will never again see with eyes of wonderment and magic, but instead will always see with eyes of annoyance and belittlement. Am I making sense? I was raised by my grandmother in the *barrio* in her little shack behind our house by the alley, and she taught me to see everything as full of magic and a gift from God. Together we'd see angels in our garden helping the corn grow. Together we'd see angels coming down in each raindrop from the heavens. Butterflies were dancing angels. Frogs were miracles of transformation. And those guys with their music took me back to those days with my *mamagrande* opening up my eyes like I was a child once again. Am I making sense? I can now see that I lost my heaven on earth when I learned to speak and that music is our best chance of . . . of getting back to that opening, our doorway to EVERYTHING! And this is why my other grandmother, on my dad's side, called God her Everything! And I'd forgotten about all this. It's like it all got ripped out of me when I started school and was told 'no Spanish and English only,' and my whole entire life was robbed from me."

I had to keep using my mother's handkerchief with the little hand-embroidered green leaves and red roses to wipe the tears from my eyes. "Now that I'm in *México* and I hear Spanish everywhere, it's like I'm able to remember all these things my *mamagrande* taught me before I started school. She was my greatest teacher but she died—I mean, passed over to the Spirit World—when I was, I guess, about four and a half years old. Balance, she always told me, was our main sense, and music was our—I don't remember which sense—I think the eighth. And it was with balance and through music that . . . that we could reach God."

"Sure, of course," she said, "that makes sense, because the word 'universe' comes from the Greek and means one verse, one song, a united . . . then we're all one note within that great symphony!" she added with excitement.

"Yes!" I said. "That's it!"

"I completely agree," she said.

I continued crying. I couldn't help it. She took me in her arms and began kissing me gently, first on the eyes as the tears ran down my face, then on my cheeks. It was so beautiful. Then she began talking, too, and she explained to me that there were words of inclusion and words of exclusion and that language not only affected the way in which we thought of reality, but became our reality. Hitler, for example, had been a genius in doing this, but, of course, for evil and that the word evil was simply "live" spelled backwards and devil was "lived" spelled backwards.

I got goose pimples. I'd never seen this before. She told me that the very basis of most religions and nations was built on a dogma of exclusion, so that the leaders of different religions and/or nations could keep their subjects under control. This was, in fact, what her father—a German Jew—had done for the Joint Chiefs of Staff, that is, figure out ways of wording things so they sounded noble and wonderful and for the protection of our nation, but in reality the words were a smoke screen so that the military could do what they really wanted to do without any interference.

"Then you mean that all this isn't just a mistake?" I said.

"Of course not," she said.

"But don't they see that this is what's pitting us against each other all over the world?"

"That's the plan," she said.

"And I'd always thought that we just didn't know any better, but our hearts were in the right place."

"And they are for most individuals," she said, "but as my dad always said, the organized are for the organized."

I suddenly felt ill. I could see she was right. I'd been a complete fool to quit the Catholic Church and go off to find God, thinking that once I found Our Real God, a God of dazzling Beauty and Pure Love—like I sometimes felt here inside of my heart and soul—I'd be invited back into Catholicism with open arms and maybe even be made the Pope.

I laughed. What a ridiculous, ignorant fool I'd been. And the reason that I had always assumed that this might happen was because I'd thought that we were all in an earnest search for Truth, for God, for Meaning. It had never entered my mind that all this had been done for the benefit of the few. Then if what she said was true, in every country the church, the government, and the military were all in cahoots with one another for the sole purpose of maintaining their own power.

Tears were now streaming down her face, too. "Year after year, wherever we went, I was so proud of my father. Generals would call him at home, and they knew my first name. But then as I grew up, I began to see what my father was really doing. He was helping our military to lie, confuse, divide, and all because it had become the arm of our dollar."

My mind EXPLODED! This made perfect sense. Then this had something to do with . . . with the Federal Reserve and the people who ran those twelve banks. People like the judge who was married to that drop-dead gorgeous young woman and had terrorized her so much that she hadn't even wanted her two kids rolling down the hillside with their grandmother and having fun. No wonder I'd never found Jesus smiling in a church. Fun was dangerous. Happiness was taboo. And sex, the biggest, most fun, happy experience in life, was evil, so blame Eve, of course, and keep all the women in line.

"Excuse me," I said. "Please repeat. I'd stopped listening."

"I was saying that my father explained to me that we have become a very different nation. Before and right after World War II, we were the good guys, but then we lost our innocence. Everything became the arm of big business, which has no loyalty except to itself. My father's actions finally caught up with him. He became very disillusioned and died a broken man after years of . . . of dedication beyond the call of duty," she added, taking in a deep breath.

"My cousin Victor was with Army Intelligence, too," I said. "He told me that one day he just quit his job and walked off into the desert and almost died."

"I understand," she said. "He was young, and when he was first assigned to Army Intelligence he'd felt honored. He thought that what they were doing was the right thing, and he had a sense of self-worth. But then he began to see the cracks in the wall, and soon he saw that it was he who was fabricating these lies and half-truths, and he just couldn't do it anymore. And it's not just us. Everyone all around the globe does the same thing. That's why we think we have to be strong and ready to do it to them before they do it to us. It's our own fears that reflect back to us. Pearl Harbor and Hiroshima did this to us globally, and my father told me that it's going to get worse. We, the public, have no idea what our monetary and military leaders have mapped out for us for the next hundred years in . . . in the name of democracy and freedom."

At first I couldn't comprehend what it was that she said, but then it hit me. "Hey, I think I know what you're talking about," I said. "In kindergarten a siren would go off, scaring us kids half to death. We'd be told to hide under our desks in case we were bombed and the roof fell on us. 'Remember Pearl Harbor,' we were told. I'd have nightmares about the Communists getting us. My God, I'd forgotten all about that. We can't just keep going on like this. Something needs to be done."

"I agree, and we can't wait too much longer," she said. "So what do you suggest?"

I looked at her and took a deep breath, then blew out. "I don't know yet," I said, "but I promise you, I'm not going to stop until I figure this out, because . . . because I've got to. I really do. We've all got to. We can't just go on like this anymore, passing our fears on to the next generation." I took another deep breath. "This is why I . . . I quit the Catholic Church. I refused to live in fear of God, and I certainly won't live in fear of . . . of my fellow human beings."

"I believe you," she said.

"Believe me?"

"Yes, that you will not live in fear and that you are going to figure out what to do about this whole mess we've gotten ourselves into."

"You do? But why?" I asked.

"My father always maintained that it's not extraordinary people who accomplish extraordinary feats in life," she said. "It's ordinary people who rise up to the occasion. You don't have the vocabulary of a normal liberal do-gooder. There's just something so unique and special about you that I do believe you might be one of those rare individuals who change the course of history. My father could have done it if he hadn't been involved with . . . with all those generals. But he, too, was very young when he became involved, just like your cousin who walked off into the desert like Jesus Christ. You do know, don't you, that we all have that DNA within us?"

"DNA?"

"Yes, that same basic genetic part of us that is of Jesus and connects us to the Source."

"Source?"

"Yes, our place of origin like the starting point of a stream. A spring, a fountain from where a stream begins. And for me," she said with a great big smile, "I prefer to use the word 'Source' when making a reference to the Almighty. Because with the word Source, I feel that we're all included and moving down stream together with ease just like the children's rhyme 'Row, row, row your boat, gently down the stream, merrily, merrily, merrily life is but a dream.'"

I was laughing with *carcajadas.*

"What is it?" she said, laughing, too.

"That was the exact same thing I was thinking when you came outside."

"The children's rhyme?"

"No, about the words we use for God that destroy God. So I was thinking that 'My Everything' was a better way for us to refer to the Almighty. But now I like this word Source even better, because then I, too, feel included, plus then we are all together and moving right along, and . . . and with such ease. 'Row, row, row your boat gently down the stream.' Not upstream and 'Merrily, merrily, merrily life is but a dream.' This goes exactly with what my parents have told me all my life, that it is in our dreams that we find the wisdom and faith to keep going, especially during hard times."

I stopped and looked at her in the eyes, then took a great big deep breath. Eyes to eyes we held, not flinching, then I blew out really slowly. "Where have you been all my life," I said.

"Where have you been all of my life?" she said, laughing. "I guess you were in diapers while I was already out exploring the world."

We took a cab home, dropped her friend Doris off, went to her place, and talked until daybreak. I'd never done this with anyone in my whole life. She knew EVERYTHING! And she didn't laugh at my questions when they sounded ridiculous. No, she actually helped me clarify what I was trying to ask. Then she told me about all the problems she'd had going to school because she was a girl and so smart. A child prodigy. When she'd speak out, saying things that were different from what other people understood, even her teachers would make fun of her, because somehow they'd find out that she had one of the highest I.Q.s ever recorded, even above that of Albert Einstein.

I roared with laughter. "I had the exact same problem," I said to her, "only in reverse. I had one of the lowest I.Q.'s in my class and was called a *burro* by the kids and stupid by our teachers most of my life."

We looked at each other in the eyes, not talking anymore. And it was so beautiful. I felt like I'd somehow finally met my other half of being. We kissed, and her lips were the softest, warmest, fullest, and most gentle I'd ever kissed.

The very next day I skipped school. It was Friday, and I decided to fly home to California and get my T-bird and drive back to Mexico City. The whole wide world had burst open for me. Words, labels, these sounds with which we communicated, weren't reality. In fact, they were the *problema.* No wonder my grandmother had always told me that in the *Yaqui* language they were taught as children that there was no word for God, that any reference to the Holy Creator was so Sacred, so Holy, that it had to be hummed or said in a soft singing whisper. But this word Source I liked. It seemed to fit so gently.

"Source," I said.

"Source," I repeated.

And strangely enough I didn't feel separated or like praying when I said this word Source. No, it was like this word took me to a whole other part of my brain, and I just felt like smiling.

"Source," I said again. "Source, Source, Source," and it felt so refreshing, like a warm summer rain and/or like the beautiful good-smelling rains we got here in the Mexico City basin every afternoon like clockwork. For the first time in my life, I felt as clean and pure with the Almighty as a spring bubbling up out of Mother Earth and running downhill with ease. Oh, God felt so much friendlier and easier to get along with, with this word Source.

It was like I'd magically returned to my *mamagrande*'s garden in the *barrio* of Carlsbad, and she was rocking me on her lap under the big luscious avocado tree. Her outhouse was right next to the tree, and this was why she had the biggest, juiciest avocados in the whole barrio *de Carlos Malo.*

I laughed. I loved my grandmama, and she was right here, holding me in her big warm arms as we rocked, flowing downstream together forever and ever and ever.

# CHAPTER THIRTY

I don't know how Paul Koner . . . a guy I hardly knew . . . found out that I was going home to get my car, but he drove up in his own navy-blue T-bird just as I was catching a cab to the airport.

"I understand you're flying home to Southern California and driving back this weekend," he said. "Would you like a fellow driver? I'm a race car driver, and I know the roads. I just came down in this car last month."

I didn't get it. He was in my Art Appreciation class, but we hardly knew each other. We weren't good friends.

"Look," he said, "I need to go home to get a few things in Brentwood. I'll pay for half the gas coming back."

This made more sense. "Okay," I said, "but I'm going right now."

"Good. I'm packed."

He went over to his car, gave the keys to the beautiful woman in the passenger's seat, kissed her, grabbed a small leather bag, got in the cab with me, and we were off. On the flight to Tijuana he told me his dad was a big-time Hollywood agent-producer and how he'd grown up traveling all over the world making movies with his father. I recognized his mother's name. She was a movie star of my parents' generation, and she'd been known as the sweetheart *de México*.

"I always meet the best and finest people wherever we go," he said. "And personally I know the greatest film directors on both continents, including Fellini and Bergman."

I told him I had no idea who these guys were, but that I had heard my parents talk about his mother. Then I explained to him that I'd grown up on a ranch in North County San Diego and had never traveled until I'd come down here to Mexico City. I told him about all the racist crap that had happened to me at school, especially when I was little.

I'll never forget what he then said. "Racism is self-inflicted. My mother is Mexican, and I was never discriminated against in any school I ever attended. I think you're either exaggerating or not being very honest with yourself."

My heart LEAPED! I felt like breaking his fucking neck! He had no idea what the hell he was talking about.

"Are you telling me," I said, "that all this racist shit we have going on in the fields in the United States and in our schools against our poor recently arrived Mexicans is self-inflicted?"

He laughed. "That's not racism," he said, "that same abuse goes on right here in Mexico. The rich all over the world take advantage of the poor. Your parents obviously have money, so face it, your racism was self-inflicted."

I was speechless. That playground teacher in kindergarten hadn't cared that my parents had money. She'd slapped us, yanked us by the hair, and told us that we didn't even belong in school because we weren't evolved enough to ever learn anything and that was why we belonged in the fields. I hardly spoke to Paul for the rest of the trip. I guess that he just assumed that his privileged, rich reality was everyone else's reality.

Two days later, coming into the outskirts of Mexico City, Paul and I were almost killed when a *burro* was hit by a bus, and cars and trucks piled up all around us. We'd been going a hundred miles an hour. The only thing that saved us was that Paul was, indeed, an excellent driver. He never panicked. He just moved right and left and gave my T-bird the gas, shooting by!

When I got back to my place in the city, I immediately went to see Eve to tell her about all the music I'd been hearing in my head ever since that night of jazz. The humming behind my left ear had expanded into a whole symphony. I now knew without a shadow of a doubt how Moses had parted the Red Sea, and it sounded so easy that I was afraid to share it with anyone, except with her. But Eve couldn't listen to any of this. She was getting evicted. She couldn't afford to pay her rent because her husband was withholding her money.

"And it's my money, not his. We opened a joint account when we married, and like a fool, I put my monies in with his," she said. She'd lost all elegance. Once more she was that frightened deer out in the middle of the road. "The Mexican banks have sided with him, because he's the *hombre*. They told me he has to go to the bank with me so I can withdraw my own money. And . . . and he won't do it, because he's still pissed at me."

I went into a rage! I remembered being told how the same thing had happened to my mother when my parents had returned to Mexico right after they'd married. In Nogales, across the border from Arizona, my father sent my mother to check on a money order they were expecting from Uncle Archie. The bank teller told my mother that not in Mexico or in the great country of China did a banker discuss money matters with a woman. My father, sick in bed, exploded with rage when my mother told him this. He staggered out of bed, got his gun, and went to the bank and rammed the snub nose .38 special into the teller's face, telling him he'd spare his life this time, but to never again lose respect for a woman or he was dead meat! Laughing, my dad told me the bank teller had actually, really shit in his pants.

"Where does your husband live?" I asked.

"Across town, with his bullfighter friend," she said.

"Come on," I said. "Let's go see him."

"But it won't help," she said. "He won't even come to the door when I go over there, and he has my furniture, too. That's why we use pillows in the living room. He does all this to spite me," she added.

"Is he the father of your children?"

"No. We dated for two years. I thought I knew him, but obviously I didn't. We were only married three weeks. I wanted to leave him by the time we—."

She stopped her words, and once more she looked as frightened as a deer out in mid-road. I knew this look well. I'd been about ten years old when we came around a curve on our way back from the Pala Indian reservation. A doe jumped out in front of us, and we hit her head-on. It was night. I saw her eyes, staring at us in bewilderment as we hit her with our big ranch truck. We killed her. My uncle

Archie jumped out, cut her throat, gutted her, and tossed her in the back of our truck. I asked my dad why he hadn't swerved and tried not to hit her. My dad explained to me that every year a lot of people were killed because they swerved into oncoming traffic, trying to avoid a deer, a cow, a coyote, or a drunk staggering down the side of the road. And so, it was best to hit the deer, coyote, or whatever than to take a head-on collision.

"Come on," I said to Eve, my heart pounding! "I have a car now. We'll take care of this right now!"

"You don't understand. See, he's still my husband, so legally there's nothing I can do, especially here in Mexico."

"I'm not talking about legally anything!" I said.

I wasn't my father's son for *nada*-nothing. Over and over my dad told me how my mother had been respected when he'd been doing his bootlegging, but once they'd quit bootlegging and had gone into legal business, the legal business world had no respect for my mother because she was a woman. The legal business world was a setup, he always said, hiding behind all this hocus-pocus bullshit geared only for men and the rich.

We went down in the elevator and got in my car. She said my T-bird was beautiful, and I thanked her, but I wasn't thinking about this. I was thinking about the snub-nosed .38 special I'd brought down to Mexico with me in case anybody tried to rob me. I hadn't brought my fine, well-balanced .357 magnum Smith and Wesson that was registered in my name. I'd brought this cheap, back-alley snub-nose that couldn't be traced back to me. This was another thing my dad had taught me. Know the law. Respect the law. And be very, very careful and well thought out when you decide to break it.

Eve's husband lived clear across town in a poor section of the city. Kids were playing soccer in the street. They stopped to stare at my car. I suddenly wished my T-bird didn't look so gorgeous. I decided to leave my gun under the dash. I was too upset, and my dad always taught me that you needed to have a cool head to handle a situation with a gun, or the whole thing could very quickly get out of hand. I could see my dad was right. If I took my gun, I'd probably just kill him. I had to force myself to use my brains.

We walked up the stairs. Her husband's place was on the roof of a three-story apartment building without an elevator. The rooftop was cluttered with clotheslines full of colorful clothes and poor-looking sheets.

"Victor," she told me as we slipped in and out of the clotheslines, "we don't have much time. I need to get back, so I can be at home when my kids get back from school."

"No *problema*," I said. "This won't take long."

"But what will you do?"

"I don't know, but we'll see."

I really had no idea what I was going to do, but I did know that it was going to work out, because there was no way on God's little green apple that I wouldn't let it not work out. I was set. I was in my circle of power.

The husband's place was small and painted bright blue. Eve knocked on the door. I got back to the side, so I wouldn't be seen when he first opened the door. We waited. No one answered. She knocked again. This time I saw the curtains move at the window at the side of the door. I got a quick glimpse of a young man's face. She didn't see it and wanted us to leave.

"No," I said, "someone is home. I saw the curtains move at the window. Knock again, and call out his name. What is his name? I hope it's not Adam."

"George," she said.

"Well, knock and call George. Go on. Do it. It's going to work. Trust me."

"How do you know?"

"Just do it, you'll see."

She really didn't want to do it, but still she knocked one more time and called out, "George, I know you're in there! I need to see you! I'm going to get evicted if you don't go to the bank with me so I can get my money!"

No one came to the door, but I swear I heard laughter. My heart exploded, and I stepped forward. This was once again those seniors back at the Academy who poured their punch on Becky's breast. This was once again Wellabussy and his racist friends. I banged on the door with the meaty part of my open left hand, yelling, "OPEN UP RIGHT NOW!"

Then I screamed when he didn't open up, and I grabbed hold of one of the clothesline posts and yanked it out of its concrete base, ruining a whole line of laundry. "I'M GOING TO BREAK YOUR FUCKING WINDOW AND come in and drag you out by your balls if you don't open this door right now!" I bellowed.

"Please," she said, "don't do that!"

"GET BACK!" I yelled at her, getting ready to ram the pole through the window when the door opened, and there stood a startled looking American guy with a Mexican guy behind him. They were both older than me, in their mid-twenties, and bigger, too, and very good-looking, but I didn't give a fat rat's ass!

"Who are you? This isn't any of your business!"

"I'VE MADE IT MY BUSINESS!" I bellowed. "Now talk to her! Don't say one fucking word to me. NOT ONE WORD!"

"What makes you think you're so tough?"

"DON'T TRY ME!" I screamed, leaping into his face and taking up my wrestling position. "I was trained by the fucking best the Marine Corps has to offer, and I'm WARNING YOU, try me and I'll CASTRATE YOU! I'll MAIM you on the FUCKING SPOT! Talk to her!"

I threw down the clothesline post and walked over to the side of the building. I was heaving for air. I was crazy*loco* with rage. I would've taken that metal post and beat the living shit out of both of them. They would have never had a chance. And I didn't care how many bulls they fought on Sundays.

It was a good thing I'd left my snub-nose in the car. I might have shot them through their window when I heard them laughing inside. And yet it was their laughter that had given me the key, because no real men with *tanates* would have laughed. They would have come out to talk and settle things.

People came out of their apartments to see what was happening. I gave money to the two women who complained that it was their laundry I'd ruined. I gave them twice the amount they'd asked for. Everyone settled down.

When Eve and George finished their talk, the bullfighter José and George brought out her furniture, and I helped take her stuff down to his VW van. Then Eve and I followed him to the bank where he helped her draw out her money.

"Look," George said to me when we got to her place and I helped him unload the furniture, "I don't know who you are, or what your plans are with Eve, but don't be so naive as to think you really know what's going on. She owes me money, but she completely forgets that. It was a financial disaster, marrying her and driving down here with her. You see where I live. I have very little money left. All the way down, every few minutes she'd want to stop to see this or that, and she'd buy all the junk in sight. It got to where we couldn't even sleep in my van anymore because of all the crap she'd bought. Did she tell you that it took us almost a month to get down here?"

"Yes, and she told me it was because you kept getting lost and wouldn't ask for directions."

He burst out laughing. "That's hysterical! She'd have me change directions so many times I didn't know what to ask anymore. I wouldn't get involved with her if I were you," he added, "especially for the kids' sake. Peter and Lauren are the two best little troopers I've ever met, but it breaks their heart the way she goes through men. You must have money, right?"

"What's that got to do with it?"

He grinned. "Do you really think she'd be putting on all her charm if you didn't?" he said.

I heard him, I really did, but also I didn't believe him. I'd seen how he'd behaved like a coward, hiding in his apartment. It took us four trips to get all of her belongings out of his VW van and into her place. He wanted to shake hands with me when he was ready to leave. I thought this was strange, but I took his hand. His bullfighter friend hadn't come with him, which was good, because I was sure he and I would have ended up in a badass fight.

After George left, Eve went to the real estate office and paid her last two months rent. She also paid a month in advance. She was so happy she invited me to go out for dinner with her and her two children. She kept telling her kids how I'd stood up and fought for women's rights and that I was their knight in shining armor. Once she asked me if I'd really been trained by the Marine Corps' best. I turned all red.

"Yes and no," I said. "*Sí, y no.* You see, I was trained by a Marine, but in wrestling. Not in combat fighting."

"Well, then, what would you have done if the two of them had attacked you?" she asked, looking slightly frightened.

I glanced at Lauren and Peter. "I don't know. I guess I would've probably turned into a rabbit and hopped away as fast as I could."

The kids burst out laughing, but Eve wasn't sure whether to laugh or not.

After dinner, Eve put Lauren and Peter to bed and asked me if I knew how to build a fire in her fireplace. I said, sure, I'd built hundreds of campfires. Then I told her how I'd been taught by my uncle Archie Freeman from the Pala Indian Reservation out by Palomar Mountain in north San Diego County, that big fire meant white man far away and little fire meant Indian up close.

She loved it and wanted to know how it had been for me to grow up on a ranch by the sea. We lay down on big fat pillows on the floor in front of the fire and talked late into the night. I'd never known anyone so interested in my life. I talked for hours, and for the first time in my life, I could see that I'd lived two very different lives ever since I'd started school. On the ranch I'd lived a life full of love and work and warm good feelings. At school I'd been treated with so much . . . physical and mental abuse that I was still filled with so much rage; it was hard for me to even think about it.

I told her about Ramón in kindergarten and how he'd been the bravest and smartest of all of us and how he'd been killed by the seventh grade, shot in a gang fight.

"But why was he in a gang," she asked, "if he was so smart?"

"For the same reason your dad joined the army," I said to her. "There's comfort and safety in numbers."

"Yes, but a gang is illegal."

I laughed. "Look," I said, "we didn't even realize it, but we started a gang on our first day of school in kindergarten in order to protect ourselves. They treated us awful, hitting us, insulting us, belittling us. I would have stayed in our gang if I hadn't had the ranch and was sent to Catholic school."

"I had no idea," she said.

"Thank you for saying that you didn't know," I said, and I went on to tell her about Paul Koner, and how he'd said that racism was self-inflicted.

She knew who his father was and of his importance in the film world. "It doesn't surprise me at all that he took that position," she said. "Remember, the organized are for the organized, especially among the wealthy."

Eve opened a bottle of wine, and we watched the little flames dancing in the fire. It was hypnotizing to watch the dancing flames and sip our wine. I'd never felt this comfortable around a girl before. Then I remembered Eve wasn't a girl. She was a very wise older woman like Mrs. Wucker. I wondered if she, too, knew all the positions Mrs. Wucker had known.

The warm glow of the wine began to come over me. The fire, the wine, and a woman who understood me felt so good deep inside. I don't know why, but I began telling Eve about the substitute teacher who had come into my life in the seventh grade.

"I'd become a bed wetter," I told her, "because I was so scared of school. But in the seventh grade, a very muscular, blonde male teacher came to school. He put a poster of someone skiing in the Rockies on our bulletin board. 'My wife and I were ski bums in Colorado, that's why we were substitute teachers,' he said, 'and we've come to California to be surf bums. This is why we'll continue to be subs'."

"I love it!" she said with a voice full of joy. "He must have felt like a breath of fresh air for you!"

"Exactly," I said. "Then he said the craziest thing I'd ever heard, and in English class, too. 'I don't care about spelling or punctuation,' he said, 'because my wife and I learned when we were ski instructors in Boulder that if you teach technique first, you can interfere with a person's natural ability. But if you put people on the slopes first, get them all excited, then when you teach technique afterwards, they will learn two hundred times faster. So what I want to do,' he said, 'is get you all so excited about reading and writing that you'll start flying through your classwork'."

"That's fantastic!" she said. "This was exactly what you needed, with that razor sharp mind of yours."

"Yes, I think you're right, because he gave me wings, and I got my first A." Tears came to my eyes. "Eve, I actually stopped being a bed wetter after that. That's also when I learned to play chess. Looking back, I don't think I ever could have learned to play chess at the level I reached if that substitute teacher hadn't opened up my mind to the possibility that I wasn't stupid. In fact, maybe I would have never even tried to learn how to play if I'd never gotten those A's for those three days he taught us. Truly, I'm beginning to see that a teacher can change a kid's life for the good, or for the bad, and so easily. Maybe Ramón would never have been killed if . . . if he'd had an angel teacher, too."

The tears were running down my face. I'd never told this story to anyone before. She took me in her arms and held me close, kissing me tenderly. Then she served us more wine, and she began to tell me about her own life. I noticed she had very little to say about her mother and spoke almost exclusively about her father, the advisor of generals.

She asked me about my drive down from California. I told her it had taken Paul and me thirty-nine hours, that we'd been flying at ninety to one hundred miles an hour and that Paul was a race car driver.

I told her how I'd been hearing a symphony of music inside my brain ever since the night that she'd taken me to hear jazz. I told her that at one point, while we were driving across the deserts of New Mexico just before we'd come into El Paso, Texas, I'd seen so . . . so clearly that . . . that . . .

"I don't quite know how to explain it," I said to her, "but Paul was driving, and we were going about 100 miles an hour. It was past midnight and the stars were out by the zillions and so big and close, and I saw so clearly that making miracles on earth is no big deal. It's the . . . the getting into harmony with the Symphony of Creation that's the big deal. Because once one person, or a group of people, raise up their voices in the exact same . . . same note, sound, pitch as Creation, then miracles are our norm. This is why Moses and all of his people lined up behind him in V-like formations. Thousands of them. And each little V pointing in the same direction. And the music in their souls harmonized with the stars, and the heavens came dancing down to earth, and it's the power of the stars in the heavens that parted the Red Sea and . . . with such ease.

"Eve, I tried to tell this to Paul, but he only laughed at me, then suddenly he sped up to over 120, went over a little rise, turned off the headlights, braked real hard, flipped a U-turn, and parked on the side of the road. 'Get down and act like you're sleeping,' he said to me, and he did it, too. And here came the police siren over that same small rise with lights flashing, shooting right past us. I asked him how he'd known about the cop. He'd said that he had built-in radar when it came to cops. I then asked him why he didn't believe me about what I'd seen so clearly about Moses and all those people in V-formations in groups of 13 and 26 and 52? He laughed at me and said, 'You saw my cop, right? Well, you show me your Moses and all his people and I'll believe you, too. Then we can make the biggest hit movie of all time!'

"Crossing the border at El Paso, Paul and I had to drive a lot slower. The roads weren't as good, and so we kept the car at about sixty and eighty. I . . . I remembered that my dad and his mother had crossed the border at El Paso, and when I looked around, I saw beauty all about me. The poor people had looked beautiful to me. The posture of the women and young girls carrying their *ollas* of water alongside the road were absolutely gorgeous. Twice I had Paul stop and back up for half a mile so I could give money to some mothers and their daughters."

Eve laughed. "The very same thing happened to me when we drove down from the States. I don't know how to explain it, but the moment we crossed the border, it was like everything changed. I saw beauty in everyone and everything, and I'd ask George to pull over so I could buy things that we didn't even need, but I wanted to share our money with them. Their things were so colorful and beautiful. The Mexican people are natural artists. Even the way they arrange their fruit or their Coca-Cola cans in their little stands. Life is art and art is living. But poor George, I was driving him crazy. He was determined to get from there to here, and that was it. No living or playing between points." She giggled. "He wanted to kill me by the second week of our honeymoon, except when we were making love, which, of course, I'm very good at," she added, laughing all the more, "so he'd, then, forgive me everything."

I looked at her, and I flashed on Mrs. Wucker. I bet that Eve was, indeed, very good at lovemaking in her skinny, delicate way. I took a deep breath and told her that I had also driven Paul crazy*loco,* because he, too, had only been interested in getting from there to here.

We looked into each other's eyes. I'd never felt this close and warm and good with . . . with . . . with anyone.

"You're so beautiful," she said.

I blushed. I'd never been told this before.

"Please don't blush," she said. "Look at me, and really, really hear what I'm saying." I looked at her. "You're so beautiful," she repeated, "so full of . . . of beauty. That's what beautiful originally meant, full of beauty."

My heart was beat, beat, beating. No one, except my mother, had ever looked at me or spoken to me like this.

"You are the most sensitive and beautiful man I've ever met," she said with tears coming to her eyes.

I took a big, deep breath. This was just too much. I couldn't believe it. I'd been called stupid and ugly for so long that this was really tough to hear. Once, I'll never forget, two seniors at the Academy had stopped me and ordered me to attention, and I'd snapped to, as we underclassmen were supposed to do. They'd walked around me, carefully inspecting my uniform, and one of them then said, "Is this the cadet?"

"Yes," said the other one.

"I agree with you, you're right," said the first one. "This is the ugliest cadet in the school!"

My chest caved in, and they'd walked off laughing and left me standing at attention. As soon as I got home, I went to the bathroom, locked the door, and looked at myself in the mirror and . . . and I could see that they were right. I had a wide face and big teeth. I definitely was the ugliest cadet at the whole school. Mexicans weren't just stupid, but also ugly people. I told the story to Eve and the tears began to stream down her face, too.

"Come with me," she said, taking my hand.

I got up, and she led me across the room, down the hallway, and into her bathroom. She had two very good smelling candles burning by the mirror.

"Look," she said, "look at yourself in the mirror and see how truly beautiful you are. I'd love to have those high wide cheekbones. You'll never have wrinkles. In fact, as you age, the more handsome you'll become."

I glanced, but then quickly looked away.

"Victor," she said, taking my chin in her fingertips, "please don't be afraid. Take a nice good long look."

"I can't."

"Yes, you can. Come on, look into the mirror, and now smile."

This I definitely couldn't do, and once more tears came to my eyes. How could I ever explain to Eve that even my mother, whom I'd always thought was so gorgeous, had become ugly to me after my first week of school? That deep, that thorough was the brainwashing job we'd received with "English only." And not just in language, but in how we saw ourselves and the whole world.

Gently, slowly she drew my face close to her face, and she began kissing me, taking the tears off my cheeks with her lips. I began to purr like a kitten. She continued kissing me on the neck, the ears, then on the mouth. Our breathing changed, and her kisses became tiny, tickling, quick nibbles, and it felt so good I began to giggle. She giggled, too.

"Now look in the mirror," she said.

I did, and I was utterly amazed. I'd never ever seen myself smiling with such happiness. I was actually grinning ear to ear.

"Is that guy handsome, or what?" she said.

I nodded. She was right. I was handsome. I wasn't ugly at all. We laughed and laughed and laughed, then we began kissing once again. This was heaven! This was WONDERFUL! Then our bodies came together and instantly my cock burst forth, pushing through her clothing, feeling her hot wetness. Her breathing quickened. Mine did too, but she suddenly pulled away from me.

"No, no," she whispered. "With you, no can do. You're too special. I want you. I really do, but no can do. You should save yourself for someone younger and pure . . . like, well, my daughter. What sign are you?" she asked.

"What sign?" I said, feeling totally confused.

"Yes, what month were you born?"

"May."

"May what?"

"May tenth, Mother's Day Mexican-style, but right at midnight, so I was put on the eleventh."

"You see, you're a Taurus," she said with a big smile, "an earth sign, just as I thought. This afternoon you handled things like your sign, the bull! Also," she added, "you are closer in age to Lauren than you are to me, so you should be hers. Not mine. See?"

But I didn't see. All I knew was that she'd opened me up, and we'd been kissing and feeling each other so wonderfully, then she suddenly stopped. I guessed that when she felt my erection, she wanted no part of it.

I went back up to my place that night, feeling completely confused. We'd drunk quite a bit of wine, and I still wasn't used to drinking alcohol, but . . . why had she stopped? We'd been really kissing very well. Was she serious about wanting to save me for her daughter? That was crazy talk. Her daughter was a child, and when she grew up, she'd figure out on her own who she wanted to be with. I fell right to sleep.

# CHAPTER THIRTY-ONE

The next day I was watching ass. I was lying on the grass in the warm sunlight, watching all the girls and guys walk past me. There were students at this university from all around the world, but mostly from the United States and Europe. I don't think that I'd ever seen a place with so many good-looking young people. I was beginning to understand why those street kids had told me—when I first arrived in Mexico City—that I walked funny, dressed funny, and spoke my Spanish in a funny way, too. I could see that most of the students walked funny, dressed funny, and spoke Spanish in a funny way compared to the locals. I could spot the students from Europe. Their funny walk seemed a little more at ease, and their asses a little looser. The asses of the Americans—no matter how beautiful or well-built—seemed to be tighter. And the girls from Brazil . . . oh, their asses seemed to sing a language of joy and sexuality as they walked past me in great colorful clothes.

I laughed, thinking that there should be a three-credit college course in Ass Watching. Sure, of course, and I began to also see that the people with the tightest asses were the ones who didn't smile very much. This made sense, a lot of sense, because two parts ass and one part brain made happiness, and two parts brain and one part ass made heavy-seriousness. I laughed with *carcajadas*! Ass watching was definitely educational!

I got up off the grass and went to my next class. There were five of us. We were studying Kant, the German philosopher, who'd lived from 1724 to 1804. I took the seat by the window, the same one I took every day. I loved this class. We only dealt with one paragraph at a time, and our professor read aloud the paragraph for us. The book we were working with was called *The Critique of Pure Reason*.

At the beginning of the course, our professor told us that some people considered Kant to have had the greatest mind of any human
being in western civilization. I was working away when our professor came to my desk and looked over my shoulder.

"What are you doing?" he asked.

"I'm correcting Kant," I said.

"You're what?!!"

"I'm going over the last paragraph you read to us, and I'm
changing a few words and removing a few others."

"But you can't correct Immanuel Kant!" he said.

"Why can't I? I bought the book, so I can do anything I want to
do with it."

"Well, yes," he said, breathing fast. "I can't argue with that, but
to think that . . . that you can . . . oh, my God!" he said, and he
stopped his words but continued speaking to me with his body.

Now he was a nervous wreck as he kept trying to light a new cigarette off his last one. His fingernails and fingers were yellowed by
his constant smoking, and his breath smelled of acid because of all
the coffee he drank. He was so upset that he finally turned and
walked out of the classroom. I hadn't meant to upset him. I'd just
seen some things that were obviously wrong with Kant's last paragraph, and I'd wanted to correct them.

Looking out our window, I could see that it took our professor
several deep breaths before he could calm down enough to light his
next cigarette. He was a real chain-smoker, going through four or
five packs a day. On our first day, he told us that he'd studied in
Spain and Italy and had a doctorate in philosophy from the University of Madrid. My fellow students and I continued to do our work
on Kant, but I was the only one writing in my book between the lines
and in the margins. Once he'd lit up again and taken a few good
puffs, our professor came back into the classroom and walked right
up to me.

"Could you please explain to me," he said, blowing smoke all
over me, "what it is that you are . . . are . . . well, changing in the
text?"

"Sure, I'd be glad to," I said. "You see, in my opinion, Kant
missed the whole boat, because—if I understand correctly—what

he's trying to say is that ultimately we can't know anything through pure reason, and therefore he can't believe in God because the concept of God is beyond human comprehension. Well, I say, bull, because our comprehension isn't limited to just what we know through reason. There are lots of things I know and comprehend, and yet I can't reason out."

"Name one."

"Almost everything. Running down a hillside on foot back home on the ranch, jumping over cactus and my feet knowing what to do all by themselves. Suddenly I freeze inside and come to a skidding stop just before I land in a nest of rattlesnakes. How is it that something inside of me knew about those snakes way before I saw them? I can't explain this rationally. It was just me being in rhythm with myself and in harmony with my surroundings as I ran down the hillside. And Kant was so old and in such bad health all his life that he never got to have any of these kinds of experiences. So there's a whole lot he didn't know. It was beyond his reason and comprehension, but not beyond mine."

"So then, are you saying that truth is relative, depending on one's own experience?"

"I hadn't thought about it like that, but yeah, I guess I am. Because the truth of a sixteen-year-old boy is very different than the truth of a man in his sixties."

"But don't you think there are truths that are absolute? Fire burns. It doesn't matter how old you are."

"Okay, I can see why you say that," I said. "But . . . I'm also beginning to see that there are exceptions to everything we know, especially when we go from one culture to another. For instance, my dad told me that when the Mexican Revolution came into their mountains *de Jalisco* and destroyed their ranches that my grandfather, a big pure-blooded Spaniard, went crazy*loco* screaming, 'It's the end of the world! God has forsaken us!' and he died. But, on the other hand, his short little mother, *una India de Oaxaca*, didn't panic when they were starving and her children were being raped and killed all about her. No, instead she got together with all the other old Indian women of the village, and they did a ghost dance. They built a huge fire of oak—which has no pitch like pinewood—and they danced on the burning coals. They took rocks in their hands, striking the stones together, summoning forth all the powers of their ancestry, and now miracles became their daily bread, because they were backed up by the heavens."

"Are you telling me that your grandmother danced on fire?"

"Sure, but that's not the big one. Now they were able to bring rain to give them water and flocks of wild birds to feed them, because—as my dad told me—they were now dancing up the wild steps of heaven."

"And you believe all this?"

"Sure, why not? You, being a Christian, believe Moses parted the sea and Jesus walked on water and healed the sick and fed the multitudes with one fish and five loaves of bread, was crucified, and rose from the dead?"

"Well, yes, of course, but that's different," he said, "because Jesus was the Son of God, and Moses was . . . "

"And what makes you think that my grandmother wasn't?"

"Wasn't what?"

"The daughter of God."

He quit smiling. "Because," he said, "Jesus is the only Son of God!"

Now it was my turn to smile. "There you did it," I said. "You used the word 'the' and then the word 'only' to crush me, to divide and conquer, to separate and exclude. Not to be open-minded and critique with pure reason like you're asking us to do in this class."

"What are you saying?" he asked.

"I'm saying," I said, "I think it's language itself that we ate from the Tree, and it's language that keeps us ignorant and in turmoil."

"And what other means of communications do we have?"

"Music," I said, "and I'm beginning to think . . . no, feel down deep inside of me that it's through music that we can really comprehend God. In fact, I'd go so far as to say that I do believe the word 'the' was invented by the Jews for the sole purpose of . . . of . . . . "

"Wait," he said. "What proof do you have that Jews invented the word 'the'?"

"I don't. But I ask you, who has benefited the most from the word 'the'? It gave the Jews the tool to call themselves 'the' chosen people."

I could see that he was thinking.

"And also through reasoning, I'm beginning to think that it was the Greeks who then popularized 'the,' and that's where the rest of Europe got it."

"Could be," he said, "they did come after the Jews. And the word 'the' certainly did give the Jews the foundation of language with which to claim they were 'the' chosen people. Where do you get all these wild ideas?" he asked.

I smiled. I was happy that he'd used the word wild. "From here," I said, pointing to my ass.

Instantly, he got mad.

"No, please don't get mad," I said. "I used to think that we got our ideas from the air, from this sea-soup that's between all things, but now I can also see that we can't access this natural attraction unless we have a relaxed ass. Truly, I'm not joking. I've been watching a lot of ass lately, and I believe that . . . that Ass Watching should be a three-credit college course, because I've come to see that to the degree that a person's ass is uptight to that degree they don't smile, laugh, and walk stiff. And to the degree that they walk with a relaxed ass, to this same degree they are free and loose and happy.

"Truly, I honestly believe that Kant's ass was so tight that he is the one who couldn't see anything beyond reason. You told us that he was seventy-eight years old when he wrote this book. He was probably so old and dried up and in bad health that he wasn't able to see any life beyond words. His brain owned him through words. That's why he couldn't see that there's no conflict between believing in God and also believing in reason and evolution. Look, all we have to do is combine the two like we combine $H_2O$. GodEvolution, make it into a new word. What does it really matter? The flower is beautiful. The butterfly is gorgeous. Get into the feelings behind the words, then we are free once more and living with reason and beyond reason at the same time just like when I play chess."

He sighed, and all the while his burning cigarette was dropping ashes on his shirt, which was dotted with little burn holes. "May I see the changes you've made?" he asked.

"Sure. Take a look," I said. "The other day I also corrected, or more precisely I updated, what Jesus is supposed to have said."

He stopped dead in his tracks. "Are you now saying that you have also corrected and updated the words of our Lord God Jesus?"

"Sure, of course," I said. "Isn't this what every new translation of the Bible does?"

"Yes, that's true," he said. His shirt suddenly caught on fire. He slapped at his shirt in a frenzy, putting out the fire. "But . . . but these men are SCHOLARS!"

"Yes, and that's the whole problem, the way I see it," I said. "They are men and they are scholars, so they will only keep seeing things as . . . as they've been trained and educated to see. And men, I do believe, the more and more educated they become, the tighter and tighter their asses get. So women, who can't hide from life because of pregnancy, are consistently looser with their asses, so they should be the ones to rewrite the Bible. I guarantee that in a few hundred years, we'll have a much kinder and better God and, hence, a much kinder and better world."

"Then God is relative, too?"

"Absolutely. It's the same God all over the world like it's the same ocean. It's just that we humans have . . ."

I stopped speaking. His whole head was jerking as if he had a kink in his neck. His eyes rolled over, showing all white, and his left hand began to shake. I didn't know what was happening. Maybe he was having a heart attack.

"And . . . and what is it that you corrected or updated about Jesus Christ?" he asked.

He hadn't heard a thing I'd said about women and God and the oceans. He was grabbing his left hand with his right and trying to stop it from shaking.

"When they say that Jesus said that 'the Kingdom of God is within all of us,' I changed the 'is' to 'starts'."

"Starts?"

"Yes, because what Jesus really meant to say was that the King-dom of God starts within all of us."

"Oh, of course. And how do you know this? Did Jesus come down from heaven and tell you?"

"No, not this time. This time I just figured it out, understanding Him the way I do. Because, you see, He never meant just to imply that that which is inside of us stays within us forever. But that which is inside of us is our Source and needs to be brought out into the world, and that this is our responsibility as human beings. And when we do this, bring the Kingdom of God out into the world, then mir-acles happen, just like Moses parting the Red Sea. You see, Moses really did part the sea. It isn't symbolism. It really, really did happen, and we can do it, too."

"And you . . . you know how to do this?" he said.

"Yes, of course, we all do once we get past our fears, because if Peter hadn't looked down and lost faith, then he, too, could have walked on water alongside Jesus. Fear is what holds us all back, because once we get past our fears, we're like, well, a void, a blank page, and the power of God can come flooding into us with such force that the parting of seas is small potatoes.

"This was our natural power back in Eden, and this is how both of my grandmothers survived the Mexican Revolution. By perform-ing daily miracles. And Moses wasn't a leader. He was a conductor. He was like, well, the lead horn of his day, and, together, all the Jews lost their fear at the same moment and harmonized into one Mighty Symphony of the Pure Love of God, got into V formations, and reached for the stars. You see, it's the stars that really parted the Red Sea, not Moses, and so easy. No big deal. Like an opera singer breaking a wine glass."

He was staring at me.

"Don't you get it?" I said. "To be able to draw even one breath without fear is the beginning of all living. Can't you feel it inside you? The Garden is still here within us just bursting to come out."

"And this doesn't bother you?" he said.

"What?" I asked.

"To be comparing yourself to . . . to the greatest, the most INFLUENTIAL PERSONS OF ALL TIME!" he shouted, eyes getting wild.

I took a deep breath. I could see that if he had a lance or sword, he would run it through me. But I'd worked too long and too hard to get to where I was, so I wasn't going to allow him or . . . or his Spanish-thinking trapped-brain to intimidate me as had been done to both of my grandmothers' people for the last 500 years. After all, this was a philosophy class, so if we couldn't discuss these things in this class, where could we?

"No," I said, "on the contrary, would my life be worth living if I didn't?"

"OH, MY GOD!" he shouted once again.

"Exactly! Oh, my God, all of us! Because the time has come when we can't just sit around anymore on the sidelines of Creation and complain! We've got to jump into the middle with both feet, take a stance, and move mountains, too!"

"And how do we do this? By following you?" he shouted.

"No, absolutely not! You follow yourself within your own Kingdom of God with the understanding that it's music, not laws, that is the True Voice of God."

He backed away from me. He looked sick. The other four students in the class were grinning. I guess they thought that the two of us were the greatest show in town.

After class, I left school. I was so upset I was trembling. I could now see why Father Williams had wanted to give me absolution. Dr. Nacozi had been right. Thinking was the scariest thing a human being could do. And why? Because we were IMPRISONED by all we knew and terrified to step outside our prison walls into the great VASTNESS OF THE UNKNOWN!

And this prison was WORLDWIDE, AND STRANGLING THE LIFE FORCE OUT OF US!

# CHAPTER THIRTY-TWO

That same afternoon Eve and I drove out of the city and into the country with her children. We turned off the paved road and took a dirt road. We drove around a hill and into a long little valley. Ahead of us in the distance was a tiny white village. It had just rained, and the tile roofs were wet and bright red. There were pine trees on the hilltops surrounding the village and palm trees down in the plaza. The whole valley smelled fresh and pure as heaven.

As we approached the village, we spotted a herd of goats being brought down from the hills by two little Indian boys. Lauren and Peter got all excited and wanted to know if they could get out of the car and help the boys herd the goats up the grassy meadow to the village. I stopped the car, got out, and talked to the boys in Spanish. I told them I'd give them each ten *pesos,* the equivalent of almost a dollar, if Lauren and Peter could help them with their herd of goats. They said yes, of course, with great big happy smiles, telling me I didn't need to pay them, that they were happy to show our two children how to herd goats. I thanked them and insisted they take the money. They did when I offered the money a second time.

My mother had taught me this. She, too, had grown up dirt-poor in the mountains of Chihuahua, and she'd explained to me that country people were very proud and self-sufficient, so it was bad manners for them to accept anything, especially when it was first offered. No matter how hungry or thirsty they were, my mother had been taught that even food and water was to be refused when offered the first time. Why? Because you never knew how much the person who was offering really needed it and was simply being courteous.

Eve was beside herself with joy, watching her two children interact with the two little Mexican-Indian kids as they moved the goats up the grassy meadow. There was a winding creek running down the middle of the valley. I thought of my dad and all the stories he told me about taking care of goats with his brother Domingo up in the highlands of *Los Altos de Jalisco* when they were little boys. I'd never realized how awful the Mexican Revolution had been until I got to the University of the *Americas* and took a course on the history of *Mexico*. The Mexican Revolution had been pre-World War One. German advisors had shown up with barbed wire and machine guns. They dug trenches to see if they could stop a cavalry charge, and they had, killing tens of thousands of Mexicans on horseback like rats in a can. In just a few years, over one million Mexicans out of a population of sixteen million died in combat, and another half a million starved to death. American advisors had shown up for the other side with the same equipment, plus airplanes with crude bombs. And in this hell on earth, my dad and mother had grown up, knowing nothing but bloodshed and starvation, and the only things that kept them going were their mothers and their stout faith in the Almighty.

When I was a little kid growing up in California, I'd always thought that my dad and mom had grown up during the time of Moses and Abraham and the enslavement of the Jews. Because the stories my parents told me were full of daily miracles, conversations with God, and goats and sheep—just like the stories of the Bible. It wasn't until I was in the fourth grade and in Catholic school that I began to understand that Mexico wasn't the Promised Land and that my father's and mother's people weren't God's chosen people. That had been very hard on me. Hell, I'd been so mixed up I'd thought that our town *Carlos Malo*, referring to Carlsbad, was the Garden of Eden, and my grandmother was *Eva*, the first woman in all the world.

Eve and I left the car and walked behind her children and the two little goatherders. Suddenly a huge swarm of orange butterflies came flying by. We were surrounded by dancing color. I stretched out my hands, and butterflies landed on my hands and arms. This was exactly what my *mamá* always told me would happen to them every year when the butterflies migrated through their Rain of Gold canyon. Eve and I couldn't stop smiling. The swarm of butterflies was so beautiful, then it was gone, moving up the valley like a magic cloud.

In the village, we watched the two boys put the herd of goats in pens for the night. Lauren and Peter then got to see the two boys milk the mother goats with their huge milk bags and feed the baby goats. I was beginning to understand how lucky I was to have been raised on a ranch. I, too, as in the Bible, knew how to milk goats and cows and to help a mother cow or goat with her birthing. I also knew how to plant corn, string beans, squash, and plant and cut alfalfa. I really did know a lot more than I gave myself credit for.

We had a wonderful, magical time all afternoon. I felt so much more at home out in the country than in the city. *La plaza* was the most beautiful little cobblestone plaza I'd ever seen. Eve told me to notice how the women weren't embarrassed to nurse their children in public.

"They're so natural and beautiful," she said. "I just love raising my kids in Mexico, where they can experience life as a whole and not compartmentalized, as we do in the United States."

Driving back to Mexico City that night, Eve drew close to me, snuggling in like a cat as we watched the last of the sunlight slip away. It felt so good. After the kids were put to bed, I shared with Eve what had happened in philosophy class and how my chain-smoking professor had become so upset with me.

She started laughing. "But can't you see how threatening that must have been for him? Poor man, he'd studied Kant all his life, and it never once entered his mind to set a pen to the text."

"But it was a philosophy class," I said, "where we're supposed to question everything." Then I told her how I'd changed a word of what Jesus had said from "is" to "starts." "And I partly did this because of the word Source that you taught me," I added.

"You're right. That does fit in very nicely with the concept of Source," she said to me, not frightened or upset. "With the word 'starts,' then we, too, become participants with Christ in row row rowing our boats gently down stream with the Kingdom of God that is within us all."

"Exactly!" I said. "Bringing the Kingdom out into the world. Ever since the night you took me to hear jazz and I saw that words are labels, it's like, well, I can now move concepts around freely. Like I can see that the Ten Commandments are out of date. Moses only used the label 'commandments' because he was dealing with a people who'd been enslaved for so long they wouldn't have been able to understand it any other way. The commandments are so full of "don't do this and don't do that," that people end up doing exactly what they are told not to do."

"I completely agree," she said, "the commandments do not work."

"What works," I said, "is to encourage people to find their balance. This is where our true power begins. Then once a person is in balance, they harmonize themselves with their surroundings. This was how Moses personally lived, in balance and harmony, and this was why he was able to see and listen to the Burning Bush. You see, the time has come for all of us to activate this place where Moses himself lived, and not just obey God but understand God, so that then we can help the Almighty in Creation just like Moses did."

She drew me close, holding my face in both of her hands, looking into my eyes, then softly, gently she began kissing me, on the cheeks and then on the lips, tickling me with her tongue. Feelings I'd never felt before came shooting up my spine. She nibbled my ears, using her lips and the tip of her tongue in quick, tiny movements. I squirmed and laughed. She laughed and undid my shirt and nibbled my nipples, blowing hot breath on them. I began breathing so fast, I was ready to burst, when she suddenly pulled away from me once again.

"No, no, please," she said, between deep breaths of her own. "Don't you see, you must be an all-time thing. Will you marry me?"

"Marry you?" I said, totally shocked. "But you're not even divorced."

"But I will be, and will you marry me then?"

I didn't know what to say. All the wind went out of my sails. I felt like I'd been set up. We'd had a wonderful time all afternoon, and then we'd stopped for a bite to eat at a *taco* stand at the outskirts of the city.

"Is it that I'm too old?" she said. "You do seem to get excited by me and you like my children. And they certainly love you."

I still didn't know what to say. It wasn't her age. No, I felt that somehow I wasn't being dealt an honest hand of cards. I mean, the daughter of that professor, she must have known her husband was coming back, and yet on the very day he'd returned, we'd made love and she told me she loved me. What was I, a plaything for these older women?

"Look, I'm sorry," she said. "This must feel pretty sudden to you, like I'm trying to trick you," she added. "But I'm not. Honestly. It's just that, well . . . we had such a wonderful time this afternoon, and you treated my children with such responsible love that I would—I guess—love for it to go on forever." She got up. "Please don't be mad. I'm sorry. I hope we can see each other again tomorrow."

She got up. I got up, and very awkwardly we hugged and kissed goodnight. I left, feeling all twisted and confused inside.

# CHAPTER THIRTY-THREE

The next day my roommate Jack Gulliver and I drove to the university, took our class of the day, then went back down the hill to our gym, the Chapultepec Club, to work out and swim. I felt so frustrated I worked out extra hard, and when four big Mexican guys with huge arms started bench-pressing to show everyone how strong they were, I almost went over to show them that I, a good sixty pounds smaller, could pop reps with what they could hardly move. But I didn't. I could see I would only make them lose face in front of the three *señoritas* they were trying to impress.

Going back to our apartment, I could sense there was something Jack kept wanting to tell me, but every time he'd start, he stopped.

"You really like Eve, don't you?" he said, getting a couple of cold Mexican beers out of our fridge.

"Yes, very much. I've never met anyone like her," I said. "She understands everything."

"Yes, she's smart," he said. "I met her type at Princeton."

His tone of voice sounded funny. "Is there something you want to tell me?" I asked.

"No," he said. "Just be careful. Don't let yourself get hurt."

"Man, you almost sound like her ex-husband."

"He's not her ex," he said. "Keep that in mind."

When I heard this, I thought I understood what Jack was trying to tell me. Maybe George was going to come back into her life, as it had happened to me with the professor's daughter. That same afternoon when I went over to see Eve, I half-expected George to be with her. But when she opened the door, she was happy to see me, and George was nowhere in sight.

"The kids and I are on our way to take a guided tour of the *Zóca-lo*," she said, trying her best to pronounce the word zocalo with a Spanish pronunciation. "Would you like to join us? We'd love for you to come, wouldn't we?" she said, turning to Peter and Lauren.

Both kids responded with a big enthusiastic yes and actually rushed up to give me a big hug. I forgot all about what Jack told me, and we went down in the elevator, hailed a cab, and drove off downtown to the *Zócalo*, the great big open square where the Palace of the President, the ruins of the Aztec temple of *Tenochtitlan*, and the main cathedral of Mexico were located. The *Zócalo* was a huge outdoor museum that stretched all over the old downtown of Mexico City. It was considered by many to be one of the ten wonders of the world. I'd walked the area many times, but I'd never had a guided tour, so I never knew what to look for.

To my surprise, our tour guide was *Carlos Esparza*, a teacher I knew from the university. He was about thirty and taught our Mexican Studies course. He immediately recognized me and thought I'd finally come down to do the required lab work. In the classroom, I'd always found him to be boring, but out here he was transformed into brilliance. Our tour group consisted of about a dozen people, and he started out by telling us that he was from *Oaxaca*, and a full-blooded *Indio*. He explained to us that when *Cortés* came to Mexico City, he found a greater trading of goods than anything that he'd seen in all of Europe, including Constantinople.

He spoke to us in English with a heavy accent. Most of the people in our group were from Europe, the others from the United States. Little by little, I began to realize that *Carlos* had told us a lot of this stuff in the classroom, but I'd never really understood it before. Now that we were here, in the actual place he'd been referring to, it was almost like the stones themselves were speaking to us. For the first time in my life, I truly began to understand how difficult it was for anyone to really believe in any of the horrors of Mexico's history unless they visited the locations. The German Holocaust of World War II was accepted by most people, because the death camps were constantly shown to us in movies and on T.V., so we all knew that those atrocities had really taken place.

But no one really gave a rat's ass about the women and children of my *Yaqui* grandmother's people who had been massacred, and the surviving men—because they were great warriors—had been told that if they took up arms in the name of the Mexican Revolution, they'd be given back their ancestral lands if they won. The *Yaqui* men fought like mighty eagles with all their hearts, turning the tide of battle after battle. But then they'd been double-crossed once the Revolution was over and their side had won and rounded up and executed, except for a few who'd escaped and crossed the border to Arizona. Telling this story, silent tears made deep crevices down my grandmother's old weathered dark-brown face, and she explained to me that what had saved her was that she'd raced out of a burning hut into her enemies' hands, begging to be spared. She was three years old when she was taken in and raised by the enemy of her own people.

Two men dressed in dark suits joined our group. Instantly I sensed danger. *Carlos* noticed them, too, but didn't stop his lecture. He told us that Mexico was still one of the richest countries in the world, that people didn't need to go to the United States for work. It was just that 4 percent of the population controlled 90 percent of the nation's wealth, and this was what caused Mexico's vast poverty and created one of the worst and lowest paid educational systems of the whole civilized world.

After we finished our guided downtown tour, we boarded a large, modern bus and were taken out to the pyramids where we were to have an evening tour and dinner, then witness a full moon dance performed by native people. I'd never been to *Teotihuacan* before. The place was enormous, much larger than I'd imagined. People looked like tiny ants as they climbed up the pyramids, especially the biggest one, which was built in honor of the Father Sun.

*Carlos* was just beginning to point out the different sights of interest when the men in dark suits showed up once again. Now there were six of them, but still *Carlos* kept calm and continued giving us so much information that it was hard for me to keep up. Then out of the blue, he said something that sent chills up and down my spine. He told us that the concept of zero had not come to Europe until the 16th century by way of the Moors from North Africa through Spain, yet this concept of zero had been known in the Americas for thousands of years. The *Toltecs,* the people of *Oaxaca,* the *Mayans,* the *Incas,* the *Navajos,* the *Pueblos* and dozens and dozens of tribes throughout the Americas had known this, and so these people had never thought Mother Earth was flat or the center of the universe. They'd figured out that Mother Earth was round and circled around Father Sun and that there were thirteen months to the year and that time was circular. Then he added that every 26,000 years the earth wiggled, changing from male to female energy, then back again, and that this was just barely being recognized by modern science.

My heart was pounding! I'd never known any of this! I'd always accepted what I'd been told in the U. S., that there were no worthwhile civilizations in the Americas before Columbus.

He went on and on, telling us that the Mayan calendar was still the most accurate calendar known to man and that written languages had existed in the Americas pre-Columbus. My heart-*corazón* was beat, beat, BEATING like a great war drum! I'd been so stupid, stupid, stupid to have ever let myself be misled. I felt like a whole con job had been done to me, robbing me of my whole cultural ancestry!

A rage started coming up inside of me like I'd never felt before. And now I didn't just want to go back to the States and kill that damn playground teacher who'd slapped *Ramón* until he'd been a bloody mess in kindergarten, I wanted to burn the libraries and kill the writers who'd written all those lies and half truths!

I wanted to MASSACRE, to TORTURE as I'd been tortured, and scream "YAQUI ONLY, you SON-OF-A-BITCHES!"

I was FLYING! I could hear a symphony inside my brain. Carlos was now explaining to us that you couldn't do higher math without the concept of zero, and so all European-based mentality was barely in the early stages of comprehending the math behind the design of the heavens. Because zero wasn't the absence of life. Zero was the foundation of Life itself. Nothing was Everything, and we could never really see and know the Almighty until we stopped using "belief" as our basis for "knowing."

*Carlos* told us that native people all over the globe didn't "believe" in God, they "knew" God, they "did" God. God was Living Life. And he predicted that our next wave of great mathematicians would come from Africa, the Americas, New Zealand, and Australia, wherever native people still lived with some traces of their indigenous understandings.

Something happened.

When I heard *Carlos* say this, something happened deep inside me. I could now feel the Kingdom of God oozing out of me. Things were beginning to make sense to me that never had made sense before. Zero was my center, my circle, my strength, and it was from this "neutral" place that I'd been able to go into my genius and do so well in chess. It was from this "neutral" place that I'd been able to solve that math problem in high school. Being *nada*-nothing was the opening through which we could all get into our Everything of *Papito Dios!* And Kant hadn't known this. He couldn't. Because his ass had been too tight to leap into the rhythms of fast chess playing. Trusting your intuition was how we got into this place of genius. Suddenly a warm, smooth feeling began enveloping me. I'd returned to the womb. I felt so happy, I couldn't stop grinning from ear to ear like . . . like I'd seen myself do in the mirror.

We went to dinner, and for the first time in my life, I started doing shots of *tequila* and downing bottles of *Dos Equis* beer. But I couldn't seem to get drunk.

"*Carlos*," I said to our guide, "my grandmother on my dad's side, *Doña Margarita*, also came from *Oaxaca*. Her father *Don Pío* was a colonel. He fought alongside *Benito Juárez*. He even knew *Don Porfirio* before he turned white and became the dictator-king of México."

"Are both your parents from Mexico?" he asked me.

"Yes," I said.

"But you were born in the States, right?"

"Yes," I said.

"What part?"

"California."

"Los Angeles?"

"No, further south, just north of San Diego."

"And you didn't speak any English when you started school and within a week you were so ashamed of being *un mexicano* that you started telling people you were Spanish," he said.

I laughed. "No, I was too Mexican-looking to do that. But some of my Mexican friends, especially the smarter ones, did do that."

He put his hand on my shoulder. "I know the story well," he said. "I have cousins in Santa Ana. And a large part of you felt like killing, eh?"

I nodded. "Oh, God, yes!"

"But who did you really want to kill," he asked, "those who'd abused you, or yourself, whom you'd grown to hate?"

My knees went weak. This had never, ever entered my mind. But he was right. I'd just never seen this before. Who had I really wanted to kill . . . those abusive teachers or myself?

"You know, there are thousands of young people who feel just like you felt, and still do."

"There are?" I said. "I'd always thought I was alone."

"No, there are tens of thousands of young people here and all over the United States who feel like killing just like you do, but they won't, and yet they are going to revolt. And," he added, "this Great Revolution will be worldwide and will not be done with weapons this time, but with music and love."

"With music and love?" I said.

"Yes," he said, "that same music you are hearing right now within your soul and you are seeing within your heart."

My eyes grew big! "You mean that you, too, can hear and see this huge symphony that's going on inside me?"

He laughed. "I wouldn't be talking to you if I couldn't hear and see what you hear and see. Truly, you are not alone," he added. "None of us are. We are finally beginning to come together all over the globe. We are the children of the future just as the Mayan calendar predicted, and we all came to earth to do a music of world harmony and peace. We are of the age that keeps our star memories. You used to draw stars when you were a child, didn't you?"

Chills went up and down my spine. "Yes, over and over again."

"What color did you color them?"

"Turquoise."

He laughed. "Of course, turquoise. You were trying to heal yourself, to keep the pure spirits of the sky and the clean waters of the world within you. Yes, I hear the music you hear and there are thousands who hear it, too, and soon it will burst forth all over the globe."

It was dark, and the stars were out by the thousands. I was drunk, and the whole world was swaying. This was when I saw that the pyramids themselves were swaying, too. They were dancing to the music I was hearing within me. This was astonishing. Could it then be that we human beings could harmonize our heartbeats with the Symphony of Creation and this was what Moses and those thousands of people had been doing in V-formations before the sea? Could it be that *Carlos* was right and there were thousands of young people just like me ready to take the words of Jesus to heart and step forth to do as He said, "This that I do, you will do and more." Could it be that the time had come for us to jazz together as brothers and sisters all over the globe and . . . and . . .

"You brought a gun with you, didn't you?" he was saying.

"Yes," I answered, wondering how he knew this, too.

"For what purpose, to protect your fancy car?"

"How do you know about my car?" I asked.

"Everyone at school knows about your Golden Bird. To use a gun to protect property is beneath you. Do you not know that with the money you paid for that car, a village could have a whole aqueduct built, with dam and all?"

"I'll give you my gun when we get back to town and sell my car," I said.

"No," he said. "Not yet. Just remember that Mexico is going to bring the Olympics to Mexico City for 1968."

"Oh? I didn't know that."

"This is where this New Revolution of music will start for us," he said.

"At the Olympics?"

"Yes, and you'll read about it in the newspapers. Many of us are going to be killed."

I took a deep breath and glanced around to see the men in suits. They were gone. I suddenly knew he was telling me the truth, just as much as when my dad had told me before I'd come on this trip about the man with the watches. Those men in suits were . . . were *Carlos'* executioners.

"And knowing this, you are still willing to go ahead with your plans and maybe die?" I asked.

"Absolutely! Like you, I've already given my life many times before, and this time I've come to give my life for my greatest work."

I took a deep breath. This was really heavy. Then did this mean we were all predestined, but some of us just didn't know it, or knew it and didn't want to accept the responsibility for what we knew about ourselves, so we were forever sabotaging our Sacred, Holy Lives?

The evening celebration had begun with people drumming and dancing. They were dressed in native clothes and spectacular head-dresses. Watching them, little by little I began to realize without a shadow of a doubt that these pyramids hadn't been built for human sacrifice but for communicating with the heavens.

This was a Holy Place where Angels and Humans interacted.

A Sacred Place where Heaven was brought down to Earth.

The history books were full of crap. These pyramids hadn't been built for human sacrifice. That would be like saying that all of Germany had been built just to exterminate Jews. The story of a nation was much greater than one simple-minded way of viewing its story.

I could see-feel that the symphony I'd been hearing inside was now oozing out of me and taking on form.

I smiled.

I laughed.

I could see-feel with every fiber of my being, that Music was, indeed, the Holy Voice of Creation. Yes, yes, yes, and this was why those jazz musicians had spoken volumes to me that night.

MUSIC WAS THE ALMIGHTY'S VOICE!

MUSIC WAS THE DESIGN BEHIND THE WHOLE ENTIRE UNIVERSE!

# CHAPTER THIRTY-FOUR

The next day I was too hung over to drive, so once more I went to class with Jack in his car. In Art Appreciation, I started thumbing through our history of art textbook. I found that the faster I turned the pages, the more the paintings and sculptures sprang to life.

Suddenly I could see that the whole history of art was the ongoing story of humanity. I could see that the pictures by Picasso and the sculptures of Henry Moore at the end of the book looked so much like the paintings in the first part of the text. Those child-like cave paintings in France looked like they'd been done by the same hand that had moved Picasso and Moore. Did this mean that *Carlos* was right when he told me last night that we humans were returning to the beginning, that we were circling back on ourselves and reuniting with our most primitive expressive instincts before going into the future with a Revolution of music and love?

I turned the pages of my book as fast as I could, using my right thumb to slow them down just enough to see the individual images. My whole head was swimming with alcohol, and I couldn't stop talking. I was so excited with what I was seeing. Time really was circular, as *Carlos* had told us at the pyramids last night. I could see that human history continuously circled back on itself, like the four seasons of the year.

Creation really did work in cycles, like my grandmother used to tell me when we planted maize every year. But while all this was going on, I could also see that Jack was going bananas. He had something important he wanted to tell me.

"Look," he said, once we were in the parking lot, ready to go back down the hill into town. "Listen to me! Stop talking, damnit! I think you should know this! You're my bud, so I think it's not right for you not to know this, since you and Eve have become so close."

I had to work hard to calm down enough to give him my full attention.

"What is it?" I said.

"Eve came up to my room last night, after you two got back from the pyramids, and . . . and, well, she climbed in bed with me," he said.

"She what?" I said. "But why? I don't get it."

"Do I have to draw you a picture?" he said. "Come on, get real!"

I could see he was really upset. "You mean that she went up to your room and got in bed with you to . . . oh, my God! But . . . but I was drunk, so, well, she was probably just . . . just, well . . . "

I stopped talking and gripped my forehead.

"Vic," he said in a calm voice, "she's been coming up to be with me almost every night since you two have been together."

This time I really heard him, and I suddenly felt my guts twist so hard I thought I was going to puke.

"But I'd thought she and I were so . . . oh, my God!"

I felt sick. I began to shake. Jack helped me into his car, and we started down the hill.

"I'm sorry," he said. "I'm really sorry. But what the hell, if it wasn't me, she would have gone to one of our other roommates."

"Honestly?"

"Yes, honestly," he said. "She reminds me of Lady Ashley in Hemingway's book *The Sun Also Rises*. I should have told you when you first started seeing her."

"Tell me what?" I said.

"That she goes on the make almost every night after she has a few drinks. She's like an alley cat in heat. It has nothing to do with you, bud. She was doing it before you moved in with us."

My eyes twisted. I threw myself over the side of his convertible and began puking.

"Jesus! Are you going to be okay?" he asked. "Maybe we better stop and get you something at a drugstore."

I didn't know what to think or do. I never wanted to see another woman as long as I lived. First the professor's daughter and now

Eve. I began to cry. My God, she'd set me up every night with all that kissing. I really was a stupid, stupid fool, and ugly, too, I guess. That was why she'd gone to Jack. He was as big and handsome as Rhett Butler in *Gone With The Wind.*

We stopped at a drugstore. Jack went in and got something for me. I took the three little pills he handed me and in a few minutes began to feel better. Then he suggested we go out for an early round of drinks and dinner. I agreed. Last night after the pyramids, Eve and I had been so close. She'd even given me a book called *The Little Prince* written by a Frenchman who'd crashed his plane in the Sahara Desert. She said she bought it especially for me, and she read the whole book to me. The book had moved us to tears, and we'd gotten so close that she'd told me she loved me, but . . . then she'd once more pulled away when we were kissing and began getting all excited.

At the restaurant, Jack ordered drinks, then went to the phone to call our roommates. They came down and joined us, and when they tried to tell me about Eve, that they, too, had been with her, I cut them off.

"Thanks, but no thanks," I said.

After dinner they all decided we should leave Jack's car at the restaurant, get a cab, and go to the red light district. I guess they figured that this would help me get over Eve. But they didn't understand. I thought I . . . I loved her. I felt closer to her than I'd ever felt to any human being in all my life.

The cab driver took us to a great big old mansion with a beautiful rose garden in the front. The place was full of antiques. They served us a special drink on a silver platter, and then a group of beautiful girls dressed in negligees came out. Everyone except me picked a girl and went off. I wasn't interested. I went to the little bar. A girl came up to me. She wasn't very pretty, but was slender and gentle looking. We talked. Then I don't know how it happened, but I started crying and told her everything that had gone on between Eve and me. She said she understood Eve. She, too, had a boyfriend who didn't know what she did for a living, so she wasn't going to bed with him.

"I'm saving myself," she said, "to be with him on our wedding night."

Hearing this, my head twisted, and I got a sharp kink in my neck, just like my professor of philosophy had when I told him I was correcting Kant. I couldn't believe what she was saying. I had to rub my neck to keep my head on straight.

"But Eve doesn't do sex for a living," I said.

"Look," she said, "please understand that we women don't have it as easy as you men. She has children, right?"

I nodded.

"And she has no husband."

I nodded once again.

"And women have urges just as strong as men, but where can they go? There aren't places like this for women to go to. And if there were, they'd be looked down on if they went to such a place. But men, on the other hand, are seen as being real *hombres* when they come here."

I kept rubbing the back of my head and neck. "You mean to tell me," I said, "that she could have really meant it when she said she loves me?"

She nodded. "Yes, and I'm sure she really does."

"But then she went upstairs to be with someone else?" I said with tears streaming down my face. "I swear for as far back as I can remember, I've never had anything but complete crazy*loco* things happen to me when I get . . . get around women," I said. "In the fourth grade I proposed to a nun and almost got killed by the mother superior and a young priest."

She laughed. "I was going to be a nun," she said.

"No!"

"Yes."

"You're kidding!"

"No, I'm serious. I was a very good student, and my *familia* is very religious. But we were poor, especially when my father started drinking and my two older brothers did the same. My mother and my six younger sisters were going hungry. So what could I do, being a woman? I gave up my studies and told my parents that I'd been accepted to a convent, and I came here to Mexico City. They think I work now as a teacher at a Catholic school, but this is how I'm able to make enough money to send some home to them each month. I think my mother knows the truth, even though we've never spoken about it." She took my hand. "Please, come to my room," she said. "I can't spend any more time talking with you, if you don't pay and come to my room."

There was a very attractive older woman watching us. I paid the young girl the hundred *pesos* she asked for, and she gave most of it to the older woman. Then we went down the hallway and up the stairs to her room. It was large and beautiful and full of antiques. The bed frame was huge and made of carved wood. The whole place was decorated in gold and blue and silver. She got a small pan and filled it with warm water, undressed me, and knelt down to wash my private parts with soap and warm water. It was so soothing. I'd never had anyone wash my private parts since I was a baby. It was heaven!

Then she undressed. She had the most beautiful slender body I'd ever seen. She pulled back the covers and asked me to lay down on the bed. But when I tried to take her in my arms, she said no and told me to put my arms back down. She began to touch me, to gently stroke my body from my feet up to my chest, but she never once touched my private parts again.

I moaned and groaned and wanted to grab her, but each time she said no. Then she undid her dark hair, which came down all about her shoulders and naked arms. Now she kissed and nibbled her way down my body to my groin. When she got there, she opened her mouth and breathed hot breath on my balls and penis. It drove me crazy*loco,* but still she wouldn't let me take her in my arms.

She kept on and on until I was ready to scream!

She kept on and on until I was dying with good-hurting pain!

She kept on and on until my vision blurred, and once more I could hear-feel that Symphony of Creation within me!

The pyramids were swaying, dancing! The whole world was moving to the Great Music that was going on inside of me!

She got on top of me.

I closed my eyes.

She took my penis and moved the tip back and forth and through the entrance of her hot juicy opening, and then just like magic, she suddenly consumed me! Devoured all of me to the hilt! I began to

SCREAM! The whole world BURST OPEN, and I came STREAK-
ING ACROSS THE HEAVENS LIKE A SHOOTING STAR!
Not STOPPING!
Never STOPPING; never, never, never STOPPING!
I was screaming, and she was laughing and riding me in and in and
out and out and she was an angel! I couldn't believe it, but it was true.
Her whole body had turned into a MAGNIFICENT ANGEL! Gor-
geous bronze-brown face framed with a wealth of luscious mink-like
black hair and huge golden-white wings, catching air at her sides as she
kept coming down on my penis slow and long, feeling so, so, so good,
then she began going up and down faster and FASTER!
I was SCREAMING!
She was laughing, and I passed out.
I don't remember anything after that. I awoke the next day in my
room at our fifth floor apartment. I couldn't remember how we got
home. But then I remembered, as though it was a faraway foggy
dream, that after dinner we'd gone to the red light district, and that
I'd been with a . . . a nun? An angel?
I got up. I couldn't quite get things straight in my head, but one
thing was very clear to me. I felt wonderful. I couldn't stop singing
as I showered. I wanted to return to that mansion and give enough
money to that angel-nun, so she, too, could stop what she was doing
and get married to her boyfriend.
I had a big breakfast of *huevos rancheros* and *chorizo,* then I
drove around for hours in my T-bird. But I couldn't find the place. I
decided to take my car back to our building, park it in our underground garage, and hire a cab. I described the mansion to the cab
driver, and he took me to several places, but none of them were in
the *Zona Rosa* district, and they all looked cheap.
"No," I said, "this is a mansion in the *Zona Rosa* district, and it
has a very well-kept rose garden in front, inside an iron fence."
The cab driver told me that houses of prostitution no longer
existed in the *Zona Rosa* district. "This section of town is now the
rich artist part of Mexico City," he said.
"No," I said to him, "you're wrong! I was there last night! I
know what I'm talking about!"

He stopped at a taxi location and asked the other cab drivers if they knew of any such place. None of them did. Then an old taxi driver drove up. My driver went over to ask him if such a place existed. The old cabbie started laughing and laughing, then came over to me with my driver following.

"Was it a huge mansion?" he asked me with a big grin.

"Yes," I said.

"Did it have the most beautiful rose garden you've ever seen?"

"Yes, exactly!" I said. "Right in front."

"And you went up thirteen stairs to go inside, right?"

"Well, I don't know how many, but it was definitely more than three or four."

"And inside they gave you a special drink."

"Yes."

"Served to you on a huge silver tray."

"Yes," I said, "that's true."

"And the girl took you upstairs to a room full of antiques and a bed carved of the finest, most elaborate woodwork."

"Yes," I said, "so can you take me there?'

"Sure, of course," he said, laughing. "No *problema*. But, my friend, we will have to roll back Father Time about thirty-five or forty years. That place was closed down right after Don Porfirio's regime."

My mind went into a spin. I couldn't understand what he was saying. "But I was there last night," I said. "The girl was . . . was . . . was . . ."

"Was an angel!" he said. "And she'd originally studied to be a nun!"

"Yes, exactly."

He couldn't stop laughing. He took off his hat, slapped his legs, and began dancing in the street. "My friend, you had a gift given to you from heaven if you were there last night! You hear me, you were presented a gift straight from God! That place hasn't existed, like I told you, for at least, well, I'd say close to forty years. I was a boy of ten or twelve when it closed down!"

"No," I said. "You've got it all wrong! I was there last night! The rose garden was lit up! The place was well kept! There was a little bar to the right as we went in where I met her, and we talked and . . . and . . ."

"Look," he said, "I've met a few others who have been there in the last few years. They swear it, and they hire taxi after taxi to take them back to that place. I'd be happy to drive you around all day and night, but *mi general,* we will never find that place. Because no one who has gone there once gets to go back for a second time. You, my *pocho amigo,* consider yourself lucky that you got to visit heaven here on earth even once!"

I didn't believe him. This couldn't be true. So I hired him to take me back to our apartment so I could talk to my roommates. After all, they'd taken me there. I'd prove to him that he was wrong. I was shocked though when they said that it had been no big deal. Yes, it had been a big old house, but no mansion, and no, they hadn't seen any well-kept rose garden in the front. I asked them to please come with me to meet the old cab driver who was waiting for me downstairs and talk to him. None of them wanted to. They all said that I'd just been too drunk to know what was going on. I went back downstairs and had the old cab driver drive me around for hours. We never found the place. We ate dinner together, and he warned me that I had to let go of it, because there were miracles in life the human mind could never understand and that I'd go crazy*loco* if I tried.

Then, as if to drive me even more crazy*loco,* who did I bump into on the street when we got back to our building, but Eve.

"Hi, there!" she said with a big happy smile. "Haven't seen you in many a moon, *amigo!*"

She came up to give me a hug and a kiss. But I didn't want her to touch me. Still, I don't know how, but I found myself hugging her and returning her kisses once I was in her arms.

"Come on up," she said. "I bought you another book."

"But I don't like books. They give me a headache."

"Not this book," she said with that infectious smile of hers. "This one is called *The Family of Man.* It has very few words. It's a book of photographs from all around the world. A good friend of mine from New York took many of the photos."

I didn't know what to say, so I followed her into our building, and we took the elevator up to her apartment. I really didn't want to get out when the elevator stopped at her floor.

"Come on," she said, holding the elevator door open. "I can't wait to see your reaction to the book."

I took a deep breath. I felt so misused. I wanted to strangle her. But she took my hand, smiling at me with so much love and excitement that I followed her out of the elevator. We went down the hallway to her place. It looked quite different now that she'd gotten her furniture back. Lauren and Peter weren't home. She told me they were visiting friends. She gave me the book, all gift-wrapped. A part of me didn't want to accept her present. I had mayhem in my heart. I wanted to grab her and violate her as she'd violated me.

"Open it," she said. "I'll get you a glass of wine so you can look at it while I cook dinner."

"I don't want any wine," I said.

"Oh, you're not drinking?"

"No, not tonight."

"But will you stay for dinner?"

"Why don't you invite Jack?"

"Your roommate?"

"Yes."

"To join us?"

"No, instead of me."

"Why would I want to do that?" she said. "Has Jack been talking to you?" she added.

I nodded.

"Oh, my dear," she said. "It's not what you think. I like Jack. He's a good friend, but I have nothing special going with him the way I do with you."

My heart was pounding so hard I thought I'd explode. But before I could grab her and scream in her face, the door opened behind me and in came the children. They were happy to see me and came rushing across the room to hug me. Ever since we'd taken that drive out into the country, they'd been very close to me. They wanted to know if I'd stay for dinner, after all they hadn't seen me since the night I danced on the pyramids.

"I danced on the pyramids?" I said.

"Oh, yes!" said Lauren, bouncing around and pretending to dance. "With your arms out, saying you were a great red-tailed eagle-hawk!"

"Then you howled at the moon and cried out that you were a coyote-dog named Shep," said Peter, laughing.

I didn't remember any of this. "Maybe I will take that glass of wine," I said.

Eve gave me a glass of red wine, and I sipped the wine as I opened the gift-wrapped book. All the photos were in black and white, and they were so beautiful and natural and haunting. They were about people all over the world. In Europe, in Africa, in the U. S., and in Asia. Little kids, big kids, adults, old people. Little by little, I began to see as I flipped through the pages why this book was called *The Family of Man*. We really were all one *familia*.

After dinner, Eve put the kids to bed and sat down on a pillow on the floor, sipped her wine, and asked what our guide and I had been talking about out at the pyramids.

"I don't remember," I said.

She looked at me. It was a whole different kind of look. She wasn't a deer caught in mid-road. She was a warrior.

"Do you want to talk about Jack?" she said in a calm, even voice.

I shrugged. "I don't know if there really is anything to talk about."

"I didn't mean to hurt you," she said. "You need to believe that. I'd been seeing him for a couple of weeks before I met you."

"But you kissed me on the mouth!" I said, my eyes filling with tears. "And you told me you love me!"

"And I do," she said, tears coming to her own eyes, "with all my heart. I've never met anyone like you," she added.

"I don't get it," I said. "Then why do you kiss me and stroke me until I'm half crazy*loco*, then stop? I don't understand."

"Because with you," she said, tears coming to her eyes, "it has to be an all-time thing, and with Jack, it's well, good, but if it wasn't him, it would be . . . "

". . . someone else?"

She nodded. "I'm afraid so."

My whole face twisted with pain, and my hands became fists. "Oh, my God," I said. I wanted to slap her, hit her, make her hurt like I was hurting.

She reached out to touch me.

"DON'T!" I said. "DON'T YOU DARE!"

"All right, whatever you say. Look, if it will make a difference to you, we can go to bed right now."

"NO!" I shouted. "That's not the point anymore! DON'T YOU GET IT? You led me on!"

"Did I? What do you think? That a woman my age with children is going to revert to being a virgin?"

"I TRUSTED YOU!" I yelled.

"And I haven't betrayed your trust. I will never see Jack again if that's what you want. He's not that important to me."

"But I am?"

"Oh, yes, most certainly. Did you see the movie *The King and I*?" I nodded. "Well, who was the king really in love with? The English woman with whom he wasn't having sex or with all the wives he was bedding?"

"I don't know," I said, getting to my feet. "That's a movie! This is life!" I began to pace the room.

"I'm sorry I hurt you," she said. "If only I'd met you before I met Jack. I swear the more I live, I see that above all else. It's really love that causes us our greatest pain. We are a very confused people when it comes to . . . to love, but not romance. Romance is easy, especially when we keep it all in our heads. But venture out of the head, and oh, boy, is it ever a rough and tumble world in that great realm of love. This is why we have wars, you know, we just don't know how to . . . to love."

"Stop it," I said. "JUST STOP IT!"

"Okay," she said, "I'll stop it, but . . . but you can stay the night if you wish. I've never asked Jack to stay the night with me. I always go to his place after the kids are asleep."

I looked at her. I really looked at her, and it was so tempting, because I really, really wanted to be with her. But also I was so angry inside. "I don't know," I said. "I just don't know. I want to, I really do, but no . . . no, NO!" I yelled.

"See. That's exactly how I was feeling," she said. "True love is scary, especially when you've failed at it as many times as I have. But the other night, when I saw your reaction to *The Little Prince* and tonight when I saw your reaction to *The Family of Man*, I finally felt safe. You see, most men just see *The Little Prince* as a children's book and nothing more, and they see *The Family of Man* as just a book of photographs and nothing more. But you, you have like, well, x-ray vision that allows you to see the soul of everything you look at."

I said nothing. I just didn't know what to say or think. I didn't know if I could ever trust her again. Her words sounded so perfect. But she was also her father's daughter, and her father had made his living by choosing just the right words with which to manipulate, not just minds, but entire nations!

"Whatever I've said tonight," she continued, as if reading my thoughts, "believe this, I do love you. Truly, I do."

My whole chest swelled up, and my eyes overflowed with tears. I now saw her in a completely different way. It was as if I could now see that she, too, was an angel, and she wasn't really trying to con me. No, she was really, really being truthful. Suddenly I wondered if this was why I'd been able to see those golden white wings on the girl at the mansion and that feathered serpent oozing out of the stone at the pyramids. Maybe when we humans see through the eyes of our soul, we see God all around us and we see the Miracle of Creation in Everything and Everyone.

"Goodnight," she said. "And please don't forget your book. Lauren and Peter helped me pick it out for you."

"They did?"

"Yes, of course."

I left her place feeling, well, not really raging mad anymore, but more like, well, very divided and confused, and yet also beginning to realize for the very first time in my life that . . . that going crazy*loco* was maybe part of being in love. In fact, maybe being crazy*loco* was the beginning of learning who I really was and who I really wasn't.

I took a huge deep breath and held. My God Almighty, it felt like one hundred thousand years had come to pass since my dad had taken me past the barn and corrals to speak with me underneath the giant pepper tree.

# ~ BOOK FOUR ~

# CHAPTER THIRTY-FIVE

For days I avoided the elevator and took the back stairs up or down from our apartment so I wouldn't see her. After several days, I asked Jack if she'd been up to see him. He said no, not since the night we'd come back from the pyramids. I carried the book *The Family of Man* everywhere I went. I would stare at one picture sometimes for hours. It was so obvious. We'd been collectively brainwashed. We really were just one *familia* all over *la Tierra Madre*. We had different cultures, different languages, different words for God and woman and child, but we were all the same people with the same *Papito* all over the *planeta*. I couldn't stop crying. We were all so lost. Eve had been totally right. We really were a very confused people when it came to love.

One afternoon I found myself in front of a little church way, way out on the edge of the city. I'd walked, I guess, twenty miles or more. I went inside and saw a large group of poor people reciting the rosary. It was so peaceful. It sounded like a song. I lit a candle, knelt down, and started praying too, but I really didn't know how to pray in a church, since I was no longer a Catholic.

Suddenly I remembered that when I'd looked up the word "catholic" in my dictionary it said, "Universal, all-inclusive, of general interest or value, hence having broad sympathies and understanding; liberal." I was stunned. Then the Holy Catholic Church had taken the word "catholic" and twisted it all around, making it narrow and conservative and not liberal at all, but . . . but kept the con job going by pretending to be universal and all-inclusive when the church was "exclusive" in its very nature.

I went outside. I looked up into the sky and took in several deep breaths. Then it hit me between the eyes like a lightening bolt. I was still a Catholic, but with a small "c". Yeah, sure, because I was open, inclusive, and . . . and . . . my whole heart suddenly felt all warm and good. I bought a hand-crafted rosary from an Indian woman selling her wares on the church's steps and went back inside to say the rosary with the other people.

It felt good to repeat the "Our Father" and "Hail Mary." I hadn't realized how much I'd missed praying in a church. There was something soothing and almost magical about running the beads through my fingers while repeating the same prayers over and over again like song.

I started back across town after I finished the rosary. I could've taken a cab, but I didn't want to. It was past midnight when I got back to our apartment building. I'd walked maybe a total of fifty miles, but I wasn't the least bit tired. I knocked on Eve's door, and she let me in. We never said a single word. We went right to bed and held each other close all night long, but we never kissed on the lips or made love. I'd never slept all night with a woman, or with a man for that matter, since I was a little kid and slept with my parents. I loved her, I really did, and she loved me, too. I could now see why she'd told me that she'd never asked Jack to spend the night with her. Sleeping with another person was the most intimate experience one could ever have and I guess . . . even more so once you were married and you made love.

# CHAPTER THIRTY-SIX

Two days later, Jack and I took off in his convertible on a hunting trip to the jungles south of Tampico on the Gulf side of Mexico. We planned to be away for over a week. We met Indians who didn't speak Spanish and, through an interpreter, we learned that there were ruins nearby that had never been seen by European eyes. Jack wanted to go. I didn't.

"Why don't you want to go?" he said. "We could be like Lewis and Clark and be the first white men to see them."

I was shocked. Jack considered me white. He didn't see me as Mexican, so how could I explain to him what I was feeling? If these ruins had actually never been seen by European eyes, there was a good reason for it, and I didn't want to disturb it.

"Let's hunt for a few days," I suggested, "then see how we feel."

He agreed. In two small motorboats, our guides took us about fifty miles from the coast up a large river. We shot turkey and deer and caught fish as long as our arms. That evening we gutted a deer and hung him in a tree to try to lure in a jaguar. That night we huddled down with our two guides with the old .12 gauge shotguns that had been supplied to us, lying in wait downwind from the gutted deer.

The jungle was very quiet. There wasn't a profusion of bird sounds like was were during the day. Then suddenly, sometime after midnight, a huge terrible scream pierced the night like a knife. It was the jaguar, we were told, who had no doubt caught the scent of the gutted deer. He screamed again, so loud I swore he was only a hundred feet from us. But our guides laughed and said he was still two or three kilometers away. It would be at least another hour before he got to us.

Jack and I glanced at each other, and we both said, "No way," at the same time, agreeing that if he was this big and loud from that far away, we didn't want to hunt him with old shotguns that didn't fire half the time. Our guides couldn't stop laughing.

That night, as we headed back to our base camp, something went flying through the treetops just above us at an incredible speed. Our guides told us that it was a band of monkeys, but it was hard for Jack and me to believe that monkeys could travel so fast.

The next day we went further up the river in our two boats to an Indian village. I told the natives about the jaguar's scream and the fast movement through the treetops. They quickly took me to the old man of the village. He listened very carefully, then assured me in a very broken Spanish that those had not been earthly sounds or earthly movements.

"Those," he said, "were the spirits of the ruins you two disturbed."

"But I never saw any ruins," I said.

"Most people don't see them," he said, "even when they're right in the middle of them."

"Why?" I said. "Because of the jungle growth?"

"Partly," he said, "but haven't you ever been with people and you see things they don't see and experience?"

I nodded and told him what had happened to me at the mansion in La Zona Rosa. Then I added what the old cab driver had told me the next day, about needing to roll back time forty years for me to be able to see that mansion again.

"So, then, you know what I'm talking about," he said. "You just aren't ready to see the ruins. Your time hasn't come."

"How does a person get ready?"

"Well, first you need to realize that time, like reality, has many faces. This is why in our native languaging we have twenty-six different words for reality, just as we have twenty-six different words for love," he said. "And . . . and each of these words prepares our mind so it can then see that particular reality and love when our life gets to that type of reality and love."

Chills began going up and down my spine. Was this what was happening to me with Eve? She was showing me a type of love I just wasn't ready to see, because simply I hadn't gotten to that part of my life at which I'd be able to see this type of love?

As if reading my thoughts, he said, "Tell me, why is it that the Spaniards could never find the Seven Cities of Gold our northern cousins kept taking them to see?"

"You mean to tell me that those Cities of Gold that Coronado searched for really do exist?"

He only laughed. "Truly," he said, "I find it astonishing that the Spanish have lasted as long as they have with only one understanding of time and only one word for love and reality. Is this also true for the English, that they only have one word for each of these three moving, changing spectacles?"

"Yes," I said.

He started laughing even harder. "I should have known this," he said. "Small wonder these poor Europeans have survived at all. For how is it possible for any society to speak of time and reality and love with only one word?" He shook his head. "They must realize—even though they have no language to express it—that there is more than just one way to see reality, just as there is more than one way to love."

"Tell me," I said, "are these different kinds of love true for women as well as for men?"

"Of course," he said. "My old wife would be all dried up if it wasn't for her young lover. This is what helps keep her young and limber and healthy."

I couldn't believe what he'd just said. Did this mean his children knew that their old mother had a young lover? This was so repulsive, especially when I thought of my own mother. But none of this seemed to bother him. Seeing me get upset, he laughed all the more, truly enjoying himself, and invited me to come and sit by him at the little fire they had going.

An elderly woman came up with a big cigar for him. He thanked her, accepted the cigar, and put a stick in the fire. Once it took on flame, he used it to light his cigar. A line of young people came up, and he puffed great clouds of cigar smoke on each of them. Then he handed me the big cigar and indicated for me to puff and blow smoke on him. I did so.

"For the mosquitoes," he said.

"Oh," I said, finally understanding, and it was true, the hungry mosquitoes immediately stopped terrorizing us.

The old man asked me if I'd grown up in the United States. I said yes. He then asked what part of Mexico my parents had come from. I told him, and he told me that it must have been wonderful for me to grow up in a country where all the people had lots to eat and the government was just and open-minded and didn't use armed forces to keep its people in constant hunger and poverty.

"But," he added, "all that comfort I would gladly give up for all the suffering I saw up there."

"Suffering? Then you've been to the United States?"

"Oh, yes, of course. As a young man, I, too, had dreams of a fine little old work truck, so I went up there to work and adventure. First I went to Texas, but it was very hard, looking as Indian as I do. So I went to Arizona, and it was much better for me. Then I went to California. I worked in Bakersfield, Fresno, Los Angeles, and Santa Ana," he added with pride. "I'd never had flour *tortillas.* They are delicious!"

"Santa Ana," I said, "that's where my parents got married."

"Are they still together?" he asked.

"Yes."

"God bless them," he said. "I saw with my own two eyes just how difficult it is for any kind of marriage to last up there with all those distractions and no way to express all the different types of love that we feel in a normal lifetime. Here, a man and woman unite for life, but they include in their union all of the loves they will live through in their lifetime. But over there, it's all about changing wives and changing husbands, searching for that one perfect *amor,* when in reality, there are twenty-six different types of perfect loves, just as there are twenty-six different types of perfect reality." He shook his head. "I saw such suffering, such desperation, but what could I say or do when even our most basic reality of all, our dreaming, is seen by the *gringos* as not a reality at all, but as something of a lesser nature.

"For us here, as your parents must have told you, dreaming is everything. That is why we have seven sacred realities of dreams alone. Because the dream reality of the oldest man in the village is so different from a young man's dream reality that the same word cannot be used, just like a young man's dream reality cannot be compared to a young girl's." He laughed and smoked. "To use the same word for all these different realities and loves causes such confusion that, I tell you, it was painful for me to see all the suffering I saw amid all that wealth. Take happiness, for instance; it was not seen as the foundation of all realities."

My mind was swirling, swimming, dissolving, and . . . little by little the strangeness of the whole world he was presenting to me began to loosen up and take on form, washing away all I'd been previously taught. I couldn't believe it, but I actually began to see that his children, knowing about their mother's young lover, maybe wasn't really that different from a kid down the street from me in Oceanside, California accepting a young stepfather after his mother divorced. In fact, I could now see that there was more stability in keeping all these loves together in one ongoing structure of marriage.

The old man told me that his youngest son was presently going to the university in Mexico City, because Carlos Esparza, the greatest of all *curanderos,* had come through their village half a dozen years ago, encouraging the youth to learn the ways of the Europeans.

"Carlos took us all through a voyage in time and showed us that in the not too distant future, three—or four hundred years—the Europeans will be no more than a memory, and we, of the Mother Earth, will be as ongoing as the rocks and the sea and the stars. But for now, we need to learn their ways."

I wondered if this old man was talking about the same Carlos Esparza I knew. And if so, was this man's son in peril of being one of the students to be killed at the Olympic Games in eight years?

I took a breath and wondered if I should warn this man of his son's predicament. But at this very moment, a jaguar SCREAMED, no more than a couple of feet behind me, not a roar like an African lion but a blood-curdling scream, like a woman being raped!

I plunged forward, grabbed a *machete*, and whirled about to defend myself. But there was no jaguar behind me. The old man burst out laughing and looked at me as if I was the most ridiculous person in all the world. But I stood fast with a *machete* in hand as the light from the flames of the fire danced all over me. Then I understood what he was saying: that the great cat was way across the river, not any-where nearby, and if he was nearby, then a dozen *machetes* couldn't defend me, because I looked very juicy and tender and just right for eating. He suggested we should all sleep with our doors locked tonight, because the great cat did sound very hungry.

Lowering the *machete*, I glanced around. I saw no doors at the entrances of their huts, much less locks. "But you have no doors or locks on your huts," I said, trying to understand what he was saying. He laughed all the more. Feeling pretty ridiculous, I put the *machete* down.

The old man explained that feeling ridiculous, as I was obvious-ly feeling, was one of the different kinds of love, and this one allowed us to be silly without any shame. And that laughter from deep inside the gut was one of the keys that enabled us to go from one love to another love and that this key love was called Love-laughter. Lovelaughter was the love that healed even the most stone-hearted of men. Then he explained to me that Lovelaughter could actually soften the hunger of the fierce jaguar and miraculously cause a little jungle pig to come out of hiding and give himself for dinner to the great cat.

Lovelaughter was the love that even softened the worst of all animal killers, man, himself. This was why most men didn't eat their own offspring anymore, even though you could still see this urge in many a man's eyes when he first saw how beautiful and soft and plump his child looked when first born.

The thought turned my stomach, until I remembered how many times I'd heard a father or mother say that their children were so cute that they could just eat them all up. I saw the old man licking his chops as he looked at me.

"You're in good shape," he said. "You have nice-looking, juicy arms and legs, but because of my bad teeth, I refrain from eating humans anymore."

My eyes must've gotten huge with fear, because he now laughed with *carcajadas* once again.

"But why does this frighten you?" asked the old man. "You Christians eat the flesh and blood of your God Jesus every Sunday.

So for us to eat you must mean we think very highly of you. We're civilized, see, just like you. We'd never take human flesh into our bodies that isn't of the finest."

Once more he eyed my arms and continued laughing so hard that tears were streaming down his face.

Jack asked me to tell him what was going on, but I didn't know how to translate all this to him, so I just said, "He says they're cannibals and that we look very healthy and juicy."

Jack stopped grinning and stared at me. Then he turned and looked at the old man with the one big tooth in his mouth, and he glanced about and saw that we were surrounded by people; they all had *machetes* and they were smiling at us with great big smiles.

"You're joking, right?" he said.

"No," I said, shaking my head, and laughing. "In fact, he says that as Christians, we eat the flesh and blood of our Jesus Christ, so it is a great honor for them to eat us."

Jack reached for his shotgun. The people around us burst out laughing. One man handed him the *machete* I'd put down. Jack took it, having no idea what to think or do.

"I suggest you loosen up and laugh," I said to Jack. "Come on, obviously they're not going to eat us tonight. Relax. We're the best entertainment they've had in months, and they don't want to spoil that. Besides, get real, they don't have enough light to butcher us correctly, and they wouldn't want to do a sloppy job on a fine piece of meat like you."

Jack's fear cracked. I saw it in his eyes. And now he, too, was laughing. Big *carcajadas* from the gut. Our collective laughter was so tremendous and contagious that soon the jungle, itself, was laughing, too!

We were all laughing in hysterics—the trees, the ferns, the huts, and finally even the Holy Stars above. This was when we once more suddenly heard a TERRIBLE SCREAM and the sharp squeal of a pig. We froze, but only for a split-second. I guess our laughter had really brought the little pig out of hiding, and he'd given himself to the jaguar.

People started saying goodnight, and made their way to their huts, still giggling, still laughing. I remembered my dad had told me that when he and his old mother and sisters had been migrating north to the United States, it had been laughter that had lessened their pains of hunger and kept them sane.

War had been going on all around them, my dad told me, cavalry charges and cannons exploding, but their dear old mother had brushed the snakes and scorpions out of the way with a branch, and she'd given them little round river rocks to suck on to keep saliva in their mouths so they wouldn't swallow their tongues. She'd get them in a circle and tell them stories of the Little She-Fox in the Stars from where we'd all come, and she'd get them all laughing with such huge gut-jerking *carcajadas* that their hunger pangs subsided. Soon they'd been able to go to sleep and travel up to heaven to be in *Papito Dios'* loving arms. My dad always told me that his mother had explained to him that *carcajadas* were the greatest healing power of all.

I lay down in one of our boats that had been pulled up on the shore. I listened to the tiny waves slapping the riverbank, and I looked up at the stars. Tears came to my eyes. I knew I was never going back to the United States. Why? Because I'd found peace here, in Mexico.

*Marina* was smart to work in New York but live in Mexico. It was the best of both worlds. I should go see her. She lived just a couple of hours north of Mexico City in *San Miguel de Allende*. I drifted off to sleep, hearing the little waves of the river gently slapping the shore. That night I dreamed of the sea waters of the universe slapping gently against the stars.

The next day I awoke knowing, without a shadow of a doubt, that I'd slept all night in *Papito Dios'* Holy Arms. I stretched, feeling great. Jack also awoke, grinning from ear to ear. We glanced at each other and saw that we hadn't been eaten, and we burst out laughing.

# CHAPTER THIRTY-SEVEN

A s soon as we arrived at our apartment back in Mexico City, I went down to see Eve, but she was gone. Her neighbors told me she'd moved to a small town about two hours north of the city and that she'd left me her address and a map. She'd moved to San Miguel de Allende, where Marina lived. This was wonderful! That very same afternoon I got in my T-bird and drove out to see Eve. I was feeling pretty good. The hunting trip had done wonders for me, and the day I'd prayed inside that little church had helped me a lot, too.

In fact, I was now praying five times a day, and it felt so, so good. I was beginning to see that I couldn't manage it alone, especially my relationship with Eve. I needed to pray and ask God for help, because the limitations of our word "love" kept trapping me inside myself just . . . just as much as the words "stupid no-good Mexican" had entrapped me years ago.

I could now see so clearly that there was a language of entrapment just as there was a language of exclusion, and both destroyed the heart and soul, even though by their very nature the heart and soul were infinite. Jesus had showed us this when He'd forgiven those who crucified Him. Love knew no boundaries. It was fear that needed boundaries in order to exist. So for love to have any chance on Earth, then being God-connected wasn't just needed, but necessary. Just as one part hydrogen and two parts oxygen combined to make water, three parts God and one part man and one part woman combined to make . . . what? I guess, a marriage.

For well over an hour I'd been driving north across flat farm country with an occasional *burro* or herd of goats crossing the road in front of me. Then coming over a little rise, I suddenly saw one of the most spectacular sights of my life. It was *San Miguel,* a sun-baked little village of white *casas* and red-tile roofs, nested up against a hillside with a valley stretching out beyond it.

I braked. I stopped. I got out of my car and let my eyes feast on the incredible beauty of this little man-made paradise. No wonder Marina said that Mexico fed her soul. No wonder Eve had come here with her children. *San Miguel* was a watering hole for the soul!

Driving down into the village, my tires made a pluck-pluck singing sound on the cobblestone road. There were beautiful potted flowers in front of every *casa*. I wasn't able to find Eve's place, even though I had the address and the handmade map she'd left for me. Then just when I was beginning to feel panicky, I spotted Lauren and Peter. They had a basket and were doing their grocery shopping in the open-air *mercado.*

I parked and walked quietly toward them. They both looked so lovely with their bright red hair and their faces full of freckles. They were speaking in Spanish to the vendors like it was their native tongue. I hadn't realized they spoke Spanish so well. Then I saw Eve. She was off to the side of the market looking at jewelry. Slowly, carefully, I came up behind her.

"We'll take it!" I said to the seller in Spanish.

She turned and saw me, and her entire face lit up with joy. "Oh, my God!" she said, gripping her breasts with her hands. "You came! The kids told me you would, but I had my doubts," she added, laughing.

The kids spotted us and came running over. We put everything in my car and crammed in like fish in a can. We drove up the steep hill to a little house on a bluff overlooking the whole town. We took the groceries inside, then Eve showed me the living area and the back, which suddenly opened out into terraced gardens decorated with colorful pots and leather chairs like the ones I'd seen in town. There was also a fountain with cascading water, and birds were singing in the treetops. It was paradise.

"Different from an apartment, no?" said Eve, beaming.

"The place is spectacular!" I said. "How'd you find it?"

"The house or the town?"

"Both."

"The town I found because people in the city kept talking about this art colony, telling me that the rent was way cheaper than the city.

We came out to see, and it's true. Rent is dirt cheap, and everyone is an artist in *San Miguel*. Every shop, every little place in every alley is full of artists at work. Just to walk down to the *plaza* is intoxicating. You're inspired, seeing all you see, and everywhere the prices are so cheap! Then at night, the music!" She gripped her breasts again. "Have you ever really listened to the words of some of these old Mexican songs? Love isn't just love. No, love has all these variations. There's painful love. There's tragic love. There's sad love, happy love, silly love, and . . ."

I started laughing. It seemed like she already knew what I wanted to talk to her about. Our souls were in sync.

"And then there's profound love," she added, making her voice deeper. "There's lasting-forever love," she added in another tone of voice. "Then there's also crazy*loco* love that knows no boundaries or limitations, plus of course, there's the basic love a mother has for her children and the love children have for their mom and dad. The list is endless, I do believe, and they are all wonderful!"

I was laughing.

"What is it?" she asked.

"This is exactly what I'd come to talk to you about. There are twenty-six different kinds of love. I learned this from an old Indian man in a village way up the river from the coast near *Tampico*. He told me that there are twenty-six different words for reality, too, just like there are twenty-six different words for love, because—this is the real kicker—God sent us here to Earth to plant His Garden of Love for Him. This is also what my grandmother used to tell me, that we are five-pointed walking stars, having come across the heavens gathering stardust to plant here on Mother Earth for God's Garden. It's for each generation to do their own share of the planting."

"This is so beautiful!" she said. "My father would have loved to hear this. I can feel him stirring in his grave. Tell me more! This is exciting!"

"I'd love to," I said, "because you see, I've decided I'm never returning to the United States. I want to stay down here and keep in . . . I guess, rhythm with my heart and soul. I was so brainwashed in the States, I once actually tried to castrate myself. But now words are never going to entrap me again. Do you see what I mean? It's a whole new ballpark. I'm free, and life is wonderful, and God is alive and all around us, just waiting for us to wake up and see Her-Him in all of Her-His Glory once again!"

"It sounds like you've come into your own," Eve said. "This is wonderful. Let's celebrate! I'll cook you up a welcome-home dinner. I'm so happy you came out!"

"Me, too," I said.

She put on a colorful apron and began chopping vegetables for dinner. The kids got right to work in the kitchen, too. It was like I'd come home to my own little *familia.* I told them that I'd be right back, that I'd promised my dad and mom I'd say hello to *Marina* the moment I got into *San Miguel.*

"But you will come back to have dinner with us?" she said.

"Yes, of course," I said. "I'm not leaving."

"Good," said Eve. She gave me a big kiss at the front door, then turned back toward the kitchen with her hands made into fists and gave a little shout of *gusto* like she was a quarterback who'd just been put into the game and threw the winning pass.

I got in my car feeling ten feet tall and drove whistling down the steep cobblestone street, past the *plaza,* and headed out of town. My God, Eve was beautiful! Those wide muscular shoulders of hers and that skinny sexy body. It was like she was an electric wire of pure energy.

I found the motel *Marina* was building a couple of miles west of town. She had just come back from *Cuba* where she'd spent nearly two weeks interviewing *Fidel Castro* for the *Washington Post.* The *New York Times* hadn't been interested in the story. She was glad to see me and told me she'd heard I was with a woman with two children with bright red hair. I was shocked.

"But how can you know this?" I asked. "I just got into town and met them at the *mercado.*"

"San Miguel is a very small town," she said, laughing, "and it's not every day that a handsome young *mexicano* drives into town in a golden car," she added with a coquettish flare.

"My God," I said, "but honestly, that only happened about an hour ago."

"In most small towns in Mexico gossip travels faster than telephone calls. Who is this woman?" she asked.

"A friend."

"What kind of friend?"

I took a deep breath. "I don't really know. But let's not talk about her. Tell me about *Castro*. My mother told me your mother told her that you've been in *Cuba. Fidel, Fidel,*" I sang, "*¿qué haces, Fidel, que los americanos no pueden con ti?*" It was a popular song of day in Mexico, especially among the young college intellectuals.

"I'd prefer people around here don't know about that," she said. "Being a journalist isn't the best thing to be in Mexico, especially when you're trying to build a motel and have to work with so many different government agencies."

We talked, and she asked me how I had been doing since I'd come to Mexico. I didn't know where to start. She asked me to stay for dinner. I told her that I already had another commitment.

"With that woman?"

I nodded.

"Be careful," she said.

I rolled my eyes. My God, what was it with everyone? Why did they all keep telling me I had to be careful? But, then, that very night I found out why.

# CHAPTER THIRTY-EIGHT

The next morning I awoke with a splitting headache. But I'd had a few hangovers before, so I knew that this wasn't just a hangover. This was something else. But for the life of me, I couldn't figure out what it was. Then little by little, I began to recall what had happened to me the night before.

I decided to take a walk to clear my head. There was a huge brown hill behind *Marina*'s motel. I walked across the flat of the valley and started climbing the tall, bone-dry hill. By midday I could see there were a couple of huts in the distance. They looked like nothing but tiny shacks made of sticks and rock and palm leaves. This was such a different country from the luscious green jungle Jack and I had hunted. As I got closer, I began to see it was a whole village, but from the road none of the huts were visible, because the structures blended so well with the trees and brush and cactus.

I stopped to catch my breath just below the first hut. Once more I tried to figure out what had happened last night and just what kind of love Eve and I had if . . . if we had any at all. I mean, last night we'd had a wonderful dinner, put the kids to bed, then drove down the hill to the *plaza*. We went to a restaurant with a bar in the inside *patio*. A man was playing the piano in the garden. He sang like an angel, and the moment we came in, he recognized Eve, gave her a big smile, and dedicated his next song to her. She was thrilled. When he finished, he came to our table, and he and Eve hugged and kissed. Then we went to another place where the guitarist also knew Eve. They hugged and kissed, too, but on the lips this time, and it wasn't just a little peck, either. No, this was a real kiss, by two people who'd already made love together. But then she stepped back from him, took my hand, and told the man that she was with me. His demeanor instantly changed, and he shook hands with me and sat us down at the bar so we could hear him play.

"Listen to the words," she said to me as if nothing had just happened. "I've learned enough Spanish to understand most of the song. Isn't it so sad and beautiful and happy all at the same time?"

My heart was pounding. Wild crazy*loco* thoughts were whirling about inside of my head. I was just finally beginning to calm down enough to get into the music, when she told me to look at the poor man at the end of the bar.

"He looks so lonely," she said. "He doesn't know anyone here. Let's go talk to him. Poor soul. Can't you just feel his loneliness?"

The next thing I knew, we were at the other end of the bar, and she was consoling the man. But I could see in his eyes, by the way he was looking at me over her shoulder, that he saw it differently. He thought she was coming on to him, and he couldn't figure out why I was bothering to hang around. When he made his move on her, she looked at him as if he was crazy. He got angry. She couldn't figure out why he was behaving like this, since she'd only meant to make him feel better.

We left that bar and went to another, and I tried to explain to Eve what I had seen and why that man had become angry. She would hear nothing of what I said, and she then began to explain to me that there were twenty-six different kinds of love, just as there were twenty-six different levels of reality, and so it was very unhealthy for me or anyone else to get stuck in just one level of reality or one type of love.

At first, I thought she was joking, but then as she went on and on and once more told me of her high I.Q. and that she knew what she knew because she was so smart, I suddenly realized that she'd forgotten that I was the one who'd told her about the twenty-six different types of love and realities.

I was shocked. What was going on? Was she drunk? Or did her mind just work in this way? Then I remembered that she'd told me this had happened to her father, that some of the generals he'd fed information to for years began to think that they were the ones who'd come up with these brilliant ideas on their own, and a couple of these generals had actually become so mixed up and paranoid that they'd suspected her father was a spy.

I was suddenly exhausted. I wanted us to go home. What I'd thought was going to be one of the most wonderful evenings of my life was quickly becoming a whole mess. But she wanted to keep going from bar to bar, so I went with her, and at each place, she'd find another poor lonely man. I began to notice that all of her poor lonely men were often the most handsome men, and they looked quite a bit like Jack. I wondered if her dad had looked a lot like Jack. I didn't want to drink anymore. I wanted to call it a night. Finally, I took her by the arm, pulled her to my car, and drove back up the hill. She was pissed, but still kept telling me about what a wonderful time we'd had. She just didn't seem to realize it hadn't been much fun for me.

She was so drunk her body was limp, and I had to help her inside and put her to bed. And yes, I knew I could have stayed and slept with her and that we would have probably ended up having sex, but this wasn't what I wanted.

I went out to her back *patio* and looked up at the stars. It was beautiful and peaceful, and down below us, the sleepy little town of *San Miguel de Allende* looked gorgeous. Tears came to my eyes. Why was I so attracted to her? This whole situation was driving me crazy*loco*. My dad had been right. Love and marriage weren't for the weak. You needed to be strong and sure of who you were and who you weren't before you got into a relationship.

I wiped the tears from my eyes. I felt so much for Eve. She was the first person who truly understood me, and this felt so good down deep inside. But was this love? Was this the type of love that a relationship could be built on? I didn't know. How could I know? Love was so new to me, and tonight her breath had smelled so bad that when she tried to kiss me as I put her to bed, I'd almost puked. And this was the way she'd gone up to Jack's place and made love to him? That wasn't love. That was . . . was bad-smelling fucking— disgusting!

I took a deep breath, loving the smell of the clean night air, and stayed outside for quite a while. Then I went back inside and sat down on the floor with my back against the wall and watched her sleep. I'd never heard a woman snore before. It wasn't a big, loud sound like I'd heard men do. It was soft and gentle, and she looked like an angel now that she was asleep. She lay naked half out of the covers, so I tucked her in, checked on the kids, and left, going to *Marina*'s motel.

That was last night. Now, I drank some water from the leather gourd I'd purchased in town the day before, and I continued up the dry brown hill. The village was larger than I'd thought. There was a whole community living up here. I guessed they were the people who worked in downtown *San Miguel*. There was no electricity or running water. This was where the poor people lived, just as they did in every large town throughout all of Mexico and the whole world, I was told. I was impressed by the cleanliness, though. The earthen floor in front of each hut was brushed clean and dampened with water to keep down the dust. I saw potted flowers at every doorway and window, and I knew that the water for these flowers had been carried by hand all the way up from the valley. These were strong proud people, just like my mother and father's people. Then I saw them, a line of young girls and older women carrying pots with water on their heads. Their backs looked straight and strong as they came up the hill with grace and dignity. I smiled. These were healthy, happy people. Maybe this was where I should be looking for a wife. I froze inside. I'd used the word "wife."

Walking into the village, I heard screeches of laughter and saw little kids running around naked. I could hear goats and roosters calling, too, and I saw a mother pig with her little ones scramble by. The little kids stopped their games when they saw me. They stared at me, not moving a muscle or coming to ask for a handout like the poor kids in Mexico City. No, these kids were watching me, as cautious as deer in the wild.

There was an old man sitting in the shade of a mesquite tree near the center of the huts. I walked up to him. He wore wire-rimmed glasses and looked very distinguished. With a wave of his hand, he invited me to sit with him.

"Good day," I said to him in Spanish as I sat down beside him on the well-swept earth.

"Good day," he answered me. "So you speak Spanish?"

"Yes, of course."

"We thought that you didn't. People from *San Miguel* never come up here to see us. It is that rare American who's studying artistry in town that comes up now and then."

"Really?"

"But, of course. You either have to be *loco* or very poor to come up that steep mountainside in the heat of the day."

I laughed. "I think you're right. I'd just planned to walk a little way up the hill, but then I saw your huts and became intrigued."

We'd been visiting for well over an hour when I suddenly noticed that he had no lenses in his wire-rimmed glasses. I saw, too, that the paper he'd been reading when I first came up was yellow with age. I picked it up to see the date. It was almost two years old.

"Look," I said, when he saw me reading the date, "why don't I bring you the latest paper tomorrow, if you'd like."

"Oh, no," he said, "please, don't do that. I like this one."

"But it's almost two years old."

"So, aren't they all just about the same?"

"Well, yes, in a way, but each day there is new news."

"Yes, I've seen that," he said, "when I've gone to town. But then, I think about it, and I see that there really isn't that much difference in the news from day to day, or even year to year. So why would people do that to themselves? It's taken me reading this same paper for almost two years now to finally find peace with what I've read. Don't you think it takes at least that long for the human mind just to digest all that a newspaper has to offer?"

I was astonished. I'd never before quite thought of it like this. But maybe he was right. We just took in too much information all the time, never giving ourselves the time to digest what we'd taken in.

"Yes, I guess you're right," I said, "if we only read the same paper for a year or two, then we wouldn't feel overwhelmed. But isn't there a part of you that at least wants to know about the latest news?" I asked.

"Why, to disturb me? No, I like taking my time in getting to know anything, not just the news."

Then he asked me about Russia and communism and the United States. He wanted to know if I thought a war was going to take place

between these two powerful nations. I said I didn't know and added
that I hoped not.

"Well," he said, "if a war does happen, I'm sure the United
States will want Mexico to help her, so I've been wondering if, well,
each of us men here in Mexico will be issued a rifle? Then after we
whip Russia and all those nonbelieving communists, I'm wondering
if we will be allowed to keep our rifles."

I almost burst out laughing, but didn't. "You know," I said, "I
don't see why not. Sure, of course, they'll allow you to keep your
rifle after we whip those nonbelieving Russians."

"Good, because with one of those new rifles, you and I can go
hunting over behind this mountain range and shoot us a big deer, and
I'll throw a big celebration here in our village. I'm the mayor, you
see, and the sheriff, too. In a few years we plan to bring up electricity from that motel where you are staying. Oh, what a pleasure it will
be to have light at night and a television for us to watch cartoons
with our children," he said joyfully.

He asked me if I could bring him extra ammunition for his rifle
after the war between Russia and the United States. I said, "Yes, of
course."

I thanked him for our visit and started back down the steep hillside. I'd no sooner gotten back to the motel when *Marina* told me
she'd heard that I'd gone up the hill behind the motel and visited
with *Don Miguel.*

"And I hear that you offered to take him a new morning newspaper every day, but that he turned you down because you didn't say
how much it would cost him."

I started laughing, not even wondering how *Marina* already
knew all about this, since I'd just managed to hike back down from
the village. "But your sources got it all wrong. I wasn't going to
charge him anything," I said. "And I only meant that I'd take him the
paper one time, not every morning."

"He thought that you were *loco* to be going up there in the heat
of the day through all that rock and cactus only wearing shorts and
sandals. They say you carried your shirt in your hand. Look at yourself, you're all sunburned."

I quit laughing. I didn't like the feeling of where this seemed to be going. "What else did they say?" I asked. It felt to me like *Marina* had an agenda going on that I knew nothing about.

"From the Indian village nothing more," she said, "but from the people in town a lot. They say you had a very difficult time last night."

My eyes narrowed.

"*Mundo*," she said to me, calling me by my family nickname Edmundo, "what are your intentions with this woman?"

"Like I said yesterday, I don't know," I said. "She's so smart, and I've learned so much from her, and yet . . ."

"She's *una americana loquita,* you know. And many *locos* are very smart. In fact, often the smartest of all, so you must be very, very careful or—I shouldn't even be talking to you about this," she said, then added, "I called your parents."

My heart leaped! "You did what?"

"I called your parents," she said once again.

I could now see that she was very upset. I'd been right. She did have an agenda going on that I knew nothing about.

"I think you're getting into something much bigger than you realize. You might think I did wrong to call your parents and that it was none of my business, but they are my godparents, and so I have an obligation to . . ."

"What did you tell them?!" My heart was pounding!

"Don't raise your voice to me. I was there when they put your first diaper on you. You're like my little brother. I didn't tell them much. I figure that this is for you to do. I simply said that maybe it was time for you to go back to the United States, and they should come down to get you immediately. Then I added the old Mexican saying, '*Dime con quién andas* y *te diré quién eres.*' Tell me with whom you walk with and I'll tell you who you are."

I was furious. "But I'm never going back!" I shouted.

"Why? Because of her?"

"No, not because of her, but because, well, I've found peace here. This is where I want to live."

"Okay, this I can understand. I feel the same way. That's why I talked my mother and father into buying this land and those old ruins at the hacienda out of town."

"But you went to Berkeley," I said. "You were the first *Chicana* to do this. You always did great in school. What problems did you ever really have? You got a job with the *New York Times*, and now you have one with the *Washington Post*."

She laughed. "I've had no problems? Give me a break. Just like you haven't had any problems because you were born rich and your father is a powerful man who's not just respected, but feared! Grow up, don't be so simplistic. I haven't had anything but major problems at every turn in my career. All my life I've had to be at least ten times better and harder working at my job than my Anglo coworkers. I can well understand what you mean when you say that you've found peace here. At first my parents were shocked, because they'd struggled so hard to go to the United States, and I wanted to return to Mexico."

The rage began to leave me, and *Marina* and I talked all afternoon. It was wonderful. *Marina* was every bit as smart as Eve, and she was also . . . I didn't know how to say it, but more, well, like rooted to Mother Earth and therefore practical and wise. I flashed on the mayor of the village I'd visited with earlier. I flashed on the old man I'd talked to on the riverbank in the jungle. There was a real big difference between being smart and being wise.

Late that afternoon, a call came into the motel office from my parents. They said they'd be flying into Mexico City that weekend with my two little sisters. I was pissed and yet kind of happy, too. I ate dinner with *Marina*, then showered and changed clothes to go into town.

"Look," said *Marina*, "a lot of *americanos* come down here, and they relax and start drinking a little bit, but then soon that's all they do, celebrate night after night. Be careful. You never used to drink, Mundo. People say you were quite drunk last night."

"How do you know all this?"

"We, the business community, all know each other," she said.

I nodded. She was right. I never used to drink. But my drinking had nothing to do with Eve. What it had to do with was all this rage and confusion I had inside of me THAT WAS DRIVING ME CRAZY *LOCO*!

# CHAPTER THIRTY-NINE

**M**y parents were on their way, and for the life of me, I felt like I should make sure my room was clean. What was it with me? I was almost twenty years old, and it still rattled me that my parents were coming to see me. I decided to go see Eve and tell her. But it had gotten so late visiting with *Marina* that I figured Eve had already put her kids to bed and gone out drinking. I didn't want to drink, but I still felt I should find her and tell her my parents were coming.

She wasn't at the first three *cantinas* we'd gone to the night before. I did find the musicians though, and they recognized me and told me she hadn't come by. I drove to her house. The lights were on in the kitchen. She was home. This was wonderful! She was spending the evening with her children, so she probably wasn't drinking. I knocked, she let me in, and I was in heaven visiting with her and Lauren and Peter. After we put the kids to bed, she apologized about the night before.

"I'm sorry," she said. "But sometimes I just lose my head after a few drinks."

I accepted her apology, and we hugged and kissed and were feeling so close that I couldn't believe it when once again she pulled away.

"No can do," she said. "You're so beautiful and pure, and you grew up on a ranch with wild horses by the sea, so no can do. You should wait for my daughter Lauren who loves horses and is so strong, smart, hard working, pure, and responsible. Because the truth is that, no matter how much I try, I just know that I'm going to end up blowing it. And I don't want to lose you," she added, looking me right in the eyes. Her eyes swelled with tears. "I do want you to be part of our little *familia* forever and ever, and I can see you'll have a much better chance of it with Lauren. She's big and very mature for her age, and strong! In five years, when she's sixteen, you two could marry on horseback by the sea and be so happy."

I didn't know what to say. She was driving me completely crazy*loco.* "But Lauren is only a child!" I said. "You have no right to . . . to be thinking of who she should marry when she gets older."

"Get real," she said to me, "arranged marriages have been going on for centuries. What I'm proposing is very smart."

"Smart," I said, "or is it that you're afraid of finding out who and what we really are to each other?" I took her hand. "It's okay for you not to have all the answers, Eve," I said. "It's okay for you to not know everything. In fact, not knowing is really where it all begins. Can you see this? Being smart doesn't mean that you necessarily know everything. You can have that high I.Q. of yours and still feel okay not having all the answers."

"Okay," she said, "you've convinced me. Then will you marry me on horseback by the sea?"

"What?" I said. "Why do you do this? Why do you keep asking that? My God, you keep putting the cart before the horse. We don't even really know each other yet."

Tears were streaming down her face. "Do you love me?" she asked.

I took a deep breath. "Yes, damnit, I guess I do!"

She started laughing. "That's exactly how I've felt since the first day I met you and those eyes of yours, then how you stood up for me with my husband. You're so brave and beautiful. Yes, damnit, I guess I love you, too. And it hurts here in my heart worse than a kick to the stomach!"

"I agree," I said.

She stopped laughing. "So what do we do?"

I stopped laughing, too. "I don't know. But you're right, what do we do?"

We looked into each other's eyes, and truly, it was as if we were seeing each other for the very first time. She reached out and touched my cheek, stroking my face so gently, so softly, then we began to kiss once again, and this time it was different. We hadn't had anything to drink. We were just getting close once again when, without warning, Lauren appeared in the room.

"Mother," she said, "I need to speak to you."

I froze. She hadn't called Eve "mom" as she normally did. She'd said "mother."

"Yes," said Eve.

"I need to speak with you in my room," she added.

"All right," said Eve. "I'll be right in."

"No, right now, mother."

Eve got up. "I'll be right back," she said to me.

"Not necessarily," said Lauren to me, and she took her mother's hand and they went up the hallway and down the stairs.

I got up and went outside. I looked up at the stars and the full Mother Moon, and the moon spoke to me. I could feel it deep inside, and I now knew what was going on. Lauren had just begun her first period, and this was why she'd needed Eve. It really wasn't that she was upset that we were kissing on the couch. I waited for about an hour and then left. The first thing the next morning, I bought flowers for both Eve and Lauren. Lauren was so happy. No one had ever given her flowers.

"Last night my little girl became a woman," said Eve with a grand smile.

"I know," I said, "the moon told me."

"The moon told you?" said Lauren. "Does this mean that everyone at school will know about my period?"

"Oh, no," said Eve, "only very special people like Vic, who has x-ray eyes and sees the soul in everyone and everything. He's a lot like you, Lauren. He's as special as you and your brother Peter."

"Really," said Lauren with that slow pronunciation of hers. She looked at me in a new way.

It was almost frightening. I could see she really had become a woman overnight. We men really had no idea what it was like to have that first blood come loose from our bodies, telling us that we could now get pregnant and could never again go back to just being children.

That morning after we took the kids to school, Eve and I had breakfast down at the main square. We went to the little outdoor restaurant in front of the church. We ordered Mexican coffee with Mexican chocolate. It was delicious. I told Eve about my parents coming that weekend.

Her eyes held and didn't flinch. "I'd love to meet them, if you're not too ashamed of me," she said.

"Why do you even talk like that?" I asked.

"Well, I have behaved pretty badly with you," she said.

"*Sí, y no,*" I said. "Yes, and no," and I just didn't know how to explain everything I was feeling inside, especially not in English. English was too sharp and exacting. Not round and smooth and easy. I felt so close to her and yet cautious, too. "Eve," I finally said, "don't you know how much you mean to me? My life didn't make any sense until I met you. You helped me see myself and my culture and even the entire world in a whole new way. I'd be honored for my parents to meet you."

Smiling, she took a sip from her chocolate-coffee. "And I was just hoping that you wouldn't be too ashamed of me. Do you really mean what you just said about your life not making much sense until you met me?"

"Absolutely."

Her face began to glow. "Here," she said, reaching into her bag. "I have a little present for you, but I keep forgetting to give it to you."

The package was beautifully wrapped. I took it, and I could feel through the wrapping that it was a book.

She was beaming. "It's Homer's *Odyssey*" she said.

I must've looked puzzled because she now said, "Don't you remember how you asked me, after you'd read *The Family of Man*, if there were any books written in words that tried to unite us globally, like those jazz musicians with their music and the book *The Family of Man* had done with photographs?"

"Oh, yes, now I remember, and you told me that some old Greek had tried to do that with a couple of volumes."

"Yes, and Homer is that old Greek," she said, laughing. "Remember you asked me if he was a local writer, and I said he was a Greek storyteller, long before Christ, and that his works were classics. You asked what a classic was, and I said, 'A classic means that it's still good'," she said in a deep authoritative voice, laughing all the more. "So here is one of those books. I got it for you here in *San Miguel* in English. They didn't have it in Spanish."

My heart began pounding so fast that I could barely hear her. Our food arrived, and after the waiter left, I said, "Eve, it doesn't really matter, English or Spanish, because . . . because I . . . I can't read in either language." I took a huge deep breath. "My parents don't even know this," I added. "It's . . . it's my darkest secret."

My whole body was trembling. I was so scared she might laugh or argue with me, trying to convince me that I did know how to read and was . . . was just exaggerating. But she didn't question me or make fun of me. She just looked at me for a long time, then said a most astonishing thing.

"Maybe this is your special gift of genius," she said. "Just as Moses' gift was that he had a speech impediment and yet he was the one chosen to speak and lead his people out of bondage, then maybe your gift, not being able to read, will lead you to write books. Hello, Moses!" she added, laughing.

I couldn't believe what she'd just said. "I didn't know that about Moses," I said, "and writing has never entered my mind. But it has crossed my mind that not being able to read saved me from getting brainwashed like my cousin."

"That and your genius," she said.

"My genius? Get real, Eve, I'm not a genius."

"But of course you are. I'm smart enough to recognize true genius."

"But . . . but I can't be. My I.Q. is almost exactly a hundred points lower than yours."

"Genius has very little to do with I.Q.s or being smart," she said. "Have you ever looked it up in a dictionary? I have many times, and it says, guardian spirit, natural ability, then it says something about an ancient Roman belief of a guardian spirit assigned to a person at birth."

"What! Then you're telling me my grandmother was right when she told me that each one of us comes into this world with a guardian angel?"

"That's beautiful," she said. "Your grandmother was right. Each of us does come into the world with a guardian spirit, and that's our genius."

My eyes welled up with tears, but I wasn't crying. No, I was happy! Big, big, BIG HAPPY!

After breakfast Eve and I drove out in the country, pulled off the road, laid out a mat and blanket, and she began to read the *Odyssey* to me. Instantly the story came to life. It was so much like the story of my father's childhood in *Los Altos de Jalisco* with a two-headed serpent that devoured children and little pigs. My grandfather, a great horseman, roped the snake and dragged it into the village where two woodsmen chopped off its head, and the heavens opened up and angels came down to Earth to sing.

For the next few days, Eve and I drove out into the country each morning after we dropped the kids off at school and . . . she'd read to me. Then in the afternoons, I would read to myself what she'd read to me, and I'd circle in pencil all the words I still didn't know, even after she'd read that section to me. It was usually forty to sixty words per page that I had no idea how to pronounce, much less knew what they meant. It was wonderful. Never before had I understood why people liked to read books. It had been completely beyond my comprehension why people sat at the beach reading a book instead of watching the surf. Books were fantastic! They could transport you to another time and place. In a couple of days I'd be driving into the city to pick up my parents and my sisters. There was so much I wanted to tell Eve, and I wanted to thank her for coming into my life, but I didn't know where or how to begin.

The next morning we drove west out of town into the country. We drove in silence, each of us lost in their own thoughts. Up ahead I saw a bunch of cattle on a hillside full of rocky cliffs and cactus and underbush. I stopped, and we got out of my car and climbed a little ways up the rocky hillside. We were about ten miles from San Miguel. Neither one of us was in very good shape. It was hot, and I began to sweat. We stopped in the shade of a couple of trees and sat down on a grassy area next to a large boulder. Eve brought the *Odyssey* out of her book bag and began to read to me. I'd never had the experience of having a whole book read to me. I was beginning to understand why . . . why I'd always had so much trouble reading. All these years it was like I'd get hypnotized by the white rivers that ran up and down a page between the words. The white rivers had been my focus, not these little insignificant chicken-markings called letters.

"Eve," I said, "please stop for a minute. I think I finally get it. As you read to me aloud, the words become alive for me, and I can see pictures in my head. But when I try to read, all those little letters just confuse me. Because it's the white of the page between the words that truly grab me. Do I make any sense? Reading, I do believe, is a very unnatural thing. But to listen to a story, like sitting around a campfire, is very natural."

She didn't laugh or make fun of me. "You're right," she said. "Reading is very unnatural. I'm sure that's why 80 percent of people all over our globe don't know how to read, and I also believe this is why Homer was a storyteller and not a writer. They now believe he was blind and traveled from town to town telling the story of the Illiad and the Odyssey. Maybe this will be your way of writing, too. To be the storyteller of all the stories your parents have told you."

I nodded. This, I could understand. My father, who could also hardly read, was a great storyteller, just as his mother had been a great storyteller, but . . . but she'd known how to read and write very well. We continued talking, and as we spoke I felt comfortable enough to tell Eve something that had been haunting me and . . . and seemed so crazy*loco*, and yet true.

"Eve," I said, "I'm beginning to see that it's not just the stars, but also the darkness between the stars that fills me with wonder just as it's the whiteness of the page that gives power and significance to each letter. I don't know how to explain it, but . . . but I'm beginning to feel that it's the silence between the notes in music that give feeling to . . . to each note."

I stopped and took a deep breath. She still wasn't laughing or making fun of me. This was wonderful.

"Eve," I continued, "I'm beginning to understand why *Carlos Esparza* explained to us at the pyramids that Europe still doesn't understand the concept of zero. Because you see, I now see so clearly that zero isn't the absence of life. No, zero and nothing are alive, and not a void but the possibilities of limitless life, and this is our center. This nothing, this white blankness of the page, this silence between the notes is . . . is our beginning. Because you see, we need to quiet ourselves long enough to see what's right in front of us, or we live our whole lives lost and full of . . . "

I stopped talking. Suddenly I was full of fear and all my instincts for survival came bursting up inside me. I glanced around. A herd of huge black cattle had come up on us.

"Don't move!" I said, under my breath. "These aren't regular cattle. These are fighting bulls!"

And how they'd suddenly come up on us, I had no idea. Unless they were the same cattle that we'd seen way up on the steep hillside from the road, and they'd come down to inspect us once they'd seen us making our way up into their territory. They were big and shiny black and solid muscle. Now they were snorting and flipping their tails to keep the flies and bugs off of their huge, thick bodies as they came in closer to inspect us.

"What do we do?" she asked.

"Keep real still," I said. "They're different from men, who get brave when they're in groups or in a gang. Bulls only get aggressive when they get cut off from the rest of the stock. They'll keep calm, I think, if we don't panic."

There were eight of them, and one was getting in so close to us that I could smell him. I doubted they'd ever seen a human being on foot. They'd probably only seen men on horseback. Very slowly, I took off my shirt.

"Are you going to bullfight all of them?" she asked.

I almost laughed. "No," I said, "I'm going to get to my feet really slowly, then throw my shirt at them if they charge, like I've done to swarms of bees that got after me, hoping they'll go after my shirt long enough for us to get away."

"Should I take off my dress?" she said. "It is red," she added.

"It wouldn't hurt," I said. My shirt was white. "But don't throw it at them until I throw my shirt, because to throw it too soon could backfire on us."

"I'm not wearing any underwear," she said.

"I don't think the bulls really care," I said.

She slipped off her elegant plain red dress. She really wasn't wearing any undergarments. Did she usually go without them or . . . had she planned for us to finally make love after we finished reading today?

"Okay," I said, "now let's start going down the hillside, but real slowly. Leave the book bag. It might give them something to sniff at."

"But I can take the book, right?"

"Yes," I said.

Slowly, carefully, with our clothing in hand, we started easing our way back down the steep rocky hillside. Once we were a good ways away from the huge black beasts, we turned and took off racing through the rock and cactus and short *chaparral*. We were both laughing hysterically by the time we got to the rock fence, climbed over, and approached the T-bird. We looked at each other. We were sweaty and naked as the day we were born, and her skinny, slender body looked so firm and strong and beautiful. I took a deep breath. Her dark brown bush looked thick and luscious. Instantly I got an erection. She smiled. I smiled. This was how I'd always dreamed of us making love, out in the wild. But then we heard a truck coming up the grade. We both laughed, and quickly began to dress. We'd just put our clothes on when the truck came around the last curve with a load of firewood and three men riding in the back. Driving back into town, we didn't say a single word. Something really big had just happened to us back there. But what it was, I had no idea.

That night Eve finished reading the *Odyssey* to me. It was one of the most exciting experiences of my life. A book really could transport a person across time and space and make those people, over there, come ALIVE!

"Eve," I said, "a book can take us out . . . out of our isolated existence and show us how people live in another culture. I feel closer to those Greeks than I feel toward my own sisters. Books are holy. They really are. I want my parents to read this book," I added. "The *Odyssey* sounds so much like the story of my father's people in *Los Altos de Jalisco* and my mother's people from the Rain of Gold canyon in *Chihuahua*. Their stories were also full of passion and wild adventure and holy spirits interacting with their people.

"Why wasn't I ever told in school that books can be exciting?" I asked Eve. "Why wasn't it ever shown to us that education can be alive and enlightening and wonderful? Why did they make everything so boring and all technical and seem so UNRELATED TO LIFE? MY GOD, EDUCATION CAN BE THE MOST EXCITING THING IN THE WHOLE WORLD!"

"You won't get any argument from me," said Eve, her eyes dancing.

"Eve," I said, "I feel so close to you. You're my godsend. When I'm with you I . . . I feel like we're the first two people on earth. You are coming into the city with me tomorrow afternoon so we can pick up my parents at the airport together, right?"

She'd looked happy and confident, but now her eyes started blinking, and once more she took on that look of a deer out in midroad. I hadn't seen this look since Mexico City.

"I don't think that's a very good idea," she said to me. "Besides, your sisters are coming, so I don't see how you'll get all of us in your car."

"I'm taking Marina's big station wagon," I said.

"Oh," she said, "but still I'm sure that . . . that no, no, no can do. I'll meet them when you come out to *San Miguel*, if you come at all."

"But we're coming out for sure. I want them to meet you," I said.

"I'll be here," she said, "for at least six more months before my money runs out, then I guess I'll be returning to La Jolla."

"Good, then you'll meet them."

"But don't force them to come out to meet me," she said. "I'm sure they'll want to stay in the city for at least a few days."

I took a deep breath and could see that she was right. We didn't speak about my parents anymore. We were both pretty nervous.

The next morning Eve and I went out for a little drive before I drove into the city. It was like we both knew that we loved each other dearly, that we'd finally found our other half of being, and yet something wasn't quite right between us. We came over a little rise, and a skinny old man was going on the trail along the side of the road with his *burro*. The little animal was loaded down with a huge stack of firewood, and the old man was yelling at the little animal and hitting him with a stick to keep him going at a good click.

Eve went berserk! "Stop!" she screamed. "Stop!" And she leaped out of the car while it was still rolling. She almost fell. "Stop hitting that animal!" she shouted at the old man. "That's not right! Stop it!"

Then she rushed up, grabbed the stick away from the old man, and began asking him how he'd like to be hit with a stick. The old man didn't know what to do. He looked at me, waiting for me to say something or do something.

"Eve," I said, getting out of the car, "please calm down. He wasn't hitting the animal that hard. He was just trying to keep his speed going, so the *burro* could get up over that next little upgrade more easily."

"He was abusing the poor beast!" she yelled.

"Eve, you're not being realistic," I said. "Take a good look at the *burro*. He's well fed. This man loves his little *burro*. He knows what he's doing. He probably raised him since a baby."

"No," she said, "you just don't want to see it! There are parents who abuse their children, and they also raised them since babies! Ask him how much he wants for the wood. I'll buy it. He doesn't have to cart it into town to sell it."

"Eve, you don't know what you're getting into," I said.

"Ask him!" she snapped. "Here, I'll do it! *Cuánto por los,* eh, sticks?"

The man was looking very perplexed.

*"La señora quiere comprar su leña,"* I said to him. "The lady wants to buy your firewood."

"Oh, okay," he said in Spanish. "I understand now. I'll deliver it to your home."

"He says fine, that he'll deliver it to your home."

"No, no, no!" she said. "Me buy, me buy, but you drop here. Tell him that!"

I told him, then I told her the man's response. "He said, sure, that he'll sell you the wood and he'll drop it off for you here, but that he doesn't think that this is a good place for you to build your fire to roast your meat for our dinner."

"Tell him I'm not going to roast my dinner here. For him to just sell me the firewood."

I told him. He agreed to sell her the wood, but she had no money, so I paid for it, a sum of two dollars. The man then picked up another stick and started yelling at his little *burro* to go on, to move it up the gulley, and he hit him on the butt again. Eve went berserk once more.

"He's hitting him again!" she yelled. "Can't he learn? What's wrong with him?"

I started laughing. But Eve didn't think it was funny. She wanted me to help her break down the load of wood so that we could take it in my car into town. This was when I said, "No can do," that I had to shower, change clothes, and go get my parents. She said fine, that she'd return with Peter and Lauren and they would carry the wood by hand if need be.

I said fine, I wasn't going to let her intimidate me or make me feel guilty as I saw her do over and over again with her kids when she didn't get her way.

All the way into the city to get my parents and sisters, I kept thinking about Eve and that *burro* and the firewood. It was like she just couldn't see the bigger picture. I took a deep breath. Tears came to my eyes. I loved her. I really did, and yet I still had no idea what to do about our situation. That poor little old man had just been doing the best he could. He hadn't been abusing that little *burro*. He'd just wanted to keep the little animal going at a good clip, so the upgrades would actually be a lot easier for him. This I knew well. After all, I'd been working with livestock all my life.

# CHAPTER FORTY

I didn't recognize my parents and my sisters when they came off the plane. My two sisters, Linda and Teresita, were so much taller and more grown-up looking than I remembered, and my dad and mom, my God, they looked so old. I'd never realized this before. I was shocked. It had only been a few months since I'd seen them.

They were all tired. It had been a long day for them. They wanted me to immediately drive them to a hotel.

"Someplace nice, but not too expensive," said my mother.

"The biggest and the best!" said my dad.

"With monkeys," said my youngest sister Teresita.

"Do they have monkeys in the city?" asked Linda. She was four years younger than me, and Teresita was ten years younger.

"Sure, they do," I said, "just look at you two. You're both a couple of monkeys!"

"You look more like a monkey than us," said Teresita. "Look at you, all suntanned and wearing real *huaraches.*"

I was impressed. I hadn't thought that my baby sister knew the Mexican word for sandals. I drove the family to the big luxury hotel right across from the main square in downtown Mexico City. The bellboys treated me like a hired driver. I thought this was funny but it angered my dad, and he told me to change clothes for dinner. We almost ended up in an argument, but to keep the peace, I went over to my place on Avenida de la Reforma, changed clothes, then came back to join them for dinner.

For three days we did all the tourist stuff in Mexico City, and every time I tried to bring up anything that had to do with Eve, the subject was always quickly changed. On the fourth day, it was decided we should drive out to the coast at *Acapulco* and stay in a big fancy hotel on the beach. It was an eight-hour drive with all the stopping we did.

In *Acapulco,* we saw the world-famous divers dive off the huge cliffs. During dinner my dad complained about his steak. My mother was embarrassed, but my dad wouldn't back off. He told the waiter to call the chef, that they didn't even know how to cut a steak. The chef arrived.

"I own a cattle ranch so I know what I'm talking about," he told the chef. "For a steak you cut the opposite of cutting for *carne asada,* where you cut with the grain of the meat. *Capiche*? For a steak, you cut across the grain so that the meat can be thick and yet still tender and juicy."

My mother was fit to be tied she was so embarrassed, but the chef remained calm and personally brought my dad a filet mignon covered with mushrooms. It was delicious. My dad was happy now, but my mother was so upset that she continued to accuse him of showing off because he had money.

An American couple from another table came over and asked my mother for her autograph, saying that she was as beautiful as they'd seen her in her movies.

"I'm not a movie star," said my mother, getting all embarrassed again.

"Be truthful, Lupe," said my dad. "You see, she just doesn't like people to know it, but she's been a big star ever since I found her."

"Then you're her agent?" asked the American woman.

"You damn right," said my dad. "I found this angel!"

"Sorry for bothering," said the man, "but my wife just thinks your wife is the most beautiful woman in all the world."

As soon as the two Americans were gone, my mother was furious and started reprimanding my dad again.

"Why do you lie like that all the time, Salvador? I'm not a movie star!" she snapped.

"You're the movie star of my life," he said. "And they're right, you are the most beautiful woman in the world. Come, let's dance."

Music had started. People were crossing the room to the dance floor.

"No," said my mother, "you know I don't know how to dance, and you always insist on embarrassing me!"

My dad took her hand, and, reluctantly, my mother got to her feet. My sisters and I watched our dad lead our mother across the huge dining room to the dance floor. It was easy to see that our mother knew how to dance very well—she just liked to play hard to get. Our parents looked so wonderful dancing together on the open balcony with the sea behind them and the sky full of stars. After all these years, our father's eyes still sparkled when he looked at our mother. I wondered if Eve liked to dance. With all her barhopping, I'd never once seen her dance.

On our drive back to Mexico City, we stopped at *Taxco* and my parents bought tons of silver, including the biggest silver punch bowl I'd ever seen, one that I personally picked out. Back in the city, I found out the hotel had actually kept my parents' rooms for them while we were gone. Everyone could smell my parents' wealth. I, too, like my mother, sometimes found it very embarrassing.

"Okay," said my dad to me once we were in our room, "we've come, we've visited, so now let's get to *el gordo del caldo*. Tell your mother and me what's going on between you and this woman."

I took a great big breath. *El gordo del caldo* was the fat of the soup, which meant the substance of the situation. My dad was never one for subtleties. He was telling me no more bullshit, that he now wanted to get down to the main reason they'd come to see me. I took another big breath.

"I don't know what's going on between us," I said.

"That's no good," he said, "a man must know what is going on with him and a woman, and right away. Pussyfooting around only leads to heartaches. She has two kids, right?"

"Yes," I said.

"And no husband?"

"Yeah," I said, half lying.

"Well, then she must know what your intentions are. She has no time to be fooling around, unless she's a fool. A woman like her with kids has a lot of big responsibilities. She either needs a man just so she can satisfy her natural urges, or she needs commitment. Right now there can be no in-betweens for her or for you. You've got to be *un hombre.*"

"Look, Salvador," said my mother. "I think you can handle this without me. I'm going to take the girls out shopping. We'll be gone for a few hours."

"You don't have to go," said my father. "It's never too early for young girls to start learning about these matters."

"No, I'm taking Linda and Teresita out of here right now," said my mother.

"Come on, girls," she said, going to the door.

"But we want to hear," said Teresita. "This sounds real juicy! How old are her kids?" she asked me.

"Her daughter Lauren is just about your age," I said to my youngest sister.

"Then she must be really old," said Linda, laughing.

"Come on, girls. We're leaving!"

My mother and sisters went out the door, and my dad and I were left alone. I was stunned by what he had said. He'd never even met Eve, and he'd already figured everything out.

How did he do this? How did he always seem to be able to get to the root of a complicated situation, and suddenly make it look so simple and easy to understand? I guess being a genius didn't mean that much. A person also had to be very wise.

"They must have explained all this to you at the Academy," said my dad, "how to handle yourself with women."

"No, *papá,* at school they never taught us anything about life, and . . . and especially nothing about men and women."

"They didn't?"

"No."

"Then what the hell did they teach at that school? And why did they have all those fancy dances? Shit, to not know how to deal with these matters of the heart leaves people wide open for the biggest mistakes of their whole *vida*! Because no matter how much wealth or power a man accumulates, he's still a baby if he doesn't know how to deal with women. And the same thing is true for women. They must know how to deal with men. Now I see why that stupid real estate millionaire back home killed himself. He had lots of schooling about business and money, but I guess none about women. This is all my old mother ever spoke to me about, always teaching me about the responsibilities of women and love and *familia,* and about God. This is why the first thing I asked your mother, when I was finally alone with her, was what were her dreams.

"I didn't try to kiss her like a fool, when we were finally alone. No, I asked her about her dreams. Dreams are the most important realities we humans have. Your mother's whole face lit up when I asked her this question. I'll never forget, her heart came forward, and we began to talk, cutting through years of courtship, because we'd gone straight to the heart of the matter of what it is to be human, which is to dream.

"Dreaming is what human beings do more than anything else in all their lives, my mother always told me. So it is with sharing our dreams that a man and woman truly come close and get to know each other. Your mother loved my question, and she opened up to me in a way that takes most relationships years, or never."

"And you did this deliberately, *papá?"*

"But of course. I had a plan all mapped out how I was going to court your mother, so she would marry me. Do you, *mijo,* have a plan mapped out for this woman?"

"Ah, well, no, I guess I don't," I said.

"Does she want to have any more children?"

"I haven't asked her."

"Do you want children?"

"Oh, yes, of course," I said.

"And yet you haven't asked her? This isn't very wise, *mijo.* These basic matters between a man and a woman must be talked about, and QUICKLY! *Capiche?* Or else, all goes to hell. In fact, this is what hell is here on Earth, all these mixed-up feelings that we've got in our hearts but don't have the *tanates* to address. My mother, God bless her soul, explained all this to me when I was a child."

"But can't a man and woman just be friends?" I asked.

"What kind of friends? Friends who satisfy each other's urges and know that this is it, and nothing more? Or friends who just keep almost doing it, but not quite," he said, turning his open palm up and then down, "and torture each other until something breaks and it gets real bad? Or friends who pretend that there really is no battle going on between men and women."

I took a huge breath and blew out. This was really tough. I only wished I'd had this conversation with my dad a long time ago. But if the truth be known, maybe I wouldn't have been ready to hear any of it. I mean, how could I? I'd never realized that all these complications even existed between a man and a woman until I was in the middle of the whole catastrophe.

"Believe me, *mijo,* to teach you how to play poker or dice and how to go to Las Vegas and win five out of six times is easy compared to teaching a man how to deal with the women in his life. And why? Because first of all, it starts with the understanding," he said, closing his eyes, "of having trust in God."

"It starts with having trust in God," I said, my mind suddenly leaping!

"But of course. There isn't a man alive who doesn't now and then want to strangle his wife to death by the neck. There isn't a woman alive who doesn't think of poisoning her husband. When two people get married, it isn't a nice *matrimonio.* It is a *matar los demonios!*" When two people get married, it isn't matrimony, it's kill the demons! "But you kill those demons with love, and patience, and the understanding that each thinks they are giving 75 percent and only receiving 25 percent. This is marriage. This is the whole catastrophe of a man and woman getting together and trying to make a home, and so, of course, trust in God is needed. Lots and lots of trust. Because no two humans can make it together without God being there in the middle, helping them to iron our their differences."

I was stunned. "But why didn't you ever tell me this before!" I was angry. With all his talking, my dad had never once mentioned any of this!

He burst out laughing. "*Mijito,*" he said, "I have been telling you this again and again since you were born."

"But I don't ever remember you telling me any of this, *papá!*"

He laughed all the more. "Remember, hearing isn't listening," he said. "This is exactly why my mother always said that it takes about a thousand times of telling the same story for it to finally sink in. *Mijito,* understand, everything we humans do, dream, hope, live, die, whatever, it all starts and ends with the Almighty. Didn't the nuns and priests teach you this? God is our Everything. All the time. Every moment. Now, about this woman who you are seeing, what does she say about her own mother?"

I took a deep breath. "Very little," I said. "She mostly talks about her father."

"This isn't good, *mijito*. We come from our mother's womb. We nurse from our mother's breasts. To not speak good and a lot about your mother means that there is a big wide hole in your heart. To speak mostly about your father is to be locked up in your head."

I couldn't believe all this great stuff my dad was telling me. "I suppose that you also told me this?" I said.

"But of course. Many times. Oh, the jewels our parents tell us, but we think we're so smart we can't even hear. Look," he said, "I once had an older woman who was my friend. She was the madam of a house up in Butte, Montana. She was a fine English lady maybe, well, fifteen years older than me, and she took me under her wing. She taught me how to dress and close my mouth when I chew, and she explained many things to me about life. But—and this is a very important but—we never once so much as held hands. No, she'd have me go with her best girls, who taught me all about the wonders of the bedroom. This, too, is a very important education, because there are many ways to peel a cat."

"Skin, *papá*," I said. "Skin a cat."

"Okay, skin a cat. So what are your plans with this woman?"

"I don't honestly know. I guess that maybe I have none."

"Okay, then you must tell her this as soon as possible so she isn't living in half hopes. Like the old Mexican saying, *cuentas claras, y amistades largas.* This old saying didn't just get made up overnight, *mijo*. No, these sayings are the fruit of generations trying to learn how to deal with all the different realities of life, *la vida*."

"Then you also think that there are many different realities in this life, *papá*, and not just one?"

"Absolutely! They must have taught you at least this in school."

I shook my head. "No, *papá*, nothing about life is taught at school." My dad had never been to school one day in his life. "Then are there many different kinds of love, too?" I asked.

"But of course, and in my mother's language from *Oaxaca,* they have a different word for each of these different kinds of love. You mean they also didn't teach you about this in school, either?"

I shook my head. "No," I said, "they didn't, and about school, I do have a plan." My heart started pounding. "I'm not ever going to go to school again," I said. "And, also, I'm not returning to the United States. I want to stay in Mexico for the rest of my life."

"And does this have anything to do with this woman?"

"No, not at all," I said. "In fact, she'll probably return to the U. S. in six months or so."

"Okay, I hear you. And what will you do here?"

"I don't know yet. But I did find a little tile factory in San Miguel that I like a lot, and . . . and it's up for sale. So I was thinking that you could help me buy it, and I could then sell that tile up in the United States for a good profit for us and for our workers."

"Okay, that's one way to peel a cat, but you're probably better off not to buy the factory, and first go to the States and find out who will buy this tile from you, then order only that amount of tile. In this way, you use a lot less capital, plus you could also, then, work with several other factories and not limit yourself."

I nodded. My God, here he was being brilliant once again. "I . . . I hadn't thought of it like that," I said. "But just wait. Hold on, *papá.* In doing it the way you suggest, then the workers will never make more money. The profits will always go to owners of the different factories and to me.

"No, *papá,*" I added with my heart pounding, "I don't want to do it that way. I want to buy the factory. You should see the tile, it's so special and beautiful! It could change the whole way people look at color in kitchens and bathrooms back in the States, especially in Southern California where there's already some Mexican and Early California architecture."

"And you like this tile business?"

"I feel it in my bones, *papá.* Colors are alive! The yellows alone can make a home feel so warm and good that . . . that disagreements won't automatically turn into arguments. Design can do this, too. I'd love to put a bunch of stores together in the United States, *papá,* so people will have the feeling that they've come into a village, like here in *San Miguel* when they go shopping. I see it all so clearly. Color and design can bring harmony and happiness into people's lives. Every town I come to, I automatically go to the *plaza* and sit by the fountain."

I flashed on the book, *The Little Prince,* and how that child prince had been walking across the universe in search of his own star. Every book Eve gave me just seemed so perfect for me. She was the first person in all my life who understood why I'd felt compelled to draw stars ever since I could remember. She'd done the same thing. I almost felt like Eve and I had come across the stars together. Maybe we should never have even kissed, and yet . . . we were so drawn to each other in such a formidable way.

"So why don't you go to school and become an architect?" said my dad. "I could help you once you got your license, and you could do very well being a builder-architect in California."

I took a deep breath. I wanted finally to come clean and tell my dad that there was no way I could ever become an architect or anything else, because I didn't know how to read. But I couldn't. I felt too ashamed.

"No, *papá*," I simply said, "I'm staying here in *México* for the rest of my life."

"But, *mijito,* be reasonable, California is now our home," he said. "That's where your two grandmothers are buried, and that's where all of our businesses are located. I could help you to do real good up there. But down here in *México*, I can't really help you, because we can never trust the government like we can in the U. S. Hell, you can't even trust the value of the *peso*."

"Look, *papá,* that's not the point," I said. "You see, I've found peace here in *México*. My stomach doesn't hurt."

"Your stomach doesn't hurt? What the hell are you talking about?" he said. "Are you sick?"

"No."

"Then you don't know shit about a stomach hurting!" he shouted. "We were starving to death when we got to the Texas border! You've got to see people dying all around you and hear children moaning and crying all night with swollen stomachs before you can talk to me about your stomach hurting!"

He was hot and went on and on.

"And I'm not saying that the United States is perfect. Not by a long shot! But with all of its shit, the States is still the best damn bet for your future! Not *México*, where every new president and all his *compadres* make it a game to *chingar* this country even worse than the president before them, when they leave office. The American presidents, they are little babies when it comes to stealing, compared to Mexican presidents!"

And he would have kept going on and on, but I cut him off.

"NO, *PAPÁ!*" I yelled, "LISTEN TO ME! I'm not going back, and that's that! All your talking isn't going to change this!"

"And why not? You tell me? We've got a good life over there in Oceanside. Why do you want to leave all that?"

I couldn't help it. I started crying. I guess there was just no way I could get away with not telling him the whole truth.

*"Papá,"* I said, "on our first day of school, they screamed at us, 'No Spanish! English only!' Then they slapped *Ramón* in the face until he was all bloody because he wouldn't stop talking Spanish. And all he was saying was 'Don't yell at me, you're not my mother,' and 'Don't be grabbing me, you have no right to do this.' He was so smart, *papá,* and so brave and noble, and they kept slapping him, again and again, until his whole face was a bloody mess."

"Why didn't you tell us? Your mother and I would've brought in our lawyer, Fred Noon, from downtown San Diego, and he would have had those teachers in jail, hanging by their thumbs! WHY DIDN'T YOU SPEAK UP?"

"Because . . . because," but I was crying so hard that I . . . I . . . I couldn't speak. My dad came close to hug me, but I pushed back away from him. I had to collect myself, so I could go on. "Because I was ashamed," I was finally able to say. *"Tenía vergüenza.* I thought it was me who was to blame. It got worse every year, *papá. Ramón* was dead by the seventh grade. And the nuns, they locked me in the closet and called me the devil and . . . and the Academy was the worst of all. Captain Moses would ridicule me every day. Then one day he changed my name from *Edmundo* to Edmund and told everyone that I was so stupid that I didn't know how to spell my own name."

"Moses? Captain Moses?"

"Yes."

"But your brother Joseph liked him, and Captain Moses always spoke to your mother and me very respectfully."

"Captain Moses is a KISS ASS! A SNEAKY SON-OF-A-BITCH SNAKE!" I screamed. "I was finally ready TO KILL HIM, *papá,* it had gotten so bad! And I would've done it, killing him with your 30/30 Winchester the day you went up to see Dr. Hoskins who was dying, but . . . but the only reason I didn't kill him was because I saw you forgive the doctor, and so I could see that . . . that I had to forgive Captain Moses, too, just like Jesus did to his executioners on the cross and you did to Dr. Hoskins."

My dad was stunned. "Truly," he said, "you were prepared to kill him?"

"Yes, truly," I said, "then I was going to kill that teacher who'd bloodied *Ramón*'s face. *Ramón, papá,* he was the best one of all of us. He really was, and they beat him down so bad that he could never get beyond his hate and want of revenge.

"Don't you see, *papá,* you had it easy compared to me. Sure, you had starvation and revolution, but here inside your head and heart, you'd also seen that our people, *los mexicanos,* were people of value and bravery, and so when you got to the U. S., they couldn't brainwash you into thinking that you were a bad, inferior, no-good person. My God, *papá,* by sixteen I was so brainwashed into being ashamed of being *un . . . un mexicano* that I . . . that I . . . I . . ." I had to bite my fist to keep from screaming. "I tried to castrate myself, so I wouldn't bring anymore inferior people into this world."

"OH, MY LORD GOD!" screamed my dad. "I never knew this! You never SAID ANYTHING!" He rammed his own fist into his mouth so that he wouldn't scream out in terror, too. The tears ran down his face. He was devastated. "And your mother and I worked so hard to get rich so you kids wouldn't suffer like we'd suffered.

"Do these teachers still live?" he asked. "We can still get them and prosecute them to the letter of the law, then hang them in the *barrio* until their bodies rot! Oh, *mijito, mijito,*" he said, and we took each other in our arms and hugged in a big strong *abrazo.*

"So you see, *papá,* this is why I can never go back to the States. Because . . . because when I was in the United States and I was a nothing and ashamed of being *un mexicano,* they could do whatever they wanted to me, and it was okay. But now, *papá,* that I've come down here and lived in *México* and have pride being *un mexicano,* I go back and I see some *gringo* mistreat a *mexicano,* or a Black or Chinese, I swear I'll kill them on the spot! I'll rip out their Adam's apple and shove it up their ass! I'll cut off their balls and force them down their throats!"

My father started laughing. *"¡Un puro Tapatío a lo Villaseñor!* This is good!" he yelled. "Very good! Let's go down to the bar and have a couple of tequilas from *Los Altos de Jalisco!* Well, I see that you haven't wasted your time down here. You got *orgullo!* That's WONDERFUL!"

I was shocked. I'd thought he was going to get all upset and tell me that I couldn't go around killing people and cutting off their balls, but instead he liked the fact that I'd found my cultural pride.

We went downstairs. The bar was empty. It was still too early for the afternoon crowd, and the lunch crowd was already gone. Plus the prices were so expensive that not too many people frequented the place. My dad and I had the whole grand old bar to ourselves. My mother was still out shopping with my two sisters. He called the barkeeper over.

"Bartender," said my dad, "this is my son *Edmundo.* We'd like to have some of your finest tequila and also some *antojitos,"* meaning appetizers.

"But the restaurant is closed right now," said the bartender.

"Look at me closely, *amigo,"* said my dad, "here is a hundred dollar bill just to start with. Thirty dollars of this is for you to put in your own pocket right now. *Capiche?"*

The bartender's whole attitude changed. Suddenly he wasn't tired anymore. "Yes, *mi general, entiendo!"* he said.

"Good, and give another twenty to the chef in back and ten to the dishwasher. That leaves forty for my son and me to drink and eat a little something."

"But, of course!" said the barkeeper. "The whole place is open for you! Which *tequila* would you like?" he added anxiously.

"*Herradura*, and a couple of *Modelo cervezas.*"

"I like *Dos Equis*," I said. "The dark one."

"Okay," said my dad, "one *Modelo* and one dark *Dos Equis*."

The bartender was flying, moving, truly enjoying the whole show.

My dad winked at me.

"Like I always say, to tip after the meal is stupid. Tip first and big, and the whole world changes."

"Is this also true in business?"

"No, not in business. In business you promise a bonus, but you don't give it until the job is done and you've inspected everything very closely."

"Why is that?"

"Because, one, a lot of businesspeople are always looking for shortcuts, and two, you can't be watching everything in business, but here, we can see what we are getting second by second."

I nodded. It always impressed me how almost anything you asked my father about why he did this or that, he always seemed to know why and in such detail. He was a very deliberate well-thought-out man. He didn't like to leave much to chance, especially when it came to gambling and business. He always said a real gambler took as much gamble out of the gambling as he could and a businessman put as much business into business as he could.

All afternoon my dad and I drank and talked and ate. It was one of the greatest times of my life.

The next day we all drove out to *San Miguel de Allende* to see *Marina* and for them to meet Eve and her two children. I'd called Eve several times in the last few days but I had never been able to reach her, so I left a few messages with a couple of her friends. Still, she didn't return my calls. I began to wonder what was going on. I hoped to God, she hadn't gotten drunk and just . . . just disappeared.

"Dear Lord God," I said to myself as I drove, "please help Eve. The two of us can't do it without You. You are our Everything. Without You, a man and a woman just can't do it."

I suddenly felt much better. I'd turned it over to *Papito,* my best Friend, my Everything, and a whole lot of weight was taken off my back.

# CHAPTER FORTY-ONE

**M**ost of the motel was still under construction, so *Marina* put my parents and sisters and me in the rooms that were the most finished. The walls were made of black lava rock, and they felt like spacious caves. Linda and Teresita found cockroaches in their room and started screaming. I ran in, saw what they were screaming at, and told them to stop it, that these were Mexican lobsters and to help me scoop them up for dinner. They both believed me, but only my little sister Teresita would help me catch the huge *cucarachas*. My mother got upset with me for tricking my sisters. My dad laughed and said he and his family had caught a lot of rattlesnakes and cockroaches during the Mexican Revolution and cooked them up for a delicious dinner. He began to sing the popular song of the Revolution of 1910. *"La cooca-rracha, la cooca-rracha, ya no puede caminar, porque le falta, porque no tiene, marijuana que fumar."*

We had dinner that first night with *Marina*, and she and my dad argued about *Fidel Castro* most of the meal. She thought *Fidel* could end up doing very good things for *Cuba*.

"He's just starting out, and he's the most charismatic man I've ever met, except, of course, for you," she said to my dad.

"Thank you *por la flor*," said my dad, "and I'm sure you're right about his charm, but in my opinion communism is just a slick new kind of dictatorship, because the ones in charge get to figure out who is going to get what, and human nature being what it is, no one man or group will behave themselves very well for very long. A system of government needs to understand that we are all basically thieves at heart. That's why we have to have checks and balances like we do in the States, or we're screwed."

*Marina* and my dad loved their disagreement and continued arguing after dinner. I went outside to sit under the stars. My mother and sisters came outside to join me.

*"Mijito,"* my mother asked me, "is it true that you told your father that you are not coming back home with us to California?"

I took a big breath. This one was really tough. "Yes, *mamá,"* I said. "That's what I told him."

Tears came to my mother's eyes. "Your father and I worked so hard to build a good home for all of you kids over there. What will your sisters do? You are the oldest. Your sister Tencha didn't marry a man we can depend on. Is it because of this woman?" she asked.

I took another deep breath and blew out hard. "No, *mamá,"* I said. "It has nothing to do with her. In fact, like I told *papá,* she'll probably be returning to the States in six months or so."

"If she didn't turn your head around, then who did?"

"Mother, it's not about anyone turning my head around. It's about me here, inside, having found peace in Mexico."

"Your father told me. Why didn't you ever tell us about all those abuses at school?"

*"Mamá,* I was little and so I thought it was me who . . . who . . . *mamá,* I can't go back. That's it! I just can't!"

She said nothing more. We just sat in the patio, looking up at the stars. They were out by the millions. The whole Milky Way could be seen as a pouring of bright stars across the heavens.

"I still think it's this woman," said my mother after a while.

I could feel that a certain meanness had come into my mother's voice. *"Mamá,* believe me, she has nothing to do with it. In fact, it's the opposite, she's the one who helped me open my eyes."

"See, it is this woman!" snapped my mother.

"Her name is Eve. Not 'this woman'," I said.

That same night I drove over to see Eve to tell her I was in town with my parents. But she wasn't home, and it was late and Peter and Lauren hadn't had dinner. They'd run out of food the day before. I got angry and took them out for dinner. We had a wonderful time. Then I bought some *tortillas,* eggs, *chorizo, papaya,* and milk from the restaurant for their breakfast and some Mexican chocolate, too. I took them home, and went out looking for their mother. I hadn't wanted to take them along in case she was drunk.

I finally found her. She was trying to sing along with a piano player. She was happy to see me, but then started insulting me by telling everyone how I'd said I loved her and would never leave her, only to run back to my parents' apron strings. I suddenly understood how things must have really been between her and her husband.

The music was beautiful. It was from *Argentina*. Eve was drunk and didn't want to leave. Finally, I lied to her and told her that her kids were waiting for us out in my car, that I'd taken them out for dinner, and they were ready to go home to bed. She quit arguing with me, told everyone goodnight, and we walked out together. At the car, she got very upset when she didn't see her kids.

"My kids aren't here!" she said.

"No, not right now," I said. "I meant to say that they were, but I already took them home."

"Are you trying to trick me?" she asked, swaying on her feet.

"No, of course not," I answered.

"Look, this was my dad's specialty. You can't pull the wool over my eyes. You go home. I'm staying."

"Eve, your kids were hungry. They had no food. You need to stop drinking and go home and get some sleep. My parents want to meet you tomorrow."

"What for? To tell me that I'm not worthy of their precious son?"

"Is this what happened with you and your ex?"

"I will not speak of the past. Go on, leave! I don't need you! Get away! My money comes in tomorrow. I'll take my kids shopping. We don't need you! Go back to mommy and daddy!"

I took a deep breath, blew out, then grabbed her to put her in the car.

"No!" she yelled.

"Do you need help?" said a man coming out of the bar. He looked like an American.

"No," I said. "I need to get her home to her kids."

He ignored me and came up to speak to her. "Is he your husband?"

"No!"

"Then I suggest you let her go," he said to me.

"She's joking," I said. "We're married."

"Which is it?" he asked Eve. "Are you two married or not?" He was big, in his thirties, half drunk, too, and ready for a fight.

"Did you say that we're married?" Eve said to me.

"Yes," I said.

"Then yes, it is," she said to the man. "Good night to you! I'm going home with my husband!"

"Good night," said the man.

I closed her door, went around to the driver's side, got in, and we took off. The cobblestone street sang loudly under my T-bird. I didn't get back to the motel until three in the morning. Eve had gotten sick, and I'd had to clean her up and put her to bed. Then she'd begun to cry and once more she'd told me I should wait for Lauren, that she was going to screw things up for me. I was beginning to finally agree with her, but . . . but still I loved her. She was so important to me. I truly wanted my parents to meet her.

"Please, Eve. Just get some sleep. I really want my parents to meet you."

"Really?"

"Yes, really."

"Okay," she'd said smiling, "I'll meet you and your *familia* at noon in the small downtown plaza in front of the *iglesia,*" she added in Spanish.

I tucked her in, we kissed, and I left.

# CHAPTER FORTY-TWO

**M**y parents and sisters and I arrived at the *plaza* at noon, but Eve wasn't there. We waited fifteen minutes, then we were just getting ready to go to lunch when I spotted her coming across the cobblestones wearing a beautiful, large hat and a long, flowing, flowery dress. She looked stunning. And she was wearing huge oversized dark brown sunglasses and dark brown Mexican sandals with straps crisscrossing her ankles. Her whole face lit up when she saw me. I guess my whole face had lit up, too, but then . . . her face collapsed. Just like that and she looked like that deer out in mid-road, caught in the headlights of an oncoming semi.

I turned around and saw my parents. And I was sure the semi-truck was the look my mother had given her. But Eve was tough. She collected herself and continued across the *plaza* toward us. My family and I were right in front of the beautiful little church of *San Miguel*. When she got close, Eve held out her hand to me. I took it and kissed her on the cheek, then I turned to face my parents and two sisters.

"Hello," Eve said to my family.

"Hi," said my dad.

"Eve, I'd like you to meet my dad, Salvador," I said, "and my mother, Lupe, and my two sisters, Linda and Teresita. And I'd like all of you to meet Eve, my . . . my very good friend."

"Glad to meet you," said my dad, putting out his hand.

"And very glad to meet you as well, *Señor Villaseñor*," said Eve in Spanish with that slightly British accent of hers. "You must be very proud of your son. Vic is going to save the world, you know," she added with a big smile.

"He what?" said my dad, not quite understanding what she'd said.

"She said that *Edmundo* is going to save the world," said my little sister Teresita, laughing.

But my dad and mom weren't laughing. They were staring at Eve as if they thought she was a *loquita americana*, a crazy *loca* American. I wondered how much *Marina* had told them.

"Oh, I'm so sorry," said Eve, lowering her head. "I assumed you knew, calling him *Mundo*, meaning world in Spanish. I'm sorry. I didn't mean to surprise you."

"What are you saying?" asked my dad.

"Oh, nothing," said Eve, "I can see I've said way too much already. I'm glad to have met you. Goodbye, now."

"But, Eve, please don't go," I said. "Please, hold on."

But her head was even lower, as if she'd been beaten, and she didn't look very elegant anymore. "No can do," she said. "They don't know about the Moses in you. I've got to go."

"Moses?" said my dad. "That teacher at the Academy?"

"What teacher?" Eve asked.

I'd never told Eve about Captain Moses. "She didn't mean that Moses, *papá*," I said. "She meant the Moses from the Bible," I added.

"Are you feeling okay?" my mother asked Eve.

"Yes, I'm fine, *señora*," said Eve. "It has been a . . . a pleasure meeting you and your daughters. But I do believe it's time for me to go. I hope you have a wonderful visit in *San Miguel*. The shops are wonderful. Everyone is an artist. *Vayan con Dios*."

She turned to go, and I could see by the back of her shoulders that she was crying. I whirled about and stared at my mother, then at my father. But I could see it was mostly my mother who'd done it. I wanted to scream. I turned and ran after Eve, catching up with her around the corner.

"Please come back," I said. "We're going to have lunch."

"No can do," she said.

"But Eve . . ."

"Go back to them. They're right, you know. I was foolish to ever think that I—how many horses do you have?" she asked, out of the blue.

"What?"

"How many horses do you have on your *rancho*?"

"Oh, I don't know. Maybe twenty or twenty-five," I said.

"And you say that they've broken loose from time to time and gone down to the sea during the full moon?"

"Yes, quite a few times."

"And you've had to round them up, chasing wild horses by the sea under the full moon?"

"Yes," I said, "lots of times."

"Lots of times?" she said, laughing.

"Yes."

"Just to be able to do that one time," she said, "to bring Heaven down to Earth for one moment would be Paradise for most human beings, and yet you are such a gift that you have been allowed to do this many times."

"I don't understand," I said.

"Of course you don't, not yet, but you will," she said, reaching out with her right hand and lightly stroking my left cheek. "I do love you," she said, "but I'm too old for you. I could see it in their eyes, especially your mother's. Go back to them. Do it right now. Please. Because I'm going to go into that bar across the street and get shit-face drunk, and . . . and I don't want you to see me do that."

"But Eve?"

"Don't 'but Eve' me, Adam!"

"Adam?"

"Sure. Don't you know, it's always been the same story. Ask your mother, she'll tell you. You get involved with me, and I'll be the one to blame for it all over again. But also being Moses, as you obviously are this time once more, I thought you'd just part the sea of fear and doubt that surrounds us with such ease that I, too, could walk across with you back to the Promised Land. But don't worry, you will do it, my love. You will. God bless you. Bye now, *mi amor*," said she, turning to go.

"NO, EVE, STOP! That's all just a bunch of old Bible stuff! This is here, right now! Come back, please!"

"No can do," she said, and she pulled back her shoulders and walked across the cobblestoned street with such elegance and beauty, it was . . . was breathtaking.

I stood there and watched her walk inside and pass through the dark entrance, into the light of the large inside *patio con flores* and birds and tables with white linen tablecloths. Tears came to my eyes.


The next day I was in Mexico City with my parents. I had it all planned out. I would take them and my sisters to the airport, then I'd turn around and drive back to *San Miguel* to be with Eve.

"So, you're not coming back with us, eh?" said my dad.

"No, I'm not," I said.

My mother and sisters had gone out for a last little bit of shopping. They were buying gifts for all of our extended *familia* back home, which was about fifty people.

"Because you've found peace here, eh? And your stomach doesn't hurt here. And if you return to the States, you're sure that you will start killing people right and left, because you've got so much rage inside of you. Eh, did I get it all?" he asked.

"Yes, you did," I said.

"Well, I've thought it over very carefully," he said calmly. "And now that I've had time to chew it over in my head . . . like the old cow chewing her cud, I say BULLSHIT!" he suddenly screamed, startling the hell out of me.

"YOU'VE GOT RAGE. THEN YOU RETURN TO THE STATES WITH THAT RAGE! YOU DON'T RUN AWAY! You saw bad, terrible things happen to you and other Mexican kids in school, then YOU DON'T CHICKENSHIT OUT! No, you go back, and you do something with that rage that will MAKE A DIFFERENCE for all those kids! That's the beauty of the United States! Even the little guy can fight back!

"We were starving when we got to the Texas border! And we thought that once we got across all our troubles were over. But we

were wrong! A new kind of war started for us of racism and preju-
dice. They treated us Mexicans worse than dogs! In Douglas, Arizona, I stole six dollars worth of copper ore from the Copper Queen
Mining Company to feed my starving mother and sisters, and they
put me in the penitentiary. I was only thirteen years old! They
wouldn't have done that to a *gringo* kid, but they did this to a Mexican kid to teach an example!"

Tears came to his eyes. "In prison those monsters tried to rape
me, but I fought back so hard that they cut my stomach open from
rib to rib," he yelled, tearing his shirt open and showing me the huge
scar that ran across his whole abdomen, going from his upper right
side to his lower left side. "My intestines came out, and they left me
for dead, but the guards found me and took me to the hospital. After
a week I awoke, and, at the end of that month, I escaped with two
*Yaqui* who'd gotten twenty years for eating an Army mule. Their
*familias* had been starving! And they'd stolen the mule to feed them!

"YOU'VE GOT NO RAGE COMPARED TO THAT, *PENDE-
JO*! There aren't enough bullets for me to kill all the racist no-good
son-of-a-bitches I've met in the United States! But—and this is a big
but—anybody can go around killing people! Any damn group of
kids can get together and kill! That takes no guts! What takes guts is
to have that rage, here inside," he said, pounding his chest, "and
decide to do something good with that rage. My revenge against this
racist two-faced country of the United States is that I got rich and
became a Republican! So now you come back to the United States,
and you do something worthwhile, AND YOU DO IT RIGHT NOW,
*PENDEJO*!

"You got me!" he added. "You don't stay down here and hide
from your rage! No, you take hold of that rage, and you grab hold of
your *tanates,* and you do something worthwhile, and not just for you
but for that boy *Ramón* you saw get hit 'til he was bloody. You hear
me? YOU DON'T HIDE! YOU STAND UP *A LO BENITO
JUÁREZ, un puro Indio de los buenos,* and you make a difference,
AND YOU DO IT RIGHT NOW, *PENDEJO*!"

I had tears in my eyes. "But *papá,* I don't know what to do
worthwhile."

"Of course you don't. You haven't been thinking like that, but you start thinking of doing something worthwhile and ideas will come to you from the heavens. Because you see, there ain't a man, woman, or child that hasn't been raped, beaten down, humiliated, or whatever. And the day they grow up and become an adult is the day they admit that they don't know what to do, and yet they decide to do something worthwhile with their lives. *Capiche?*

"Becoming an adult is making the decision that you are a person of value. You stand up, pull back your shoulders, and do something worthwhile even in the middle of your own personal disasters! In a few days you will be twenty years old. You are not a boy anymore. You are *un hombre,* and a man has got to know who HE IS AND WHO HE ISN'T BY NOW, or you are going to SCREW UP your life! THERE ARE NO EXCEPTIONS!"

"But *papá,* I still don't know who I am or who I'm not," I said with tears streaming down my face.

"How can you?" he said. "You've been running! Hiding! You haven't been thinking with a whole deck of cards. But when you decide to take this rage and do something worthwhile with it, believe me, THE HEAVENS ABOVE WILL OPEN UP AND MIRACLES WILL START TO POUR DOWN TO YOU, then you will know who you are and who you aren't without a shadow of a doubt! I know! Just days before my wedding to your mother, my old mother had to take me out and teach me a thing or two. You are coming home, *mijito,* to the United States, and you are going to do something worthwhile, and THAT'S THAT! YOU DO NOT ABANDON *RAMÓN!*" he bellowed.

Tears were pouring down my face in rivers. He was right. I could see that he was absolutely right. I was not going to abandon *Ramón.* I was going to take up the flag that he'd dropped in his death, and I was going to go forward in his honor. I had been hiding like a selfish little chickenshit coward, and I wasn't going to do that anymore.

That afternoon, my dad and I drove my mother and two sisters to the airport, and they boarded the plane. My dad had decided to stay with me so we could drive back to the States together. I wanted us to go by *San Miguel* to see Eve, but I could never get an answer to my phone calls.

"Look," said my dad, "she's coming back to the States in six months, you say, so you can see her up there, if this is what is meant to be. Let her go for now. *Que será, será*, and trust that when it's all said and done, it's all really in the hands of *Papito Dios*."

I took a deep breath. He was right. This was what I was learning more and more, ever since the day I'd walked way out to the outskirts of Mexico City and bought that hand-crafted rosary and prayed inside the church. A human being really, really, really did have to let go and put Her-His trust in the hands of the Almighty. We just couldn't do it alone.

# CHAPTER FORTY-THREE

After seeing my mother and sisters off, my father and I picked up all the stuff I needed from my room and drove out of the basin of Mexico City, heading north to the U. S. Our first night, we stopped in a little town and took a hotel room with a bathroom so tiny the shower was directly over the toilet. The second day, we hit the road at daybreak. Back then, there were no freeways in Mexico, and once you got away from the main cities, all of the major roads were little two-lane affairs. It was late afternoon, and I was driving fast when we came over a little rise and suddenly right in front of us was a *burro* loaded down with firewood crossing the road. And a woman was walking on the left shoulder of the road with a child at her side and a basket of wash on her head.

I started to brake, but realized I'd never be able to stop in time. I thought of giving it the gas and seeing if I could somehow, magically, slip between the *burro*'s nose and the woman whose back was to me. But then I could also see that just a little way ahead of them was an old narrow bridge with concrete sides, and a bus full of people was coming down the hill from the village on the other side and they were getting ready to cross the bridge.

I was moving at sixty-five miles an hour, and there was just no way on God's little green apple that I could ever brake fast enough to avoid hitting the *burro* or the woman. If I honked, I'd startle the *burro* and the man herding the animal, and I'd also frighten the hell out of the woman with the child.

In that millionth of a second, I remembered what Paul Koner had done when we drove down from the States and a bus had hit a *burro* right in front of us and cars piled up all around us. I decided not to honk, not letting the animal or the woman even realize that I'd just come over the little rise.

I smashed the gas pedal to the floor, pulled to the left, slipping under the *burro*'s neck, then I cut right, barely missing the woman and child by inches. I was on the bridge, and there was no way the bus could stop in time to let me cross first. I gave the Thunderbird all the gas again, flew across the narrow old bridge at over a hundred miles an hour, managing to slip past the right side of the bus just as it came on the bridge. I hit the uphill at a hundred and twenty miles an hour, spraying dirt and rock as my right rear tire went off the road.

Then it was over!

DONE! FINISHED! All behind me!

I took a huge long breath, blew out, braked, and braked again, getting back down to sixty-five as we approached the village ahead of us. My entire body was shaking. My dad had never made a sound through the whole ordeal. I turned and looked at him, and he, too, was trying to catch his breath.

"Why did you speed up?" he asked, and I noticed that he didn't yell. No, he asked this so calmly. "Why didn't you brake, instead?"

"Because I could see that it would never have worked," I said, slowing down to thirty miles an hour as we entered the village. "I would have lost control of the car if I'd tried to brake that hard, and I'd have ended up just scaring the hell out of the *burro* and the woman with my screeching tires. I don't know what they might have done, so I would have probably killed one or both of them."

"And by speeding up, you thought you could keep control of the car and not scare that *burro* and the woman?"

"Yes," I said. "I learned from Paul Koner when we drove down from California, that you can actually gain more control of the car by speeding up. So I figured I could pass the *burro* and the woman before they even realized we'd just come over that little rise in the road."

"Okay, but what about that bus and the concrete bridge?" said my dad. "If that driver hadn't slowed down for that little bit, you would have hit him head-on at over a hundred miles an hour, and we'd both be hamburger."

I took a big breath and another deep breath to steady myself. "Yeah," I said, "I thought of that, too, but I also figured I'd be better off to gamble on him, because he's a professional bus driver, so he'd probably see and figure out what I was trying to do and give me that split-second I needed."

"And all of this you saw in your head?" asked my dad.

"Yes, I guess I did," I said, braking down to fifteen miles an hour as we came into the busy section of the village. "And, also, on the other side of the bridge, I could see it was uphill into the village, so I figured when I'd be at my highest speed, I'd be okay and still in control, and then I'd be able to slow down real fast because of the uphill grade."

"And all of this you didn't really have time to think in words, did you? But you did have time to see all this in flashes inside of your *cabeza*-head, and you felt sure of what you saw inside of you, right?" he said.

"Yes," I said, "that's right, *papá.*"

"And feeling sure, you were willing to put both of our lives on the line?"

"*Papá,*" I said, "truthfully, when all that was happening, I'd forgotten you were even in the car with me."

He nodded. "So you're telling me you were so much into what you were doing that you forgot me. You forgot about everything in the world, except for what you were doing?"

I took another deep breath. It sounded pretty awful, but this was, in fact, what had happened. I'd forgotten everything, except what I was intent on doing. "Yes, *papá,*" I said, expecting him to get angry.

But he didn't. Instead, he said, "Good! I like that, because this is how to live life, *mijito.* This is exactly what I do when I gamble. This is how I become *aprevenido.* You've got to feel it so strong that you see it all in your *cabeza*-head. This is when we are able to see what's going to happen before it happens. *Mi mamá,* she explained to me that this is how all people used to live back in the Garden. That back then, we could all see what was going to happen before it happened, because we lived in a blessed state of grace *con Dios.*

"You did good, *mijito,* very good! Someone else might have lost faith, and we'd be pieces of dead meat scattered all over the place.

You kept your faith. You felt it, saw it, and didn't back down. No, instead, you grabbed hold of your *tanates* and jumped in with all the gas to the pedal, knowing down deep in your soul that you are blessed, that it is no accident you are here on this *tierra madre* at this time, and that all these awful, scary things that come your way are no accident, either.

"*Capiche?* You didn't hide this time, *mijito,* because the going got tough. No, you realized that the God that knows how to rule the heavens certainly knows how to step in and help us when we don't lose our faith, and we stay connected in His blessed state of grace.

"So, *mijito,* you now go back to the United States with this rage, with this *rabia,* and I guarantee you that your instincts will help you—not just to avoid all disasters like your instincts helped you to do back there at that bridge—but your heart and soul will then connect you directly to *Papito Dios,* who in turn will help you to do MIRACLES BEYOND YOUR WILDEST DREAMS!

"But—and this is the biggest but of all—you've got to want it! You've got to open your *ojos*-eyes and want it! You've got to ask and want, and also pray. Get it? A dozen things could have gone wrong back there. You could have hit that *burro* and we'd both be dead. You could have gotten past the *burro* but killed that woman and her child and we'd both be dead. Or you could have gotten past these two, then crashed head-on into the concrete bridge or that bus full of people. But none of these disasters happened. No, it all went as smooth as clockwork. And why? Because the Holy Hand of God came down from the Heavens and guided us through the valley of death as easy as drinking a good cold *cerveza*—and why? Because you had faith. You had trust. You knew that God was with you, so you got hold of your *tanates* and did it *a lo chingón*! This is living life! This is knowing who you are and who you aren't! Because without this knowledge, WE ARE NOTHING! Understand, *nada, nada, nada! Capiche?*"

This time, I did *capiche.* I really did. But what I couldn't understand was how just seconds ago, my dad and I had almost been killed, and here he was already talking about this whole matter as if he'd had two or three days to think about the whole thing. How could he do this? It was incredible.

"*Papá,* weren't you scared?"

"Of course."

"Then how can you even be thinking about all this? I mean, who are you, *papá?*"

"I'm glad you asked," he said, smiling, "I've been waiting for you to ask me this question for years, and I'll answer this question for you just like my mother answered it for me. *Mijo,* I am the tick up your SPIRITUAL ASSHOLE! I am that awful gnawing you feel up your asshole every time you chickenshit out and lose faith in the WONDERS OF GOD! This my mother said to me, and now I say it to you, anytime you feel your asshole too tight and itching, it means that you are not listening to your ancestry from the other side! *Capiche?*"

I was laughing. I was howling with big huge *CARCAJADAS!* And here I'd thought that I'd invented Ass Watching. My dad must have gotten his doctorate on watching ass to know all this. I could now see that I still had a shitload to learn from *mi papá* and *mi mamá* about living life, *la vida.*

"And about love, *papá,* do we also have to have this same faith in our instincts like I had back there, or is it a different matter with *amor?*"

He took a big deep breath. "With love, *mijito,* believe me, it is more about faith and these feelings that you feel deep inside of you than with anything else. Here, let me tell you about the first time I laid eyes on your mother."

So my dad began to tell me the story of how he met my mother. I'd already heard this story a hundred times, but as I listened now, I realized I'd never really heard the story before. I guess I'd had to live enough and grow up enough, so I could really take in all that *mi papá* was saying to me. This time I really listened to what my dad said. In fact, driving back north to the United States, *con mi papá* became one of the finest and most memorable times of my entire life.

At the border town of *Ciudad Juárez,* my dad showed me the hill where the sandstorm almost killed him and his mother and two sisters. "Even the ants went underground," he said. "Lots of people died, and some . . . were never found. But *mi mamá,* that bag of Indian bones, she got us through that storm." Tears ran down his face. "She was my EVERYTHING!"

Little by little, I began to see that all of my dad's stories were true, and it was I who'd become the doubting Thomas since that first day of kindergarten when my language and culture had been ripped out of me with "English only."

ENGLISH ONLY WAS THE END OF THE UNITED STATES!

All over the globe in every country we had to start learning two and three languages, so we could expand our brain and open our eyes and see what was right here in front of us, we were all one *familia!* There were different cultures, but we were all the same race—the human race—all over the world!

Crossing the border into *El Paso*, meaning "the passage" in Spanish, I felt very strange. Both of my parents had crossed this border half a century ago, hoping for a new life and here . . . here I was doing the same thing, and yet it was all different. I'd been born and raised in the States, and I wasn't crossing the border for safety or for economical reasons. No, I was crossing to . . . to—my heart began beat, beat, BEATING like a huge drum—TO DO BATTLE!

TO CAUSE CHANGE!

TO KICK ASS!

Because the United States was my home, too, and I wasn't going to allow my home to be taken over by people like Moses and Olbase and Wellabussy and his rich, spoiled, racist, elitist, ignorant friends!

And how I'd accomplish this, I had no idea, but . . . but I was not going to let *Ramón's* death pass unforgotten. He'd been the bravest and the best of all of us! I'd been the coward! I'd been the bed wetter!

I started to make the sign of the cross over myself as we crossed the bridge into the U. S., but I couldn't, so I simply said, "God, please help me. I'm scared and I can't do this alone. I need your help. I really, really do."

Instantly I heard a loud screech, and I looked skyward, and there above us was a huge magnificent red-tailed hawk, circling and giving us greeting.

I smiled.

I laughed.

My brother Joseph was with me, and I could see that he had always been with me. After all, it was his big belt buckle that stopped that bullet from killing me. I took a big deep breath and my Red Eagle Brother kept screeching, and I knew that he was telling me that if I just didn't chicken out, kept faith, and remembered that even our dollar bill said, "In God We Trust," I'd be fine. I was not alone. I had a whole army of Spirit Guides at my side. I laughed, and I couldn't stop smiling.

# ~ BOOK FIVE ~

# CHAPTER FORTY-FOUR

The first thing I did when I got home was to go across the grass and past the barn and corrals to the huge old pepper tree. "Hello, I'm home," I said to the great tree, and I hugged her. She purred and sang and her limbs danced in the sea breeze. I laughed. We were so happy to see each other. I told her that I'd missed her, too.

Then suddenly, like a lightning bolt, it hit me between the eyes. All of my life I'd been searching for the Tree of Knowledge, and here was the Great Tree of Eden right in front of me all this time!

We really, really, really couldn't see what was right in front of us until we relaxed our asses and quieted our minds long enough to see-feel the silence between the notes, see-feel the wonder of the darkness between the stars, see-feel the whiteness of the page. We really did need to go to zero before we could see-feel the LIMITLESS possibilities that surrounded us in LIVING LIFE!

I smiled.

I laughed.

The Sacred Tree of Knowledge had always been right here in front of me. My eyes filled with tears. I was so happy. BIG HAPPY! And I remembered how my Yaqui *mamagrande* always told me that every woman needed her crying tree and every man needed his big boulder. Because women came from Tree and men came from Rock. Did this then mean I was more of a woman than a man? Or . . . or did this mean that I was a balanced man, *un hombre* who'd balanced his male and female energies into a whole other kind of energy just . . . just like when you combined $H_2O$ to make water?

I sighed.

I took several deep breaths and looked up at the tall ancient tree who was speaking to me just as ancient trees had been speaking to humanity since time began. I couldn't believe it. I'd been searching everywhere for the Holy Tree of Knowledge, and it had been right here at my very own home, staring at me all this time. No wonder I'd wanted to have a moment of silence for that big tree at the Academy. As a child I'd been raised to know to the marrow of my bones that old trees were Holy and filled with Sacred Knowledge, and just bursting to share their knowledge with us humans.

I gently ran my open hand up and down the tree's rough brown bark, then I carefully climbed up into the fork of the tree's huge thick branches. I lay down in the nest between the branches and closed my eyes, breathing real easy. I felt like I'd returned to the womb. It had only been four years since my dad had walked me from the house to this tree and told me that it wasn't enough for a man to know right from wrong. That a man also had to know who he was and wasn't or his life would be like a fish out of water. It seemed more like ten thousand years ago.

I must have gone to sleep, because the next thing I knew the sun was going down. I sat up, stretched, and decided to go up to the corrals and say hello to the livestock. Midnight Duke came up to me and I petted him and brushed him out. Then I asked him if he'd like to go for a ride and when he said yes, I bridled him and leaped on him bareback and we went running down the canyon toward the beach. It felt wonderful to be on horseback once again. I flashed on Eve and her kids. It would really be great to go horseback riding with them down this canyon some day.

At Buccaneer Beach I turned north. It was low tide and I said hello to the big black rock where I'd last seen my brother Joseph and Jesus just beyond the breakers. I'd never noticed it before, but the big rock looked a lot like an African lion lying in the waves, facing south. The rock, the sea, the whole place seemed magical. Midnight Duke and I continued galloping north, in and out of the surf. It was HEAVEN!

Getting to the pier, I looked at the two big brown Rorick houses up on the bluff. I wondered if Nick and Clare were home? And I wondered if they were both going through as much crazy*loco* stuff as I was. I truly missed Clare. Her words "together" and "don't worry about it. We'll do better next time" still rang like music in my ears. Suddenly I remembered that my dad had asked me if Eve spoke much about her mother, and when I'd said no, he'd then told me that a person had a big hole inside their hearts if they didn't talk a lot about their mother. Clare, I remembered, loved to talk a lot about her mother and her father, too. I guess this meant that she was balanced between her female and male energies.

Tears came to my eyes and I felt like charging up the hill on my horse and grabbing up Clare in my arms and tell her that my heart soared like an EAGLE every time I thought of her. But no, not yet. I had quite a few major battles I had to fight first. I nudged Midnight Duke with my knees and we headed back down the beach toward home.

The next day my friend John Folting came by. John had grown half a foot taller since I'd last seen him. He took me out to the little San Luis Rey airport where he worked and he took me up for a plane ride. He had gotten his single engine pilot's license and I could see he was thrilled to be flying. We headed south. The tiny plane was so slow that the traffic below passed us. We were flying so low I could spot the rabbits hiding in the brush from the noonday sun. John couldn't stop smiling.

"This is what I'm going to be doing for the rest of my life," he shouted to me over the engine noise. "I feel like I'm free as an eagle when I'm flying! All the problems of the world just disappear!"

I laughed. This was exactly what was starting to happen to me, too. I was beginning to feel like I was finally learning how to fly like an eagle with all my heart and soul. A lot of my old problems with the world had disappeared. I was no longer that frightened, confused kid who'd been afraid of God and sex and going to hell and all that other fear-crap that had been put into my head ever since I could remember. No, I was feeling pretty free now.

We passed canyons and hills and two-lane country roads. Up ahead we came to a great big beautiful mountain and a valley just beyond it. I'd never realized that there was still so much open land in San Diego County. But also from up here, I could see that most of the building took place alongside the major roadways.

John dipped our right wing, and we started back.

"No, wait!" I shouted. "Let's just go a little further. I want to see that little, beautiful green valley on the other side of the big mountain."

"That's Mexico!" he shouted back at me.

"What?"

"Mexico! I can't cross the border without a permit!"

"But I don't see any border!" I yelled back. "The brush on this side looks just like the brush on that side. The trees, the rocks, they all look exactly the same, John!"

He laughed all the more. "What did you expect to see, a great big cement border up here in the sky?" he shouted.

It hit me like a ton of bricks. Yes, I guess I had. I really had expected to at least see some kind of concrete distinction between our two countries. Then I saw it clearly. Borders weren't natural. They were man-made. They really were, and so for us to have peace on earth, we had to stop looking at each other across our man-made borders and start looking skyward. Up into the huge vastness of the whole sky, then just like Moses and his thousands of people we, too, could lift up our hearts and souls beyond all our earthly fears and limiting thoughts and simply see ourselves as ONE *FAMILIA* OF HUMAN BEINGS REACHING FOR THE STARS!

Not Mexicans!

Not Americans!

BUT HUMAN BEINGS REACHING FOR THE GREATER GLORY OF GOD, HAND IN HAND WITH OPEN HEARTS AND A VISION OF WORLD UNITY! Why? Because we really were one *familia* all over the globe. We really, really were once we got out of our fear-based brainwashed heads and started jazzing together.

We flew back to the little airport of San Luis Rey in no time at all. Being free to cut across roads was so much faster—even in a slow-moving plane—than following the winding, stopping, twisting roads laid down by mankind. Truly, I could now clearly see that looking down from the air opened up my mind and changed EVERYTHING!

The next day my dad invited me to go with him to El Camino Country Club, which was only a couple of miles east of our *rancho*. My dad didn't play golf. He played poker. He introduced me to his poker-playing friends, and none of them even knew that he had a son, because, I guess, I'd kept away from people and stayed on the ranch so much.

"Do you golf?" one of my dad's friends asked me. There were five of them, smoking and playing poker. "Maybe you'd like to join our club."

"I played a few times down at Mission Valley in San Diego," I said, "when I was going to school last year, but I'm not really much of a player."

"What's your handicap?"

"I don't have one. But on nine holes, I usually shot in the low forties."

"Pretty good. Not too bad."

My dad was drawing chips so he and I could sit down to play poker with his friends when a young blondish guy came in with his golf clubs. He wore white shoes, and they were covered with mud. He seemed to know everyone and sat down and began taking off his shoes. He was real slender and full of jokes and charm and happiness until the man who'd asked me if I golfed told him that he should get together with me so we could golf together.

"This is Sal's son," the man added, "and last year he played for his university down at Mission Valley."

Instantly, all my instincts for survival came SCREECHING UP INSIDE OF ME! I could feel it in my bones! The young man, who was probably only two or three years older than me, wanted no part of me. I could see it in his shoulders. He froze for a split second. But then, instead of addressing that and facing me, he slipped off his shoes and shouted at Jimmy, the old black man who was cleaning up the place. He threw his shoes at him and reprimanded him for not having cleaned his white shoes thoroughly enough last time.

I LEAPED OUT OF MY CHAIR! I couldn't believe it. He'd used the "n" word. And back in 1960 there weren't many Blacks in Oceanside, and my family and I knew Jimmy very well. Every year he and his whole *familia* came to our Christmas celebration of *Las*

*Posadas.* And this skinny, blondish guy with a long neck and large Adam's apple had mouthed-off at the dignified old man like . . . like it was business as usual.

My heart was beat, beat, BEATING! And everyone was looking at me, even my dad. They weren't looking at the racist shithead. I didn't know what to do. But then, I saw that Jimmy was telling me with his eyes to calm down, to please not embarrass him. I turned and quickly walked out of the clubhouse.

In the parking lot, I SCREAMED BLOODY MURDER TO THE HIGH HEAVENS! What had pissed me off wasn't just that the skinny white guy had mouthed-off, but how Jimmy, such a distinguished-looking old black man—no, DISTINGUISHED-LOOKING HUMAN BEING—had accepted that . . . that skinny asshole's shit! And . . . and I could now see that I, too, had done this same thing all my life in the States.

Tears were streaming down my face. So help me, God, I wasn't going to start doing this again. I would not lower my head and act like I didn't understand what was going on when people put me or others down.

I'd KILL FIRST!

I'd MASSACRE!

I took off running. I ran all the way home to our *rancho* and got my .357 magnum Smith and Wesson and a box of ammo. The sun was going down, but I figured I still had enough time to get back and kill that skinny guy with the big Adam's apple. Then after I killed him, I'd explain to my dad's poker-playing friends why I hated their guts for not speaking up and allowing this shit to happen, and so this was why they, too, were going to die.

I opened the gun cabinet, took out an over-and-under 30/30 and 12 gauge, an excellent weapon for what I intended to do. I filled my vest with ammo, too. I took off running up the railroad tracks, heading east, but then at El Camino, I didn't turn right and go up over the hill to the country club. I continued straight ahead at a good pace toward Vista. What would I really gain by killing that guy with the Adam's apple and my dad's poker-playing friends? Would the world really learn anything, or would all that bloodshed just be looked at

as . . . as the act of another crazy*loco,* stupid-*pendejo* kid? AND
YET, I HAD TO DO SOMETHING!

Coming into a grove of huge eucalyptuses right alongside the
railroad tracks, I surprised a couple of deer. I killed them both and
then I came across a *coyote* further up the tracks and killed him, too.
I pulled out my hunting knife and started to skin the *coyote.* He was
dead, but his eyes were still wide open. I'd taken him by complete
surprise. He hadn't been able to figure out what I was because I'd
come upon him so fast. The poor *coyote,* he'd looked so beautiful, a
lot like my brother's dog Shep, and he hadn't done anything to me,
so why had I killed him?

"I'm sorry," I said to the *coyote.* "There was no need to kill you.
Please, forgive me."

I swear that *coyote* winked at me as I said this.

An icy-cold chill snaked up and down my spine. Was I halluci-
nating or was I just crazy*loco* out of my skull? I took a big deep
breath, blew out hard, and began skinning the *coyote.* Then I went
back down the tracks, skinned the two deer, and headed for home.

I'd only been back in the U. S. three days, and my stomach was
already in knots. At home, I was in the bathroom washing the blood
off me when I looked in the mirror and leaped back in fear! My God,
my eyes looked COMPLETELY CRAZY*LOCO* INSANE! I had to
get out of town before I ended up killing Captain Moses and that big
mean-ass kindergarten playground teacher. Those two had been the
worst. Quickly I packed a couple of thousand rounds of ammo in my
old Chevy pickup, got a sleeping bag, a bunch of rifles, shotguns,
and pistols, and took off.

I drove east staring straight ahead like I was in a trance. I went
through Bonsall, Temecula, Riverside, and San Bernandino. I drove
on through Las Vegas, Nevada, still staring straight ahead. I ate in an
all-night diner at St. George, Utah, then turned, going north. I saw a
herd of mule deer in a big alfalfa field just outside of Salt Lake City.
I drove through a corner of Idaho, then turned east across the great
rolling plains of Wyoming. I had absolutely no idea where I was
headed. All I knew was that I needed to get as far away from all people as quickly as possible, because if I didn't and . . . and I . . . I saw
even the slightest injustice, I'd start killing.

Oh, I would have loved to have gut-shot that blond golfer and watched him suffer. The look that had come on his face when his dad, I guess, had suggested that we get together to golf had said it all, even before he'd used the "n" word. I was a greaser, a chile-belly, a lowlife, a no-good Mexican. How dare his dad tell him that he should get together with me to golf. He must have known of my dad's formidable reputation, and so when he was told I was Sal's son, he couldn't very well attack me, so he'd turned on Jimmy . . . Jimmy who'd boxed in the Navy. Jimmy who was a wonderful, thoughtful Human Being, a real asset to the world. Oh, I would have loved to gut-shoot that racist bastard, cut his balls off, and shove them down his throat while he squirmed in agony.

Once I stopped, got out of my truck, and looked up at the sky, seeing more stars than I'd ever seen in all my life. I pissed, drank some water, and then broke down crying. "GOD!" I screamed, "I NEED YOUR HELP! What's wrong with You? CAN'T YOU SEE THAT! I don't know what to do! Please, dear Lord God, help me! I'M LOST! I'M CRAZY *LOCO*! I can't do it here on earth WITHOUT YOU!"

I must have stood there in a trance for a long, long time, because the next thing I knew, Father Sun was coming up in the distance in front of me. I'd never seen a sunrise spread out across the flat plains. It was magnificent. I got back in my truck and continued driving east. I hadn't passed a town in hours. I was out in the middle of nowhere.

Suddenly a herd of pronghorn antelope ran across the road in front of me. I slammed on my brakes, pulled off to the side of the road, grabbed my gun belt, my 30/06 Winchester model 70, my day pack, and took off after them.

American pronghorns are the fastest antelope in the world. Faster than any antelope in Africa. They've been clocked at sixty-five miles an hour, the same speed as the African cheetah. They have a leg bone four times smaller than that of a cow, but eight times stronger. I cut down an *arroyo* running away from them, like I'd seen my brother's dog Shep do a thousand times, and then once I was out of sight, I started back around toward them, running as fast as I could. I knew that my running away from them had confused them so they'd stop and not go too far. I guess I ran two or three miles, then I came crawling up an *arroyo* on my belly. Sure enough, just as I'd figured, here was the herd of antelope out in front of me. This was perfect. I took a deep breath. My heart was pounding, and I had to calm down to make clean shots. I'd killed many a deer at ranges like this, about three hundred yards. Once I'd actually dropped some big muleys right outside of Meeker, Colorado, in Strawberry Canyon on the run at six hundred yards. I was an excellent shot.

After catching my breath, I took aim on the farthest animal, not the closest, so when they saw him drop, they'd think the shooting came from the other side, and they'd spook and come running toward me. I could get three or four more of them with my '.06, and then, if they were still running scared and coming to me, I'd get a bunch more with my .357 magnum. But my hands were shaking. What was wrong with me? I'd done this before. I was a great hunter and a fantastic shot.

I took a big breath, breathed out half, stopped shaking, took aim, and started to squeeze off my first round. But then, I just couldn't do it. The whole herd looked so peaceful, like family, and the rolling green hills all about them were so beautiful, and the snow-capped mountains in the distance were drop-dead gorgeous. I wasn't hungry, so why did I want to kill them? Tears started pouring down my face. Then it hit me. What I really wanted to kill was all this hate I'd been carrying inside me since my first day of kindergarten. This was what I really wanted to kill, all this hate and rage and confusion that I'd been keeping in my heart and soul for as long as I could remember.

I wiped the tears from my eyes. Some of the pronghorn had spotted me. And a couple of yearlings were coming over to see what I was. I guessed these yearlings had never seen a human being before. I took off my Stetson, which had three feathers tucked into its rim, and raised my hat up in the air. One of the yearlings stopped, the other one kept coming toward me. I waved my hat, and the yearling who was coming toward me started trotting. I smiled. This was amazing. But maybe we all come into the world full of innocence and curiosity, just like this yearling.

Then something happened.

The yearling coming toward me at a trot wasn't an antelope anymore. He was now a Human Being. I rubbed my eyes. I thought that my vision had blurred or had somehow gotten all mixed up. But when I looked again, the whole herd was no longer antelope. Now they were all a tribe of Indians migrating with their horses and drag poles.

I took a big deep breath, and I could now see that the yearling, who'd come toward me, was . . . was none other than . . . than *Ramón*, my friend from kindergarten, and he was waving at me with a big smile. I waved back at him, and he turned and ran after the rest of his people.

I took another great big deep breath and glanced around. I could now see that the whole world all around me had become alive in a way I'd never seen before. I got up, and when I looked at the tribe of Indians migrating north, they were antelope once again. Something very big had just happened deep inside me, but what it was, I didn't know.

I turned and headed for my truck. I felt like I was walking in . . . in a trance. Maybe this was what the old man in the jungle outside of *Tampico, Mexico*, had been talking about when he said there were twenty-six different realities on earth. Did this mean I was now starting to see realities that I'd never been ready to see before? Did this mean that the heavens were opening up for me as my dad had told me they would if I kept faith and didn't chicken out?

I took a deep breath and realized that I'd been walking for a long time, and I still hadn't come to my truck. In all directions, as far as the eye could see, there was nothing man-made to give me a point of reference. I'd never been so far out in the middle of nowhere in all my life. I stopped walking and blew out. I could feel myself starting to panic. I was lost.

"Just wait," I said aloud to myself. "Hold on to your reins, *amigo*. You're not lost. You're right here where you've always wanted to be, at nowhere, at zero, and remember this is good. In fact, this is wonderful. All you have to do is quiet yourself long enough to see what's right in front of you." I took a big deep breath, held, then blew out real fast and took another big deep breath, and another. I finally began to feel myself getting quiet inside.

"There," I said to myself, "feeling better, eh? Yes," I answered myself, "I'm feeling better, and I can now see that . . . that I'm strong and . . . and healthy and young, and I have a rifle, a handgun, a knife, and a backpack with a real good windbreaker, matches, water, jerky, and dried fruit. I'm set, *hombre.* THERE'S NO PANIC HERE!" I shouted. "I CAN WALK ACROSS THIS ENTIRE CONTINENT! NATIVE PEOPLE HAVE BEEN DOING THIS FOR . . . FOR HUNDREDS OF THOUSANDS OF YEARS!"

A warm, good feeling came up through me. It was true. Really true. Indigenous people had been walking across this continent and the whole world for hundreds of thousands of years, maybe even millions. Also, strangely enough, it felt like somehow the shouting had gotten the information into the deepest crevices of my brain, and this felt good and solid. Really real.

I laughed and turned south and started walking. I figured I'd eventually come to the road I'd been traveling on, because I'd been going just about directly east when the herd of antelope had run across the road in front of me. And if I didn't, that was fine with me, too. I was good. I was centered. Hell, I could walk all the way back to Mexico or to California.

I came to the edge of a tall flat piece of land called a *mesa* in Spanish. It had always amazed me how there were so many words in English that had originally come from Spanish, *patio, plaza, arroyo, mesa, rodeo,* the list went on and on, and yet we didn't acknowledge any of this. "English only" was such a bad, lousy, stupid, lazy joke!

Below me lay a long narrow valley that cut down around the *mesa* with a little river. I guess I'd walked a lot further than I'd thought. I started down the face of the *mesa,* and a bunch of soil came loose as I made my way down. I saw that there were some little white seashells in the soil.

"What does this mean," I said to myself, "that the ocean used to be up here in Wyoming thousands of years ago?"

I slid further down the *mesa,* and this time some pieces of Indian pottery came up with the loose soil. I stopped and looked at this, too, but I didn't pick it up. I didn't do that. "Does this mean," I said aloud once more, "that there used to be an Indian village up here in Wyoming with beachfront property?"

My mind EXPLODED, just as it had back in Mexico City on the night I'd heard the jazz. Suddenly I saw that there were thousands and thousands of Indigenous Tribes that had come and gone all over Mother Earth and that we knew nothing about them.

We didn't know who built Stonehenge in England. We didn't know who made those great big designs on the high plateau of Peru. We didn't know who carved and moved those huge rock-faces on Easter Island or how the ruins at Macchu Picchu had been constructed. But . . . but we did know a lot about one tribe called the Jews, because the Jews had a book called "the" Bible, and this book anchored them to Creation and made them "the" Chosen People of God. And the Jews were persecuted century after century, but they never fell apart. No matter how much hell they went through, they just kept getting back up with confidence and genius.

THEN I SAW IT!

I saw it with utter clarity. We were all God's Chosen People, not just the Jews. It was that the rest of us hadn't yet written down our stories of Creation.

Tears began pouring down my face.

I now knew why I'd seen those antelope become humans. Through God's Holy Eyes we were all Human Beings. Each and every Tree, each and every Rock, each and every Animal, each and every Insect was a Human Being made in the Supreme Being's Holy Image, too. So, this meant that I'd glimpsed those antelope through God's Eyes. I'd seen those antelope as God saw them, just like back home when I'd finally seen our old pepper tree as God saw that Sacred Holy Tree.

I breathed and breathed again, and I now knew without a shadow of a doubt that the Garden of Eden was here all around us, once we began to see through the Almighty's Holy Eyes. And we were all His Chosen People once we saw through His Eyes.

Then I saw-felt it even deeper. Sure, of course. No doubt about it. The time had come in Human Being Development for each and every Tribe of People to take flight. To get up in the air as I'd done with John Folting and see the whole world differently. Beyond all of our manmade borders and barriers and then write down our own Story of Creation.

YES, THIS WAS IT! So simple, so easy, because this was the only thing that was keeping us from coming together all over the Earth as ONE UNITED *FAMILIA!*

"Okay, God, I see it all so clearly," I said out loud. "You're telling me that each of my grandmothers had their own Bible-like story of Creation, and . . . and . . . You're also saying that their stories need to be written down. Yeah, I get it. I really do. This would instantly bring peace and harmony—well, not instantly, but over a period of, well, about five hundred years—to us human beings all over the globe. And, also, it would take the Jews off the hook, so people won't be jealous and hate them anymore."

My eyes continued watering, but I wasn't crying. I was happy. Big, big, BIG HAPPY!

"What? Then You're also telling me that You, God, never chose the Jews. It was the Jews who chose You when they decided to put their oral story into written form? Did I hear You right? This is really big, God. This is major stuff, I hope You know."

I heard laughter.

The Almighty was laughing.

I started laughing, too. Her-His laughter was contagious.

"Why are We laughing?" I asked. "Yeah, sure, it feels good, and I know it's healing, too, but—I mean, it's—what? What did You say? Please talk a little slower, God. I'm what? I'm Your Son, too? Oh, no, thanks. That's too much, God. What? Well, okay, that I can accept. Then I'm Your son, but with a small 's' like I'm now a catholic with a small 'c'. Yeah, this I can handle. You've got to be careful, God. Remember, I'm still in a human body, so there's only so much I can take in at a time."

God burst out LAUGHING WITH *CARCAJADAS!* I did, too. Now I got it. She-He was laughing because I'd finally, really completely gone over the hill. I was now advising God—not generals—on what to do and not to do. This was WONDERFUL! God loved that I was finally, totally, CRAZY*LOCO* OUT OF MY SKULL AND LISTENING TO HER-HIM without question and/or any petty man-made thoughts. Because now Her-His laughter LEAPED, EXPLODED, and the WHOLE LAND began to SING and DANCE, and the faraway snow-capped mountains of the great Tetons, named the great titties by a French mountain man, began to loom and sway like great gorgeous juicy breasts!

Instantly, I leaped AN ERECTION!

I wanted to MAKE LOVE TO THE WHOLE MOTHER EARTH!

An eagle screeched, and I looked skyward. A huge Golden Eagle was circling overhead. I'd never seen one before. It was way, way bigger than the Red Eagle. I continued laughing along with God, and the little white clouds above me rejoiced and whirled and danced. I now knew why Jesus had been smiling such a big smile when He'd come walking across the water just beyond the breakers with my brother Joseph. Like any good Son, Jesus was constantly listening to the Almighty's contagious laughter.

That old man in the jungle outside of *Tampico, Mexico*, had been right once again. LoveLaughter was the key to all the other loves we humans had, and it was LoveLaughter that connected us directly to God!

I really couldn't remember ever laughing with such wild, insane, CRAZY*LOCO CARCAJADAS!* I was free! FREE! FREE as the eagle above me, and it was WONDERFUL!

The rocks were free and laughing, too.

The grass, the trees, the plains, and the mountains were free and laughing.

We were all free beyond words and labels and limiting thoughts, and we were now all LAUGHING TOGETHER WITHIN GOD'S HOLY VOICE OF *CARCAJADAS!*

The whole wide world and I were now deep into each other and making love! This was how we human beings accessed the Kingdom of God, by making CRAZY*LOCO* LOVE BEYOND ALL RHYME AND REASON!

Yes, yes, yes! I could see it, feel it, and hear it! And we couldn't get into this kind of *amor* until our asses were totally relaxed and HAPPY!

*Carlos Esparza* had been absolutely right! A revolution of music and love was starting to take place all over the world, and this revolt was the music and love I was see-feel-hearing right here, right now, and I'd saw-felt-heard at . . . at the pyramids outside Mexico City. I got it now! I really, REALLY DID!

God was joy!

God was happiness!

*Papito Dios* was lovelaughter!

"Thank you, God!" I said.

"THANK YOU, *PAPITO DIOS!*" I shouted. "Thank You! Thank You! Thank You! THANK YOU!

"Thank You, Allah!" I added.

"THANK YOU, *PAQUA-GISH-CHEE-OJO!*" I screamed! I shouted! And I had absolutely no idea where this last name for God had come from, and . . . and I didn't care.

They were just words. Hollow, empty, incomplete labels and really had very little to do with the feelings, the magic, I was feeling deep inside of me.

I giggled.

I laughed.

And I was so happy, I was crying. I continued laughing until my erection subsided, and I was done, spent, all gone.

"Yeah, I get it now, *Papito,*" I said. "I really do. This is why it says in the Bible that in the beginning was the word, and before the word there was chaos and void. The word is referring not to You or to the Universe's beginning, but to the beginning of . . . of our human consciousness? Of this crazy*loco* love consciousness in which I am, right now.

"You know, God, this is pretty good. Yeah, and I can now also see that You were right when You had me change Your Son's word from 'is' to 'starts,' because You're telling all of us that Your Kingdom, within each of us, really does need to be activated. Yeah, I hear You," I said, laughing. "You've really got a good sense of humor, God. Yeah, I like it. A whole new world with relaxed asses and Your Son Jesus smiling that big smile of His, and His mother laughing, too, and Magdalena looking sexy and elegant and as beautiful as royalty. Yeah, I hear You, God. I really do. A 4-H Club of the whole globe! HAPPY! HEALTHY! HARMONIOUS! HORNY!" I shouted. "I get it! I'm with you! No more Jesus with a sad, tormented face. THAT'S OUT OF DATE!"

The laughter grew and EXPLODED ONCE AGAIN!

"All right, God," I continued, "thanks! This is really great. *Gracias!* Thank You very much. What? Oh, no, You've got to be kidding," I said. "You mean that You're showing me all this because You want me to get the ball rolling and write the stories of my two grandmothers so that other people can start doing their own Holy Books, too. Oh, no, God. You made a real big mistake. This ain't funny. You bring me to this mountaintop so I can see Your Vision, then You tell me that I'm supposed to become a writer?

"Look, God, don't get senile on me! I'm not my brother Joseph. I'm the dumb one, remember? *El burro* who can't read. So how in hell—excuse me, I mean, how in Heaven—do You expect me to become a writer, eh? Let's get real, God. What? Okay, I hear You, so Moses had a speech problem, and I've got a reading problem, and You'll help me. BUT THIS ISN'T FAIR! BOOKS GIVE ME SPLITTING HEADACHES! SO WHY DON'T YOU JUST GO GIVE THIS JOB TO SOMEBODY ELSE? Remember, You're God, so You can do anything You want. You don't need me. You can pick someone else better qualified for this!"

I stopped. I could hear the laughter once again. But this time I kind of felt like God was laughing at me, instead of with me. Well, I didn't think this was funny one little bit. "I'm out of here! Bye, God! Thanks, but no thanks." And I continued on down the *mesa.* This was when I suddenly tripped over nothing and went rolling halfway down the *mesa,* almost breaking my neck. I leaped up! I was PISSED!

"YOU TRIPPED ME, GOD!" I yelled. "NOW WHAT ARE YOU DOING?!! You gonna keep tripping me up until I agree to do what You want me to do? This isn't fair! I thought we had free will. What? I'm the one who's been asking You for this all along? Well, yeah, maybe I have, but . . . but never in a million years did I really think that You'd actually hear me and come down to Earth to talk to me.

"God, remember, I'm really like Peter. I'm the one who got scared and pissed in my pants in kindergarten. I'm not *Ramón* who was brave and smart, and I'm not my brother Joseph—who even when he knew he was dying—never panicked. I'm, well, a big bluffer, You know that. I don't know what I would have done if Eve's husband and that bullfighter had taken me on. I probably would have turned into a rabbit and hopped away as fast as I could.

"What? You don't buy that? Why not? Because of the day I was going to castrate myself. Because of the day I pissed on my father when I was still in diapers. Because of—okay, stop it, God, I hear You, but I don't like it. What? You want me to think back and remember the substitute teacher I had in 7th grade. Sure. I remember him. He was an angel. Wait. Hold on. You mean to tell me that he was really, really an angel?"

Then I saw it, and my mouth dropped open. God wasn't pulling my leg. I could now see so clearly that that substitute teacher—Mr. Swift, I do believe—was not only an Angel, he was Archangel Gabriel, himself!

My eyes flowed with tears. Suddenly I saw that I'd been Angel Protected and Angel Guided through my entire life. We all were. Everyone of us. All we had to do was open up our heart-eyes to see-feel this fact that was staring at us before our very own *ojos*-eyes.

"Okay, God, I see it now," I said, "and since I, too, am Your beloved son, but with a small 's', then I'll accept. I'll do it. I really, really, really will, but I'm still pissed off at You, God, for all the crap I've had to go through and all the crap I see in the world, so I'm not going to kneel down to make this deal with You. I'm through with that! I'll stand up and deal with You, one on one. Okay?"

"Okay," I heard a voice say deep within me.

"All right, *Papito,* then You help me become a writer, as great as Homer or better, and I swear to You, *Papito,* that I'll do my part and I'll never give up. I swear it. I'll never give up, and I'll never marry, and I'll never accept any more money from my parents until You and I pull this off.

"DO YOU HEAR ME!" I now screamed to the heavens, driving this information into the deepest crevices of my mind. "I, VICTOR EDMUNDO VILLASEÑOR, TAKE THIS HOLY OATH BEFORE YOU, GOD ALMIGHTY, as your son, to write my people's story WITH ALL MY HEART AND SOUL! I'll write! I'll do my part with all the power and intensity that I put into wrestling, hunting, trying to castrate myself, and chess! BUT, THEN, YOU'VE GOT TO DO YOUR PART, TOO, GOD. Okay? You accept? Then it's a deal, God, and remember, a deal is a deal, so no chickening out on me now."

I took a deep breath, held, then blew out really fast. What in the hell—I mean, in heaven—had I just done? This was crazy*loco*! I'd just made a deal with God to become as great a writer as Homer or better, and I didn't even know how to read. This was totally, absolutely insane!

My knees got weak. I dropped to the ground.

I guess I must have fallen asleep, because the next thing I knew, I awoke and it was late in the day. I sat up, rubbed my face and eyes, took off my pack, drank some water, ate some jerky and dried fruit, chewing real slow as I stared off into the distance. I could feel humming going on at the back of my head, so I knew I wasn't alone. God was keeping His part of Our bargain and sticking by me.

"Thank you, *Papito*," I said. "I guess this is it then. No backing out now for either One of Us."

The humming got stronger and I guessed that God was doing His share. Then it hit me, and I knew what had been missing the day Eve and I had run naked down that hillside away from the fighting bulls. God had been missing. I saw it so clearly now. Yes, we'd been a man and a woman out in the Garden of Eden, naked as the day we were born, but we hadn't taken God into our *amor*.

This was what marriage was really all about, a man and a woman bringing God and family and friends into their union. This wasn't fucking. This was making love in its deepest, most sincere form of union, body to body, heart to heart, and soul to soul.

"Eve and I should have prayed together," I said. "We should have done a lot of praying, instead of all that drinking and high-level thinking and talking. We should have shut up and just looked into each other's eyes until we saw the light of God within each other."

"Yes," I heard God say within me, "that's it, Adam."

"What?" I said. "You mean Eve was right when she said that it's all the same story ever since the beginning. I'll be damned. I mean—excuse me, God—I'll be heavened! Then Eve really does know her business." My eyes filled with tears. "And she's so beautiful, God, and so . . . so . . . ."

I stopped and took a huge breath, held, then blew out really fast. The tears were pouring down my face.

"I love her, God," I said. "I really do, and yet I'm afraid that it can never work out between us. What? That's not the purpose of love. Love is simply to be loving. Oh, wow. You know, God, You keep this up, and we really are going to become a writer as great as Homer or better. No doubt about it. Together, we kick ass, God! What, that's the plan?"

I smiled.

I laughed with *CARCAJADAS,* got to my feet, reshouldered my pack, got my .06, and started off to look for my Chevy truck. But my hat wouldn't stay on. It kept falling off. I guess it must've shrunk in size lying in the sun as I'd slept, or . . . or . . . or could it be that my head had grown larger? Could it be that God had come down to Mother Earth while I was asleep and . . . and performed an operation on my skull? Sure, why not? GodEvolution could be one word. God could certainly step in at times like this if She-He wished and give us humans more brains, so we would have the ability to do what it was She-He had sent us down to do in the first place. Sure, of course, why not? Miraculous Christlike Intervention by the Almighty.

I laughed and kept on walking, carrying my hat half the time. The sun was going down. The whole western sky was painted in beautiful colors of pink and orange and turquoise blue. And there was my truck, right in front of me.

"Thanks," I said to my Partner God.

Walking up to the Chevy, I took off my pack and put my Winchester away. I wasn't going to go east any further. I'd found my answer. I was now a writer in full Partnership with God. This was who I was and who I wasn't . . . I wasn't lost anymore. And I wasn't a coward either, because I hadn't blamed Eve this time. No, I'd stood up like a balanced male-female human being and proved to the Almighty that I wasn't afraid of hell or damnation or anything else. Why? Because I loved Him. Simple as that. I loved *Papito* with all my heart and soul and . . . and I had faith that God was my best *AMIGO,* with a capital "A". And when a Human Being was best friends with the Supreme Being, then this was Heaven, right here, right now, Forever. I was Blessed. We all were once we got past our fears of the Almighty.

Making a U-turn, I started back for home. The last of the Father Sun was going. It was just about dark when I came into a little town. I decided to stop and gas up, even though I had two five-gallon ex-Army tanks of gas in the truck bed. As I was gassing up, I saw that there was a little bookstore across the street.

After paying for the gas, I went into the tiny station's bathroom, washed, pissed, filled my Stetson with water, let it soak in a little, then dumped the water out. I put my hat back on, and with both hands I pulled it down real hard, trying to stretch it out to fit my new head size. But it was really tough. It felt like my head had become longer in the back and wasn't round anymore. I guess God had come down and added bulk to my brain, making it larger in the back where the humming went on. I was finally able to stretch it out enough so it would stay on my head. I looked in the mirror. I looked okay. My eyes were no longer crazy*loco* insane. In fact, I looked kind of handsome. I really did. I dried my hands and walked across the street to the bookstore.

The little bell that was hooked on the door gave a jingle as I went in. It was nice and warm inside. Wyoming got freezing cold once the sun went down. A tall handsome man in his early thirties came out from the back of the store. I was the only customer in the place.

"Can I help you?" he said with a big smile. I thought that I detected a slight accent from the East Coast.

"Yes," I said. "I just decided to become a great writer a little while ago, so I'd like to know if there have been any great books written lately?"

He looked at me as if I'd just asked the dumbest question in the whole world.

"Well, yes, of course," he said, "there have been many great books written lately. You'll have to be a little more specific," he added.

"Look, let's not make a big deal out of this," I said. "Just tell me what great books have been written lately that you have in this store."

"Well, uh," he said, glancing around at his inventory, "I have a lot of very highly respected books in my store that have been written lately. But what is it that you like? What have you read in the past?"

I could feel that I was getting angry. "Look," I said, "I don't like books. I've never really read any of them. So just give me any one of these books that you personally consider to be great and was written lately!"

"Okay," he said. He seemed to be getting nervous. "I can do that." He walked past me over to a bookshelf near the front window.

"This book, *Ulysses* by James Joyce, is considered one of the greatest books of modern times," he said, taking a great big fat book off the shelf.

"Hold on!" I said. "That book is too damn thick! I don't hardly know how to read. Don't you have a skinnier great book?"

He stared at me. "You barely know how to read and you have decided to become a great writer?" he said to me in a voice full of shock and arrogance.

I'd finally had enough of him. "Yes!" I bellowed, going into my wrestling stance. "I don't know how to read, and I've decided to become a great writer—WHAT OF IT!"

"No, nothing, nothing," he said. "That's fine with me. Fine." He quickly put the big book back and pulled out a much smaller one. "This," he said, "*Portrait of the Artist as a Young Man*, is also by James Joyce and very highly regarded, too," he added.

"Good, I'll take it!" I said.

I just wanted to get the hell out of the store. We went to the counter, and I paid him for the book in cash. He put it in a paper bag, and I went out. I wasn't going to allow anyone, anywhere to dampen or question my decision to become a great writer. This was strictly between God and me, and there was no turning back.

I climbed into my truck, took my gun belt off, and put it on the passenger's side of the front seat along with the book. Across the street, I could see that the bookstore owner was turning off his lights and locking up. I started my motor. He looked different. Somehow he didn't quite look like the same man that I'd just seen inside of the store when I was buying the book.

I put my truck in gear and drove slowly out of town. It was getting dark. The first stars of night were just coming out, but I didn't turn on my headlights. I was the only vehicle on the long straight highway. Then it hit me. That bookstore owner had looked different because he was also an angel, just as my seventh grade substitute teacher had been an angel. Yes, I really, really got it now. Each and every Human Being I came in contact with was an angel sent down by the Holy Creator to help me plant my seeds for Her-His Holy Garden.

I laughed.

This was great. Then even that no-good racist bastard back in Oceanside at the El Camino Country Club had also been an angel, because without my interaction with him, I would never have gone on that killing spree, then ended up coming here to Wyoming. Oh, life was really CRAZY*LOCO*!

It was getting darker and darker, and the stars were getting brighter and brighter as I drove up the deserted highway. Did this mean that all these bad awful things and people that came my way were the darkness that gave light to my stars? Then was it up to each and every one of us to open up our *ojos*-eyes and see-feel life, *la vida,* through God's Holy Eyes?

I continued driving without headlights and soon it looked like I was driving right up into the stars themselves. Yes, it was all beginning to make sense to me and . . . and I could see why I'd been sent down here to this *tierra firme.*

I smiled.

I laughed.

It truly felt very good deep inside of me to be headed home, knowing who I was and who I wasn't and what I was going to do with my life. Simply, I could now see I was a Human Being with a capital "H" and a capital "B" and that all my other labels were small letters; catholic, mexican, american, everything else was small potatoes. We were all Human Beings above all else, and God was Supreme Being and when We jazzed Together We were BEING with all capitals.

I now remembered what we'd been told in Art Appreciation class about Michelangelo cutting stone away for years, then one day here was David standing before him in all of his dazzling beauty. Well, maybe this was what I'd been doing to myself all along, too. With all of my mistakes, I, too, had been cutting away the stone of who I wasn't and finding out little by little who I was. It was like we were all our very own self-sculptor, and maybe one day, in the not-too-distant future, I, too, would stand before a mirror and see a dazzling figure, just as Michelangelo had. Sure, why not? Stranger things have happened. I laughed and the purring at the back of my head continued as I drove up into the stars from where we'd all come.

Thanks, *gracias,* God Bless,

Victor Edmundo Villaseñor

# AFTERWORD

**W**hen I got home to the *rancho*, it was all still very clear in my head, so I quickly told my parents that I was a writer. That this was who I was and what I was going to be doing for the rest of my life. And so I would not be going into our family business or any other kind of business. Now it was my dad who went berserk and started yelling at me. Then when I told my mother I was no longer a Catholic with a large "C," but with a little "c" and that, I, too, was the son of God with a small "s," all hell broke loose.

"What happened to your tile factory?" yelled my dad. "Hell, I'll buy the little factory for you! You can't just put all of your eggs into becoming a writer. Half of them never get recognized 'til they're dead!"

"You need to go to church and pray for guidance," said my mother. "You're talking crazy, *mijito!*"

"No," I said. "I told you, I'm no longer a Catholic with a big "C," so I don't need to go to church to pray. I can pray directly to God anywhere."

"It was that woman!" said my mother. "She's the one who put all these wild ideas in your head!"

"No, *mamá.*"

"She was evil! I saw her!"

I began to cry, and it went from bad to worse. My mother said the devil had taken my soul, and my dad slapped me across the face, telling me to shut up. But I kept talking. He slapped me until my face was bloody. Still I wouldn't quit. He'd told me to find out who I was, and who I wasn't and I had. My parents ran down the hallway and locked themselves in their bedroom. For three days and nights, I continued talking to my parents. Finally they calmed down enough to see that maybe, just possibly, I wasn't possessed, and they began to understand what I meant with a small "c" for catholic and a small "s" for being the son of God.

Next I went to see Captain Moffet at the Academy, and I told him that I'd decided to become a great writer, as great as Homer or better. I told him about my vision in Wyoming, and he wasn't shocked. In fact, he pointed to the poster in his classroom wall that said, "Whatever you can do or dream you can do, begin it. Boldness has genius, power, and magic." Then he went behind his desk, brought out a book, and read to me. "What lies before us and what lies behind us are small matters compared to what lies within us. And when we bring what is within out into the world, miracles happen."

"That's it!" I shouted. "These two people know! They really do!"

He told me the first writer was Johann Wolfgang von Goethe and the second one was Ralph Waldo Emerson.

"You anchor these two things to what Jesus said about the Kingdom of God being within us all," I said, "and you have the foundation about everything I'm talking about. Thank you, sir! Thank you! This is great, sir!"

Captain Moffet's face was glowing, and we talked the whole afternoon. He gave me tips on how to become a writer, but the biggest thing he told me was that I was going to have to learn how to read. That was when I realized he'd always known my secret. He told me to start with fourth grade books and work up to a seventh or eighth grade reading level before I started to write.

I went to the Oceanside library as he suggested and checked out fourth grade books for "my cousin from Mexico" who was visiting for the summer and wanted to learn English. Three months later on the 16th September 1960 at six a.m., I began to write. I wrote about what I knew well. How to catch and calm down a nervous, dangerous stallion by keeping so quiet and calm that he finally trusted you. I wrote about how the local Indians hunted rabbits and skinned them and cooked them over an open fire with their guts still intact. They were all one-page stories. I'd work on one story all day, week after week. Then that winter I tried to write about the old man I'd met behind *Marina*'s motel in *San Miguel* that hadn't had any lenses in his glasses. For well over six months I wrote, but the more I learned about writing, the more I began to doubt everything I'd seen so clearly in Wyoming. Finally I began to think that God had never spoken to me. It got so lonely I felt like a complete fool. This was when I decided that I had to move out of my parents' house and become a monk if I ever wished to hear the Voice of God again.

I rented a little shack in Ocean Beach for fifty dollars a month near where my cousin Victor—who'd moved back to San Francisco—had his apartment. I began waking up in the middle of the night sweating and thinking I really was crazy*loco*. Not only had God never spoken to me in Wyoming, I also began to doubt all the things that had happened to me in Mexico. That old man in the jungle had never existed, and that mansion with the angel had just been my imagination. But then I'd look at my brother's big belt buckle and see how it was all bent in the middle, and I knew some things had really happened. It couldn't all just be that I was crazy*loco* and my imagination.

I decided to go see Father Williams. Maybe he could help me as Captain Moffet had helped me. I couldn't find him. At the main office, they told me that he was on a sabbatical. I asked when he'd be back. They told me that they didn't know. I asked for his address so I could write to him. The priest in charge of the office came out and looked very sternly at me. He told me that it was best that I didn't try to contact Father Williams. A chill went up and down my spine. Then my cousin Victor came down from San Francisco for the holidays. I shared with him what had happened to me when I'd gone to the university and tried to see Father Williams.

"Of course they don't want you to see him. He had a nervous breakdown after dealing with you."

"What are you saying?"

"I'm saying that you're destroying people. Look at your own father and mother. They're suffering. They don't know what you'll do next."

"Wait! Hold on! Don't try to saddle me with Father Williams' nervous breakdown, if he really even had one! I saw how women came on to him and how he'd look at their asses!"

"And your parents? What rationale do you have for them?"

I turned and walked away. It hurt, it really did, but I wasn't going to allow anyone or anything to turn me. I had to keep my center. This was the only way I'd be able to keep the deal I'd made with God. Maybe Father Williams was . . . was better off not being a priest. Maybe he should be a married professor instead. Ultimately it was his call. His decision. Between him and God.

Eve moved back to La Jolla. She was real and so were her kids. I told her what was happening to me and that I'd . . . I'd decided to go six months without speaking. Maybe this would help give me back the Voice that was deep within me. She completely agreed with me. I was in my second month of not speaking when I discovered Sonny Rollins, the master jazz man, and he taught me that silence was, indeed, the power between each note, giving significance and feeling to his music. Suddenly I began to remember all these wild thoughts I'd had in *México* and I understood that it was this silence, this blank space within me, within my thinking that I needed for my writing. Instantly I felt a soft, warm glow come into me, and the humming began behind my left ear. Oh, I'd been so crazy*loco* that I hadn't understood that the silence of God's Voice was my spot, my center, my beginning, my opportunity, my "start" of the Kingdom of God that was within each of us. This was why it said in the Bible that before the word there had been chaos. Oh, this was wonderful! She-He God had so much faith in me that She-He had gone silent.

I LEAPED!

I SCREAMED!

I began to love the blank page. I began to see that the no-words on the page were what set up what I put down on the page. I began to love short sentences, and paragraphs were so beautiful they were an art form. This was when my writing room began to fill up with writing guides. It was like now that I loved and appreciated the silence of God's Voice within me, all these spirit forces could come to me. And they weren't just ordinary spirits. No, these were the masters who'd come to me through the Kingdom of God.

Every morning by three a.m. I couldn't sleep anymore. Homer was in my room and anxious for us to get "started" and so was Confucius, Shakespeare, *Cervantes*, Anne Frank, *Azuela*, Emerson, Goethe, Tolstoy, Dostoevsky, and Joseph Smith, who had spoken to me outside of Salt Lake City on my way back from Wyoming, and a guy named Norman Mailer.

One day, visiting the little bookstore in Ocean Beach, I discovered that Norman Mailer was still alive. This was very strange, so I wrote Mailer a letter telling him that I was destined to be a writer as great as Homer or better. Then I explained to him who were my writing guides, especially Shakespeare who was so bossy that I now had little notes all over my place telling Bill to stay the hell away until I found my own human voice. I also told Mailer that he was my only guide who was living.

"So my question, Mr. Mailer, is how can you—who hasn't passed over to the spirit world—have the ability to come to me like my other spirit guides who are all over on the other side?"

He never answered my letter. I wrote to Mailer one more time in case his publisher hadn't forwarded my letter to him. Still he never answered me, so I finally just said to hell—I mean, to Heaven—with it. He was coming to me almost every morning along with Bill and Cervantes and Anne Frank, explaining to me all these things about modern writing and nonfiction, so what did I really care if his living self didn't answer me. His spirit-soul-self was answering me quite regularly.

The years passed, and sometimes just before I . . . I awoke, I'd hear music going on inside of my head. I'd lay perfectly still, not moving, not waking, and the music would spread all through my body, just as it had done at the pyramids outside of Mexico City. Finally I'd leap out of bed and start writing like a madman. Ten, twelve, fifteen hours a day. It was just pouring out of me. It was limitless! And when I couldn't stand its power anymore, I would run out of my shack and down to the beach, but the music would follow me, haunting me. *Carlos Esparza*'s words took on new meaning. Tens of thousands of young people really could hear this music that was oozing out of us, and we were going to . . . to revolt . . . to cause change. And not with guns. But with music and love. Why? Because love and music were the True Voice of God!

The sea would sing to me!

The early morning dump trucks with their big noisy equipment would be an orchestra of music as they moved the big dumpsters!

The whole world was alive with music, just as those people had become alive with song when they'd been saying the rosary at that little poor church back in Mexico City. Oh, music was everywhere and in everything and in everyone! All we human beings had to do was open up our Heart-Eyes and see the world through GOD'S HOLY EYES AND THEN ALL WAS ALIVE WITH MUSIC!

My writing became a SYMPHONY! I could hear music with every word, every sentence, every paragraph. I WAS FLYING! It got to be that I'd sometimes find myself up by the ceiling of the room looking down on me as I wrote at the kitchen table. It was almost like there were two of me and each with his own center. One "here" and another one "over there."

Then I received my military papers and went into the Army. Being in great shape, I loved boot camp, and I met all kinds of Americans that I'd never known before. The United States truly was a huge diverse country, and yet in . . . in some crazy*loco* way, we were all Americans.

I was overseas when Jack Kennedy was assassinated. I broke down crying and served out my last few months of enlistment at the military Presidio in San Francisco. I'd walk the streets at night. Music was exploding all over the place. The revolt had begun with all these young crazy*loco* musicians. Jack's death had broken the dam. My cousin Victor came to see me at the Presidio. He asked me if it was true that I'd completed a book. I guessed that my parents had talked to him. I said yes. He asked if he could see it. Reluctantly, I gave him the manuscript. It was 800 pages and was called *Witness A Loco Pendejo*. He came back the following week, and we took a walk down to Fisherman's Wharf. He was really upset.

"What is it?" I asked.

"It's your book!" he said angrily. "I couldn't sleep! I read it three times!"

I took a big breath, preparing for him to tear my book apart. But what came out of his mouth next, truly shocked me.

"It's great!" he said. "It's TREMENDOUS! You keep this up and you're going to end up being a world-class writer like . . . like Dostoevsky!"

"You really mean it?" I said with tears coming to my eyes.

"YES, DAMNIT!" he shouted. "The brutal honesty with which you write! The simple, direct sentences you use. I don't know how you did it. You're not educated! You're not smart! I should be the writer of our family! NOT YOU! You're a BARBARIAN! I've seen you castrate pigs and slaughter innocent cows! I'm going to tell your parents! They have nothing to worry about! You really are destined to . . . to be a great writer! But . . . but why, I'll never know."

"You really mean it?"

"Yes, damnit! AND I HATE YOU FOR IT! Congratulations!"

I opened my arms and we hugged, holding each other heart to heart. I couldn't believe it. Victor, my cousin, of all people, was the first person in all my *familia* to give me encouragement. Everyone else thought I was a crazy*loco* fool. We became close friends.

Then I got discharged and I began to work as a laborer in construction in San Jose. Four months of labor would give me enough money for eight months of writing time down south in a shack at Ocean Beach. But the more I wrote, the more I came to realize how easy it was for me to turn into a Doubting Thomas. It was tough to keep the faith. My cousin's words had helped me, but still it was hard to keep going. Then one day I read that Vincent Van Gogh said, "If you hear a voice within you say 'You can't paint,' then paint, and that voice will be silenced." That was it. Van Gogh was right. So I kept writing and writing, and finally that negative voice was silenced.

In 1968 the Olympics did, indeed, come to Mexico, and a couple of days before the games, it came out in the news that there was a massacre of students and young professors in Mexico City. I called *Marina*. She told me that she'd been there when it happened, and while she couldn't talk on the phone, she said that the situation was far . . . far worse than any news that was getting out. I asked if the students had been playing native instruments and singing about world harmony and peace? She said yes and asked me how I knew.

"I was with them," I said, and I began to tell her about my other "over there" self and *Carlos* when the phone went dead. I redialed, but couldn't get through. I decided to take a walk on the beach. My God, *Carlos Esparza* had been right. He'd known the future just as my dad had known the future when I'd gone down to Mexico and that man with an overcoat full of watches approached me. I hoped *Marina* was okay.

The next morning at three a.m. there was only standing room in my writing room, the place was so jammed full of Spirit Guides. The Music within me EXPLODED, and once more a part of me was up by the ceiling and this "other me" could see myself writing at my kitchen table. This time I knew what was going on. I was at "one" with my Guardian Angel who was at "one" with God. Sure, of course, it was my Guardian Angel Self who was up by the ceiling and was giving me this view, this consciousness of my own conscious. Because when we are "one" with our Angel, then we are Angel Connected to all other Angels, and this was how my writing guides came to me, including Norman Mailer who was still alive. Dead or alive really didn't matter once we are Angel Connected, because when we are Angel Connected, we are Totally, Completely within the Kingdom of God. Understanding this, my writing now became a GREAT SYMPHONY OF SOUND!

Each word, every sentence took on LIVING LIFE! No, I had not abandoned *Ramón*, and I would now not abandon *Carlos*! Because once we were conscious of our consciousness, then we could see what was right in front of us—we were all Spiritually Connected in a World of Limitless Abundance for all! Scarcity only existed in the world of separation.

Month after month, I continued writing like a madman. The years passed, and I accumulated 265 rejects before I sold my first book in 1970 called *A La Brava*, which my New York publisher changed to *Macho!* It was published in 1973 and reviewed by the L.A. Times comparing it to the best of John Steinbeck. I was finally on my way. And it had only taken me ten years. I could finally get . . . get married. For years, once a week, I'd set a table for two and have a candlelight dinner alone, thinking of my future wife.

I met my Sophia Loren at my publisher's office in Hollywood. Her name was Barbara, and she'd gotten into Berkeley at fifteen and did her graduate work at Radcliffe at nineteen. She understood writing, and it didn't frighten her that I was a crazy*loco* writer. We dated for a year, then my parents met with her parents, and they formally asked for their daughter's hand in marriage. Her parents said yes. My father butchered our finest steer under the big pepper tree, and her father had both a rabbi and a priest do our wedding. One year later we got pregnant. It was now time for me to start our big book. I didn't want our child coming into the world without our own Holy Book connecting us to Creation, too.

Check my website: victorvillaseñor.com. Every year we have a free concert potluck at the *rancho* in Oceanside at one p.m. the Sunday before Thanksgiving for world harmony and peace. Admission is that you bring a dish for twelve that you made with your own hands with patience and love. Over 2,000 people come every year. At sunset we light candles and have a minute of silence, sending goodwill and *amor* around the whole globe. We need one thousand locations by 2012, one hundred thousand by 2026, and a million by 2052. Moses parted the sea, and so can we, parting the sea of doubt and fear all over the world! Come and join us, or set up your own Power-Spirit-Center at your own local church, school, and/or service club. You, me, we weee weeeeee are all Angel Connected and we have the whole world in our hands!

Thank you, *gracias,* God bless,

Victor E. Villaseñor

# Also by Victor Villaseñor

*Estrellas Peregrinas: Cuentos de Magia y Poder*

*Macho!*

*¡Macho!*

*Rain of Gold*

*Walking Stars*